# Banking on Beijing

China is now the lender of first resort for much of the developing world, but Beijing has fueled speculation among policymakers, scholars, and journalists by shrouding its grant-giving and lending activities in secrecy. Introducing a systematic and transparent method of tracking Chinese development projects around the world, this book explains Beijing's motives and analyzes the intended and unintended effects of its overseas investments. Whereas China almost exclusively provided aid during the twentieth century, its twenty-first-century transition from "benefactor" to "banker" has had far-reaching impacts in low-income and middle-income countries that are not widely understood. Its use of debt rather than aid to bankroll big-ticket infrastructure projects creates new opportunities for developing countries to achieve rapid socioeconomic gains, but it has also introduced major risks, such as corruption, political capture, and conflict. This book will be of interest to policymakers, students, and scholars of international political economy, Chinese politics and foreign policy, economic development, and international relations.

Axel Dreher is Professor of International and Development Politics at Heidelberg University, Germany. He is also Fellow at CEPR, CESifo, and AidData.

Andreas Fuchs is Professor of Development Economics and Director of the Centre for Modern East Asian Studies at the University of Göttingen, Germany. He is also Director of the Kiel Institute China Initiative.

Bradley Parks is Executive Director of AidData, a research lab at William & Mary. He is also Non-Resident Fellow at the Center for Global Development.

Austin Strange is Assistant Professor of International Relations at the University of Hong Kong.

Michael J. Tierney is Professor of Government and Director of the Global Research Institute at William & Mary.

# Banking on Beijing

*The Aims and Impacts of China's Overseas Development Program*

Axel Dreher
*Heidelberg University*

Andreas Fuchs
*University of Göttingen*

Bradley Parks
*William & Mary*

Austin Strange
*University of Hong Kong*

Michael J. Tierney
*William & Mary*

CAMBRIDGE
UNIVERSITY PRESS

# CAMBRIDGE
## UNIVERSITY PRESS

University Printing House, Cambridge CB2 8BS, United Kingdom

One Liberty Plaza, 20th Floor, New York, NY 10006, USA

477 Williamstown Road, Port Melbourne, VIC 3207, Australia

314–321, 3rd Floor, Plot 3, Splendor Forum, Jasola District Centre,
New Delhi – 110025, India

103 Penang Road, #05–06/07, Visioncrest Commercial, Singapore 238467

Cambridge University Press is part of the University of Cambridge.

It furthers the University's mission by disseminating knowledge in the pursuit of
education, learning, and research at the highest international levels of excellence.

www.cambridge.org
Information on this title: www.cambridge.org/9781108474108
DOI: 10.1017/9781108564496

First published 2022

*A catalogue record for this publication is available from the British Library.*

ISBN 978-1-108-47410-8 Hardback
ISBN 978-1-108-46339-3 Paperback

# Contents

# Figures

## Appendix Figures

# Tables

# Acknowledgments

John F. Kennedy is credited with popularizing the saying that "victory has a thousand fathers." He might have said the same about this book. While there are five names on the cover, this book could not have been written without the assistance of hundreds of other people over the past nine years. To say that we are grateful for the support of many other people is a huge understatement. The open-source, project-level dataset that provides the foundation for this book has been a collaborative effort, drawing upon the expertise and labor of researchers from multiple universities on four continents. But the inspiration for this dataset came from Austin Strange, who at the time was an undergraduate student at William & Mary.

In 2008, with support from the William & Flora Hewlett Foundation and the Bill and Melinda Gates Foundation, AidData[1] began systematically collecting data on development projects financed by a wide variety of international donors and lenders. This work involved extensive outreach to two groups of nontransparent donors and lenders. The first group did not oppose the idea of making their data publicly accessible in a format that met international standards, but it lacked the know-how or the time and resources to do so. This group included bilateral development institutions in Brazil, Poland, and Taiwan, as well as multilateral development institutions such as the African Development Bank and the Nordic Development Fund. These funders cooperated with AidData to make their project-level information available, which AidData then crosswalked into a format that researchers could use for statistical analysis.[2] A second group of funders (including Libya, Russia, and Turkey) refused to work with AidData to make their data publicly accessible. China is an unapologetic member of this second group; when a group of researchers

---

[1] AidData is a research lab at William & Mary. See www.aiddata.org/.
[2] For a detailed description of the original AidData dataset (which lacked information on Chinese development finance) and an introduction to a special issue of *World Development* that used these data to revisit old questions with better evidence, see Tierney, Nielson, Hawkins et al. (2011).

x

from AidData initially asked the authorities in Beijing (in 2009) if they might be willing to share their official, project-level development finance data, a representative of the Chinese government told them that "everyone who needs to know how generous we are already knows."[3] So, even though researchers and policy practitioners around the world recognized that China was an increasingly important donor and lender with a rapidly growing portfolio of development projects, AidData's first publicly accessible dataset (released in 2010) did not contain any projects financed by the Chinese government.[4] In 2010, several researchers affiliated with AidData were able to document and publish a small portion of the Chinese government's foreign aid portfolio from 1990 to 2005 by digitizing information found in the China Commerce Yearbooks.[5] However, these project-level data did not contain monetary amounts. Nor did they capture the universe of Chinese development projects during that time period.

In the spring semester of 2012, Austin returned from two years of study in Beijing and asked Brad Parks if he would oversee an independent study course to document existing efforts by scholars, think tank researchers, and policy analysts within international organizations to track the scale and distribution of Chinese development finance. Austin quickly concluded that there was limited agreement on what to count, how to count it, or what sources to use. He directly contacted many of the people who were doing this work and, even as an undergraduate student, was disappointed to learn that almost no one was willing to share their data or disclose their methods and sources. However, late in the semester, several World Bank staff members agreed to share their preliminary dataset of Chinese infrastructure projects in Africa as well as the procedures that they followed to assemble it. As luck would have it, these World Bank staff members were under pressure from above to stop doing this research. At that time, China was an increasingly powerful and assertive member state, and it was none too pleased that the World Bank was shining a light on its overseas development finance activities. At this point, Austin approached Brad and Mike Tierney and asked if he could recruit a team of ten research assistants to work over the summer in the attic of Blow Memorial Hall in an attempt to refine the World Bank's data collection methods and broaden the approach to cover all sectors of Chinese development finance in Africa. The pilot project during the summer of 2012 yielded a new method of open-source data collection

[3] Phone interview with MOFCOM official in August 2009.
[4] For detailed discussion of limitations and the first analysis using these data, see Dreher, Nunnenkamp, and Thiele (2011).
[5] See Hawkins, Nielson, Bergevin et al. (2010).

and the 1.0 version of AidData's Chinese Official Finance to Africa dataset.

At the same time that AidData was piloting new open-source data collection methods, roughly 6,660 kilometers across the Atlantic, Axel Dreher and Andreas Fuchs, two development economists from Heidelberg University, were piecing together multiple data sources stretching back to the 1950s to address the question of whether China was a "rogue donor." They used the previously mentioned data from the China Commerce Yearbooks along with declassified reports from the CIA and a Cold War dataset from the German sinologist Wolfgang Bartke, which used Chinese media reports to reconstruct the historical record. While they were able to squeeze an impressive amount of blood from these stones, they also left the exercise disappointed in the quality and the reliability of the hybrid dataset they were able to construct. Since Axel was already one of the leading researchers analyzing project-level aid data and Andreas was studying a range of non-Western donors and lenders, they seemed the ideal collaborators for a project designed to build a robust time-series dataset of Chinese development projects. The five of us joined forces during the fall of 2012 with Vijaya Ramachandran at the Center for Global Development to write a working paper that introduced the beta version of the dataset in April 2013.[6]

The fact that we now had a multidisciplinary team broadened the range of methods we could bring to bear and the types of questions we attempted to answer with these new data. And while this book and our previous publications address a wide range of questions – related to the aims and impacts of China's overseas development program – this is still a narrower range of questions than others have sought to answer with our dataset.

In fact, a key contribution of this book is to introduce people to AidData's project-level dataset of Chinese development finance and highlight the value of an open data policy. Rather than privately holding these data until we could finish publishing with them, we made them available in a series of data releases, each of which was made public shortly after we finished collecting and cleaning the data. As a result, they have been used not just by economists and political scientists but also

---

[6] Strange, Parks, Tierney et al. (2013). An updated version of that first working paper was eventually published in the *Journal of Conflict Resolution* in 2017. It also showed that the availability to Chinese government financing lowered the probability that civil war would occur as a result of "aid shocks" when Western donors walked away (Strange, Dreher, Fuchs et al. 2017). Of course, previous research was not able to include Chinese development finance in these aid shock models because there was no comprehensive source of high-quality data on Chinese development finance.

by computer scientists, epidemiologists, geographers, sinologists, sociologists, journalists, and policy practitioners. These folks had very different ideas than we did about how to use these data to generate insights in their own work. We have benefited immensely from this uptake since those who use the data have frequently helped correct our errors, asked questions that reveal where we could be clearer, and made specific suggestions about additional variables to include in the dataset. While we have worked with one another (and many other coauthors, highlighted later), people outside our small circle of coauthors have written the vast majority of journal articles, books, policy reports, and media publications that have used these data. Dozens of studies have already been published with these data, and we consider this to be one of the most significant contributions of our nine-year collaboration. This book pulls together what we have learned over the previous decade and puts it all in one place in a more accessible format than the dozen-plus journal articles, book chapters, and policy reports that we draw upon and supplement in these pages.

Over the past nine years, we have worked together on multiple journal articles, working papers, and policy notes where one or more of us were contributors. In this book, we draw heavily upon the methods and insights from these articles, but we have added more data (often expanding the analysis from the African context and testing claims using the new global dataset) and qualitative evidence, which we use to further explore our arguments from the articles or to bring the narrative to life. We list these papers here and thank our coauthors who taught us a great deal in the process.

Edwin Muchapondwa from the University of Cape Town and Daniel Nielson at the University of Texas helped us "ground-truth" our remotely sourced data in a 2015 article published in the *Journal of Development Studies*. We build upon this work in Chapter 3.

Our analysis in Chapter 8 draws upon collaborative research with Ariel BenYishay, Daniel Runfola, and Rachel Trichler, all researchers affiliated with William & Mary. "Forest Cover Impacts of Chinese Development Projects" was published as an AidData working paper in 2016.

In "Tracking Underreported Financial Flows," published in the *Journal of Conflict Resolution* in 2017, we describe our data collection methods and use the dataset to replicate and extend previous work on the links between aid shocks and civil war. We revisit and further develop these themes in Chapters 3, 4, and 8.

In "Apples and Dragon Fruits," published in *International Studies Quarterly* in 2018, we distinguish between different types of Chinese official finance and show that in Africa, the allocation of the two types of development finance is driven by different factors. We build upon this previous research in Chapters 4 and 5.

In an article written in collaboration with Roland Hodler from the University of St. Gallen and Paul Raschky from Monash University, titled "African Leaders and the Geography of China's Foreign Assistance," published in the *Journal of Development Economics* in 2019, we explore the allocation of development finance at the subnational level in Africa. We draw upon and extend the analysis from that article in Chapter 6.

In follow-up work with Roland and Paul, we analyze the economic effects of politically motivated development projects from China in Africa in an article titled "Is Favoritism a Threat to Chinese Aid Effectiveness?" which was published in 2021 in *World Development*. This research contributed to our analysis in Chapter 7.

With Richard Bluhm, a development economist at Leibniz University Hannover, we explore the diffusion of economic activity at the subnational level in localities that receive Chinese transport infrastructure projects. This work is published as a 2020 AidData working paper focused on "Connective Financing." We extend these ideas in Chapter 7.

In "Aid, China, and Growth," published in the *American Economic Journal: Economic Policy* in 2021, we introduce our global project-level dataset and explore the impact of Chinese development finance on economic growth in recipient countries at the country level. We refine and extend these ideas in Chapters 7 and 8.

In "Chinese Aid and Health," a CESifo working paper published in 2020 with John Cruzzati and Johannes Matzat from Heidelberg University, we explore both the national and the local effects of Chinese development finance on health outcomes. We address similar issues in Chapter 7.

We are also grateful to Gerda Asmus, Angelika Budjan, and Vera Eichenauer who co-organized the workshop "Tracking International Aid and Investment from Developing and Emerging Economies" in Heidelberg in September 2017. This event engaged researchers with the beta version of our global dataset prior to its public release and provided us with invaluable feedback. Our special thanks go to David Dollar and Helen Milner who agreed to act as keynote speakers at this event.

In addition to those already listed, we have benefited from comments on this book manuscript and previous papers. For comments on previous articles and working papers listed earlier, we thank Anupam Anand, Kurt Annen, Channing Arndt, Owen Barder, Sarah Bermeo, Jean-Marc Blanchard, Deborah Bräutigam, Bruce Bueno de Mesquita, Pasita Chaijaroen, Chuan Chen, Marta Curto-Grau, Samantha Custer, Xinyuan Dai, Harsh Desai, Simone Dietrich, Helen Ding, Vivien

Foster, Patrick Francois, Martin Gassebner, Erik Haustein, Fang He, Cullen Hendrix, Anke Höffler, Christopher Holtz, Sebastian Horn, Yi Huang, Robert Inklaar, Ryan Jablonski, Lennart Kaplan, Christopher Kilby, Andreas Kotsadam, Mathilde Lebrand, Gregory Lévieuge, Quan Li, Jamus Lim, Yannick Lucotte, Takaaki Masaki, Anna Minasyan, Josepa Miquel-Florensa, Scott Morris, Ibrahim Okumu, Nataliya Pushak, Ferdinand Rauch, Gina Reinhardt, Phil Roessler, Marina Rudyak, Justin Sandefur, Mona Sehgal, Xiang Shao, Duncan Snidal, Arvind Subramanian, Bann Seng Tan, Heiwai Tang, Zhigang Tao, Finn Tarp, Joe Thwaites, Christoph Trebesch Laura Malaguzzi Valeri, Yan Wang, John Watkin, Lukas Wellner, Eric Werker, Franck Wiebe, James Williams, Tianyang Xi, Yang Yao, Zhejin Zhao, Yu Zheng, and Ekkart Zimmermann.

A special round of thanks is due to the participants in our pre-pandemic book workshop that was funded by William & Mary's Global Research Institute and held in Vancouver, Canada, in February 2020. These experts in the political economy of development, applied econometrics, and Chinese politics not only provided substantive feedback on the entire manuscript, but they also persuaded us to write the book in a way that would make it more accessible to the nonspecialist. We sought to make our quantitative tests come alive with reference to cases that not only illustrate the underlying logic of our arguments but also highlight the politics and the real-world effects of Chinese development finance. For moving us toward our "hummable tune" and for providing us with hundreds of specific suggestions, we thank Ryan Briggs, Ryan Jablonski, Erasmus Kersting, Christopher Kilby, Sooyeon Kim, Xiaojun Li, Dan Nielson, Christina Schneider, and Alexandra Zeitz. We are not certain that any of us are cut out to write for a nonacademic audience, but at the urging of workshop participants we have attempted to write a book that is accessible and engaging to readers beyond the ivory tower. We benefited enormously from the assistance of our editor Heath Sledge. She not only helped translate our turgid prose into simpler English but also taught us a great deal about the power of narrative that will inform our own writing instruction as we teach our graduate and undergraduate students.

In addition to academic colleagues, this project relied on the outstanding assistance of ten professional staff members at AidData: Sid Ghose, Brooke Russell, Mengfan Cheng, Harsh Desai, Seth Goodman, Joyce Lin, Brian O'Donnell, Miranda Lv, Charles Perla, and Scott Stewart. They refined our data collection procedures, implemented an elaborate data quality assurance plan, oversaw a small army of research assistants, and provided professional project management services.

This book benefited from tens of thousands of hours of painstaking data collection, coding, and quality assurance by a very large number of research and team assistants at William & Mary, the National University of Singapore, Heidelberg University, the University of Göttingen, and the Kiel Institute for the World Economy. In addition to the work they did for this book, many represent the next generation of researchers on this topic. We offer huge thanks to Faith Achan, Melanie Aguilar-Rojas, Rashid Ahimbisibwe, Omar Alkhoja, Immaculate Apio, Katherine Armstrong, Bilal Asad, Isabelle Baucum, Zach Baxter, Rachel Benavides, Ellie Bentley, Liliana Besosa, Abigail Bilenkin, Allison Bowers, Abigail Britton, Peter Byambwenu, John Wycliff Byona, Ariel Cadby-Spicer, Emma Cahoon, Bree Cattelino, Alex Chadwick, Ava Chafin, Anissa Chams-Eddine, Tina Chang, Harrison Chapman, Wen Chen, Yining Chen, Yuning Chen, Michelle Cheng, Tiffanie Choi, Sarah Christophe, Miranda Clarke, Kate Connors, McKay Corbett, Graeme Cranston-Cuebas, Catherine Crowley, Hali Czosnek, Jenna Davis, Alex DeGala, Hannah Dempsey, Rohan Desai, Justin DeShazor, Isabel Docampo, Joseph Dobbels, Weiwei Du, Ashton Ebert, Caleb Ebert, Aili Espigh, Claire Etheridge, Alexandria Foster, Jordan Fox, Robert Francis, Ze Fu, Wesley Garner, Melanie Gilbert, Elizabeth Goldemen, Jaclyn Goldschmidt, Sara Gomez, Zijie Gong, Grace Grains, Liz Hall, Thompson Hangen, Sarah Harmon, Ethan Harrison, Lauren Harrison, Michael Hathaway, Tobias Hellmundt, Collin Henson, Jasmine Herndon, Skye Herrick, Elizabeth Herrity, Gabrielle Hibbert, Carlos Holden-Villars, Keith Holleran, Weijue Huang, Daniel Hughes, Evelyn Hytopoulos, Torey Beth Jackson, Jiaorui Jiang, Qi Jiang, Emmaleah Jones, Amar Kakirde, Simon Richard Kalema, Naixin Kang, Rachel Kellogg, Connor Kennedy, Ibra Kibare, Ciera Killen, Ian Kirkwood, Warren Kirkwood, Emily Koerner, Dylan Kolhoff, Hayley Kornblum, Lidia Kovacevic, Martyna Kowalczyk, Mirian Kreykes, Dinu Krishnamoorthi, Isabella Kron, Heike Kullmann, Karthik Kumarappan, Marko Kwaramba, Robert Kyaligonza, Daniel Lantz, Caroline Lebegue, Patrick Leisure, Jade Li, Yuwei Li, Xiao Liu, Steven Livingston, Yaseen Lofti, Adriane Lopez, Flynn Madden, Nyasha Mahonye, Dominick Margiotta, Sarah Martin, Janet Mbambu, Kevin McCrory, Emily McLenigan, Paul Michel, Alex Miller, George Moss, Henry Muhaire, Samson Mukanjari, Marie Mullins, Vincent Mutegeki, James Muyindi, Jennipher Nakabugo, Will Nelson, Albert Ngageno, Qiuyan Ni, Jack Nicol, Brendan O'Connor, Olasubomi Obadeyi, Paul Stephen Obuya, Daniel Overbeck, Alexandra Pancake, Henrique Passos Neto, Carol Peng, Grace Perkins, Sophia Perrotti, Victor Polanco, Andrea Powers, Laura Preszler, Han Qiao, Emily Qiu, Kamran

Rahman, Sarah Reso, David Rice, Sara Rock, Ann Rogers, Elizabeth Saccoccia, Natalie Santos, Dominic Sanzotta, Faith Savaiano, Dominic Scerbo, Rebecca Schectman, Mark Schoeman, Leigh Seitz, Ryan Septon, Lu Sevier, William Shangraw, Kaitlan Shaub, Samuel Siewers, Andrea Soleta, Kyra Solomon, Scott Stewart, Lauren Su, Yifan Su, Elizabeth Sutterlin, Catherine Tabingwa, Mahathi Tadikonda, Joanna Tan, Wenxia Tang, Emily Tanner, Nate Tanner, Brittany Tennant, Becca Thorpe, Pius Tibaingana, Austin Trotta, Felix Turbanisch, John Collin Twaya, Anna Umstead, Jessica Usjanauskas, Julia Varoutsos, Emily Walker, Yale Waller, Katherine Walsh, John Paul Wanambwa, Xinyi Wang, Wendy Wen, Nicolas Wesseler, Matt Westover, Tom Westover, Amber Will, James Willard, (Jiacheng) Jason Xi, Hanyang Xu, Darice Xue, Erya Yang, Gaohang Yao, Antonio Tianze Ye, Lincoln Zaleski, Jack Zhang, Yue Zhang, Echo Zhong, Joana Zhu, and Junrong Zhu.

Large collaborative projects like this one require more than good ideas and sweat equity on the part of the coauthors. They require real resources to make initial investments in new ideas, fund data collection and field research, and pay for the time of professional staff. We have been particularly fortunate in this regard, for we have received financial support from a large number of philanthropic foundations and government agencies. Given the sensitivity and potential controversy surrounding this topic, we made a conscious decision not to take any money from the US or Chinese government until after we were well along in the project and had already published several peer-reviewed studies demonstrating the quality of our methods and research in this area. In addition to receiving substantial support from our home universities, we received external support from the William & Flora Hewlett Foundation, the John D. and Catherine T. MacArthur Foundation, Humanity United, the Smith Richardson Foundation, United Nations University-WIDER, the Academic Research Fund of Singapore's Ministry of Education, and the German Research Foundation.

Finally, we would like to thank our editor at Cambridge University Press. John Haslam has been insightful, creative, and kind in all our interactions, but what stands out most is his patience. Our original promise to John was that we would deliver a completed manuscript in the spring of 2018. To put it mildly, John has been more lenient with deadlines than we are with our own students. We are hopeful that the extra time he provided has also made this a better book.

While we have accumulated many debts and benefited from the generosity of so many other people and institutions over the past nine years working on this project, all remaining errors in the manuscript are our responsibility.

# Abbreviations

| | |
|---|---|
| ADB | Asian Development Bank |
| ADM1 | First-Order Administrative Unit |
| ADM2 | Second-Order Administrative Unit |
| AEI | American Enterprise Institute |
| AfDB | African Development Bank |
| AIIB | Asian Infrastructure Investment Bank |
| ASEAN | Association of Southeast Asian Nations |
| ATI | Access to Information |
| BCL | Non-Preferential Buyer's Credit Loan |
| BRD | Battle-Related Deaths |
| BRI | Belt and Road Initiative |
| BUILD Act | Better Utilization of Investment Leading to Development Act |
| BYU | Brigham Young University |
| CAITEC | Chinese Academy of International Trade and Economic Cooperation |
| CCCC | China Communications Construction Company |
| CCP | Chinese Communist Party |
| CDB | China Development Bank |
| CDC | Commonwealth Development Corporation |
| CESifo | Center for Economic Studies and Ifo Institute for Economic Research (the Munich Society for the Promotion of Economic Research) |
| CIA | Central Intelligence Agency |
| CIDCA | China International Development Cooperation Agency |
| CIDRN | China International Development Research Network |
| CMPH | China Merchant Port Holdings |
| COMPLANT | China National Complete Plant Import & Export Corporation Ltd. |
| CPEC | China-Pakistan Economic Corridor |
| CRBC | China Road and Bridge Corporation |
| CRS | Congressional Research Service |

| | |
|---|---|
| CSIS | Center for Strategic and International Studies |
| DAC | Development Assistance Committee |
| DFA | MOFCOM's Department of Foreign Aid |
| DFID | Department for International Development |
| DHS | Demographic and Health Surveys |
| DPP | Department of Public Prosecutions |
| DSF | Debt Sustainability Framework |
| DSSI | Debt Service Suspension Initiative |
| ECCOs | Economic and Commercial Counselor Offices |
| EIA | Environmental Impact Assessment |
| EIB | European Investment Bank |
| EU | European Union |
| EURIBOR | Euro Interbank Offered Rate |
| Eximbank | Export-Import Bank of China |
| FCDO | Foreign, Commonwealth and Development Office |
| FDI | Foreign Direct Investment |
| FYDP | Five-Year Development Plan |
| G-7 | Group of Seven |
| GADM | Database of Global Administrative Areas |
| GCL | Government Concessional Loan |
| GDP | Gross Domestic Product |
| GHSL | Global Human Settlement Layer |
| GMM | Generalized Method of Moments |
| GNI | Gross National Income |
| IAD | Inter-American Dialogue |
| IATI | International Aid Transparency Initiative |
| IBRD | International Bank for Reconstruction and Development |
| ICRG | International Country Risk Guide |
| IDA | International Development Association |
| IFAD | International Fund for Agricultural Development |
| IMF | International Monetary Fund |
| JAST | Joint Aid Strategy for Tanzania |
| JICA | Japan International Cooperation Agency |
| JRC | Joint Research Center |
| KfW | German Development Bank |
| LIBOR | London Interbank Offered Rate |
| LTTE | Liberation Tigers of Tamil Eelam |
| MCC | Millennium Challenge Corporation |
| MDGs | Millennium Development Goals |
| MFA | Ministry of Foreign Affairs |
| MOFCOM | China's Ministry of Commerce |

NAM               Non-Aligned Movement
NBSC              National Bureau of Statistics of China
NCF               National Conference Party
NDRC              National Development and Reform Commission
NORINCO           China North Industries Group
OBOR              One Belt, One Road
OECD              Organisation for Economic Co-operation and Development
ODA               Official Development Assistance
OF                Official Financing
OFDI              Outward Foreign Direct Investment
OOF               Other Official Flows
OP                Operational Policy
PBC               Preferential Buyer's Credit
PGAR              Provisional Government of the Algerian Republic
PLA               People's Liberation Army
PRC               People's Republic of China
ROC               Republic of Congo
SAFE              State Administration of Foreign Exchange
SAIS-CARI         School of Advanced International Studies - China Africa Research Initiative
SGR               Standard Gauge Railway between Mombasa and Nairobi
Sinosure          China Export and Credit Insurance Corporation
SMS               Short Message Service
SNPC              Société Nationales des Pétroles Congolais
SPLA              Sudan People's Liberation Army
SPVs              Special Purpose Vehicles
TPP               Trans-Pacific Partnership
TTL               World Bank Task Team Leader
TUFF              Tracking Underreported Financial Flows
UNDP              United Nations Development Program
UNECA             United Nations Economic Commission for Africa
UNEP              United Nations Environment Program
UNESCO            United Nations Educational, Scientific and Cultural Organization
UNGA              United Nations General Assembly
UNSC              United Nations Security Council
USAID             United States Agency for International Development
USGS              United States Geological Survey
WGI               Worldwide Governance Indicators
WHO               World Health Organization

# 1 Why Do We Know So Little about the Aims and Impacts of China's Overseas Development Program?

### From "Hide and Bide" Donor to Lender of First Resort

Over the past two decades, Beijing has achieved something truly extraordinary: it has established itself as the lender of first resort for many low-income and middle-income countries.[1] In doing so, it has become "public enemy number one" in the eyes of many Western governments and multilateral institutions. According to the US government, China is deploying a US$3 trillion war chest of foreign currency reserves to gain the upper hand in a zero-sum competition for global influence. The 2018 US National Defense Strategy asserts that "[t]he central challenge to US prosperity and security is the reemergence of long-term, strategic competition ... [with] revisionist powers."[2] It calls upon the development, diplomacy, and defense agencies of the US government to "out-think, out-maneuver, out-partner, and out-innovate" these powers and singles out China as a "strategic competitor" that "us[es] predatory economics to intimidate its neighbors."[3] The US National Security Strategy is even more direct in its criticism, arguing that "Chinese practices undermine ... long-term development by corrupting elites, dominating extractive industries, and locking countries into unsustainable and opaque debts and commitments."[4]

The US Agency for International Development (USAID) operationalized these strategies through its 2018 adoption of a "Clear Choice Framework," which sought to distinguish the American and Chinese value propositions and proactively communicate these differences to the

---

[1] During the summer of 2020, the World Bank took the unprecedented step of publishing data on public and publicly guaranteed debt stocks and debt service by creditor country. These data are available for sixty-five of the poorest countries that participate in the World Bank's Debtor Reporting System (DRS). The publicly available debt stock data from the DRS indicate that China is the single-largest bilateral lender to forty-six of these sixty-five countries. See https://datatopics.worldbank.org/debt/ids/, last accessed November 10, 2020.

[2] US Department of Defense (2018: 2).   [3] US Department of Defense (2018: 1).

[4] Office of the President of the United States of America (2017: 52).

leaders of low-income and middle-income countries.[5] US legislators from different ends of the political spectrum followed suit. In October 2018, they passed the Better Utilization of Investment Leading to Development (BUILD) Act, which established a "full service" development finance institution to help the US government compete with China around the globe. Then, in September 2019, they voted unanimously to create a US$375 million "Countering Chinese Influence" fund.[6]

China has faced an equally relentless barrage of criticism from European governments and multilateral institutions. Some have warned that Beijing bankrolls economically inefficient but politically expedient "white elephant" projects. Others have raised concerns about China saddling its overseas borrowers with unsustainable debt burdens. Another common refrain is that, in its zeal to help partner countries install the "hardware" of economic development (e.g., highways, railroads, dams, bridges), China prioritizes speed over quality, green-lighting projects without appropriate environmental, social, and fiduciary safeguards or monitoring and evaluation systems.

The Belt and Road Initiative (BRI) has provided a focal point for these concerns. Launched in 2013 by Chinese President Xi Jinping, the BRI is a US$1 trillion global infrastructure program that the *New York Times* describes as having "little precedent in modern history."[7] Before it was announced, Western diplomats and leaders of multilateral organizations questioned the aims and impacts of China's overseas development program from the sidelines with a sense of bemusement. Beijing's role in the global development finance market was a popular topic at cocktail parties and roundtable discussions governed by Chatham House rules.[8] But their concerns did not spill into public view – or inform official policy – until they understood the true scale, scope, and ambition of the BRI.

In June 2019, the president of the World Bank, David Malpass, faced questions about the wisdom of the BRI. He responded by admonishing China for the secrecy surrounding its global infrastructure program and emphasizing that "[i]f debt is executed in an opaque manner, it is difficult

---

[5] USAID's Clear Choice Framework characterizes the "American model" as one that privileges transparency, accountability, financial sustainability, the right to self-determination, and free-market principles. By contrast, it characterizes the "Chinese model" as one that privileges authoritarian governance, state-led capitalism, opaque and unsustainable debts, and subordination to the dictates of a foreign power (Igoe 2018a; USAID 2018; Green 2019).

[6] In September 2019, the US Senate Committee on Appropriations voted 31–0 to create this fund "to combat malign Chinese influence activities and increase transparency and accountability associated with the Belt and Road Initiative."

[7] Perlez and Huang (2017).

[8] According to Chatham House rules, participants can freely use and speak about the content of discussions without attributing it to any specific participant.

for other lenders to know the conditions, making it difficult for them to invest in the business, which ultimately hinders the development of the borrowing countries."[9] In January 2020, a top International Monetary Fund (IMF) official doubled down on this admonishment. He announced his organization's "number one message" to the Chinese authorities in Beijing: "[i]f you are a big lender, there is no free-riding.... If you fail to be transparent, you make it more difficult for everyone else."[10] Two months before this dressing down, Japan and Australia announced that they would join forces with the United States to launch the "Blue Dot Network" to counter the BRI. They established this network to "evaluate and certify nominated infrastructure projects based upon adherence to commonly accepted principles and standards" and to "promote market-driven, transparent, and financially sustainable infrastructure development in the Indo-Pacific region and around the world."[11]

The fact that we have reached the point where China's overseas development program inspires awe and contempt from international donors and lenders is extraordinary – and puzzling. Just fifteen years ago, China was a *net recipient* rather than a net donor of aid.[12] So, how did we get here?

The central claim of this book is that during the first two decades of the twenty-first century, China has undergone a major transition from a "benefactor" to a "banker," and this shift has had far-reaching impacts in low-income and middle-income countries that are not yet widely appreciated or understood.[13] During the twentieth century, China's international development expenditures were roughly on par with those of a small, Northern European donor like Denmark. Beijing kept an especially low profile during the 1980s and 1990s, adhering to the principle of "hide your capabilities and bide your time," put forth by Deng Xiaoping, China's former paramount leader.

But everything changed in 1999, when Beijing adopted a "Going Out" strategy. That was the point at which the government tasked its state-owned

---

[9] Kawanami (2019).    [10] Zettelmeyer (2020).

[11] International Development Finance Corporation (2019). In a high-profile speech laying the groundwork for this new initiative, US Vice President Mike Pence said, "as we're all aware, some are offering infrastructure loans to governments across the Indo-Pacific and the wider world. Yet the terms of those loans are often opaque at best. [The] projects they support are often unsustainable and of poor quality. And too often, they come with strings attached and lead to staggering debt" (Pence 2018).

[12] Chin (2012) estimates that China became a net donor in 2005 or 2006.

[13] Throughout much of this book, we use "China" or "Beijing" as a shorthand term to refer to all of the Chinese government institutions, state-owned banks, and state-owned enterprises that provide development finance to low-income and middle-income countries.

"policy banks" – China Eximbank and China Development Bank – with helping Chinese firms gain a foothold in overseas markets.[14] The Going Out strategy came into existence because of several challenges that Beijing faced at home. First, the country suffered from a domestic industrial overproduction problem because its state-owned steel, iron, cement, glass, aluminum, and timber companies were over-leveraged, inefficient, and unprofitable.[15] Beijing viewed domestic industrial overproduction as a threat to the country's long-term growth prospects and a potential source of social unrest and political instability.[16] It wanted to reduce domestic supply (through the off-shoring of industrial input production facilities) and increase international demand (by encouraging foreign buyers to purchase more industrial inputs from China). Second, Beijing faced a foreign exchange oversupply problem: annual trade surpluses facilitated a rapid expansion in foreign exchange reserves, and the country risked macroeconomic instability (inflation or a currency revaluation) if it allowed these reserves to enter the domestic economy, so the authorities decided to instead look for productive overseas outlets where they could park their excess dollars and euros. Third, Beijing recognized that to sustain high levels of domestic economic growth, it would need to scour the globe for those natural resources that it lacked in sufficient quantities at home.[17] To address these challenges, the Chinese government enlisted the support of its policy banks; they were given a mandate to support overseas projects focused on industrial production, infrastructure, and natural resource acquisition and to facilitate the participation of Chinese firms in these projects. In the fifteen-year period (2000–2014) following Beijing's adoption of the Going Out strategy, China's overseas development spending skyrocketed.

During this period, the *nature* of Beijing's participation in the global development finance market also changed in a fundamental way. At the turn of the century, China mostly offered Renminbi-denominated grants and interest-free loans to its counterparts in the developing world. It used

---

[14] China Development and China Eximbank are state-owned banks that pursue profit and national policy objectives.

[15] The Chinese government characterizes the problem as "industrial overcapacity," which is a term that usually refers to the difference between domestic production capacity and actual production for the domestic market. However, for the sake of clarity, we prefer the terms "industrial overproduction" and "excess industrial production" because China overproduces industrial inputs relative to demand on the domestic market. It then attempts to sell its overproduced industrial inputs to foreign buyers (often in developing countries) because of its domestic overcapacity problem.

[16] More specifically, they feared that if this problem was not resolved, some of the country's biggest employers would lay off large numbers of Chinese workers, which could in turn lead to public antipathy toward the government and the Chinese Communist Party (CCP).

[17] These natural resources included oil, gas, copper, and cobalt, among others.

its largesse to cultivate and cement diplomatic ties and political alliances with other countries, constructing projects such as presidential palaces, parliamentary complexes, and soccer stadiums. However, over time, Beijing began to behave less like a benefactor and more like a banker. As we explain in Chapter 2, China's own experiences with outbound and inbound development finance during the last two decades of the twentieth century paved the way for this transition. But China did not fully embrace its role as a major international lender until the turn of the century, when it saw that doing so could help it address the challenges of industrial overproduction, excess foreign exchange reserves, and limited access to the natural resources needed to sustain high levels of economic growth. In response to these challenges, China's policy banks made three changes: they ramped up foreign currency-denominated lending at or near market rates, they contractually obligated overseas borrowers to source project inputs (such as steel and cement) from China, and they made it easier for countries to secure and repay loans with the money that they earned from commodity sales to China.

Consequently, after 2000, Beijing's overseas development spending became less focused on aid and more focused on debt. Only 23 percent of China's overseas spending between 2000 and 2014 met the Organisation for Economic Co-operation and Development's (OECD) definition of official development assistance (ODA) – that is, aid in the strict sense of the term. China used debt to finance most of its overseas projects. By contrast, the members of the Development Assistance Committee (DAC) of the OECD – wealthy, industrialized countries that dominated the international development finance market during the last five decades of the twentieth century – devoted nearly all (~90 percent) of their overseas spending to ODA between 2000 and 2014.

The blurring of the distinction between Chinese aid and debt has far-reaching implications that are not well understood by many politicians, journalists, or researchers. Indeed, much of the controversy about China's overseas development program arises from a failure to differentiate between projects financed with grants and low-interest loans (aid) and projects financed with loans at market or close-to-market rates (debt). Beijing's critics and rivals characterize China as a rogue actor that uses its largesse for nefarious purposes: to purchase the loyalty of ruling elites in corrupt and authoritarian regimes, to exploit natural resources without concern for environmental consequences, and to create unfair commercial advantages for Chinese firms in overseas markets. Beijing's allies and clients take issue with this characterization; they view China as a flexible and demand-driven financier that is willing to bankroll and build big-ticket, high-impact projects.

How should we evaluate these competing narratives? We address this challenge by separately analyzing Chinese development projects financed with aid and Chinese development projects financed with debt. To this end, we have assembled a granular and comprehensive dataset of Chinese government-financed projects around the globe that allows for such parsing. Our analysis of the dataset suggests that China is neither the "hero" promoted by its allies and clients nor the "villain" caricatured by its rivals and critics.

Beijing, we argue, uses financial instruments that are *fit-for-purpose*. If its objective is to buy foreign policy favors from another government, it provides financing on favorable terms through grant and zero-interest loan instruments. If its objective is to maximize investment returns or secure natural resources, it uses commercial financing instruments, such as loans that are priced at or near prevailing market interest rates. Chinese aid and debt are means to different ends, and when this distinction is ignored, policymakers, journalists, and researchers misunderstand the motivational factors that guide Beijing's overseas spending and the impacts that its projects achieve in low-income and middle-income countries.

Our findings also suggest that, in some ways, China and its OECD-DAC counterparts have more in common than they realize. We find that Chinese aid is no more likely than US aid to flow to corrupt or authoritarian regimes. Beijing does use aid as a tool to secure influence at the United Nations and other venues, but so do Western donors. Also contrary to conventional wisdom, Chinese aid does not flow disproportionately to countries with abundant oil and other extractable resources. In fact, Beijing relies heavily on one of the same aid allocation criteria used by Western donors: a country's per capita income level. Those with higher levels of need get more aid, regardless of whether it comes from Washington, London, Brussels, or Beijing. Similarly, China and its OECD-DAC counterparts are guided by the same motivation when they issue loans that are priced at or near market rates: ensuring repayment. The biggest difference that we found between China and its Western peers is which tools they use the most: China relies heavily on debt to finance its overseas development program, while OECD-DAC countries rely on aid.

But it is still difficult to directly compare the overseas spending practices of China and its OECD-DAC counterparts because the former is a state-led economy and the latter represents a group of market-led economies. As such, China's approach is fundamentally different from that of its peers and competitors in the OECD-DAC. In market-led economies, the government expects a decentralized set of actors in the private sector to pursue profit and lend with the objective of maximizing investment returns, and there is no strong rationale for government involvement in commercial lending activities. By contrast, in China, the government is a major economic actor that pursues profit, so the country's state-owned banks are heavily engaged in commercial lending activities; the lending behavior of China's state-owned banks resembles that of private sector banks in OECD-DAC countries.

Another major source of debate among policymakers and practitioners is how Chinese development projects affect social, economic, environmental, and governance outcomes in low- and middle-income countries. Beijing's critics claim that it bankrolls ill-conceived and risky projects that would not be funded by Western aid agencies or multilateral development banks. In the words of *The Economist*, "China seems to be repeating many of the mistakes made by Western donors and investors in the 1970s, when money flowed into big ... infrastructure projects that never produced the expected economic gains."[18]

Here, too, our empirical findings suggest that China and its OECD-DAC peers have more in common than they think. When we separately analyze aid-financed and debt-financed development projects, we find that projects financed with grants and low-interest loans consistently boost economic growth in the countries where they take place, regardless of the funding source. Both Chinese aid and OECD-DAC aid promote economic growth in low-income and middle-income countries.[19]

Previous research demonstrates that Western development projects achieve different effects in different settings, and our empirical findings suggest that the Chinese development projects are no different. Their effects depend upon the choices and characteristics of host countries. Chinese development projects consistently improve economic development outcomes in Africa, but not necessarily elsewhere. They reduce political instability in some countries that experience sudden withdrawals of Western aid, but not in others. They accelerate environmental degradation in jurisdictions where the enforcement of environmental laws and regulations is weak, but not in localities where economic actors generally comply with environmental rules.

---

[18] *The Economist* (2017a).

[19] A more complex pattern emerges when we analyze Chinese and OECD-DAC projects financed with loans at or near market rates. Due to the short time series of data we have available, we can only investigate the short-run effects of development finance. Our results are thus not directly comparable to studies that investigate the long-run effects of aid on growth. Results across such studies are mixed, finding no statistically significant effects of aid on growth in the medium to long run or small positive effects. For surveys, see Werker (2012); Dreher, Lang, and Ziaja (2018); and Doucouliagos (2019).

In a nutshell, our argument in this book is that much of the conventional wisdom about Chinese development finance that is published by international media, promoted by think tanks, and accepted by governments outside China rests on untested assumptions, individual case studies, and incomplete data sources. The primary reason why we know so little about the aims and impacts of Chinese aid is that Beijing shrouds its overseas portfolio of grants and concessional loans in secrecy. It does not disclose comprehensive or detailed information about its aid projects. Nor does it publish a country-by-country breakdown of its foreign aid activities. It considers its foreign aid program a "state secret" and ranks dead last among the forty-seven international donors evaluated by Publish What You Fund in its 2020 Aid Transparency Index.[20]

China keeps its commercial lending activities equally secret. The BRI aims to develop an overland "belt" of road, rail, port, and pipeline projects that will create an infrastructure corridor from China to Central Asia and Europe, as well as a "Maritime Silk Road" that will consist of deep-water ports along the littoral areas of the Indian Ocean that will link China to South and Southeast Asia, the Middle East, and Africa. This initiative, which is being largely financed with Chinese debt, is shielded from public scrutiny. As explained in the *New York Times*, "China has never released any official map of Belt and Road routes nor any list of approved projects, and it provides no exact count of participating nations or even guidelines on what it means to be a participant."[21]

Social science research on the aims and impacts of Chinese development finance remains in its infancy because of Beijing's unwillingness to share detailed information about its overseas development program. To close this evidence gap, we have spent the past nine years working with AidData to systematically assemble a comprehensive dataset of Chinese aid- and debt-financed development projects around the globe. We are dyed-in-the-wool empiricists, and many of the chapters of this book are based on statistical analyses of this new dataset. But we want our analysis to be readable and accessible to those who are not statisticians. We therefore describe our methods and findings in simple, clear language, avoiding statistical jargon wherever we can. For readers who would like to review our methods and findings in greater technical detail, we have added technical appendices to several chapters. At the beginning of most chapters, we will also refer these readers to a list of peer-reviewed journal articles that we published before writing this book. Readers who wish to be spared these technical details should feel free to simply skip these appendices and journal articles – or consult them only as needed.

[20] Bräutigam (2009: 2); Publish What You Fund (2020).    [21] Mauk (2019).

Before we "zoom out," looking at major patterns and trends in our dataset (covering 138 countries and five regions of the world), let's "zoom in" on two countries – Sri Lanka and Tanzania – where China has used its aid and debt instruments for different purposes and with different results. These two cases are consistent with the notion that China is neither the hero promoted by its allies and clients nor the villain caricatured by its rivals and critics.

China's benefactor-to-banker transition has dramatically raised the stakes for developing countries. Its willingness to bankroll big-ticket infrastructure projects creates new opportunities for host countries to achieve rapid socioeconomic gains, but it also introduces major risks, such as corruption, conflict, and environmental degradation. The cases of Sri Lanka and Tanzania demonstrate that there is a tension between *efficacy* and *safety* in Chinese development finance, and some countries are more effective than others at managing these risks and rewards.

## When the Risks of Banking with Beijing Exceed the Rewards: The Cautionary Tale of Sri Lanka from 2005 to 2015

Until recently, Hambantota was a small, seaside village at the southern tip of Sri Lanka with roughly 12,000 residents. Hambantota District is the birthplace of Mahinda Rajapaksa, who represented it as a Member of Parliament (MP) for sixteen years before being elected president of Sri Lanka. During his tenure as president (2005–2015), Rajapaksa attempted to transform his home district into an international shipping hub and a major urban center at a "breakneck pace."[22] He designated the town of Hambantota as one of the country's five public investment priorities and promoted the idea of making it a "second capital," using "bombastic propaganda through highly paid advertising agencies, including widely disseminated computer-generated videos."[23] His twenty-three-year-old son, Namal Rajapaksa, oversaw these efforts and succeeded him as the MP responsible for Hambantota District.

The Rajapaksa family convinced Beijing's policy banks to support their rather peculiar vision for the country's future: China Eximbank and China Development Bank issued loans worth approximately US$1.5 billion for the construction of a deep seaport in Hambantota, US$200 million for the construction of a nearby airport, US$412 million for a road from the seaport to the airport, and US$180 million for an expressway connecting Hambantota to the capital city of Colombo. With

---

[22] Fowler (2010).    [23] Peebles (2015: 22).

support from Chinese state-owned companies, the Rajapaksa administration also fast-tracked the construction of a state-of-the-art international convention center, a 35,000-seat cricket stadium, a 300-acre botanical garden, a 235-acre "Tele Cinema Park" for TV and film production, an oil refinery, a sports complex, and a string of luxury hotels and housing developments in Hambantota.[24]

President Rajapaksa's push to transform this remote part of the country into a second capital was part of a broader effort to cement domestic political support for his administration by implementing highly visible infrastructure projects in the country's southern and predominantly Sinhalese region.[25] To do so, the president and his allies needed access to external financing, which they traditionally received from Western donors. However, when a ceasefire with the secessionist Liberation Tigers of Tamil Eelam (LTTE) collapsed in 2007, Rajapaksa pursued a military solution, plunging the country into civil war. This decision alienated the country's Western donors, precipitating a sharp reduction in Western aid.[26] Beijing stepped into the breach and made the 50 percent contraction in Western aid seem almost inconsequential. It dramatically increased its financial support to Sri Lanka during the Rajapaksa administration, committing a total of US$12.4 billion between 2005 and 2014.

By most accounts, Chinese government-financed infrastructure projects were an important driver of rapid economic growth in Sri Lanka during the first seven years of the Rajapaksa administration (2005–2011); the country's economy grew at an average annual rate of 8 percent during this period. However, some parts of the country benefited far more than others: Hambantota District experienced particularly rapid economic

---

[24] *The Economist* (2010); Crabtree (2012); Shepard (2016). In a 2010 interview, Rajapaksa explained that the Hambantota port project "was offered to India first. I was desperate for development work. But ultimately the Chinese agreed to build it" (Velloor 2010). On China-India competition in the realm of development finance, see Asmus, Eichenauer, Fuchs, and Parks (2021).

[25] Athukorala and Jayasuriya (2013: 20) refer to the southern (Sinhala) region of Sri Lanka as "the heartland of the electoral support base of the Rajapaksa family." In a 2009 cable dispatch, the US Embassy in Colombo characterized "the Hambantota [port] project [as] a huge deliverable to the President's home region and his electoral base" (Fowler 2009). It also warned that "some donors believe the Rajapaksa government is intentionally trying to steer aid and investment toward the Sinhala south while neglecting the north and east" and that "disproportionately [channeling resources] to peaceful [Southern] areas could exacerbate ethnic inequities and fuel the conflict" (Blake 2007).

[26] In the first year of the Rajapaksa administration (2005), OECD-DAC donors gave the country approximately US$1.1 billion of ODA (see Box 1.1 for a precise definition). However, by the last year of the Rajapaksa administration (2014), OECD-DAC ODA had contracted to less than US$500 million a year. During the same period (2005–2014), the average annual level of government financing from China to Sri Lanka was approximately US$1.2 billion.

growth and poverty reduction gains, which fueled grievances about political bias in the subnational distribution of public investments.[27]

Critics of the administration warned that the projects in the president's home district were "white elephants" that would produce short-lived benefits and long-term, recurring costs. One particular project financed by China Eximbank – the new international airport just ten miles from Hambantota – became a focal point for public scorn and political opposition. The Rajapaksa administration envisioned major international carriers bringing travelers from Beijing, Chennai, Dubai, Riyadh, and Bangkok to Hambantota for sporting events, international conferences, ecotourism, and nightlife, and the 12,000 square meter terminal building was designed to support as many as 1 million travelers per year. However, the Mattala Rajapaksa International Airport eventually became known as "the world's emptiest international airport."[28] Sri Lanka's aviation minister reported to parliament in 2014 that the airport had only earned US$123 in revenue in a single month; when a visiting journalist asked a senior government official about the airport, he indicated, "[w]hen I visited the airport there, I asked the sole immigration officer how many passports she'd stamped that day. She said, 'One.'"[29]

These problems were foreseeable. In a 2007 cable dispatch from the US Embassy in Colombo, Ambassador Robert Blake reported as follows:

The problem ... is that the projects are being driven from the top down. President Rajapaksa wants big improvements to happen quickly and has chosen large projects that will attract a lot of attention and praise for him and his party. Unfortunately, little thought has been put into what Hambantota District actually needs, what types of projects would provide jobs that locals can fill, and what would raise standards of living.... An empty port, an empty airport, and an empty vast convention center would not generate the benefits that Hambantota needs, and may, if constructed, be considered the President's folly.[30]

Cost overruns and corruption plagued many of the infrastructure projects that Beijing bankrolled during the Rajapaksa administration. One project financed by China Eximbank – a thirty-kilometer road connecting the president's home district to the capital city – earned the dubious distinction of being the single most expensive road project (in unit cost

---

[27] Athukorala and Jayasuriya (2013); Newhouse, Suarez Becerra, and Doan (2016: 15–16); Lim and Mukherjee (2017).
[28] Shepard (2016); see also Larmer (2017).
[29] Bearak (2015). Within only a few years of becoming fully operational, the airport was running an annual financial loss of US$18 million (Shepard 2016).
[30] Blake (2006).

terms) ever built in Sri Lanka.[31] A former chair of the country's National Transport Commission sounded the alarm, noting that "[t]he extension of the [China Eximbank-financed] Southern Highway from Matara to Beliatta … appears to be in a class of its own being over-priced by an astounding 545%."[32] He noted that road construction projects awarded to contractors without competitive bidding "were 55% costlier than those that were bid competitively" and explained that "[t]he common denominator of all these projects is that they were funded with Chinese borrowings and contracts have all been awarded … without calling for competitive bids."[33] Shortly thereafter, civil society organizations in Sri Lanka came forward with evidence that government officials and Chinese companies were colluding by artificially inflating contract prices and sharing the proceeds – the difference between the estimated and actual costs of the infrastructure projects.[34] A 2010 cable dispatch from the US Embassy in Colombo reported that President Rajapaksa and his inner circle were the likely beneficiaries of the corruption accompanying these projects.[35]

Making matters worse, some of the most expensive projects were not financed with grants but with loans priced at market or close-to-market rates. By the end of the Rajapaksa administration, the country had accumulated approximately US$8 billion of debt to China. "White elephant" projects – such as the Mattala Rajapaksa International Airport – were particularly damaging because they failed to generate revenue that would enable loan repayment. To avoid a crippling debt burden, the Sri Lankan authorities resorted to a fire sale. They began selling national assets in exchange for debt relief. They granted China a major ownership stake in and a ninety-nine-year lease to operate Hambantota's deep-water port in exchange for US$1.1 billion of debt forgiveness.[36] They also pursued

---

[31] According to Kumarage (2014), Sri Lanka's "[per kilometer] costs for 2013/14 [express-way construction] projects are double that of Vietnam, quadruple that of Pakistan and are generally 5–10 times more expensive than India."

[32] Kumarage (2014).

[33] Kumarage (2014) focused on four Chinese-financed infrastructure projects and reported that "[t]he loss arising from these projects alone is estimated at [US$1.3 billion]."

[34] *Sri Lanka Mirror* (2017). The cost of the China Eximbank-financed Southern Highway from Matara to Beliatta was reportedly inflated by 40 percent. Sri Lanka's neighbor to the south has also criticized China's approach for artificially inflating project costs and thereby saddling borrowers with unsustainable debt burdens. Mohamed Nasheed, who served as the president of the Maldives from 2008 to 2012, claims that "[t]hey came in; they did the work and sent us the bill. So it's not the loan interest rates as such but the costing itself. They over-invoiced us and charged us for that and now we have to repay the interest rate and the principal amount.… I can't see how our development can be rapid enough to have the amount of savings to re-pay China" (*The Economic Times* 2019).

[35] Fowler (2010).

[36] Schultz (2017); Abi-Habib (2018); IMF (2018). The seaport in Hambantota became operational in 2010. It reportedly received only twenty-four ships in 2011 and 2012,

a debt-for-equity swap to address the commercial failure of the airport in the president's home district.[37]

By 2014, President Rajapaksa's decision to ally himself with China and focus public investment in the country's southern region looked less like a political asset that would help him consolidate power and more like a political liability. Against a backdrop of rising populist antipathy toward China, an opposition politician named Maithripala Sirisena challenged Rajapaksa in the 2015 presidential election. His campaign manifesto read: "It is true that there was always corruption and fraud.... But the extent of corruption in Sri Lanka in the last few years is unprecedented.... If a total of [US$40.2 million] is spent per [kilometer] on the construction of the [China Eximbank-financed] Kadawata-Kerawalapitiya highway, the amount pilfered is [US$28.6 million]."[38]

Beijing's response made a bad situation worse. For nearly a decade, it had plied Rajapaksa with lavish support for his domestic political priorities; in return, it counted on his administration to consistently support China's foreign policy positions: Sri Lanka voted in lockstep with China at the UN General Assembly (UNGA) between 2006 and 2014. On a measure of UNGA voting similarity that varies between 0 percent and 100 percent, Sri Lanka's average score between 2006 and 2014 was 99 percent.[39] Beijing decided to take active measures to preserve its alliance with Rajapaksa, anticipating a less fruitful and more adversarial relationship with Sirisena. In the final months of the presidential campaign, China's ambassador to Sri Lanka openly campaigned for Rajapaksa; worse still, one of its state-owned companies was caught delivering nearly US$8 million in cash payments to Rajapaksa's personal residence and his campaign aides.[40] However, much of the damage was already done: even before Sirisena's presidential campaign was in full swing, China had suffered major losses in the court of public opinion; according to the Gallup World Poll, 42 percent of the Sri Lankan population expressed approval of the Chinese government's leadership performance in 2006, but by the end of Rajapaksa's term in 2014, this measure of public support had fallen to 23 percent.[41]

---

failing to generate enough revenue to enable repayment of the Chinese government loans that financed its development (Chowdhury 2015; Lim and Mukherjee 2017).

[37] Lim and Mukherjee (2017); Srinivasan (2017). As of 2017, the airport was reportedly generating US$300,000 of revenue a year. However, the loan that financed its construction required annual payments of US$23.6 million a year (Larmer 2017).

[38] Sirisena (2014).     [39] Voeten, Strezhnev, and Bailey (2009).     [40] Abi-Habib (2018).

[41] Gallup (2017).

Sirisena's policy position on China resonated with a large swathe of the Sri Lankan electorate. In particular, it struck a chord with Tamil and Muslim voters in the northern and eastern parts of the country, who resented the favoritism that Rajapaksa and his Chinese patrons had demonstrated toward the "Sinhala South."[42] When Sirisena was elected president in January 2015, one of his first orders was to allow Sri Lankan Airlines to cancel all flights to Mattala Rajapaksa International Airport.[43] His administration also launched a review of possible "irregularities" in major Chinese infrastructure projects. Among other project suspensions and cancellations, a high-profile US$1.4 billion Colombo Port City project backed by the Chinese government was mothballed.

Recognizing the strong political headwinds in Sri Lanka, Beijing sent a diplomatic shot across the bow to the new administration. Li Keqiang, its premier, announced that "China is willing, along with Sri Lanka, to steadily promote the construction of the Colombo Port City, Hambantota port, logistics and industrial zone and other projects in accordance with market and commercial principles." But he emphasized the need for local buy-in, noting that China "hopes the Sri Lankan side can [create] a good legal, policy, security and public opinion environment for [our projects]."[44]

Beijing also sought to cement its relationship with the Sirisena administration by taking a page out of the same playbook it had used with Rajapaksa. Beijing approved a US$100 million grant for the construction of a modern hospital in the President's home district of Polonnaruwa.[45] At the ribbon-cutting ceremony for the new facility, President Sirisena revealed that "[w]hen the Chinese ambassador visited my house to fix the date for [the opening of the hospital], he said that . . . Xi Jinping sent me another gift. . . . He has gifted 2 billion yuan [US$295 million] *to be utilized for any project [that I] wish.*"[46]

---

[42] Lim and Mukherjee (2017).

[43] The national carrier also released a public statement that read: "[T]he reality is Mattala Rajapaksa International [Airport] is not needed and is a distraction in Sri Lankan's efforts to turn itself around. . . . [SriLankan Airlines] continues to be highly unprofitable and having to meet the political requirement of developing and operating a second hub [in Hambantota district] will make it even harder to meet its targets for financial improvement" (cited in Shepard 2016).

[44] Reuters (2017). In response to efforts by the Sirisena administration to investigate corruption in Chinese-financed infrastructure projects, China's ambassador to Sri Lanka said that the "Sri Lankan people and government should have some gratitude for the things given" (Aneez 2016).

[45] Wijedasa (2016). Also see DiLorenzo and Cheng (2019), who provide empirical evidence that China strategically increases the provision of aid to new leaders and governments shortly after they come to power.

[46] Reuters (2018), emphasis added.

### Tanzania's Attempt to Crack the Code: Maximizing the Rewards and Minimizing the Risks of Banking with Beijing

Nearly five thousand kilometers across the Indian Ocean in Tanzania, China's track record and reputation as a development partner look very different. Shortly after the East African nation declared independence in 1961, the Julius Nyerere administration approached the donor community with a proposal to finance an ambitious project: a 1,860-kilometer railway that would run from Kapiri Mposhi in Zambia to the port of Tanzania's largest city, Dar es Salaam. The Tanzanian authorities argued that the TAZARA railway – a key pillar of the country's five-year national development plan – would increase economic growth by connecting the country's Southern Highlands and the copper mines of Zambia with a major seaport, thereby increasing maritime trade and reducing trans-shipment costs.[47] The construction of the railroad represented an extraordinary engineering challenge; it involved, among other things, moving 89 million cubic meters of earth and rock and constructing 22 tunnels, 320 bridges, and 2,225 culverts.[48] The Soviet Union declined to bankroll the project, and the United States, Britain, the World Bank, and the United Nations all questioned its economic viability.[49]

China stepped forward and offered to finance the railroad to the tune of US$415 million. It launched the project in October 1970 and sent an estimated 30,000–40,000 Chinese workers by boat to work alongside tens of thousands of Tanzanian workers. Jamie Monson, a professor of African History at Michigan State University, has done extensive research on this project, and she explains that "[s]trenuous working conditions were made more difficult by the determination of the Chinese authorities to finish the project well ahead of schedule. The Chinese management was willing to push the workforce night and day to show what could be achieved – and to build African confidence – at a time when the world was watching."[50] By the end of 1973, just twenty-seven months after construction began, the railroad was effectively

---

[47] Government of Tanzania (1969); Mwase (1983); Monson (2006).

[48] See the Tanzania-Zambia Railway Authority website at https://tazarasite.com/our-history, last accessed February 23, 2018.

[49] Song (2015). Two feasibility studies commissioned by the World Bank and the United Nations in the early 1960s "concluded that the proposed [1,860 km] rail link would be neither economically feasible nor sustainable" (Monson 2009: 15). The project was also characterized as a "bamboo railway" by the *Washington Post*, which prompted a Tanzanian railway spokesperson to clarify that TAZARA was in fact being built with steel rather than bamboo and construction would be of the "highest quality and long durability" (cited in Monson 2009: 7).

[50] Monson (2009: 52).

complete on the Tanzanian side of the border.[51] The project was her-
alded as a shining example of "the poor helping the poor" by the Chinese
and Tanzanian authorities.[52]

Over time, the railway encountered a number of operational, maintenance, and sustainability problems,[53] but it also had far-reaching and long-
lasting positive impacts on economic development patterns in Tanzania.
Monson explains in her book that "[u]pon its completion, the TAZARA
railway formed the backbone of a new spatial orientation for agrarian
production and rural commerce."[54] It promoted a large-scale resettle-
ment of rural villages along the rail line, attracted migrants in search of
wage labor opportunities to these villages, increased agricultural intensi-
fication near the settlements along the railway corridor, and strengthened
linkages between rural and urban markets.[55]

Several decades later, China stepped into the breach a second time to
help the Tanzanian authorities pursue a national development plan that
did not have broad support among OECD-DAC donors and lenders.
Tanzania was a "donor darling" of the West during the 1990s, and by the
turn of the century it was heavily dependent upon external sources of

[51] Construction then began in earnest on the Zambian side. Eventually, the railway connected communities near the Zambian copper mines and the harbor in Dar es Salaam.

[52] Monson (2009: 3). In 1973, China's average per capita income was approximately
US$254 (in constant 2010 US dollars). See https://data.worldbank.org/indicator/NY
.GDP.PCAP.KD?locations=CN, last accessed December 1, 2020.

[53] Chinese-built locomotive engines had difficulty hauling heavy loads and routinely broke
down. Spare parts were in short supply. Heavy rainfall also damaged the railway line,
leading to major service disruptions. The project had originally planned to haul 2 million
tons of cargo a year with seventeen trains running each day, but nine years after the
project began, only two trains were running and they were only able to haul 865,000 tons
a year. By the mid-1980s, TAZARA was in serious need of rehabilitation, and a coalition
of donors (including China, the United States, Sweden, and Norway) stepped forward
with a US$150 million bailout (Monson 2009: 102). China agreed to restructure
Tanzania's debt in 1993 (Song 2015: 60).

[54] Monson (2009: 8). She explains that the railway "provided a transportation infrastructure that enhanced physical mobility for goods and people across varied ecosystems,
economic opportunities, and concentrations of settlement. Yet the train was much more
than this. It was a resource around which people ... structured their survival" (Monson
2009: 95).

[55] Wei Song, a research fellow at the Chinese Academy of International Trade and
Economic Cooperation, notes that "[t]he operation of the [TAZARA] railway facilitated
the flourishing development of an agricultural economy along its route, and local areas
changed dramatically after its completion. Wastelands and jungles were transformed into
farms of rice, corn, and bananas. The railway also promoted the circulation of commodities. Besides effectively solving the problems confronting the export of copper, the
TAZARA railway ... revitalized domestic trade by speeding up the transportation of
light industrial products between different localities and made travel much easier than
before for the local people" (Song 2015: 59). Similarly, Monson (2009: 122) points out
that "economic development in the TAZARA corridor ... radiated outwards into the
surrounding regions."

assistance.[56] Aid agencies and development banks were enmeshed in so many aspects of government decision-making that the Tanzanian authorities believed their policy autonomy had been compromised.[57] However, as Haley Swedlund of Radboud University Nijmegen explains in her book *The Development Dance: How Donors and Recipients Negotiate the Delivery of Foreign Aid*, the Tanzanian government continued to work with its Western benefactors on a series of shared strategy documents between 2000 and 2010 to avoid alienating them.[58] These efforts culminated in the adoption of a so-called Joint Aid Strategy for Tanzania (JAST), which placed a strong emphasis on poverty reduction through social sector investments. The members of the OECD-DAC committed a substantial amount of funding for the implementation of JAST.[59]

However, unbeknownst to the OECD-DAC donors, the Planning Commission in the President's Office had been secretly working in parallel on a separate, five-year development plan (FYDP) that focused more narrowly on unleashing the country's economic growth potential through a set of targeted infrastructure and industrial development investments.[60] The authorities presented this plan to OECD-DAC donors in June 2011 as a *fait accompli*.[61] Benno Ndulu, the governor of the Bank of Tanzania and a principal architect of the plan, explained its purpose: "our aim is to accelerate growth through the enhancement of data services using optical fibre, the appropriate application of resources and agriculture, the enhancement of port facilities, and the improvement of our central railway corridor. We also hope to make Mtwara [a harbor city in southeastern Tanzania] a growth base." When asked about how Tanzania's traditional development partners received the plan, Ndulu said, "DAC Donors are not pleased by this plan. But the fact is [DAC] ODA is not flexible." Likewise, the chief economist of Tanzania's Planning Commission indicated that "DAC donors have [the] MDGs [Millennium Development Goals], but the Government's orientation is growth."[62]

Faced with the challenge of financing their national development plan without jeopardizing access to billions of dollars of support for social sector investments from Western donors, the Tanzanian authorities found their solution in China: a deep-pocketed lender that was willing to provide flexible, demand-driven support for big-ticket infrastructure

---

[56] Annual ODA from Western donors represented approximately 80 percent of the government's development budget and 40 percent of total government expenditure (Harrison, Mulley, and Holtom 2009).

[57] Helleiner (2002).     [58] Swedlund (2017a: 66).     [59] Swedlund (2017a: 48–49).

[60] Swedlund (2017a: 67).     [61] Furukawa (2018: 7).

[62] All of the direct quotes in this paragraph are drawn from Furukawa (2018), who previously served as deputy resident representative in Tanzania for the Japan International Cooperation Agency (JICA).

projects. Western donors had agreed to channel their funding through Tanzania's Ministry of Finance and align it with JAST, but the Chinese government felt no obligation to these channels or criteria. Therefore, the Tanzanian authorities decided "to construct new mechanisms and management systems to absorb Chinese contributions ... in order to break ground in strategic fields that [would] drive the growth the Government desire[d]."[63] The government decided that China would directly negotiate with the President's Office, the institutional home of the Planning Commission responsible for the FYDP. This arrangement provided a formal channel through which the Chinese and Tanzanian authorities could discuss FYDP priorities and project proposals.[64]

Shortly after the Tanzanian government made its surprise announcement, China dramatically scaled up its financial support. In the eleven years prior to the publication of the FYDP, China had provided approximately US$65 million a year to Tanzania (mostly through grants and highly concessional loans). However, during the first four years of the FYDP (2011–2014), China provided roughly US$2.9 billion – US$725 million *per year*, on average. The vast majority of this funding supported projects closely aligned with FYDP investment priorities: US$1.3 billion to build a natural gas pipeline from the gas field in Mtwara to Dar es Salaam, US$409 million to help lay more than 10,000 kilometers of fiber optic cable that reached each of the country's 169 districts, US$725 billion for the construction of a new seaport on Zanzibar and an expansion of the Dar es Salaam seaport, and nearly US$65 million for the rehabilitation of the TAZARA railway.[65]

China Eximbank and China Development Bank provided a mix of commercial, concessional, and semi-concessional loans to finance these projects, which reportedly helped Tanzania realize some of its most important goals under the FYDP.[66] During the implementation of the plan, private sector investment increased sharply and the country registered an average annual economic growth rate of 7 percent.[67] The Tanzanian authorities insist that neither Western aid agencies nor multilateral development banks would have been willing or able to bankroll the

---

[63] Furukawa (2018: 12).
[64] As we explain in Chapter 6, the establishment of a direct channel to political officeholders is quite common in Chinese government-funded projects.
[65] Furukawa (2018: 10).     [66] IMF (2015).
[67] Ministry of Finance and Planning (2016: 5, 87–88). Private sector investment was a key objective of the FYDP. The key metric monitored by the government of Tanzania was gross fixed capital formation by the private sector as a percentage of gross domestic product (GDP).

large-scale infrastructure projects envisaged under the FYDP, much less implement them within a relevant time frame.[68]

China's reputation for getting things done quickly made it the development financier of first resort for the Tanzanian government during this period.[69] Swedlund describes the differences between the timelines of traditional donors and the Chinese government: "[o]ne donor official recounted going to the Tanzania Investment Centre and having it explained to him that, if a traditional donor wants to build a road in 2012, the process needs to start in 2007. If the Chinese are going to build the same road, they start in 2011, and it is finished in 2012."[70]

One reason why Beijing was able to quickly implement big-ticket infrastructure projects is that its policy banks approved loan agreements with the Tanzanian government without requiring a competitive bidding process for contractor selection; as in Sri Lanka, China Eximbank and China Development Bank encouraged its borrower to follow sole-source procurement procedures and work with a preselected set of Chinese contractors.[71] The fact that the Tanzanian government did not consider alternative proposals from firms outside of China aroused suspicions of corruption and cost inflation.[72] Public prosecutors launched several probes to investigate whether Chinese contractors had colluded with Tanzanian government officials by giving them project proposals to pitch to Beijing – without any contractor fingerprints on them – at artificially high prices, thus allowing Chinese contractors to capture

[68] Li, Newenham-Kahindi, Shapiro, and Chen (2013); Makundi, Huyse, and Develtere (2017); Swedlund (2017a, 2017b); Furukawa (2018). There is some evidence of political bias in the subnational distribution of Chinese development projects in Tanzania – for example, a primary school and a water project were implemented in President Kikwete's hometown (Makundi, Huyse, and Develtere 2017). However, this problem was far more severe in Sri Lanka than Tanzania.

[69] The World Bank's International Debt Statistics database demonstrates that China is Tanzania's single-largest bilateral creditor. See https://datatopics.worldbank.org/debt/i ds/DSSIMTables/M-DSSI-TZA.htm, last accessed January 31, 2020.

[70] Swedlund (2017a: 128–129). During this period, the Chinese government was deliberately seeking to position itself as a participant in South-South cooperation rather than as a traditional donor or creditor. As one Chinese government official in Tanzania told a group of visiting researchers, "[w]e know the root causes of poverty in developing countries. Our firsthand experience has put us in a comparative advantage to address issues here" (Li, Newenham-Kahindi, Shapiro, and Chen 2013: 307).

[71] Sole-source procurement is the rule rather than the exception in China Eximbank and China Development Bank loan agreements. In fact, their loan agreements almost always reference a specific commercial contract with a specific Chinese firm and strictly instruct the borrower to use the proceeds of the loan to finance only the commercial contracts that are referenced in the loan agreement (Gelpern, Horn, Morris et al. 2021).

[72] Brazys, Elkink, and Kelly (2017); Makundi, Huyse, and Develtere (2017); The Citizen (2017).

"super profits" and cover the expense of illicit payments to their Tanzanian collaborators.[73]

The same vulnerability in China's project preparation system helped Rajapaksa get fast-track approval for white elephant projects in his home district. However, unlike the Sri Lankan government, the Tanzanian government took several steps to prevent Chinese state-owned enterprises and their local collaborators from gaming the system in this way. The president demanded an investigation of irregularities in the award of a tender to a consortium of Chinese firms to build a standard-gauge railway line with support from China Eximbank. He also suspended the director general of a government-owned railway assets holding firm that was implicated in the scandal. The former director general of the Tanzania Ports Authority, who awarded a fraudulent tender to a Chinese firm for the China Eximbank-funded Dar es Salaam seaport expansion project, was sentenced to three years in jail.[74]

Another reason why China's policy banks were able to rapidly implement big-ticket infrastructure projects was that they did not insist that their contractors or Tanzanian government counterparts adhere to the environmental standards and safeguards of Western aid agencies and multilateral development banks. Instead, China Eximbank and China Development Bank asked the parties involved in project implementation to follow the principle of compliance with host country environmental laws and regulations. China's policy banks expect all of their borrowers and contractors to follow this principle, so the environmental impacts of Chinese development projects can vary widely depending on the strength of environmental protection policies in the jurisdictions where the projects take place. In Tanzania, the law requires that large-scale development projects with potentially adverse environmental impacts be subjected to environmental impact assessments (EIAs).[75] These assessments pinpoint the specific environmental risks posed by a development project and how those risks can be mitigated.[76] Chinese development projects posed a particularly high risk of deforestation in Tanzania; however, in ecologically sensitive areas that enjoyed formal protection under

---

[73] Makoye (2014); Policy Forum (2018).

[74] Ng'wanakilala (2015); Andreoni (2017); Policy Forum (2018); *The Economist* (2018).

[75] BenYishay, Parks, Runfola, and Trichler (2016).

[76] For example, EIAs might instruct the parties involved in project implementation to create a nature reserve alongside an infrastructure corridor; build an overpass or underpass to facilitate wildlife migration near linear infrastructure; ensure that there is proper drainage underneath newly constructed infrastructure to avoid changing the flow and salinity of water in a way that might degrade aquatic and terrestrial biodiversity; or offset expected habitat loss by supporting compensatory protected areas or other ex situ conservation activities (Buchanan, Donald, Parks et al. 2018).

Tanzanian law, Chinese development projects ultimately had little or no effect on deforestation.[77]

In short, the Tanzanian government cracked the code: it figured out how to take advantage of China's unique way of designing, approving, and implementing development projects, using it to fuel an economic growth strategy that traditional donors and lenders were reluctant to support. It also effectively mitigated some of the biggest risks posed by Chinese development projects.

Of course, like any other foreign donor and lender, China was not a disinterested party; it hoped to secure certain benefits from the Tanzanian government. In exchange for the development projects that it bankrolled, Beijing secured approval for a Chinese firm – Sichuan Hongda Corporation – to launch two of the largest commercial investment projects ever undertaken in Tanzania: a coal-mining project in Mchuchuma and an iron ore mining project in Liganga worth approximately US$2.7 billion.[78] Beijing also secured important political concessions: it won Tanzania's foreign policy support on several high-priority issues, including opposition to the South China Sea arbitration process at the Permanent Court of Arbitration in The Hague.[79] Furthermore, Tanzania consistently supported China's foreign policy positions in the UNGA.[80] Between 2000 and 2014, the two countries cast identical votes 90 percent of the time.[81]

Casual observation suggests that Chinese-financed development projects may have also helped sway Tanzanian public sentiment and elite opinion in favor of Beijing.[82] In 2014, an Afrobarometer survey found that a majority of the Tanzanian adults polled believed that China's

---

[77] BenYishay, Parks, Runfola, and Trichler (2016).

[78] Li, Newenham-Kahindi, Shapiro, and Chen (2013: 309). Several of the Chinese government-financed development projects included in this "package deal" were designed to increase the likelihood that the mining investment projects in Mchuchuma and Liganga would succeed (Li, Newenham-Kahindi, Shapiro, and Chen 2013: 310).

[79] Lipin (2016). On the relationship between Tanzania's receipt of Chinese development finance and foreign policy support for China, see Song (2015: 59) and Cooper (2016: 12).

[80] Elsewhere, we have demonstrated that in Africa, there is a strong relationship between Chinese aid provision and voting with China in the UNGA: a 10 percent increase in a country's UNGA voting similarity with China is associated with an 86 percent increase in Chinese ODA, on average (Dreher, Fuchs, Parks et al. 2018). We return to this in Chapter 5.

[81] Voeten, Strezhnev, and Bailey (2009). Tanzania and China voted together 100 percent of the time for eight years during this fifteen-year time period.

[82] Of course, these descriptive patterns should not be over-interpreted as direct evidence of Chinese development finance influencing Tanzanian public opinion. On the causal relationship between Chinese development projects and public opinion in host countries, see Wellner, Dreher, Fuchs et al. (2020); Blair, Marty, and Roessler (2021); Eichenauer, Fuchs, and Brückner (2021).

economic development assistance did a very good or somewhat good job of meeting the country's needs.[83] When asked which country they thought provided the best model for the country's future development, more Tanzanians singled out China (35 percent) than the United States (30 percent), South Africa (10 percent), the United Kingdom (6 percent), or India (4 percent).[84] By contrast, across the full sample of 36 African countries that participated in the survey (from 2014 to 2015), the United States was most frequently identified as providing the best national development model.[85] Similarly, a 2014 survey of development policymakers and practitioners in 126 countries, including Tanzania, asked respondents which donors and lenders had the most influence over their government's development policy priorities. Across the global sample, China registered relatively low levels of development policy influence, but the opposite was true in Tanzania: there, China was seen as equally if not more influential than OECD-DAC donors.[86]

## Why China's Unique Approach to International Development Finance Produces Winners and Losers

Sri Lanka and Tanzania are not outlier cases. They are textbook examples of China's approach to international development finance. China asks political leaders, rather than technocrats, to propose development projects. It then subjects these proposals to due diligence procedures that are not particularly cumbersome or time consuming. Once projects are approved, they tend to be implemented quickly because Chinese lending and grant-giving institutions do not require host countries to coordinate other donors and lenders or to comply with "gold-plated" social and environmental safeguards. They also encourage – and, in many cases, even require – that sole-source contracts be issued to Chinese companies, which further streamlines project implementation.

Traditional suppliers of international development finance have trouble making sense of China's approach because it ignores many of the standard "best practices," such as international competitive bidding

---

[83] Afrobarometer (2015).    [84] Afrobarometer (2015).

[85] Lekorwe, Chingwete, Okuru et al. (2016). The survey data from the Gallup World Poll provide a more direct comparison of public opinion of China in Tanzania and Sri Lanka. On average, 33 percent of Sri Lankans approved of the job performance of the leadership of China between 2006 and 2014. The average level of approval expressed by Tanzanians during the same period of time was 62 percent.

[86] To generate these development policy influence estimates, we aggregated and weighted the respondent evaluation-level data from the *2014 Reform Efforts Survey* for more than 100 Western and non-Western donors and lenders (see Masaki, Parks, Faust et al. 2021 for methodological details).

and the use of a common set of social, environmental, and fiduciary safeguards. But there is a reason why Beijing does not pay much attention to international best practices: its overseas lending program is tethered to China's own economic needs and challenges. Beijing issues foreign exchange-denominated loans to overseas borrowers to manage its annual trade surpluses, which create excess foreign exchange reserves that could create inflation or a currency revaluation. It requires sole-source contracts to Chinese companies to give these firms a competitive edge in overseas markets. It obligates its borrowers to purchase construction inputs that are oversupplied in China to alleviate some of the problems that plague its state-owned enterprises.

China's unique approach to international development finance therefore presents risks and rewards for low-income and middle-income countries. As the cases of Sri Lanka and Tanzania show, its approach can produce very different results in different countries. A casual reading of the cross-case evidence suggests that China simply made more unforced errors in Sri Lanka than in Tanzania: the two countries had different levels of political bias in the selection and subnational distribution of development projects, different levels of success in project implementation, and different public opinion outcomes after projects were completed. However, upon closer inspection, these two cases reveal several remarkable consistencies. In both countries, China aligned its financial support with the economic development priorities of the political leadership and bankrolled projects that Western and multilateral development partners were either unwilling or unable to support. In both countries, China's policy banks offered borrowers a blend of concessional, semi-concessional, and non-concessional debt to quickly ramp up support for large-scale infrastructure projects that could accelerate near-term economic growth.[87] And, in both countries, Chinese development projects suffered from a similar set of problems – specifically, political bias in the selection and design of projects, preferential rather than competitive awarding of construction contracts, artificial inflation of project costs, and illicit payments from Chinese state-owned enterprises to host government officials.

It is the severity rather than the nature of these problems that differentiates the observed outcomes in these two countries. In Sri Lanka, site selection bias, waste, and corruption associated with Chinese development projects reached exceptionally high levels, and the country's political

---

[87] Interestingly, both countries also credit China for helping them achieve their short-run economic growth goals (Li, Newenham-Kahindi, Shapiro, and Chen 2013; *Daily News* 2014; Makundi, Huyse, and Develtere 2017; Swedlund 2017a, 2017b; Furukawa 2018).

leadership responded to public grievances with indifference and impunity, which in turn made Rajapaksa's alliance with China a "voting issue." In Tanzania, Chinese development projects suffered from similar problems, but some of the most egregious abuses of power resulted in criminal investigations and penalties, and public sentiment toward China never soured.[88]

The cases of Sri Lanka and Tanzania suggest that the choices and characteristics of host countries can either amplify the strengths or accentuate the weaknesses of China's "on demand" approach to international development finance. As Deborah Bräutigam – a development researcher at Johns Hopkins University – once put it, "[i]n the final analysis, the developmental impact of Chinese aid ... will almost certainly vary country by country and sector by sector. The deciding factor in each case is likely not to be China, but individual ... countries and their governments."[89] For better or worse, Chinese development projects will have far-reaching impacts as long as Beijing remains the global financier of first resort. However, until we have detailed our comprehensive data on the nature, timing, and geographical distribution of Chinese government-financed development projects around the globe, we will not be able to measure these impacts – or document how they vary across sectors and geographic space.

### The Aims and Approach of This Book

Our ambition in this book is to bridge this empirical gap. The Chinese government holds its financial cards close to its vest. It does not publish detailed information about its overseas development activities. In fact, it considers this information to be a state secret. Consequently, much of the existing policy debate about China's overseas development program is guided by opinion and conjecture. Previous attempts by researchers to track financial flows from Chinese government institutions have suffered from over-counting, mis-categorization, incomplete coverage, and heavy reliance on individual sources. We attempt to overcome these challenges by employing a new set of data collection methods that paint a more detailed, comprehensive, and accurate picture of China's overseas development program. By carefully collecting and analyzing these data, we seek to provide decision-makers with a stronger evidence base that can guide their policies and potentially even facilitate more constructive dialogue between China and Western donors and lenders.

---

[88] The country's political leadership demonstrated concern about the problems plaguing Chinese development projects and real resolve to address them (Andreoni 2017; Policy Forum 2018; The Economist 2018).
[89] Bräutigam (2009: 21).

In collaboration with AidData, we have developed a new methodology called Tracking Underreported Financial Flows (TUFF), which is a systematic, transparent, and replicable set of procedures for collecting large volumes of open-source data from four main sources: data and documentation from Chinese ministries, embassies, and economic and commercial counselor offices (ECCOs); the aid and debt information management systems of finance and planning ministries in counterpart countries; case study and field research undertaken by scholars and NGOs; and English, Chinese, and local-language news reports. TUFF standardizes and synthesizes large volumes of information from these sources to generate detailed financial, operational, and locational information about Chinese government-funded projects – projects that have not been voluntarily recorded in international reporting systems, such as the OECD's Creditor Reporting System or the International Aid Transparency Initiative (IATI).

The implementation of the TUFF methodology has facilitated the construction of the most comprehensive and detailed source of project-level information on China's global development footprint ever assembled. The dataset that we introduce in this book captures approximately US$354 billion worth of Chinese government-financed development projects that were officially committed, in implementation, or completed between 2000 and 2014. It consists of 4,368 projects in 138 countries and territories across five regions of the world: Africa, the Middle East, Asia and the Pacific, Latin America and the Caribbean, and Central and Eastern Europe. It provides a bird's-eye view of China's twenty-first-century transition from benefactor to banker and an empirical basis for studying the aims and impacts of China's modern overseas development program.

Social science, at its best, involves scholars painstakingly and even-handedly assembling evidence and exposing it to empirical disconfirmation. However, until recently, the study of Beijing's international development program did not follow basic scientific principles. Contributors to the field rarely defined essential terms and concepts (like "aid"). They seldom disclosed the data and methods they use to arrive at their conclusions.[90] Nor did they rely on common datasets or test the replicability and generalizability of previous empirical studies. For the better part of the past two decades, this field of inquiry has been dominated not by social scientists but by public intellectuals and think tank researchers.

---

[90] By only disclosing highly aggregated information about its overseas development activities, China has made this problem worse, fueling suspicions and making it far more difficult for researchers and policy analysts to confront false and exaggerated claims with potentially exculpatory evidence. The fact that China does not disclose which of its international financial transfers meet the internationally accepted criteria for development aid has further complicated this problem.

Consequently, it has been easy for those who wish to portray China as either a hero or a villain to cherry-pick evidence that supports their views. Policymakers have also had the luxury of "shopping around" for research findings that comport with their prior beliefs.[91] This state of affairs benefits no one – with the potential exception of researchers who choose not to fully disclose their methods and data or subject their empirical findings to independent replication. To achieve a common understanding of the aims and impacts of China's overseas development projects, we need to establish a community of social scientists who are willing to voluntarily expose their data, methods, and findings to independent review and replication. As Gary King of Harvard University puts it, "the only way to understand and evaluate an empirical analysis fully is to know the exact process by which the data were generated and the analysis produced."[92]

The dataset that we have generated in collaboration with AidData provides a foundation upon which a cumulative social science research program can be built. An important feature of this dataset is the fact that it distinguishes between "aid" and "debt." Three problems arise when these different types of government funding are conflated. First, it becomes nearly impossible to make apples-to-apples comparisons of Chinese development finance with other sources of development finance, including any member of the OECD-DAC. Second, it becomes more difficult to understand Beijing's motivations for bankrolling different types of projects. Third, when different types of projects produce inconsistent results, it becomes less likely that these differences will ever be uncovered.

Our definitions of "aid" and "debt" are drawn directly from the OECD-DAC standards and definitions, which clearly differentiate between ODA and Other Official Flows (OOF). According to the OECD-DAC, grants and low-interest loans that governments or intergovernmental organizations provide to developing countries for the purpose of improving socioeconomic conditions qualify as ODA. Loans and export credits that governments or intergovernmental organizations issue and price at or near market rates qualify as OOF. Also, if a government or intergovernmental organization provides funding to a developing country for any reason other than the improvement of its socioeconomic welfare (e.g., the promotion of a donor country's culture, a lender's pursuit of profit), the OECD-DAC classifies such financial flows as OOF rather than ODA. We use the term "aid" to refer to ODA and the term "debt" to refer to OOF. Our dataset also allows users to separately analyze projects financed with aid and debt from Chinese government institutions (see Box 1.1). In the coming chapters of this book, we will demonstrate that this feature of our dataset is essential to understand

---

[91] Banuri, Dercon, and Gauri (2017).    [92] King (1995: 444).

## Box 1.1  Our Terminology in This Book

During the period of time covered by the dataset that we use in this book (2000–2014), the OECD defined ODA activities as those provided on highly concessional terms (with a minimum grant element of 25 percent) and with development intent (i.e., activities oriented toward the promotion of economic development and welfare in the recipient country).[a] It defined OOF as activities provided on less concessional terms (with a grant element below 25 percent) and/or activities without development intent (i.e., activities oriented toward commercial or representational objectives).

ODA projects are widely considered to be "development aid" in the strict sense of the term. Therefore, when we refer to ODA, we use the term "aid"; when we refer to OOF, we use the term "debt" or "credit." When we discuss the total amount of financing from a particular government – the sum of ODA and OOF – we term it Official Financing (OF) and refer to it with the terms "development finance," "development projects," "funding," and "projects."

For the purposes of calculating ODA and OOF estimates, the OECD has traditionally counted the face values of loans rather than their grant elements. We adhere to this practice (which the OECD recently discontinued) because it was the official OECD methodology during our period of study (2000–2014). Likewise, we use a unified 25 percent grant element threshold to determine concessionality, despite the OECD's 2018 decision to adopt different grant element thresholds (and discount rates) for countries in different income brackets.[b]

We refer to Western-dominated multilateral donors, such as the IMF and the World Bank, and bilateral members of the OECD-DAC as "Western," although this group includes non-Western bilateral donors like South Korea and Japan and multilateral organizations with Western and non-Western member states.[c]

---

[a] The grant element of a financial transfer varies from 0 percent to 100 percent. Loans provided on market terms have a grant element of zero. Pure grants have a grant element of 100 percent. To calculate the grant element of a loan that is provided on below-market (concessional) terms, one needs to calculate the discounted cost (or "net present value") of the future debt service payments that will be made by the borrower. We address this measurement issue at greater length in Morris, Parks, and Gardner (2020).

[b] See www.oecd.org/dac/financing-sustainable-development/development-finance-standards/officialdevelopmentassistancedefinitionandcoverage.htm#Notes, last accessed January 31, 2020.

[c] Note that Western bilateral donors mostly provide development finance via ODA. For example, between 2000 and 2014, the United States provided US$394.6 billion of official financing to other countries; 93 percent (US$366.4 billion) of that qualified as ODA and only 7 percent (US$28.1 billion) as OOF. Between 2000 and 2014, the OECD-DAC as a whole provided US$1.753 trillion of official financing to other countries; 80.6 percent of these flows (US$1.413 trillion) qualified as bilateral ODA and only 19.4 percent (US$339.2 billion) as OOF. (Data were retrieved from http://stats.oecd.org/ and AidData's Core Research Release, Version 3.1 on October 6, 2017.)

Beijing's "split personality" as a benefactor and a banker. It also provides an objective way to benchmark China's performance vis-à-vis its OECD-DAC counterparts.

By measuring and analyzing Chinese aid and debt separately, we hope to make future debates about China's overseas development program more productive.[93] Some policymakers and researchers think of ODA as representing "aid" in the strictest sense of the term, while others prefer to use it as a catchall term for any type of government financing (including ODA and OOF). Our dataset seeks to impose discipline by requiring analysts (including ourselves) to be explicit about whether their analysis is based on a narrow or broad definition of aid.

Making this distinction between aid and debt has been foundational to our understanding of Chinese development finance. Disaggregating Chinese development finance into its constituent parts has helped us document China's twenty-first-century transition from benefactor to banker. It has allowed us to compare the scale and composition of funding from the Chinese government and its peers and competitors.[94] With separate measures of Chinese aid and debt, we can also puncture several popular myths about Beijing's motivations, produced by research that conflates these two types of government financing. Another advantage of using methods and measures that are consistent with those followed by the OECD-DAC is that we can compare and contrast the effects of Chinese and non-Chinese development projects on various outcomes of interest, including economic growth, inequality, child mortality, democratic accountability, corruption, and environmental degradation.

The comprehensive scope of this book is also unique. Although the subject of Chinese development finance has attracted a great deal of attention from political scientists, economists, geographers, and area studies specialists, virtually all of these studies have narrow scopes of empirical inquiry. For example, the Inter-American Dialogue (IAD) and the Global Economic Governance Initiative (GEGI) at Boston University have published data on Chinese government loans to fifteen countries in Latin America and the

---

[93] In Strange, Dreher, Fuchs et al. (2017: 5–9), we argue that unsystematic measurement of Chinese government financing has led to wildly different estimates of "Chinese aid," making it difficult for researchers and policymakers to draw meaningful inferences about the nature, scale, and scope of Beijing's overseas spending.

[94] For example, researchers have previously compared Western ODA (the strict definition of aid) with Chinese "aid and related activities" (Lum, Fischer, Gomez-Granger, and Leland 2009) or Chinese "aid and government-sponsored investment activities" (Wolf, Wang, and Warner 2013).

Caribbean.[95] The Lowy Institute for International Policy has published data on Chinese government-funded aid projects to eight countries in the Pacific.[96] The China-Africa Research Initiative at the Johns Hopkins University School of Advanced International Studies (SAIS-CARI) has published data on Chinese lending to fifty-six African countries.[97] Boston University also maintains a dataset of energy sector projects financed by two Chinese state-owned banks (China Eximbank and China Development Bank) in sixty-five countries.[98] The piecemeal nature of these datasets has resulted in analyses and conclusions that are relevant only to specific regions and types of financial flows. Our approach is different: we have developed the most comprehensive, project-level dataset ever assembled on the nature, scale, and scope of twenty-first-century Chinese development finance. This first-of-its-kind dataset tracks aid and debt from Chinese government institutions to more than 138 countries over a fifteen-year period. The broad geographical and temporal coverage of the dataset provides a stronger basis for identifying generalizable insights about Beijing's overseas development program.

Another unique feature of this book is that it empirically evaluates the allocation and effects of Chinese development finance at subnational scales. A "geospatial awakening" is underway in development research and policy: scholars and policymakers are increasingly aware of the fact that major knowledge gains can be achieved with geocoded data on development projects with spatially referenced data on outcomes like poverty, disease, conflict, governance, and environmental degradation.[99] We contribute to this literature by subnationally geocoding our dataset of Chinese development projects. When we merge these data on the precise locations of Chinese development projects with satellite and household survey observations, we can evaluate the localized impacts of Chinese development projects on economic development, health, conflict, and environmental

---

[95] The data published by IAD and GEGI do not include any other types of financial transfers or in-kind transfers from the Chinese government. See www.thedialogue.org/map_list/, last accessed February 3, 2020.

[96] The data published by the Lowy Institute for International Policy do not include any other types of financial transfers (e.g., non-concessional loans) from the Chinese government. See www.lowyinstitute.org/chinese-aid-map/, last accessed February 23, 2018.

[97] The data published by the SAIS-CARI do not capture any other types of financial transfers or in-kind transfers from the Chinese government. Also, the lending data that it publishes are available at only aggregate levels, not disclosed at the level of individual projects (loans). See www.sais-cari.org/data, last accessed February 3, 2020.

[98] See www.bu.edu/cgef/, last accessed February 3, 2020.

[99] BenYishay, Runfola, Tricher et al. (2017); Custer, DiLorenzo, Masaki et al. (2018); Parks and Strange (2019).

quality outcomes. With geo-referenced data, we are also able to determine how Chinese government-financed projects are allocated within countries and whether they are vulnerable to domestic political manipulation.

Throughout this book, we pair our analyses of Chinese development finance with parallel analyses of World Bank development finance. The World Bank is an ideal comparative case and benchmark institution for three primary reasons. First, unlike many other Western suppliers of international development finance, it has two funding windows: its International Development Association (IDA) offers poor countries access to funding mostly in the form of grants and highly concessional loans, while its International Bank for Reconstruction and Development (IBRD) chiefly offers loans on non-concessional terms. In other words, the IDA provides aid-financed projects (ODA) and the IBRD provides debt-financed projects (OOF). This structure mirrors China's overseas development program, which offers developing countries access to both aid and debt. This symmetry allows us to make apples-to-apples comparisons between the motivational drivers and effects of Chinese development finance and those of the world's largest international development finance institution.[100]

Second, the World Bank represents a "tough test" against which to benchmark China's performance. The World Bank uses a transparent set of criteria to allocate its resources across countries, and these criteria are considered to be significantly more "allocatively efficient" than those that guide the decisions made by bilateral aid agencies.[101] It is also an industry leader staffed by world-class development professionals; its project design, due diligence, and monitoring and evaluation standards and procedures are emulated and envied by other bilateral and multilateral aid agencies.[102] Due to high levels of shareholder oversight, the World Bank also has a reputation for producing policies and programs that are, as a general rule, carefully designed to maximize development impacts and minimize negative, unintended impacts.[103] Therefore, regardless of how one defines "performance,"[104] the World Bank provides an objectively high benchmark.

---

[100] Between 2000 and 2014, the World Bank channeled 64 percent of official financing flows through the IBRD and the remaining 36 percent through the IDA (we retrieved the World Bank data from https://data.worldbank.org/ on September 12, 2017).

[101] Easterly and Pfutze (2008); Knack, Rogers, and Eubank (2011).

[102] Jenkins (1997); Clemens and Kremer (2016); Mitchell and McKee (2018).

[103] Nielson and Tierney (2003); Buntaine (2016); Buchanan, Donald, Parks et al. (2018).

[104] Definitions might include the efficiency with which scarce public resources are allocated; the achievement of development impacts; the ability to mitigate risk and avoid negative, unintended impacts, etc.

Third, we have detailed and comprehensive data on all aid- and debt-financed projects from China and the World Bank in Asia, Africa, the Middle East, Latin America, and Central and Eastern Europe over our entire period of interest (2000–2014). We have also pinpointed the precise locations (latitude and longitude coordinates) of all World Bank and Chinese projects, which will enable a novel analysis of the subnational allocation and effects of development finance from these two sources.

This book has eight additional chapters. After providing a history of Chinese aid (Chapter 2) and introducing the methods by which we have assembled our dataset of twenty-first-century Chinese official financing (Chapter 3), we address a set of substantive questions at the heart of current academic and policy debates:

- What are the broad contours of China's global development program? Which countries and sectors receive which types of Chinese development finance (Chapter 4)?
- Which factors influence the allocation of Chinese development finance across the world, and how do these motivations compare with those of traditional donors and creditors, such as the World Bank (Chapter 5)?
- What determines the allocation of Chinese development finance across different subnational localities within recipient countries, and how does this compare with the subnational distribution of funding from the World Bank (Chapter 6)?
- How does Chinese development finance impact economic growth and other development outcomes at the national and subnational levels? How do these effects compare with the development interventions sponsored by the World Bank? Are the economic effects of politically motivated Chinese development finance significantly different from those of other types of Chinese development finance (Chapter 7)?
- What are the positive and negative externalities of Chinese aid – for example, on violent conflict, corruption, democratic accountability, the natural environment, and the effectiveness of Western development projects (Chapter 8)?
- Finally, how will Beijing reconcile the tension between its stated desire to "multilateralize" the BRI and its traditional disregard for international development rules and standards (Chapter 9)?

Our core argument in this book is that China's newfound position as the global development lender of first resort has created new opportunities and new risks for low-income and middle-income countries. China is a pragmatic development partner that pursues a diverse set of economic and political interests. Sometimes these interests complement the interests of recipient countries and other development partners. At other times, Beijing's interests conflict with those of recipient countries and other donors and lenders. Consequently, China's overseas development projects have uneven impacts, creating both winners and losers.

Our analysis reveals a composite portrait of Beijing's motivations, actions, and impacts that is nuanced and complex. China is neither the hero nor the villain of global development. It resembles neither the Western development world's caricature of the "rogue donor" nor the Chinese government's own self-narrative of a benevolent "fellow traveler" who is uniquely able to understand and address the challenges facing poor countries. We argue that for Western donors and lenders to work effectively with (or compete against) China, they need to better understand these nuances and complexities. China, for its part, needs to better understand its comparative advantages and disadvantages vis-à-vis traditional suppliers of international development finance and the risks that its existing policies and practices pose (so that they can be actively monitored and managed).

# 2 The Journey to Global Creditor
## A Brief History of Chinese Development Finance

### Faster, Higher, Further

The Karakoram Highway is one of the world's most treacherous roads. The 1,300-kilometer thoroughfare runs from the capital city of Pakistan (Islamabad) to Kashgar in China's Xinjiang Uyghur Autonomous Region. It is known as the "Eighth Wonder of the World" because of the exceptionally difficult conditions under which it was built. One section of the highway crosses the Khunjerab Pass at an elevation of 4,700 meters, making it an extraordinary feat of civil engineering. Since its initial construction began in 1959, politicians from both countries have invoked the "Sino-Pakistani Friendship Highway" as a symbol of their "all-weather friendship."[1]

As one of China's first major foreign assistance projects, the Karakoram also serves as a figurative bridge between China's past and present experiences as a financier of development. In 1966, Beijing donated machinery, fuel, tools, and other supplies – worth approximately 50 million Renminbi – to support the construction of the Pakistani portion of the highway.[2] In 1968, after finishing the construction of its portion of the Karakoram, the Chinese government began overseeing work on Pakistan's side due to slower-than-expected progress. The Pakistani segment was completed in two phases (in 1971 and 1978) with Beijing's help: the Chinese government provided additional machinery, equipment, and small armies of technicians. Hundreds of Pakistani and Chinese workers died during the construction of the Karakoram Highway, and they are now memorialized atop Khunjerab Pass.[3]

More than forty years after the construction of this thoroughfare, the Chinese government continues to provide financial support for its maintenance and rehabilitation. But now the Karakoram is only one of many

---

[1] Chaudhuri (2018).

[2] This was equal to roughly US$20.3 million (current); Zheng (2009). 30 percent of the highway lies in China and the other 70 percent lies in Pakistan.

[3] Copper (1979); Zheng (2009); Small (2015).

Chinese-funded, big-ticket infrastructure projects in Pakistan. Many of these new projects are financed through President Xi Jinping's signature BRI; in fact, Pakistan's role in the BRI has become so significant that it now has its own brand: the China-Pakistan Economic Corridor (CPEC) initiative.[4] Recent work on the Karakoram – widening and resurfacing the highway, rerouting certain sections to make them safer, and elevating other sections to avoid landslides and seasonal flooding – has been funded through a combination of Chinese aid and debt. In 2008, China Eximbank provided a US$327 million concessional loan; in 2010, a US$259 million preferential buyer's credit; and in 2016, a package of loans and export credits worth roughly US$1.3 billion. In total, the Chinese government has provided approximately US$2 billion dollars over sixty years to make the highway a viable trade route for cargo-carrying trucks.

Beijing's consistent support for the construction, maintenance, and upgrading of the highway over six decades highlights several important points about the way that it approaches its role as a provider of international development finance. First, it has a long-standing interest in financing the "hardware" of economic development, such as major transportation corridors that can reshape patterns of economic activity. Upon completion, the Karakoram reportedly increased overland Sino-Pakistani trade flows and expanded each country's access to Central and West Asian transportation networks.[5] Chinese officials now characterize it as a key node in CPEC that links markets and communities in both countries.[6]

The history of the Karakoram also demonstrates that Beijing is often willing to go where other donors and lenders are not – and sometimes for reasons that are not purely economic – even if that means bankrolling the construction of a highway in an extremely challenging physical environment.[7] Today, a popular argument in many Western capitals is that Beijing is more interested in propping up its geostrategic allies than funding bankable projects. But Chinese development projects from the Cold War era remind us that this criticism is not new.[8] Western donors and lenders questioned the economic viability of the Karakoram Highway project, much like the Tanzanian TAZARA railway project that we

---

[4] CPEC is an ambitious plan to create stronger economic links between China and Pakistan through a set of energy and infrastructure projects (Craig and Denyer 2015; Boyce 2017).
[5] Copper (2016: 74–75).    [6] Yao (2019).
[7] In her book on Chinese state capital in Zambia, Lee (2017) uses the term "encompassing accumulation" to refer to Beijing's multidimensional objectives in supplying development capital.
[8] Large (2008); Hirono and Suzuki (2014).

described in Chapter 1.[9] Beijing certainly uses its aid to advance geostrategic goals.[10] The Karakoram Highway is the only overland route between Pakistan and China. Its location in Kashmir, a disputed area between Pakistan and India (and a swathe of disputed land that Pakistan ceded to China in 1963), and its direct connection to Xinjiang – China's highly sensitive northwest region – also make it especially valuable.[11] In addition, Pakistan is a key ally, both in the region and internationally, and as we will demonstrate through statistical analysis (in Chapter 5), Beijing uses foreign aid to cultivate and cement political alliances.

But the history of the Karakoram also illustrates how China has evolved as a supplier of development finance. Since the turn of the century, Beijing has responded to a set of domestic challenges (which we describe in detail in the section "'Going Out' and China's Rise as a Global Development Banker [1999–Today]") by reorienting its overseas development program away from a nearly exclusive focus on grants and low-interest loans (aid) and toward loans and export credits that are priced at or near market rates (debt). China's current support for the Karakoram reflects this shift away from highly concessional forms of development finance: unlike the grants and interest-free loans that supported its initial construction, more recent funding for highway upgrades has come with significantly harder terms.

Consider the "mixed credit" package of US$1.3 billion that China Eximbank green-lit in 2016 to support the rehabilitation of three segments along the thoroughfare. While neither the Chinese government nor the Pakistani government has disclosed exact borrowing terms, we know that this package consisted of a government concessional loan (GCL), a preferential buyer's credit (PBC) loan, and a non-preferential buyer's credit loan (BCL). GCLs are Renminbi-denominated loans that are usually issued with twenty-year maturities, five-year grace periods, and 2 percent interest rates.[12] PBCs are denominated in US dollars and are

---

[9] Even today, analysts continue to question the Karakoram's long-run sustainability and China's underlying motivations for supporting it. Andrew Small, a Transatlantic Fellow with the Asia program of the German Marshall Fund, argues that the highway "would have been killed off quickly if its economic value had been the only thing it had going for it" (Small 2015: 106). After a recent visit to the highway, he noted that "[w]hat you see little of is *trucks*. For anyone familiar with bustling Chinese border posts by Kazakhstan or even North Korea, the relative calm is striking" (Small 2015: 99, emphasis added). A 2018 *Wall Street Journal* article also reported low levels of vehicular traffic (Page and Shah 2018).

[10] Fuchs and Rudyak (2019).

[11] Copper (1981). It is also wide enough to accommodate a range of military ground vehicles.

[12] China's Ministry of Finance calculates the difference between the interest rates attached to these loans and the central bank's benchmark rate and reimburses Eximbank accordingly (Morris, Parks, and Gardner 2020).

typically offered on less generous terms than those of GCLs but more generous than those of purely commercial loans. BCLs are commercial loans; they have significantly shorter maturities and grace periods, and they are tethered to a (floating) market interest rate, such as the London Interbank Offered Rate (LIBOR) or the Euro Interbank Offered Rate (EURIBOR).[13] They also incorporate an additional "margin" to account for borrower-specific risk and repayment capacity.[14] Given that only 15 percent of the 2016 mixed credit approved by China Eximbank came from a highly concessional lending instrument (a GCL) and the remaining 85 percent came from less concessional lending instruments (a PBC and BCL), Pakistan is clearly receiving less favorable terms than when the Karakoram was initially constructed and rehabilitated.

From the perspective of developing country governments, this shift by Chinese state-owned banks toward semi-concessional and commercial lending (denominated in foreign currency rather than Renminbi) has created opportunities and risks that were not present during the twentieth century. On one hand, the sheer scale of financing that low-income and middle-income governments can now access from Beijing has created more opportunities to pursue big-ticket infrastructure projects. While the Karakoram highway project was once the definitive symbol of Sino-Pakistani economic relations, it is now just one of two dozen big-ticket infrastructure projects being implemented and promoted under the auspices of CPEC and BRI. These other large projects include a US$6.4 billion mixed-credit package from China Eximbank for two nuclear power plants in Karachi, a US$2.8 billion mixed-credit package from China Eximbank for the widening and rehabilitation of the 470-kilometer Multan-Sukkur section of the Karachi-Peshawar Motorway, and a US$1.62 billion China Eximbank loan for the construction of the Lahore Metro's 27-kilometer Orange Line.[15]

On the other hand, when countries accumulate excessive amounts of foreign currency-denominated debt, they have to deal with a new set of risks. If they use most of their foreign exchange to repay external debts,

---

[13] LIBOR and EURIBOR are the benchmark interest rates at which major banks lend to each other.

[14] The size of this margin is usually expressed in terms of "basis points." For example, if a BCL is offered at LIBOR plus 250 basis points and the prevailing LIBOR rate is 3 percent at the time that the loan is contracted, the "all in" interest rate is equivalent to the sum of the LIBOR rate (3 percent) and the additional margin (2.5 percent). The interest rates on BCLs often fall somewhere in the 4.5 percent to 6 percent range (Morris, Parks, and Gardner 2020).

[15] Other projects include a US$1.3 billion China Development Bank (CDB) loan for an 878-kilometer power transmission line from Matiari to Lahore and a US$1.49 billion syndicated loan for a 1,320-megawatt coal-fired power plant in Balochistan, as well as many other solar, wind, hydroelectric, and coal-fired power generation projects that involve billions of dollars of additional Chinese loans.

they may experience import shortages or sluggish export growth. Excessive borrowing can also create expectations of inflation and exchange rate depreciation and deter foreign investment. High levels of indebtedness to China can also become a political liability for the leaders of borrower countries. We saw this in Chapter 1 when we reviewed the transition from the Rajapaksa administration to the Sirisena administration in Sri Lanka. The Pakistani authorities have encountered a similar challenge. According to Adnan Aamir, a journalist based in the country's restive Balochistan province, the opaque nature of Chinese lending has provoked a public backlash: "Pakistan's government has not made public the details of project agreements with China, which contain information about the financing models," and this has produced "mounting public discontent and intense criticism."[16]

The changing nature of China's project portfolio in Pakistan also reflects the benefactor-to-banker transition that has taken place during the first two decades of the twenty-first century: Beijing's state-owned banks increasingly lend to special purpose vehicles (SPVs) rather than to the Pakistani government itself. An SPV is an independent legal entity created for the express purpose of designing, financing, and implementing a specific project. SPVs are established for projects that will create or maintain revenue-generating assets, such as railways that generate ticket sales, highways that collect toll revenues, and power plants that charge residential and industrial consumers based on their electricity use. They are especially attractive to commercial banks – and other banks guided by the pursuit of profit – when the project in question is expected to generate enough revenue to fully repay the loan principal and interest, thereby making a repayment guarantee from the host government unnecessary.[17] The fact that Chinese lending to SPVs in Pakistan now rivals Chinese lending to the Pakistani government indicates that Beijing's objectives in Pakistan are of an increasingly commercial, rather than geopolitical, nature.

This shift is also a sign of the broader changes that are taking place in the way that Beijing bankrolls development projects around the globe. In the remainder of this chapter, we zoom out, moving from the specific example of how Chinese grant giving and lending have evolved in

---

[16] Aamir (2018).

[17] SPVs are attractive to public sector borrowers because they allow them to fund big-ticket infrastructure projects "off balance sheet." However, if a host government issues a sovereign guarantee for a loan that a creditor has issued to an SPV, the host government effectively places a *contingent* liability on its balance sheet. One of the key questions surrounding Chinese debt-financed projects in Pakistan is the size of the contingent liabilities created through the use of SPVs and sovereign guarantees (Schwemlein 2018).

Pakistan to a broader account of China's evolution as an international development financier over the past seven decades. This historical survey contextualizes China's evolution from benefactor to banker and anchors the subsequent chapters of this book, which focus on twenty-first-century Chinese development finance.

We organize the remainder of this chapter into four important phases of China's evolution from benefactor to banker:[18]

- Historical Foundations and the Early Years (1949–1959)
- Aid as Politics: Mao's Revolutionary Foreign Policy (1960–1977)
- Reform-Era Recalibration: Foundations for a Shift from Benefactor to Banker (1978–1998)
- "Going Out" and China's Rise as a Global Development Banker (1999–today)

Many of the insights from this chapter draw upon earlier studies that tracked and analyzed Chinese development finance. While these datasets provide different levels of coverage over geographic space and time and were assembled with diverse methods and lacking a uniform definition of "development project," they are crucial for understanding China's evolution as a supplier of international development finance during the twentieth century. One of the first attempts to track Chinese development projects was by the German sinologist Wolfgang Bartke. He created a global dataset of Chinese foreign development projects from 1956 through 1987.[19] The OECD later built upon Bartke's work to produce its own project-level dataset on Chinese aid activities between 1953 and 1985.[20] Teh-chang Lin's doctoral dissertation at Northern Illinois University extended these studies and produced data on China's global aid commitments from 1953 to 1989.[21] Around the same time, the US Central Intelligence Agency (CIA) declassified several documents containing project-level data on Chinese aid to developing countries during

---

[18] Previous research has similarly periodized the development of China as a global donor. For example, Lin (1993) divides China's development program into four periods: 1953–1963, 1964–1971, 1972–1978, and 1979–1989. Kobayashi (2008) divides it into three phases: net donor (1953–1978), net recipient (1978–1995), and emerging donor (post-1995). Dreher and Fuchs (2015) divide Chinese aid into five periods: 1956–1969, 1970–1978, 1979–1989, 1990–1995, and 1996–2005. They see the first phase as being dominated by political and ideological considerations, the second phase by political motives, the third by economic motives, the fourth – in search of support after the 1989 Tiananmen Square events and the "One-China policy" – again by political considerations, and the fifth again by commercial motives. Cheng and Taylor (2017) divide China's assistance to Africa into four periods: the beginning (1955–1963), the development (1964–1970), and the outrageous (1971–1978), followed by an initial reform (1978–1993) period.
[19] Bartke (1989).    [20] OECD (1987).    [21] Lin (1993).

the Cold War.[22] Darren Hawkins and a group of collaborators from Brigham Young University (BYU) subsequently published data on Chinese aid projects undertaken between 1990 and 2005 from yearbooks published by China's Ministry of Commerce (MOFCOM).[23] Two of the authors of this book then synthesized the data from Bartke, the CIA, the OECD, and BYU and supplemented them with information on food aid from the World Food Program and on the number of medical teams from Chinese government yearbooks.[24] More recently, using a set of data collection procedures inspired by our own TUFF methodology, Pippa Morgan of Duke Kunshan University and Yu Zheng of Fudan University created a dataset of nearly 2,000 Chinese-funded projects that were undertaken in approximately fifty African countries between 1956 and 1999.[25]

Figure 2.1 illustrates the geographical rollout of Chinese development projects from 1953 to 1999, drawing on data from several of the datasets described earlier. Each recipient country in the map is shaded according to the first year in which it received a Chinese government-financed aid project. We have also integrated our own dataset (described at greater length in Chapters 3 and 4) to highlight the geographical expansion of Chinese development finance from 2000 to 2014. One can see that China initially focused its development finance on Africa, the Middle East, and countries in its regional neighborhood, but with the passage of time, its project portfolio expanded into Latin America and the Caribbean, as well as Eastern and Central Europe.

## Historical Foundations and the Early Years (1949–1959)

China is sometimes called a "new" or "emerging" donor. However, China's overseas development program is not new; it has existed almost since the establishment of the People's Republic of China (PRC) in 1949, and it has important "antecedents" from earlier periods of pre-1949 Chinese history that inform Beijing's current approach as a foreign aid donor.[26] These antecedents include traditional Confucian culture and values; tribute relations between imperial China and surrounding Central and East Asian polities; and, more recently, China's "Century of

---

[22] CIA (1975-76, 1981-84).    [23] Hawkins, Nielson, and Bergevin (2010).
[24] Dreher and Fuchs (2015).    [25] Morgan and Zheng (2019).
[26] Lengauer (2011); Markovits, Strange, and Tingley (2019). Scholars of Chinese development finance have cited famed journeys by Ming Admiral Zheng He's fleets to East Africa as the earliest instances of China-Africa relations, though the nature of many of these exchanges and their implications for Chinese foreign policy remain heavily contested (Wade 2005; Alden and Alves 2008; Large 2008).

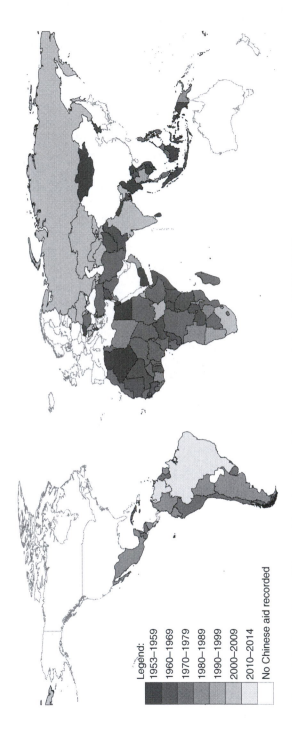

Figure 2.1 Year of first Chinese aid project by recipient country and decade (1953–2014)
*Notes:* This figure is adapted from Fuchs and Rudyak (2019). Data are sourced from Lin (1993); Dreher and Fuchs (2015); and Authors.

Legend:
1953–1959
1960–1969
1970–1979
1980–1989
1990–1999
2000–2009
2010–2014
No Chinese aid recorded

Humiliation." The Century of Humiliation arguably has the strongest connection to Beijing's contemporary global development strategy. During this period, China was invaded and occupied by foreign powers. After England defeated China in the First Opium War in 1842, the Qing dynasty's maritime economy was forcibly opened and subjected to decades of quasi-colonization and economic coercion by Western imperial powers. Then, China suffered a brutal Japanese occupation and civil war, which lasted for most of the first half of the twentieth century. This extended period of exploitation shaped China's post-1949 identity as a new nation-state, which emerged alongside colonial independence movements in the developing world. This historical sequence of events also helped position China as a rhetorical champion of the "Global South," a diverse collection of low-income and middle-income countries with a shared history of subjugation by foreign powers. The Chinese government still references this shared history as a basis for its solidarity with other developing countries.[27]

These events and a new set of geopolitical realities after World War II helped set the stage for China's entry into the global development finance market and its use of aid as a political tool. During the 1954 Geneva Conference, Beijing signaled the future orientation of its foreign policy by associating itself with a group of newly independent states in Africa and Asia. China's leaders saw their nation as an exemplar for how African and Asian states could oppose Western oppression and exploitation. In the run-up to the 1955 Bandung (or Asian-African) Conference, China's premier and head of government Zhou Enlai and India's prime minister Jawaharlal Nehru in 1954 jointly introduced the "Five Principles of Peaceful Coexistence": mutual respect for states' territorial integrity and sovereignty, mutual nonaggression; mutual noninterference in states' internal affairs, equality and mutual benefit, and peaceful coexistence.[28] At the Bandung Conference, the principles were incorporated into a joint statement that provided a set of foreign policy guidelines for China and the broader bloc of nations that joined the Non-Aligned Movement (NAM).[29] Even today, Beijing maintains that its foreign assistance policies are guided by these five principles.

---

[27] Other scholars have similarly argued that China's Century of Humiliation, bookended by the First Opium War and World War II, made its leaders keenly empathetic to the plight of newly independent nations that were highly sensitive to concerns over national sovereignty (Wu 2001); they argue that China pursued close relations with these states to counter any future imperialist aggressions (Taylor 1998).

[28] Qiang (1992); Ministry of Foreign Affairs (2014a).

[29] Zhou also met African leaders in Bandung, and these leaders would be important contacts after the Soviet-Sino split several years later (Alden and Alves 2008). For

As China cultivated these relationships in Asia and Africa, it was also forming an alliance with the Soviet Union to form a communist bloc against Western imperialism, a strategy known as "Lean to One Side." During this period, China received substantial amounts of military support and technical expertise from the Soviet Union,[30] and it channeled the bulk of its own outgoing aid to communist nations. In 1958, the Central Committee of the CCP released a "Report on Strengthening Foreign Economic and Technical Cooperation" that characterized aid as a "serious political mission" and emphasized China's "internationalist obligation to brotherhood and nationalist countries."[31] Before 1960, much of China's financial support went to wartime governments in North Korea, Vietnam, and Mongolia. Shortly thereafter, it began to provide modest amounts of assistance to other anti-colonial and communist movements abroad, such as the one that was underway in Albania. Communist movements in farther-flung places like Africa or Latin America were less of a priority, but Beijing still provided some aid to African countries (including Algeria, Egypt, Guinea, and Tanzania) as part of a unified strategy with the Soviet Union to spread communism and oppose imperialism (see again Figure 2.1). During the 1950s, China's preferred instruments of foreign influence were covert operations and propaganda campaigns;[32] however, as the delivery of military and economic assistance strengthened its alliances, it began to more fully appreciate the value of aid as an instrument for achieving its foreign policy objectives.

### Aid as Politics: Mao's Revolutionary Foreign Policy (1960–1977)

China's foreign aid program was increasingly used for political purposes after 1960, when the country's bilateral relationship with the Soviet Union soured, culminating in the "Sino-Soviet split." The dissolution of this key alliance coincided with the spread of independence movements across former African colonies. These events invigorated Chairman Mao Zedong's desire to create a powerful bloc of like-minded governments that would help China resist both Soviet

---

many participants, particularly weaker and smaller non-Western states, Bandung was an opportunity to counter perceived marginalization in the international community and oppose the double standards employed by major powers, which both create and violate norms (Acharya 2014). China was, of course, one of several powerful regional participants, along with India, Indonesia, and Japan (Lee 2010).
[30] Zhou and Xiong (2013).    [31] Cheng and Taylor (2017: 24).
[32] Alden and Alves (2008).

and American influence and create a new, socialist world order.[33] He articulated a "Three Worlds Theory" that divides the international system into three tiers of countries: major powers (namely, the United States and Russia); other industrialized powers (Japan and European states); and a Third World of exploited nations in Africa, Asia, and Latin America.[34] He placed China in the latter group and invested heavily in building solidarity with other Third World nations, often sending aid to countries with different political institutions and ideologies.[35]

During this period, foreign aid became one of China's most important foreign policy instruments. Indeed, it became the primary focus of China's bilateral relationships with many developing countries in Asia and Africa.[36] Beijing provided material support and training to dozens of African revolutionary groups in the 1960s, including those in Angola, Congo-Brazzaville, Ghana, South Africa, and Tanzania.[37] In Southeast Asia, it used aid to support communist movements in neighboring anti-communist countries such as Malaysia, Thailand, Singapore, and the Philippines.[38] All of this was taking place as Mao implemented increasingly radical domestic policies: the Great Leap Forward, a disastrous economic campaign designed to transform China's economy beginning in 1958, and the Cultural Revolution, an equally damaging political upheaval that began in 1966 and upended China's political bureaucracy and social order (while conveniently purging the system of Mao's enemies).

The official data that exist highlight the extraordinary scale and broad reach of China's overseas aid program during the 1960s and 1970s. The upper panel of Figure 2.2 presents the overall size of China's foreign aid budget over the past six decades. One can see that China invested heavily in its foreign aid program during the two decades bookended by the Sino-Soviet split and China's economic opening. The sharp increase in spending between 1965 and 1973 – the peak period of China's revolutionary diplomacy efforts during the Cultural Revolution – is especially striking. During this nine-year period, China's average per capita income was not much more than US$200 (in constant 2010 US dollars), but the government spent approximately US$12 billion on foreign assistance

---

[33] Yu (1977).    [34] Kim (1979); Ministry of Foreign Affairs (2014b).

[35] Though China did not officially launch its Three Worlds policy at the UN until 1974, the scope of its aid financing in the ten years prior was historically unprecedented.

[36] Poole (1966). Zhou visited thirteen of these countries during a three-month trip that began in December 1963 (Cheng and Taylor 2017).

[37] Alden and Alves (2008); Eisenman (2018). African states received nearly 60 percent of China's foreign assistance budget – roughly the same share they receive today.

[38] Taylor (1974).

Aid Budget (2014 US$ billion)

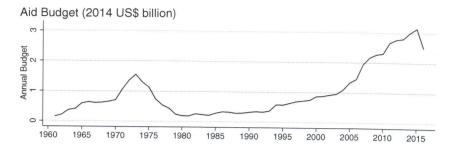

Aid as Share of Budget (%)

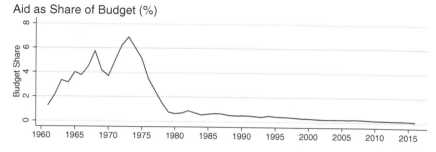

Figure 2.2  China's foreign aid budget, 1961–2016

*Notes:* (1) Data on China's foreign assistance budget are provided in the *Finance Yearbook of China* published by the Ministry of Finance. These data are unavailable for years before 1993, as the publication of these yearbooks began in 1994. See Ministry of Finance (1994: 349; 1995: 343; 1996: 463; 1997: 391–393; 1998: 354; 1999: 386; 2000: 338; 2001: 282; 2002: 295; 2003: 283; 2004: 275; 2005: 279; 2006: 313; 2007: 315; 2008: 337; 2009: 407; 2010: 371; 2011: 355; 2012: 362; 2013: 326; 2014: 312; 2015: 260; 2016: 258). Data are in terms of annual final accounts (决算数).

(2) Data through 1992 are not readily available via these yearbooks. Fu (2003) worked in China's Ministry of Finance and was responsible for aid budgeting and measuring (Zhang 2011b), and his doctoral research provides estimates for this period. Fu's (2003) data are in final account disbursements, and they are therefore consistent with Ministry of Finance data.

(3) Funds are reported in million US$ official exchange rates (Renminbi per US$, period average) provided by the World Bank. See https://data.worldbank.org/indicator/PA.NUS.FCRF?locations=CN, last accessed December 1, 2020. Note that China had a constant, pegged exchange rate before 1972.

(4) We take national budget expenditures from the National Bureau of Statistics (1999) for the years until 1978, and data for 1978 onwards from the National Bureau of Statistics (2017: 204).

activities.[39] When China's year-by-year outbound financial flows are measured in constant dollar terms (to account for inflation), one can see that its aid budget did not return to revolutionary levels until 2005 – more than thirty years later.[40] The lower panel of Figure 2.2 shows the proportion of China's government budget devoted to overseas development activities between 1960 and 2014. Overseas spending steadily increased after 1970 and reached an all-time high in 1975. More than 5 percent of the government's budget went to overseas development funding during this period.[41] (By way of comparison, in the United States, foreign aid as a share of the total federal budget is usually less than 1 percent.[42])

The size of China's revolutionary foreign aid program during the 1960s and early 1970s helps put contemporary debates about the scale of Chinese aid in perspective. It was not until 2005 that China (again) became a net donor, meaning that it provided more development finance than it received.[43] However, as we previously noted, China is not a new or emerging donor: it has been a net donor for a longer period of time than it has been a net recipient.[44] It was also one of the first countries to donate aid while still being a major recipient of aid itself.[45]

Perhaps the most remarkable feature of Chinese government financing during this period was its concessional nature, which was likely a function of its political rather than economic rationale. Unlike more recent periods of Chinese development finance, most of Beijing's pre-1978 overseas spending was given in the form of grants and interest-free loans.[46] This approach placed a heavy burden on China's national budget, since a relatively small percentage of these outgoing financial flows were repaid.[47] During this period, Beijing bankrolled several mega-projects – like the TAZARA railway in Tanzania and Zambia – and redoubled its

---

[39] Between 1965 and 1973, China's average per capita income was approximately US$212 (in constant 2010 US$). See https://data.worldbank.org/indicator/NY.GDP.PCAP.KD?locations=CN, last accessed December 1, 2020.

[40] Around the time of China's 19th Party Congress in October 2017, President Xi Jinping declared that China had provided a cumulative total of 400 billion Renminbi (US$60 billion) in foreign assistance between 1950 and 2016 (China Daily 2017).

[41] Note that this only includes foreign assistance as defined by China's government; it does not include the less concessional loan-based flows that have proliferated since 2000, which are a focal point of this book.

[42] Shapiro (2000). In the United States, foreign aid expenditure as a share of the federal budget reached approximately 3 percent in 1962.

[43] Chin (2012); Copper (2016).    [44] Kobayashi (2008).    [45] Budjan and Fuchs (2021).

[46] Horvath (1976).

[47] These Renminbi-denominated, interest-free loans were issued with very generous repayment terms (usually twenty-year maturities and ten-year grace periods). Therefore, most of them had grant elements in excess of 75 percent. Many of these interest-free loans were ultimately restructured or forgiven by the Chinese government during the 1980s, 1990s,

financial support for friendly regimes and leaders in Albania, Cuba, North Korea, and Vietnam. By the early 1970s, China's political leadership concluded that the government was fiscally overextended because of its overseas entanglements.

Beijing's costly efforts to finance revolution produced mixed results. It was successful in some places like Zanzibar and mainland Tanzania.[48] The completion of the TAZARA railway (see Chapter 1) was seen by many, including Tanzania's leaders, as proof that Western imperialists held outdated and misguided development policy beliefs.[49] However, in other countries, Beijing encountered complex realities that forced it to make difficult compromises. In places like Angola and Mozambique, China had to reconcile its revolutionary socialist policy goals with those of multiple domestic insurgent groups.[50] Many Chinese aid recipients were also reluctant to overtly oppose their biggest financial patrons – the Soviet Union and the United States – who had censured Mao.

Mao was not only interested in using aid to finance socialist revolution. He also used it to engage in a diplomatic tug-of-war with the Taiwan-based Republic of China (ROC) as the PRC sought to replace Taiwan as China's sole representative in the United Nations. When the leaders of foreign governments abandoned diplomatic recognition of the ROC and established diplomatic ties with the PRC, he rewarded them with lavish spending on stadiums, theaters, museums, presidential palaces, and parliamentary buildings.[51] The ROC engaged in similar tactics to strengthen its international alliances. This turf war was particularly intense in Africa because of the many newly independent states in the region.[52] Indeed, when the UN voted in 1971 on China's permanent representative to the international body, more than two dozen African governments voted in favor of the PRC, helping it secure a momentous victory.[53] China's strategy of using aid to gain diplomatic dominance over Taiwan continues to this day. As of 2020, there were only fifteen countries that still diplomatically recognized Taiwan.[54] Beijing has recently managed to "flip" El Salvador, São Tomé and Príncipe, the Gambia, the Dominican Republic, Panama, Kiribati, and the Solomon Islands. It has done so by supplying the

---

and 2000s, so it is unlikely that Beijing received significant reflows during the 1960s and 1970s (Bräutigam 2009: 127–128; Acker, Bräutigam, and Huang 2020).
[48] Burgess and Lee (2010).    [49] Monson (2009, 2010).    [50] Jackson (1995).
[51] Copper (2016: 149–151). China has also consistently penalized countries that recognize Taiwan by denying them access to any development funding other than emergency humanitarian assistance (see Chapter 5).
[52] Kao (1988).    [53] Wei (1982: 382–390).    [54] Ministry of Foreign Affairs (2020).

leaders of these countries with promises of cash and big-ticket infra-structure projects, a strategy we examine in Chapter 5.[55]

During the 1960s and 1970s, China's aid program also became some-what more institutionalized. Zhou introduced the country's Eight Principles of Foreign Economic and Technological Assistance (identified in Appendix 2.A) in 1963, and these principles remain central to China's foreign assistance doctrine.[56]

### Reform-Era Recalibration: Foundations for a Shift from Benefactor to Banker (1978–1998)

A major course correction took place after Mao's death in 1976 and Deng Xiaoping's ascendance to the leadership in 1978. The Mao-Deng transi-tion made China's foreign policy less ideological and more economically pragmatic,[57] and many of the country's radical domestic and inter-national policies were abandoned. Beijing imposed fiscal discipline by, among other things, dramatically reducing the size of the country's devel-opment budget. The costly and grandiose projects that had been emblem-atic of aid in Mao's era gave way to projects that placed more emphasis on economic feasibility and sustainability.[58] At the same time, China's own economic opening during the late 1970s and 1980s resulted in major aid inflows. During this period, China actually received far more foreign aid than it provided.

In the final years of Mao's rule, China's leaders were preoccupied with the intensifying Cultural Revolution, and overseas spending began to contract – even before Deng took over. Then, under Deng, who was reinstated into the country's top leadership echelon after the purge that took place during the Cultural Revolution, China's foreign policy shifted from an expansionary approach to a quieter, growth-first approach. Deng championed the principle of "biding one's time and hiding one's capabilities." Under Deng's leadership, the country "paid more attention to the economic and

---

[55] As a general rule, China avoids providing development finance via cash payments, but it makes a special exception to this rule when it engages in an active competition with Taiwan to win diplomatic recognition. This became especially clear in 2007 after "a court order . . . forced the Costa Rican government to publish the actual diplomatic agreement underpinning its decision to break diplomatic ties with Taiwan and establish them with Beijing" and "[i]ncluded in the agreement was a pledge of a grant of [US]$30 million in cash that would be delivered over two years, along with another [US]$100 million grant in the usual form of Chinese turn-key project" (Bräutigam 2009: 125).

[56] Ministry of Foreign Affairs (1990). China's experience as a recipient of aid, primarily from the Soviet Union, according to some, made it sensitive to issues of recipient autonomy and self-reliance (Watanabe 2013).

[57] Kim (1981); Jacobson and Oksenberg (1990); Zhao (2004).      [58] Copper (1979).

long-term effects of aid projects."[59] In 1980, this shift in attitude was formalized when the Ministry of Foreign Economic Liaison issued new guidelines making economic considerations as important as political ones in the design and delivery of Chinese development projects.[60]

Deng's pragmatic approach helped refocus China's overseas development program on commercially viable projects that would better serve the country's own economic growth needs. One way that he pursued this goal was by issuing a formal reinterpretation of the Eight Principles of Foreign Economic and Technological Assistance (see again Appendix 2.A), which allowed China to help maintain projects it had already funded. Many of the projects developed from the 1950s through the 1970s were so-called turn-key projects: ready-to-use development projects (such as sugar mills, textile factories, and hydroelectric power plants) that could be simply handed over to the host country. However, by the time that Deng assumed power in the late 1970s, a significant number of these projects had fallen into a state of disrepair.[61] His administration's clarification of the Eight Principles stated that Chinese involvement in the management of already completed projects would not constitute disrespect for the sovereignty of the recipient country (or interference in its internal affairs). Rather, this type of maintenance honored one of the other eight principles – helping recipient countries strive for self-sufficiency.[62]

---

[59] State Council (2011). The early reform era was also a period during which China began to more fully join the UN's primary development institutions. In 1972, it had already joined the United Nations Environment Programme (UNEP), the World Health Organization (WHO), and the United Nations Educational, Scientific and Cultural Organization (UNESCO), but during the reform period, it began contributing higher volumes of multilateral development finance through these and other institutions (Xiong 2017).

[60] Shi (1989).

[61] Beijing did not want to see projects go to waste, but it did not believe it could intervene. For example, the Chinese government built a hydroelectric power plant for Equatorial Guinea one year before Deng's government reinterpreted the Eight Principles. An economic officer from the Chinese embassy reported to a World Bank official in Equatorial Guinea that "[i]n 1982 we turned over to the Guineans the hydroelectric center which we had built. It was theirs to run. We agreed to provide a few teachers to train the Guinean technicians. After the ceremony the Chinese delegation spoke to President Obiang about the administration of the facility, how it could make money if it were well run. He said 'De acuerdo.' But in reality ever since then the administration has been very bad. ... After three to five years the Bata plant will need big repairs. The Guineans think the Chinese will do it again for them, or maybe they don't think at all. They're just glad to have electricity. So you see on our shoulders there are always placed burdens" (Klitgaard 1990: 96).

[62] Indeed, Bräutigam (2009: 57) notes that "[t]hroughout ... the 1980s and well into the 1990s, China focused the bulk of its assistance on rehabilitating the dozens of former development projects that had collapsed or were barely limping along, and developing

This reinterpretation of policy in Beijing had far-reaching consequences: turn-key projects that suffered from neglect and mismanagement during the 1950s, 1960s, and 1970s were brought under the oversight and administration of Chinese technical experts during the 1980s and 1990s, and many of them became more efficient and sustainable.[63] This policy continues to inform the way that China thinks about its foreign aid program in the twenty-first century. After making capital investments that result in the construction of a physical asset (like a hospital, school, or factory), Beijing often provides ongoing support for the operations and maintenance in the form of technical assistance, supplies and equipment, and additional funding. For example, the People's Palace – the parliamentary complex in the Democratic Republic of the Congo – was constructed in the late 1970s with a US-$100 million interest-free loan from the Chinese government. Beijing has subsequently approved ten consecutive technical cooperation projects to maintain and renovate the facility.[64] Similarly, after financing the construction of dozens of hospitals around the globe, Beijing has institutionalized the practice of stationing Chinese medical teams in these hospitals. The doctors and nurses who are dispatched to these facilities not only provide medical service to patients but also operate and maintain the on-site medical equipment.[65]

But Deng did not launch his most ambitious foreign aid reform until 1982. In that year, the Chinese government established a Foreign Aid Department and gave China National Complete Plant Import & Export Corporation Ltd. (COMPLANT) – a state-owned enterprise – primary responsibility for implementing overseas development projects. In doing so, his government laid the groundwork for a longer-term transition away from politically motivated projects backed by grants and interest-free loans and toward more commercially viable projects backed by interest-bearing loans.[66]

One way that China facilitated this transition was by blending debt and investment through joint ventures. Rather than continuing to lend to cash-strapped governments that were already struggling to repay Chinese loans from the three previous decades, Beijing encouraged partnerships between Chinese state-owned enterprises and host country firms. These partnerships resulted in the creation of new legal entities

---

ways to make their initial benefits sustainable. For every new project launched during this period, three were being consolidated (repaired, renovated, reconditioned)."

[63] Bräutigam (2009: 58).     [64] The Karakoram Highway is another case in point.

[65] In many cases, these teams operate and maintain medical equipment that was previously donated by the Chinese government.

[66] Cheng and Taylor (2017: 39).

that could develop, own, and operate projects.[67] Beijing then issued loans to these joint ventures, which were typically majority-owned by Chinese state-owned enterprises.[68] This strategy made it easier for the authorities in Beijing to manage loan repayment risk. It also created new commercial opportunities for Chinese firms – something Deng had already begun to prioritize following his 1992 Southern Tour and the subsequent 14th Party Congress.[69] More generally, it paved the way for the introduction of a more diverse set of debt instruments that would more closely align the country's international development finance program with its domestic economic development needs.[70]

In the late 1980s, Chinese researchers began to call upon the government to reserve interest-free loans for the very poorest countries and begin issuing interest-bearing loans for profitable projects and borrowers with higher levels of repayment capacity.[71] Interest-bearing loans promised several benefits to China. First, they offered a way to integrate aid, investment, trade, and contracting and to encourage Chinese enterprises to more fully participate in the country's overseas development finance program.[72] Second, they provided a means by which the country could expand the scale and scope of its overseas development finance budget without creating an unsustainably large fiscal burden. Third, by issuing these types of loans, the Chinese government could begin to build bilateral relationships based on commercial criteria rather than political ideology and geopolitical criteria alone.

Beijing began issuing some interest-bearing loans in the early 1990s, but it did not institutionalize this approach until it created China Eximbank in 1994.[73] Prior to 1994, Bank of China – then the country's de facto import-export bank – was a market-based bank that valued liquidity, profitability, and security. However, it was not particularly well equipped to back risky but strategically important projects over

---

[67] This approach is similar to China's current emphasis on lending to special purpose vehicles under the BRI.

[68] Beijing also began to encourage host governments to provide sovereign guarantees for these loans, thereby creating contingent liabilities on the balance sheets of host governments. These practices foreshadowed the creation of the China Export and Credit Insurance Corporation (Sinosure) in 2001. Sinosure is now a central player in the BRI: when host countries do not offer sovereign guarantees, it often steps into the breach by selling insurance to Chinese lenders, who then pass these additional costs on to their borrowers (Chin and Gallagher 2019).

[69] Hong and Sun (2006). Even earlier in 1986, Beijing allowed and even encouraged investment by non-state-owned enterprises in other countries (Wong and Chan 2003).

[70] These instruments were phased in over time, and they included export seller's credits (出口卖方信贷款), overseas investment loans (境外投资贷款), overseas contracting project loans (对外承包工程贷款), and project finance (项目融资).

[71] Jin (1988); Li (1992); Zeng (1996).    [72] Zhu (1997).    [73] Fuchs and Rudyak (2019).

long time horizons.[74] In May 1995, the State Council announced that the newly established China Eximbank would create, administer, and oversee the promotion of foreign aid loans (援外优惠贷款), which were later renamed government concessional loans (GCLs).[75] These were originally offered at 4 percent to 5 percent interest rates, but uptake by overseas borrowers was low, and the bank was criticized for extending credit on insufficiently favorable terms.[76] Consequently, China Eximbank's total overseas lending portfolio remained small until 1999. Its expansion began when the government adopted the Going Out strategy (described in Chapter 1), and the bank substantially lowered the standard pricing of its GCLs to 2 percent interest rates, twenty-year maturities, and five-year grace periods.[77]

Several years later, China Eximbank developed another important instrument: a lending product called a preferential buyer's credit (PBC, 优惠出口买方贷款).[78] PBCs, like GCLs, are provided to government borrowers at below-market interest rates. However, unlike GCLs, they are denominated not in Renminbi but in US dollars.[79] China Eximbank's use of these credits quickly outpaced its use of GCLs because they helped the country address a foreign exchange oversupply problem.[80] We discuss this issue in more detail later in the section titled "'Going Out' and China's Rise as a Global Development Banker (1999–Today)."

As China reoriented its twenty-first-century development finance strategy toward bankable projects, it drew upon its own experience as an aid recipient during the late 1970s, 1980s, and 1990s. Its relationship with Japanese donors and creditors had an especially profound

---

[74] Ji (1992).

[75] Fuchs and Rudyak (2019). Beijing continued to offer the grants and interest-free loans that had characterized its aid giving during the 1950s, 1960s, 1970s, and 1980s, but these instruments were refocused on projects that would cement diplomatic and political ties with other governments, such as presidential palaces and parliamentary complexes.

[76] Zhu (1997).    [77] China Eximbank (2002).

[78] China Eximbank had offered buyer's credits during the 1990s on non-preferential (i.e., market) terms. However, Iran and Indonesia were the first two recipients of preferential buyer's credits in 2001 and 2002, respectively (see Export-Import Bank of China [China Eximbank] (n.d.). China Eximbank codified the PBC as one of its core lending instruments in 2004. See www.chinca.org/cms/html/files/2013-12/16/201312161029488729 30302.pdf, last accessed December 1, 2020.

[79] Some low-income and middle-income governments favor preferential buyer's credits because they are denominated in relatively stable US dollars, while GCLs from China Eximbank are denominated in less stable Chinese Renminbi (e.g., Government of Sri Lanka 2012: 70). Therefore, the introduction of preferential buyer's credits also helped China address a problem on the borrower demand side of the equation.

[80] By 2010, China Eximbank was providing roughly as much funding through preferential buyer's credits as GCLs, and after that point, the US$-denominated credits grew at a substantially faster rate than the Renminbi-denominated GCLs. See Export-Import Bank of China [China Eximbank] (n.d.) and Duo (n.d.).

influence.[81] At the time, Tokyo funded large-scale development projects through a "request-based" system of project identification and approval. Japanese companies would develop project proposals and pitch them to officials of the host government, who would then request support for the proposals from Japanese development finance institutions.[82] Beijing eventually embraced a similar approach. As a general rule, its aid agencies and state-owned banks will not green-light a development project unless they first receive a formal request from the host government. This feature of the project approval system ensures that Chinese government-financed projects are responsive to the needs and preferences of political leaders in host countries. However, it also makes these projects vulnerable to political capture, corruption, and artificially inflated costs. All of these problems were present in Japan's twentieth-century request-based system, and they now plague twenty-first-century Chinese development projects (an issue we discuss in greater detail in Chapters 6 and 8).[83]

Japan's aid program also introduced China to the idea of commodity-backed loans, which would eventually become another one of Beijing's workhorse lending instruments during the twenty-first century.[84] Deborah Bräutigam tells this story in her book *The Dragon's Gift*. She explains that in response to the 1973 oil crisis, Japan sought to secure access to reliable oil supplies, which it found in China's Daqing oil fields. Japanese concessional loans financed the export of Japanese technologies to China and were repaid with Chinese oil exports. Bräutigam notes that "by the end of 1978, Chinese officials had signed seventy-four contracts with Japan to finance turn-key projects that would form the backbone of China's modernization," all of which "would be repaid in oil." According to Bräutigam, the Chinese authorities never perceived these commodity-backed loans to be coercive or exploitative. They simply saw them as a convenient way of hastening the economic modernization process.[85]

Although Beijing reoriented its overseas lending portfolio toward commercial objectives during the 1990s and the start of the twenty-first century, it never abandoned the idea of using aid to achieve diplomatic and geostrategic objectives. After the Tiananmen Square incident in

---

[81] Kragelund (2011); Johnston and Rudyak (2013).     [82] Bräutigam (2009: 141).
[83] Zhang and Smith (2017).
[84] Nowadays, Chinese state-owned banks issue two types of commodity-backed loans: in some cases, borrowers are allowed to repay their loans by depositing the cash proceeds from commodity export sales into bank accounts that can be accessed by their lenders; in other cases, the cash proceeds from commodity export sales are deposited into lender-controlled bank accounts and serve as collateral that can be seized in the event of default.
[85] Bräutigam (2009: 47, 50–51).

1989, China found itself diplomatically and economically isolated on the world stage as Western economies reduced arms sales, trade, and investment in China. In response, the authorities in Beijing dusted off an old playbook: using grants and interest-free loans to curry favor with developing-world leaders. They plied politicians in poor countries with lavish spending on pet projects – like presidential palaces and parliamentary complexes – and other amenities in urban centers that disproportionately benefited governing elites (e.g., theaters, museums, stadiums, and convention centers). Many of these countries were reluctant to criticize Beijing for human rights abuses stemming from the Tiananmen incident – perhaps because of their own illiberal policies or the fear of alienating a generous patron.[86]

In summary, China's pursuit of geopolitical advantage, fiscal sustainability, and commercial gain during the twentieth century laid the foundation for its twenty-first-century approach to overseas development finance. Beijing learned that its grants and interest-free loans could create large political benefits but also large economic costs, which paved the way for the creation of new development finance instruments. By the turn of the century, Beijing had a basket of assorted development finance instruments – including grants, interest-free loans, concessional loans, export buyer's credits, export seller's credits, joint venture loans, overseas investment loans, and overseas contracting project loans – in place to pursue an increasingly diverse set of political and economic interests. (The shift from solely political to a mix of economic and political motives is also visible in historical aid data, as we discuss in Box 2.1.)

---

**BOX 2.1 Comparison of China's Aid Allocation Across Five Phases of China's Development Program**

In a study entitled "Rogue Aid? An Empirical Analysis of China's Aid Allocation," two authors of this book used quantitative data to analyze broad historical developments in China's foreign development program. We collected information on the share of Chinese development projects received by 132 countries from 1956 to 2005 and then computed conditional correlations with a set of political and economic variables that capture Beijing's potential motivations for aid provision. Our regression results are summarized in Table B2.1. The results largely reflect the historical developments that we describe in this

---

[86] Taylor (1998).

**BOX 2.1 Cont**

chapter. They show that economic motivations played no significant role in China's early years of aid giving: China's export patterns did not correlate positively with its allocation of development projects across countries prior to the period of economic reform overseen by Deng Xiaoping but turn out to drive aid patterns in later periods. However, geopolitical considerations did play an important role in all five phases of China's foreign development program. Countries that voted with China in the United Nations General Assembly (or against the Republic of China on Taiwan prior to the PRC's admission to the United Nations in 1971) received larger project shares, as did countries that did not recognize the Republic of China (Taiwan) as an independent country. We also found some evidence that China allocated more projects to countries with lower levels of per capita income, which could reflect either a sensitivity to need or the lower price of purchasing foreign policy support from poorer countries (on this point, see Chapter 5). Finally, Beijing allocated development projects without much consideration of the natural resource endowments and institutional characteristics of recipient countries. In Chapter 5, we examine whether and how China's motivations for providing aid – and credit – changed during the twenty-first century.

Table 2.1  *Five phases of China's development program*

|  | Phase 1 1956–1969 | Phase 2 1970–1978 | Phase 3 1979–1989 | Phase 4 1990–1995 | Phase 5 1996–2005 |
|---|---|---|---|---|---|
| GDP per capita | 0 | – – | – – | – – | – – |
| Democracy | 0 | 0 | – – | 0 | 0 |
| Taiwan recognition | 0 | 0 | – – | – – | – – |
| UNGA voting | + | ++ | ++ | ++ | 0 |
| Exports | – | 0 | ++ | 0 | ++ |
| Oil production | 0 | 0 | 0 | 0 | 0 |

*Notes:* Summary of results in Dreher and Fuchs (2015), Table 1. Results based on regressions with Fractional Logit, with standard errors clustered by recipient country. All regressions include time period dummies, and all explanatory variables are interacted with these dummies. "++" ("– –") stands for a significant positive (negative) relationship (at least 5 percent level of significance) and "+" ("–") stands for a weakly significant positive (negative) relationship (10 percent level of significance) of the respective variable in a given phase of China's development program. "0" stands for insignificant coefficients. The regressions also control for a recipient country's geographic distance to China, population size, and natural disaster exposure.

## "Going Out" and China's Rise as a Global Development Banker (1999–Today)

Beijing was already beginning to behave less like a benefactor and more like a banker during its first two decades of economic reform (from 1978 to 1998). However, this transition rapidly accelerated at the turn of the century: 1999 was a watershed year. In anticipation of slower growth at home, the government adopted a "Going Out" strategy that sought to build "national champion" firms, reduce the cost of transporting goods to and from other countries, increase external demand for Chinese goods and services, wean the country off high levels of domestic infrastructure investment, acquire advanced technologies, and secure energy and raw materials.[87] Beijing's singular focus was on creating more favorable conditions for continued economic growth at home.

Due to annual trade surpluses, the country was rapidly accumulating foreign exchange reserves, which created a problem: if the government allowed these foreign exchange reserves to enter the domestic economy, it would increase the risk of inflation and a currency revaluation.[88] In response, the authorities decided to move more of the country's foreign exchange reserves abroad. China had traditionally parked excess foreign currency in US Treasury bonds. However, as these bond yields declined, Beijing began to look further afield for other assets that could produce more attractive returns.[89] Chinese state-owned banks were given a mandate to dramatically increase foreign currency-denominated lending to overseas borrowers.[90] With the country's foreign exchange reserves yielding only a 3 percent annual return at home, the government had an incentive to price its foreign currency-denominated loans to overseas borrowers above this reference rate.[91]

China's overseas lending skyrocketed after 1999, but the *composition* of its international development finance portfolio also changed dramatically. (We analyze this in detail in Figure 4.1 of Chapter 4.) Renminbi-denominated grants and zero-interest loans for overseas projects did not

---

[87] Downs (2011); Gallagher and Irwin (2014); Djankov (2016).       [88] Zhang (2011a).

[89] Downs (2011). China also had an incentive to lend and invest overseas because of a dwindling number of bankable projects at home (Ansar, Flyvbjerg, Budzier, and Lunn 2016).

[90] Dreher, Fuchs, Parks et al. (2021). As the country's foreign exchange reserves soared from roughly US$200 billion in 2000 to US$4 trillion in 2014, this incentive to invest in overseas assets strengthened (Park 2016). By 2009, the country's leadership tacitly acknowledged that its motivation for engaging in large-scale overseas lending was related to its surplus of foreign exchange reserves. Wen Jiabao, then-premier of the State Council, stated that "[w]e should hasten the implementation of our 'going out' strategy and combine the utilization of foreign exchange reserves with the 'going out' of our enterprises" (Anderlini 2009).

[91] Kong and Gallagher (2017).

decline in absolute terms; however, as a percentage of China's total overseas development finance portfolio, they became far less significant. US$-denominated loans and export credits – priced at or near market rates – soared to unprecedented levels.

Outward foreign direct investment (OFDI) flows also increased sharply – from nearly zero in 2000 to more than US$120 billion in 2014.[92] Based on its long-standing principle of "mutual benefit," Beijing began to bundle aid, debt, and OFDI together as part of a "package deal" to ensure that benefits accrued to both China and the host country.[93] The benefits sought by developing countries typically included grants, loans, or export credits for projects that would otherwise be difficult to bankroll; the benefits sought by Beijing usually involved investment opportunities and commercial advantages for Chinese firms, such as no-bid contracts and concession licenses to extract specific natural resources.[94]

The Going Out strategy also catapulted China into a dominant position within the global infrastructure finance market.[95] At the turn of the century, China suffered from domestic overproduction of industrial inputs – aluminum, cement, glass, iron, steel, and timber – because many of its state-owned companies were over-leveraged, inefficient, and unprofitable.[96] The authorities realized that this problem threatened the country's long-term growth prospects. If these firms could not find buyers for their excess production, they would be more likely to default on their loans and shutter their factories, thereby creating higher levels of unemployment. China lacks many of the social safety nets that are found in some Western industrialized democracies,[97] so the authorities

---

[92] Guerrero (2017).

[93] Drawing upon interviews with government and company officials in Tanzania, Li, Newenham-Kahindi, Shapiro, and Chen (2013: 306–307) provide evidence that "[t]o obtain [FDI] deals in the natural resource sector, the Chinese government normally offers a package of multiple-purpose [development] projects in various sectors (e.g., infrastructure, agriculture, manufacturing, healthcare, and education) together with loans to develop these projects." Also see the online appendix of Bunte, Desai, Gbala et al. (2018).

[94] Holslag (2011: 371–372); Li, Newenham-Kahindi, Shapiro, and Chen (2013: 310–312). In some cases, these outward foreign direct investments, development finance, and trade finance activities are packaged together but are unrelated, as when the Chinese government offers development projects to the host government while trying to secure a concession license for a Chinese firm to extract natural resources (Bunte, Desai, Gbala et al. 2018). In other cases, the constituent parts of the financial package are tightly interconnected, as when the Chinese government offers to fund an infrastructure project with a commodity-backed loan that is securitized against the net present value of a future revenue stream from a productive asset, such as the profits from a joint investment venture between a Chinese and host country firm (Mthembu-Salter 2012; Jannson 2013; Bräutigam and Gallagher 2014).

[95] Foster, Butterfield, Chen, and Pushak (2008); Mwase and Yang (2012).

[96] Stanway (2015).     [97] The Economist (2012).

feared that a wave of layoffs by some of the country's biggest employers could trigger social unrest or political instability.[98]

To address this problem, the Going Out strategy sought to reduce domestic supply and increase international demand. At home, China prohibited the development of new production facilities, expedited the closure of inefficient operations, increased the prices of key inputs such as water and power, and imposed higher product quality standards.[99] Abroad, it stoked global demand by offering concessional and non-concessional forms of government funding – grants, loans, and export credits – for infrastructure projects and making its funding *conditional upon the purchase of Chinese industrial inputs*.[100] Box 2.2 uses the example of a single Chinese government-funded infrastructure project in Kenya to explain how this international demand stimulation has worked in practice. Another key element of Beijing's strategy involves the offshoring of industrial input production facilities.[101] With foreign aid and credit, it has generously subsidized joint industrial production ventures between Chinese state-owned enterprises (facing excess production problems at home) and local firms to reduce its domestic production of industrial inputs.[102]

---

**BOX 2.2  How Beijing Uses Foreign Aid and Credit to Address Its Industrial Overproduction Problem**

China's lending operations in Kenya help illustrate one of the most important ways that Beijing has employed to increase international demand for its domestically oversupplied industrial inputs. Between 2010 and 2014, the China Eximbank sharply increased lending for road, rail, and bridge projects in Kenya. Chief among these infrastructure projects was the Mombasa-Nairobi Standard Gauge Railway (SGR), which received two loans from the China Eximbank worth approximately US$3.5 billion. This 475-kilometer railroad required extraordinary amounts of steel, cement, stone, sand, timber, and glass. It also required the acquisition of manufactured goods that depend upon industrial inputs, such as locomotives, train

---

[98] Anderlini and Lau (2009).      [99] State Council (2013).

[100] Chinese state-owned banks contractually require their borrowers to preferentially source project inputs from Chinese firms. They do so by only allowing borrowers to use the proceeds of their loans to finance a specific commercial contract with a specific Chinese firm that is signed prior to the signature of the loan agreement (see Gelpern, Horn, Morris et al. 2021).

[101] Kenderdine and Ling (2018).

[102] Indeed, in the dataset that we introduce in Chapter 4, we find that the Chinese government financed the creation or expansion of more than fifty-three cement factories, steel mills, glass plants, and other industrial input production facilities in twenty-seven countries between 2000 and 2014.

**BOX 2.2  Cont**

wagons, electricity transmission pylons, and cables.[a] The Chinese government took several steps to ensure that the vast majority of these project inputs would be sourced from China. The China Eximbank added a clause to its loan agreements with the Kenyan government that required the borrower to source project inputs from China on a preferential basis.[b] China Road and Bridge Corporation and its Chinese subcontractors also received generous tax exemptions that Kenyan firms did not enjoy, making it substantially more difficult for local firms to supply project inputs. Consequently, the "construction [of the SGR] used negligible local steel and imported all other materials."[c] China's support for the SGR is broadly illustrative of how its grant- and loan-financed development projects have worked since the adoption of the Going Out strategy. They typically involve physical construction; they usually require construction inputs that are oversupplied in China; and they often obligate recipients to import these inputs on a preferential basis.[d]

[a] Republic of Kenya (2014a, 2014b); Sanghi and Johnson (2016); Wissenbach and Wang (2017).
[b] Okoth (2019).
[c] Sanghi and Johnson (2016: 35–36). The implementation of the SGR coincided with a major increase in steel imports from China (KNBS 2015, 2017). At the time, the manager of a Kenyan logistics company told a local newspaper that "[w]e have been experiencing an influx of steel imports from China since 2013, the onset of the construction of the SGR" (Business Daily 2018). He explained that this sudden surge of Chinese steel imports had forced his firm to stop using 120-meter ships and begin using 180-meter ships capable of holding 20,000 tons of steel (Business Daily 2018).
[d] Mattlin and Nojonen (2015); Copper (2016); Ghossein, Hoekman, and Shingal (2018).

Beijing has recently incorporated this two-pronged strategy of international demand stimulation and industrial production offshoring into the BRI and codified it in a set of official statements and policy papers.[103] However, in Chapter 4, we provide statistical evidence that this rationale for Chinese aid and credit provision existed long before the BRI was introduced. Between 2000 and 2014, China was already calibrating the size of its overseas development program in response to changing levels of domestic industrial overproduction (and foreign exchange oversupply). In Chapters 7 and 8, we take advantage of these idiosyncratic motivations for aid and credit provision to unpack the cause-and-effect relationships

[103] State Council (2013, 2015a, 2015b, 2015c); He (2014); Stanway (2015); Shi (2018).

between Chinese development projects and various outcomes in host countries.

However, China's rapid rise as a global donor and lender is not due entirely to these domestic factors. It has also grown increasingly frustrated with the policies, decision-making procedures, and voting shares of the Bretton Woods institutions (IMF and World Bank), a set of international economic institutions designed to rebuild the world economy and promote interstate cooperation after World War II. China has worked with other emerging powers to build an alternative set of international financial institutions, which include a US$100 billion reserve fund alternative to the IMF, a "New Development Bank" with US$100 billion of operating capital, and an Asian Infrastructure Investment Bank (AIIB) with operating capital of another US$100 billion.[104] As China has grown more confident on the international stage, it has also signaled dissatisfaction with some of the principles, policies, and practices that were established by and for Western donors and lenders. The list of issues on which Beijing has diverged from these Western institutions is long and varied. It includes how to measure debt sustainability in borrower countries, which countries should be eligible for concessional financing, how social and environmental safeguards should be designed and implemented, whether it is appropriate to blend development and trade finance, how to select the firms that implement projects, and what types of details about government-financed projects should be subjected to public disclosure requirements.[105]

Yet another factor that has contributed to the expansion of China's overseas development program during the twenty-first century is Beijing's growing desire to project influence around the globe.[106] The 2008 global financial crisis created a unique window of opportunity and an inflection point. As Western countries entered a period of economic retrenchment and their foreign aid budgets shrank, Beijing stepped into the vacuum by ramping up its overseas spending (as we will see in Figure 4.1) and publicly positioning itself as a reliable source of development finance for low-income and middle-income countries. Since taking office, President Xi Jinping has doubled down on this strategy of using aid and credit to cultivate goodwill around the globe. His signature foreign policy initiative – BRI – is a stark contrast to the "hide and bide" philosophy of Deng Xiaoping in that it involves a public campaign to win the "hearts and minds" of citizens in host countries. Shortly after the BRI was launched,

---

[104] Biswas (2015).
[105] Beattie and Callan (2006); Tran (2011a, 2011b); Hook and Rumsey (2016).
[106] Brazys and Dukalskis (2019); Wellner, Dreher, Fuchs et al. (2020); Blair, Marty, and Roessler (2021); Eichenauer, Fuchs, and Brückner (2021).

Xi announced that "[w]e should increase China's soft power, give a good Chinese narrative, and better communicate China's message to the world."[107] The Chinese government also became more intentional about building its "brand" and broadcasting positive messages about its generosity and the efficacy of its development projects. This public diplomacy campaign represents a tacit acknowledgment that Beijing can no longer afford to narrowly cater to the parochial interests of foreign leaders. As a great power and global financier of first resort, it now has to account for the fact that public opinion can "filter up and influence political elites to be more [or less] amenable to China's interests."[108] In Chapter 9, we will return to this issue of whether the BRI ultimately becomes a reputational asset or liability.

## Conclusion: A Long Way from Mao

In a 2015 speech to Pakistan's Parliament, President Xi invoked a phrase originally used by Geng Biao, a former senior official and Chinese ambassador to Pakistan. He suggested that the "traditional friendship between China and Pakistan would spread far and wide, just like the Karakoram Highway."[109] His invocation of the Karakoram Highway is a reminder of the fact that China is not a new international donor or lender; it has been in the business of giving grants and loans to other countries for nearly seventy years.

This history matters because contemporary Chinese development finance is, in many ways, a product of its past. This chapter's review of the history of China's overseas development program highlights important continuities and changes in Chinese policy and practice over the past seven decades. As we have seen, there are many direct links between China's past and present experience as a donor and lender. China continues to frame its relationships with developing countries in historical terms, and Chinese leaders have always understood the strategic value of aid or other gift-like foreign policy tools.[110] Many central principles of Chinese aid, such as respect for sovereignty, noninterference in other states' internal affairs, emphasis on government-to-government aid, and self-reliance, have remained rhetorically intact and have been reinterpreted to fit China's evolving strategic objectives.

However, it is China's recent past that helps us understand most clearly its modern development finance policies. As this chapter has also shown,

---

[107] People's Daily (2014).     [108] Brazys and Dukalskis (2019: 567).
[109] Xinhua (2015). Geng himself attended the Karakoram Highway inauguration in 1978 (Chen 2016).
[110] Alden and Alves (2008).

China's development finance is increasingly commercially oriented and multidimensional in motivation. Both China's early overreliance on highly concessional grants and interest-free loans and its experience as an aid recipient prompted it to reorient its development finance portfolio toward commercially viable projects after 1978. Beijing's Going Out strategy breathed life into this new approach and vastly increased the scale and scope of its overseas spending, a trend that we unpack in Chapter 4. While China certainly still values the foreign policy dividends of its bilateral foreign assistance to other countries, its portfolio has become increasingly dominated by more commercial forms of state financing designed to access natural resources, raw materials, military or other strategic assets, and a financial return on investments.

The Karakoram Highway also reflects the changing set of consequences for recipients of Chinese development finance – issues we explore in Chapters 7 and 8. The increasing market orientation of China's overseas development program, particularly for large infrastructure projects, offers new opportunities for recipients but also presents new risks. Unlike earlier eras of Chinese development finance, the financial conditions attached to contemporary Chinese development finance increasingly resemble market-like offers, and these can present difficult decisions for recipient governments. Chinese state-owned enterprises and other contractors, like the China Road and Bridge Corporation (CRBC) that is implementing work on the Karakoram Highway today, have become powerful commercial actors that require economic returns for their work on Chinese-financed projects abroad.

Both recent research and anecdotal evidence illuminate these risks. Pakistan is among the most vulnerable of BRI countries to debt sustainability issues, linked in part to large Chinese loans with relatively high interest rates.[111] The consequences of China's shifts between political and economic interests and its post-2000 proliferation of state-backed loans are also being experienced in many other countries; its changing role as a development provider is reflected in its changing relationships with early PRC aid recipients such as Egypt, Ghana, Guinea, and Indonesia.[112] More generally, developing countries are finding that Chinese "patient capital," which is often financed with longer planning horizons and unconventional mechanisms such as resource-backed

---

[111] It is clear that Pakistani officials are already wary of this possibility, as evidenced by high-level debates during Pakistan's 2018 general elections about whether and how to apply for another IMF bailout and how to address outstanding Chinese debt. In November 2017, the Pakistani government withdrew a Chinese loan request, reportedly for US$14 billion, for a hydroelectric dam (Smith 2018).

[112] Bräutigam and Hwang (2019).

credit, can create attractive opportunities if it is invested prudently in bankable projects; however, if it is not carefully invested, Chinese capital can create major liabilities.[113] Given these challenges, we argue that it is crucial for policymakers and academics to understand the details of different types of contemporary Chinese development finance instruments. In the next chapter, we introduce a method to track China's development footprint across the globe.

## Appendix 2.A
## China's Eight Principles of Foreign Economic and Technological Assistance

| | |
|---|---|
| 中国政府一贯根据平等互利的原则对外提供援助,从来不把这种援助看作是单方面的赐予,而认为援助是相互的 | The Chinese government always provides foreign assistance based on the principles of equality and mutual benefit, and never views this type of assistance as a one-sided gift but rather views aid as mutual. |
| 在提供对外援助的时候,严格尊重受援国的主权,绝不附带任何条件,绝不要求任何特权 | When providing foreign assistance, [China's government] strictly respects the sovereignty of the recipient country, never attaches any conditions, and never demands any special privileges. |
| 以无息或者低息贷款的方式提供经济援助,在需要的时候延长还款期限。以尽量减少受援国的负担 | [China's government] provides interest-free or low-interest loans as economic assistance and extends the repayment period when needed in order to lower the burden of the recipient as much as possible. |
| 提供外援的目的是帮助受援国逐步走上自力更生、经济上独立发展的道路 | The goal of foreign assistance is to help recipient countries strive for self-sufficiency and independent economic development step by step. |
| 帮助受援国建设的项目,力求投资少,收效快,使受援国政府能够增加收入,积累资金 | [China's government] tries to help recipient countries build projects that require little investment and offer quick returns and results in order to allow recipient governments to increase their income and accumulate capital. |
| 中国政府提供自己所能生产的质量最好的设备和物资,并且根据国际市场的价格议价, | China's government provides the best quality equipment and materials it can manufacture based on international |

---

[113] Kaplan (2016).

*(cont.)*

| | |
|---|---|
| 如果中国政府所提供的设备和物资不合乎商定的规格和质量,中国政府保证退换 | market prices. If the equipment and materials provided by China's government are below the specifications and quality agreed upon, China's government guarantees to replace them. |
| 中国政府对外提供任何一种技术援助的时候,保证做到使受援国的人员充分掌握这种技术 | When China's government provides any type of technical assistance, it ensures that recipient country personnel are able to fully master the technology or technique. |
| 中国政府派到受援国的专家,同受援国自己的专家享受同样的物质待遇,不容许有任何特殊要求和享受 | Experts sent by the Chinese government to recipient countries receive material treatment equal to that of experts in the recipient country and are not allowed to have any type of special demands or amenities. |

*Source:* China Daily (2010).

# 3   Counting and Comparing Apples and Dragon Fruits

## Official and Unofficial Efforts to Uncover a "State Secret"

In the waning months of 2011, a large group of official donors, lenders, recipients, and borrowers converged upon Busan, South Korea, for the High-Level Forum on Aid Effectiveness. All of the usual suspects were represented: the United States, European, Japanese, and Australian governments and the United Nations; the World Bank; and the regional development banks. But this meeting was unusual because the Chinese government and other non-Western suppliers of development finance also came to the negotiating table.

A partnership agreement was endorsed by all parties, but it papered over an unresolved conflict between the "incumbents" and "challengers" of the prevailing global development finance regime. Western powers urged China and other emerging donors to join the International Aid Transparency Initiative (IATI) and voluntarily comply with transparency standards of the OECD-DAC. China flatly rejected this proposal, stating that the "principle of transparency should apply to north-south cooperation, but ... it should not be seen as a standard for south-south cooperation."[1]

Beijing's position during the Busan negotiations came as no surprise to us. Two years earlier, in 2009, we had arranged a phone call with an official from China's MOFCOM – the government agency responsible for coordination of the country's foreign aid program – in hopes of persuading the authorities to open up their books. We posed a question that had proven helpful in brokering data-sharing agreements with other

---

This chapter draws selectively upon prose and arguments from two prior studies: Muchapondwa, Nielson, Parks et al. (2016) and Strange, Dreher, Fuchs et al. (2017). These articles include more detailed links to previous research than we reference here.

[1] Tran (2011a). The final agreement included carefully worded language that effectively allowed China to avoid making any meaningful or verifiable commitments: "We will work to improve the availability and public accessibility of information on development cooperation and other development resources, building on our respective commitments in this area." See www.oecd.org/dac/effectiveness/49650173.pdf, last accessed January 31, 2020.

non-Western donors: "Don't you want the world to know how generous you are?" The MOFCOM official's terse response signaled that Chinese authorities had no interest in sharing the information that we requested: "everyone who needs to know how generous we are already knows."[2]

The High-Level Forum on Aid Effectiveness in Busan was not the first time the members of the OECD-DAC had tried to convince China to participate in the international regime for reporting, monitoring, and coordinating development finance. In 2006, the Paris Club invited China to join as a full-fledged member because of its increasing importance as a sovereign lender. China rejected this offer, instead choosing to engage as an "ad hoc participant," a status that placed it "under no obligation to act in solidarity with Paris Club members or even to inform the Paris Club about the management of its credit activities."[3] In 2009, a DAC-China Working Group was established to increase mutual understanding and trust between China and Western donors. It exposed China to OECD-DAC reporting standards. However, Beijing expressed little interest in joining the OECD's Creditor Reporting System, a mechanism for information sharing and coordination that is open to both OECD-DAC and non-OECD-DAC donors. At the country level, Western donors also made a habit of inviting China to local aid coordination meetings, but China spurned nearly all of these requests. It favored a go-it-alone approach.[4]

Beijing's secrecy about the "who, what, where, when, and how" of its overseas development program poses a major challenge for both scholars and policymakers. Scholars have historically studied the allocation and effects of foreign grants and loans based on data that governments make available through a voluntary disclosure regime. This reliance on voluntarily disclosed data worked well when regime compliance was high, and most major international donors and lenders were members of the OECD-DAC. However, China does not participate in international reporting systems, so scholars have no way of using official data to study how Chinese development finance is allocated over space and time. Nor can they use official data to measure the effects of China's development

---

[2] Phone interview with MOFCOM official in August 2009. For a more contemporary measure of the lack of transparency in China's overseas development program, see Publish What You Fund (2020).

[3] For greater context, see Willard (2007) and Hurley, Morris, and Portelance (2019: 155). Permanent members of the Paris Club agree to abide by the club's debt-rescheduling rules and principles, and they do not make decisions about rescheduling debt without consensus among the participating creditor countries. Ad hoc participants are allowed but not required to participate in a debt-rescheduling agreement for a given borrower country and are invited on a case-by-case basis to participate in country-specific discussions. See www .clubdeparis.org/en/communications/page/permanent-members and www.clubdeparis.org /en/communications/page/ad-hoc-participants, last accessed January 31, 2020.

[4] Grimm (2013); Xu and Carey (2014); Bigsten and Tengstam (2015); Furukawa (2018).

projects on economic growth, poverty reduction, human health, literacy, or environmental sustainability. Social scientists need alternative methods of data collection to understand the aims and impacts of Beijing's overseas development program.

China's decision to opt out of global reporting systems has also vexed traditional donors and creditors. As Beijing's development finance footprint has grown, members of the OECD-DAC and multilateral institutions have become more aware of the potential benefits of coordinating with China. For example, establishing a common set of social, environmental, and fiduciary safeguards with China would discourage "race to the bottom" pressures that pit funders against one another.[5] Similarly, working together to ensure that borrowers engage in responsible debt management would make it easier for all bilateral and multilateral lenders to manage repayment risk.[6] But coordination requires information about where, when, and how the Chinese government is financing, designing, and implementing projects – information that Beijing has shown little interest in disclosing. We return to this issue in Chapter 9 when we consider the tension between China's stated desire to "multilateralize" the BRI and its traditional disregard for the rules and norms of the prevailing international development finance regime.

Recently, Beijing has demonstrated some degree of willingness to increase coordination with Western powers through "trilateral cooperation" schemes and a newly established Multilateral Cooperation Center for Development Finance.[7] But these are small signs of progress that have come only after many years of Western donors and creditors trying to

---

[5] By way of illustration, Laurance, Peletier-Jellema, Geenen et al. (2015: R261–R262) point to the German Development Bank (KfW), which "is proposing to pave and upgrade a number of low-grade roads through Cambodia's greatest biodiversity hotspot, the Seima Protection Forest, to service indigenous villages there. [KfW] recognizes the large potential for environmental problems from the road upgrades, such as increased poaching and illegal logging. It has asked conservation scientists working in the area to advise them on potential mitigation measures. Although they are greatly concerned about the project, the scientists see no alternative but to support it, because otherwise they believe that Chinese proponents would do it more cheaply and without environmental mitigation, leading to a greater level of illegal logging and forest encroachment than would occur under a KfW-supported project."

[6] G-7 (2006); BBC (2009); Hernandez (2017); Lagarde (2018); Strauss (2018); Kawanami (2019). For other examples of Western leaders and analysts articulating the benefits of increased coordination with China, see G-7 (2006); Hernandez (2017); Lagarde (2018); Kawanami (2019).

[7] In 2019, China established a new Multilateral Cooperation Center for Development, collaborating with eight multilateral and bilateral development finance institutions to (a) invest in project preparation work; (b) build the capacity to mitigate risks related to procurement, corruption, and environmental and social issues; and (c) facilitate greater

convince China that greater information sharing would serve its own interests. China remains the least transparent major player in the global development finance market.[8]

Beijing's opacity also strains its relationships with host country officials. As we constructed the dataset for this book, we saw signs of rising discontent among host government officials who monitor and manage external sources of aid and debt. For instance, when we submitted a request for information about Chinese grants and loans to a senior official in the government of Gabon who is responsible for tracking incoming development finance, he responded: "I can tell you it's not easy to give you such data. There's a big problem of transparency on Chinese information." He explained that he would try again to obtain the information, but three months later, he sent us the following update: "It's incredible: I have no more information about [Chinese grants and loans to Gabon]. For three months, I can meet no one from [the] Chinese Embassy!... I'm very sorry for you and for us."[9] Separately, a senior official from Liberia's Ministry of Finance and Development Planning told us that "[we] should be solely responsible for tracking grants and loans coming to Liberia, but there are challenges tracking such information especially when it comes to China. We recently met with some Chinese delegations and we registered our serious concern about the lack of information from their end."[10]

## Why China's Overseas Development Program Is Not Transparent

Despite the cumulative weight of these external pressures, Beijing still treats its foreign aid program as a "state secret."[11] There are three key reasons why it chooses to shield these expenditures from public scrutiny.

information sharing and coordination between Chinese and non-Chinese development finance institutions (Zhou 2018; Parks 2019).

[8] Publish What You Fund (2020).

[9] Author correspondence with a senior official in Gabon's Office of the Prime Minister on March 2, 2018.

[10] Author correspondence with a senior official in Liberia's Ministry of Finance and Development Planning on April 30, 2018. Likewise, in Rwanda, Grimm (2013: 94) found that a common complaint was that "the Chinese approach [is] characterized by the lack of transparency of aid flows, due to the reluctance to report in a regular and complete way to the Rwandan Government." These experiences at the country level are difficult to reconcile with the assertion that "African governments themselves already know how much aid and development finance they are getting from China" (Bräutigam 2010a: 34). However, the Chinese government usually does share information on project design and implementation issues with a small number of counterparts within the office of the recipient country's president or the prime minister (see Chapter 6 of this book).

[11] Bräutigam (2009: 2).

First, the Chinese government is less constrained than its OECD-DAC counterparts. Donor countries with strong democratic institutions face legislatures that demand comprehensive, detailed, and accurate information about public expenditures. Beijing does not face these constraints. It has substantially greater flexibility to decide what types of expenditure data to disclose.[12]

Second, China has weak domestic political incentives to reveal the full scale of its overseas spending activities.[13] Despite its impressive growth rates over the past four decades, China is still a poor country in per capita terms, and there is little public support for the country's foreign aid program. In a 2010 survey of 62,000 Chinese respondents, only 23 percent of respondents said that China should provide overseas aid, while 77 percent of respondents said that it should not.[14] Domestic political support for China's foreign aid program is particularly weak in the western provinces and in other areas with high poverty rates.[15]

Previous disclosures about China's overseas development program have fueled popular discontent and forced the central government into a defensive posture. For example, in 2011, Beijing faced strong and sustained domestic criticism when the public learned that it had donated twenty-three school buses to Macedonia, a country that is wealthier than China in per capita terms. This donation became public knowledge just "two weeks after a fatal crash of an overcrowded school bus in [China's] impoverished Gansu province," and the "incident fueled domestic debate about the size and direction of China's aid [program]."[16] Beijing faced similar public outrage in 2018 when President Xi Jinping announced US\$60 billion of new lending to Africa. Chinese citizens voiced their disapproval on social media, and one Chinese blogger questioned whether taxpayer funds should instead fund the country's resource-

---

[12] Deng, Peng, and Wang (2013: 954) note that "[e]ven though the Secrecy Law was revised in 2010, there was no substantive change in terms of the hurdles the law throws up for open government information, including budgetary information. The parameters for defining a state secret are so broad and generic that pretty much everything the government is involved in can be considered a state secret." For additional context on the incentives of autocratic donors in general, and China in particular, see Andreula, Chong, and Guillen (2009); Wehner and de Renzio (2013); Magee and Doces (2015); Vadlamannati, Cooray, and Brazys (2018); Budjan and Fuchs (forthcoming).

[13] Foreign aid is one of the most unpopular forms of public expenditure in both democracies and autocracies (e.g., Pew Research Center 2013; Ross 2018). The fact that foreign aid is least popular among the poor and unemployed highlights that skepticism about aid is rooted in the economic anxieties of voters and taxpayers (Paxton and Knack 2012). However, unlike democratic donors, autocratic donors are better able to keep public information secret (Hollyer, Rosendorff, and Vreeland 2011; Vadlamannati and de Soysa 2016; Wallace 2016).

[14] See Tan-Mullins (2016).    [15] Cheng and Smyth (2016).
[16] Zhang and Smith (2017: 2342).

starved Ministry of Education.[17] The government tried to contain the issue by censoring the most critical online posts and using a state-run tabloid to scold angry taxpayers: "[the] Chinese people should ... be aware that major powers must fulfil their obligations. Otherwise, they can hardly stay where they are for long, not to mention going forward."[18]

A third reason why it is difficult to obtain information about China's overseas development program is the highly decentralized manner in which its foreign grants and loans are approved and implemented. Dozens of central and subnational government institutions are involved in the design and delivery of Chinese development projects.[19] MOFCOM provides grants and interest-free loans for small- and medium-sized projects. The country's policy banks (the China Eximbank and China Development Bank) and state-owned commercial banks (Bank of China, Industrial and Commercial Bank of China, China Construction Bank, Agricultural Bank of China, and China CITIC Bank) provide concessional and non-concessional loans for large-scale projects. Chinese state-owned enterprises – like ZTE, CATIC, China North Industries Group (NORINCO), Poly Technologies – provide supplier credits to help foreign governments buy their goods and services.[20] The Ministry of Education oversees scholarship programs, language programs, teacher training programs, and the country's global network of Confucius Institutes.[21] The Ministry of Health (now integrated into the National Health Commission) oversees training programs for health officials and the deployment of Chinese medical teams.[22] Other central government institutions – including but not limited to the Ministry of

---

[17] In 2013, when we released an early, Africa-specific version of our dataset of Chinese development projects, a popular domestic news site called Wangyi ran a feature story, and it became the most popular news item throughout mainland China. More than 2,500 visitors commented and almost 120,000 users participated in the online discussion by either commenting or "dinging" (similar to "likes"). Much of the commentary questioned the need for an overseas development program with so many pressing domestic issues, like school fees and public sector corruption.

[18] Quote as cited in Hornby and Hancock (2018).

[19] Zhang and Smith (2017); Rudyak (2019).

[20] Supplier credits are also known as "vendor financing." The terms of these loans vary, but they usually have shorter maturities and grace periods, and interest rates are often tethered to LIBOR plus a margin. In some cases, China Development Bank or China Eximbank will first offer an export seller's credit to the Chinese state-owned enterprise, and the Chinese state-owned enterprise will in turn use the proceeds from the export seller's credit to on-lend to its foreign customer (through the provision of a supplier credit).

[21] MOFCOM is generally responsible for school construction projects, the provision of educational materials and equipment, and nondegree training programs (Reilly 2015).

[22] MOFCOM generally oversees the construction of medical facilities, such as hospitals and health clinics (Wang, Liu, Liu et al. 2013). For details on these other institutions, see Xue (2014) and Varrall (2016).

Agriculture, the Ministry of Science and Technology, the Ministry of Culture, the General Administration of Sport, the State Administration of Religious Affairs, the National Development and Reform Commission, the State Oceanic Administration, the State Administration of Cultural Heritage, and China Women's Federation – oversee international activities in their respective areas of specialization. The Foreign Affairs Office of the Ministry of National Defense, the People's Liberation Army (PLA), and the Ministry of Civil Affairs oversee the administration of humanitarian assistance programs.[23] The Ministry of Finance is responsible for making most decisions related to the provision of debt relief and the country's financial contributions to various multilateral institutions. And there are thousands of subnational government institutions, private and public enterprises, NGOs, universities, and hospitals involved in the implementation of Chinese government-financed projects around the world.[24]

As a result of the highly decentralized way in which projects are managed and monitored, China's statistical system for tracking its overseas portfolio of grants and loans remains underdeveloped. China does not have a "master database" of its government-financed projects around the globe. Before the creation of the China International Development Cooperation Agency (CIDCA) in 2018, MOFCOM was responsible for coordinating the country's bilateral aid program. However, in practice, its ability to supervise the full scope of China's bilateral aid activities was extremely limited.[25] The government tacitly acknowledged this problem in December 2014, when it released official guidance directing MOFCOM to develop a project-level aid database.[26] But MOFCOM was never given a mandate to track China's contributions to multilateral institutions or its semi-concessional and non-concessional financial flows from the country's policy banks or state-owned commercial banks.[27]

The State Council has published three "White Papers" on the country's foreign aid program – in 2011, 2014, and 2021 – that provide summary statistics on the total amount of aid China gave to five regions of the world.

---

[23] For more details, see Kobayashi (2008); Bräutigam (2009); Zhou and Xiong (2013); UNDP (2015); Carter (2017).

[24] Reilly (2012); Shen and Fan (2014); Xue (2014); Varrall (2016).

[25] Lancaster (2007); Xue (2014). The fact that MOFCOM's Department of Foreign Aid (DFA) had only 70 employees highlights the severity of its capacity constraints (Varrall 2016: 26).

[26] See MOFCOM (2014a).

[27] See Zhang and Smith (2017). This is noteworthy because the vast majority of Chinese official financing comes from the country's policy banks and state-owned commercial banks, in the form of loans at or near market rates and export credits. On this point, see Horn, Reinhart, and Trebesch (2019) and Dreher, Fuchs, Parks et al. (2021).

As discussed in the previous chapter, the Ministry of Finance has also published data on the country's total foreign aid expenditure through its website and a publication called the *Finance Yearbook of China*. However, neither of these official sources provides a project-level or country-by-country breakdown of foreign grants and loans.[28]

Before we began writing this book, we made one final attempt to obtain access to data from the Chinese government on its overseas portfolio of grant- and loan-financed development projects. We traveled to Beijing and conducted interviews with MOFCOM officials in late 2018, inquiring about the status of the project-level database that it was tasked with building in late 2014. We were informed that an internal "information system" exists, but that "it's not really a database" and there are no plans to make it public.[29] We were stunned to learn that some MOFCOM officials had resorted to using the dataset that we had assembled for this book.

## From State Secret to Scientific Dysfunction

In the absence of official data from the Chinese government, a number of research groups have stepped into the informational breach with datasets of their own. Some of the most widely used datasets include those from the China Africa Research Initiative at the Johns Hopkins University School of Advanced International Studies (SAIS-CARI), Boston University's Global Development Policy Center, the RAND Corporation, the US Congressional Research Service (CRS), the Lowy Institute, the American Enterprise Institute (AEI), Inter-American Dialogue (IAD), the Japan International Cooperation Agency (JICA) Research Institute, and the Reconnecting Asia Project at the Center for Strategic and International Studies (CSIS). However, all of these datasets

---

[28] In previous years, MOFCOM published a *China Commerce Yearbook* and *Almanac of China's Foreign Economic Relations & Trade*. These yearbooks and almanacs disaggregate China's foreign assistance program into several categories, including "numbers of medical teams dispatched," "numbers of technical assistance projects aided by China," "comprehensive projects assumed/undertaken," and "comprehensive projects completed." However, MOFCOM only publishes project-level data for one of these four categories ("comprehensive projects completed"), and the project records that are reported lack monetary amounts or the terms on any loans. Therefore, these yearbooks and almanacs do not provide a comprehensive picture of China's foreign assistance activities at the project level (Hawkins, Nielson, Bergevin et al. 2010). For a refresher on concessional vs. non-concessional sources of development finance, see Box 1.1 in Chapter 1.

[29] It is telling that nearly identical guidance calling for the creation of a project-level aid database appeared in a policy document that CIDCA published in November 2018 (Rudyak 2019).

have significant limitations. Some are specific to individual regions or types of financial flows. Some suffer from over-counting, mis-categorization, incomplete coverage, and heavy reliance on individual sources (particularly English-language media sources). Some provide "black box" financial estimates at the country level that do not enable analysis by sector, financial modality, financier, implementing agency, subnational locality, or other attributes that can be usefully categorized at the project level. Others fail to provide enough information about their methods and sources to enable replication and building upon their work. Table 3.1 compares these data collection efforts along several important dimensions.[30]

Our goal, as we indicated in Chapter 1, is to develop and sustain a long-term, cumulative research program on the causes and consequences of China's global development program. Therefore, we have taken a different approach. To facilitate empirical analysis of China's *global* portfolio of development projects, we have constructed a granular, project-level dataset that covers all sectors, all major world regions, and all types of government financing (grants, loans, export credits, technical assistance, etc.). To make our dataset comparable to the official development finance data published by other international donors and lenders, we have relied on internationally accepted terms and definitions (e.g., official development assistance [ODA] vs. other official flows [OOF], OECD sector classification). We have also published all of our sources, methods, data, and statistical code to promote independent replication of our research findings.

As Table 3.1 demonstrates, many of the existing datasets that measure Chinese development finance are not particularly useful to social scientists because they are either not published at the project level or include very few project-specific variables. For example, the Lowy Institute's dataset of Chinese aid projects in the Pacific includes nine variables. The China-Latin America Finance Database, produced by Inter-American Dialogue and the Global Development Policy Center at Boston University, tracks five variables. The SAIS-CARI

---

[30] We compared each of these datasets in January 2020. Several of them, including AidData, have been updated to cover more years, countries, and sources since that time. For the most recent version of AidData's project-level dataset, see https://china .aiddata.org/ as well as the postscript to this book. As Table 3.1 demonstrates, there are some project-level datasets that cover years after 2014, but the type of analysis we conduct in Chapters 5–8 requires more granular information about project characteristics (e.g., subnational locations or "aid" versus "debt") than is available from any of these other data sources. While a shorter and less contemporary time series is a cost, the benefit of more granular and detailed data justifies our use of AidData's Global Chinese Official Finance Dataset, 2000–2014.

**Table 3.1** *Features of existing datasets on Chinese government financial flows*

| Data Source | Unit of Observation | Public Disclosure at Unit of Observation Level | Public Disclosure of Dataset as .xls, .csv, .dta, .sav, .txt, .rdata, or .rda | Sector Coverage | Country Coverage | Time Coverage | Financial Flow Type Coverage | Number of Variables | Source Types |
|---|---|---|---|---|---|---|---|---|---|
| China's Global Energy Finance Database (GDP Center) | Loan | Yes | No | Energy | 62 | 2000–2017 | Loans from China Development Bank and China Eximbank | 12 | Media reports; company filings and bond prospectuses at security exchanges; Chinese and host government sources |
| China–Africa Loan Database (SAIS-CARI) | Loan | No | Yes (but only at country-year level) | All | 56 | 2000–2015 | Loans from MOFCOM, China Development Bank, China Eximbank, Chinese private/commercial banks, and Chinese state-owned enterprises (SOEs) and private enterprises | 14 | Media reports; Chinese and African government sources; company filings and bond prospectuses at security exchanges; websites of Chinese contractors, subcontractors, and suppliers; IMF Article IV reports |

Table 3.1 *(cont.)*

| Data Source | Unit of Observation | Public Disclosure at Unit of Observation Level | Public Disclosure of Dataset as .xls, .csv, .dta, .sav, .txt, .rdata, or .rda | Sector Coverage | Country Coverage | Time Coverage | Financial Flow Type Coverage | Number of Variables | Source Types |
|---|---|---|---|---|---|---|---|---|---|
| China–Latin America Finance Database (IAD and GDP Center) | Loan | Yes | No | All | 13 | 2005–2016 | Loans from China Development Bank and China Eximbank | 5 | Media reports; company filings and bond prospectuses at security exchanges; official gazettes of host countries; Chinese government websites |
| China Global Investment Tracker (AEI) | Investment and construction contract | Yes | Yes | All | 150 | 2005–2017 | Investment projects and construction projects (financed with or without Chinese government financing) | 11 | Media reports; corporate press releases |
| US Congressional Research Service (CRS) | Project | No | No | All | 62 | 2001–2008 | Foreign aid and government-sponsored investment activities | 14 | Media reports |

| | | | | | | | | | |
|---|---|---|---|---|---|---|---|---|---|
| RAND Corporation | Project | No | No | All | 93 | 2000–2011 | Foreign aid and government-sponsored investment activities | 8 | Media reports |
| Chinese Aid in the Pacific (Lowy Institute) | Project | Yes | No | All | 8 | 2006–2014 | Foreign aid (excluding scholarship, trainings, China Red Cross donations) | 9 | Media reports; Chinese government websites and official statements; host government documents; Chinese contractor websites/annual reports; site visits; face-to-face interviews and electronic correspondence with project personnel and stakeholders |
| JICA Research Institute | Global Aggregates | Yes | No | NA | NA | 2001–2015 | Foreign aid | NA | China's Ministry of Finance |
| Reconnecting Asia (CSIS) | Project | Yes | No | Infrastructure | 43 | 2006–2018 | Road, rail, and port projects (financed with or without Chinese government financing) | 14 | Government agencies in host countries, development banks, and project contracts |

Table 3.1 (cont.)

| Data Source | Unit of Observation | Public Disclosure at Unit of Observation Level | Public Disclosure of Dataset as .xls, .csv, .dta, .sav, .txt, .rdata, or .rda | Sector Coverage | Country Coverage | Time Coverage | Financial Flow Type Coverage | Number of Variables | Source Types |
|---|---|---|---|---|---|---|---|---|---|
| AidData's Global Chinese Official Finance Dataset, 2000–2014, Version 1.0 (our contribution) | Project | Yes | Yes | All | 138 | 2000–2014 | All types of Chinese government financing (e.g., grants, loans, export credits, debt relief, scholarships) | 54 | Media reports; data and documentation from aid and debt management institutions in China; annual reports of lending and granting institutions; websites of Chinese embassies and economic and commercial counselor's offices (ECCOs); case studies and field reports by researchers and NGOs; IMF Article IV reports |

China-Africa Loan Database collects individual loan-financed projects, but as of January 2020 it only published data on aggregate amounts of Chinese lending to African countries. This lack of detail dramatically narrows the set of empirical questions that can be addressed. When Chinese government-financed projects are systematically categorized according to their modalities, purposes, and levels of concessionality, researchers can determine which types of financial instruments the Chinese authorities use to achieve different goals.[31] When researchers can identify the subnational locations where Chinese government-financed projects take place and differentiate between projects that have entered implementation and those that have not, they can identify the impacts of these projects on various outcomes of interest, including economic development, inequality, human health, educational attainment, corruption, environmental degradation, local conflict, trade union membership, and public opinion.[32] But without detailed information about the characteristics of individual projects, almost none of these questions can be answered in convincing ways.

Another major challenge with existing datasets is that they do not use internationally accepted definitions for key terms and concepts or employ common measurement standards. Instead, they rely on idiosyncratic concepts that can lead to misleading or inaccurate comparisons. The definition and measurement of "aid" is a case in point. As we explained in Chapter 1, an internationally accepted definition and standard for measuring aid is called Official Development Assistance (ODA). However, apart from the dataset that we have created in collaboration with AidData, none of the datasets identified in Table 3.1 uses the formal definition of ODA to determine which Chinese government-financed activities qualify as aid in the strict sense of the term.[33] Consequently, some analysts claim that China's aid giving rivals that of other major donors, while others claim that China is a relatively small player in the aid market. These disagreements are rooted in basic definitional and methodological differences.

---

[31] Dreher, Eichenauer, and Gehring (2018).
[32] See, for example, BenYishay, Parks, Runfola, and Trichler (2016); Brazys, Elkink, and Kelly (2017); Blair and Roessler (2019); Dreher, Fuchs, Hodler et al. (2021); Gehring, Kaplan, and Wong (2019); Isaksson and Kotsadam (2018a, 2018b); Marty, Goodman, Le Few et al. (2019); Bluhm, Dreher, Fuchs et al. (2020); Cruzatti, Dreher, and Matzat (2020); Knutsen and Kotsadam (2020); Martorano, Metzger, and Sanfilippo (2020); and Eichenauer, Fuchs, and Brückner (2021).
[33] For example, the Lowy Institute excludes scholarships, training programs, and some types of humanitarian assistance, all of which are included in the formal definition of ODA (see Box 1.1).

Another limitation of existing datasets is that they are rarely transparent about their sources and methods. By way of example, consider the China Global Investment Tracker, which is produced by the American Enterprise Institute and the Heritage Foundation. It provides a database of Chinese investments and construction contracts worldwide but does not disclose the sources or methods used to construct the individual project records. From direct correspondence with the lead researcher responsible for the dataset, we learned that the underlying information is sourced from "business wires, corporate press releases, and local journalism from countries where such are considered reliable, e.g., Reuters, the Sinomach website, and The Australian."[34] However, these sources are not published with the dataset. Nor does the team responsible have any intention of publishing a methodology document: they worry that "imitators" will try to produce a similar product.[35]

The fact that the American Enterprise Institute and the Heritage Foundation are averse to public disclosure reveals a broader challenge: in spite of the scientific benefits of transparency and replicability, researchers who collect data on Chinese aid and debt have a disincentive to disclose their sources or methods to preserve reputational benefits and the commercial value of their data.[36] This is problematic because knowledge is usually generated, refined, and improved by consolidating data and using a common set of rigorous, transparent, and replicable methods and procedures to analyze these data. Those of us who do empirical research on China's overseas development program should be held to a higher standard: we should consistently publish the replication datasets and computer code that other social scientists need to independently validate our results. However, this kind of research transparency is surprisingly rare; with the exception of a growing community of social scientists that use the dataset that we showcase in this book, those who study China's overseas development program generally do not publish their replication datasets and computer code. If we are aiming to

---

[34] Authors' email correspondence with a member of the China Global Investment Tracker team, October 9, 2012.

[35] Authors' email correspondence with a member of the China Global Investment Tracker team, October 9, 2012.

[36] Among area studies specialists who study Chinese development finance, there is also a lack of appreciation for the central role of replicability in the advancement of science. When we published the first TUFF-based dataset of Chinese official financing in 2013, Deborah Bräutigam, who is a leading expert on China-Africa relations, clearly stated the nature of her reservations about our aim of replicability: "The authors are striving for a database that can be replicated by anyone. But that's the problem. This is not research that can be done by just anyone" (Bräutigam 2013). Elsewhere, she and her colleague wrote that "[t]he 'forensic internet sleuthing' methods that we employ cannot easily be replicated" (Bräutigam and Hwang 2016: 7).

create a healthier ecosystem for social science research on development finance from China, we need to make a course correction.

It is useful to consider how knowledge accumulates elsewhere in the social sciences: economists who study economic growth rely on the Penn World Tables and remotely sensed nighttime light data from the National Oceanic and Atmospheric Administration; political scientists who study democracy rely on the POLITY, DD, and V-DEM datasets; and scholars of interstate and intrastate conflict rely on the COW, UCDP, PRIO, and ACLED datasets.[37] All of these datasets were constructed and refined over time by researchers who employed transparent, systematic, and replicable procedures. Also, among those who use these datasets, it is standard practice to expose one's analysis to independent review and replication. This "open research" culture has made it substantially easier to flag – and correct – calculation errors, sample selection bias, influential outliers, selectively omitted null findings, and results that are sensitive to alternative model specifications. It has also allowed social scientists to extend and refine the work of their colleagues and promote the development of a cumulative body of scientific knowledge.[38] As a result, researchers and policymakers have learned a great deal about the causes and consequences of economic growth, democracy, and conflict over the past several decades.[39]

However, scholarship on China's overseas development program has not benefited from these practices; as a consequence, we still know relatively little about the nature, allocation, and impact of Chinese development finance. This lack of research transparency does a disservice to those who formulate public policy. In *Check the Numbers: The Case for Due Diligence in Policy Formation*, B. D. McCullough and Ross McKitrick warn that "practices that obstruct independent replication, such as refusal to disclose data, or the concealment of details about computational methods, prevent the proper functioning of the scientific process and

---

[37] For transparent and replicable measures of conflict, democracy, and economic growth, see Suzuki, Krause, and Singer (2002); Cheibub, Gandhi, and Vreeland (2010); Raleigh, Linke, Hegre, and Karlsen (2010); Coppedge, Gerring, Lindberg et al. (2015); Pinkovskiy and Sala-i-Martin (2016); Van Holt, Johnson, Moates, and Carley (2016); Jenke and Gelpi (2017); Bjørnskov and Rode (2020).

[38] As Gary King of Harvard University has explained, "[t]he replication standard is extremely important to the further development of the discipline. The most common and scientifically productive method of building on existing research is to replicate an existing finding – to follow the precise path taken by a previous researcher, and then improve on the data or methodology in one way or another. This procedure ensures that the second researcher will receive all the benefits of the first researcher's hard work" (King 1995: 445).

[39] Search results from Google Scholar reveal that since these datasets were first released, tens of thousands of social scientists have used them to conduct empirical analysis.

can lead to poor public decision making."[40] Indeed, when researchers shield their data and statistical code from external scrutiny, they effectively make it impossible for their peers in the scientific community to evaluate the reliability of their conclusions, thereby short-circuiting the knowledge accumulation process and encouraging policymakers to "shop around" for research findings that comport with their prior beliefs.[41] Those who wish to portray China as a villain can do so by simply cherry-picking the evidence that supports the policy positions that they wish to defend, and those who wish to portray China as a hero can selectively draw upon the evidence that is useful for their preferred arguments.

To help address these problems, we have spent the past nine years working with AidData to construct a new dataset of Chinese government-financed development projects in five major world regions (Africa, the Middle East, Asia and the Pacific, Latin America and the Caribbean, and Central and Eastern Europe). The dataset includes 4,304 Chinese aid- and debt-financed projects in 138 countries and territories and it covers a fifteen-year period (2000–2014).[42]

We have created a publicly available methodology called Tracking Underreported Financial Flows (TUFF) that facilitates the collection of detailed financial, operational, and locational information about government-financed development projects by standardizing and synthesizing open-source materials. The TUFF methodology triangulates information from four types of sources – English, Chinese, and local-language news reports; official statements from Chinese ministries, embassies, and economic and commercial counselor offices (ECCOs); the aid and debt information management systems of finance and planning ministries in counterpart countries; and case study and field research undertaken by scholars and NGOs – to minimize the impact of incomplete or inaccurate information.

### Stress Testing TUFF: A Ground-Truthing Exercise in South Africa and Uganda

We initially used the TUFF methodology to identify Chinese development projects in one region of the world (Africa) from 2000 to 2011. When this preliminary dataset was published in April 2013, it caused quite a stir.[43] It

---

[40] McCullough and McKitrick (2009: 2).     [41] Banuri, Dercon, and Gauri (2017).

[42] The data that we have collected – AidData's Global Chinese Official Finance Dataset, 2000–2014 (Version 1.0) – can be publicly accessed at www.aiddata.org/data/chinese-global-official-finance-dataset.

[43] AidData's pilot methodology for tracking underreported financial flows was initially called "Media-Based Data Collection" (see Strange, Parks, Tierney et al. 2013).

was extensively covered by international media outlets like *Reuters*, *Financial Times*, and *The Guardian*. They ran stories with splashy headlines like "Revealed: $75 billion in previously secret Chinese aid to Africa."[44] Deborah Bräutigam argued on her blog that our aggregate estimates of Chinese government financing to the continent were "way too high." She also wrote,

> The main problem is that the teams that have been collecting the data and their supervisors simply don't know enough about China in Africa, or how to check media reports, track down the realities of a project, and *dig into the story* to find out what really happened. You can start with media reports, but it is highly problematic to stop there.[45]

We took issue with this characterization of our methodology.[46] Even the earliest (1.0) version of the methodology sought to triangulate as many publicly available sources of information as possible for each project over the course of its lifecycle. Media reports were used to identify the potential provision of a Chinese government grant or loan, but we never relied on them exclusively. The earliest version of the dataset also drew upon official sources and field research.

Our public disagreement with Bräutigam highlighted the fact that we come from two very different research traditions. She thought it was a bad idea to publish the dataset and expose our methods and sources to public scrutiny. She warned that "[d]ata-driven researchers won't wait around to have someone clean the data. They'll start using it and publishing with it and setting these numbers into stone."[47] We acknowledged at the time that some people might misinterpret or misuse the dataset, but we thought that the benefits of transparency would ultimately outweigh the costs. You cannot spot and fix errors until you know that they exist, so we thought then (as we do now) that encouraging scrutiny of our data would be the best way to promote scientific knowledge accumulation. Also, several of us had been involved in a larger effort to collect and publish project-level development finance data from a variety of international donors and lenders between 2003 and 2013; during that period, we routinely found errors in the data from official sources.[48] Therefore, we

---

However, upon publication of the initial dataset and methodology, it became clear that this name was misleading because it implied that AidData's approach relied exclusively on media reports. As we explain in the codebook, the methodology involves extensive triangulation of information from official and unofficial sources. For the updated codebook, see Strange, Ghose, Russell et al. (2017).

[44] Fernholz (2013).     [45] Bräutigam (2013), emphasis in original.     [46] AidData (2013).

[47] Bräutigam (2013).

[48] Tierney, Nielson, Hawkins et al. (2011). In Strange, Ghose, Russell et al. (2017), we demonstrate that official data on Chinese government-financed projects are not more complete or reliable than the data generated using the Tracking Underreported

were skeptical of the assertion that official data on Chinese government-financed development projects are necessarily more reliable or more complete than the data generated by the TUFF methodology.

At the same time, we recognized that some of Bräutigam's criticisms had merit, and we took these critiques seriously. One of her most valuable suggestions, made before the first version of the dataset was published, was that we collect data on the status of each project in our dataset based on available sources. Users of our dataset, she noted, ought to be able to determine if a project has been "pledged" but not officially committed through the signing of a grant or loan agreement. She also urged us to inform users if a project that was backed by an official commitment had never reached implementation or completion or was ultimately suspended or canceled. To address this concern, we included a "status" variable in the first version (and all subsequent versions) of our dataset to ensure that we would systematically track the current status of every project.

Bräutigam's admonition to "*dig into the story* to find out what really happened" also inspired us to test whether an alternative approach – field-based data collection – might be superior to the remote and electronic method of data collection that we had developed.[49] Before applying the TUFF methodology to a substantially larger sample of countries beyond Africa, we tested its reliability through field research on the ground in developing countries.

There are several reasons why field-based data collection might provide more complete or accurate data on Chinese government-financed development projects. Field-based methods could pose a lower risk of data "contamination" since information flows directly from a project site to the researcher, rather than being interpreted by

Financial Flows (TUFF) methodology. We cross-checked a database of incoming aid flows managed by Malawi's Ministry of Finance with data generated by the TUFF methodology. Malawi's Aid Management Platform (AMP) contains data from thirty donor agencies and US$5.3 billion in commitments (current US$), representing approximately 80 percent of all external funding reported to the Ministry of Finance since 2000. Out of 2,584 projects in the AMP database, only two records (for projects in 2008 and 2009, totaling US$133 million in current US$) listed the People's Republic of China as the donor entity. Both of these projects are included in AidData's Chinese Official Finance to Africa Dataset, Version 1.1. However, AidData's TUFF-based dataset identified twenty-one additional Chinese government-financed projects in Malawi, totaling US$195 million in commitments. Collectively, these newly identified projects more than doubled the total monetary amount of recorded commitments of Chinese official financing to Malawi.

[49] Bräutigam characterizes her method of data collection as "checked across multiple sources, mostly official, [and] backed by interviews and field research" (Bräutigam and Hwang 2016: 22).

a third party. These methods also provide firsthand information that requires researchers to make fewer judgment calls than when they face conflicting remotely collected reports from different electronic sources. Field-based data collection methods could also reveal more projects or project details in countries and subnational jurisdictions that have low levels of press freedom or little coverage from media outlets.

To "stress test" the TUFF methodology and benchmark its reliability against field-based data collection methods, we collaborated with Edwin Muchapondwa from the University of Cape Town and Daniel Nielson from the University of Texas on a ground-truthing exercise in Uganda and South Africa.[50] Working with a team of professional enumerators, we decided to investigate each of the ninety-four Chinese government-funded projects identified by the TUFF methodology in these two countries.[51] We chose South Africa and Uganda because we wanted to test the reliability of the TUFF methodology in a country where we anticipated it would be relatively easy to obtain information about Chinese government-funded projects and a country where we anticipated it would be more difficult.[52]

We first developed a set of protocols to familiarize enumerators with publicly available information about Chinese government-financed projects and guide the conduct of their site visits and interviews with project stakeholders. We then trained nineteen professional enumerators in Uganda and four in South Africa on the use of these protocols.[53] Box 3.1 describes the training protocols that we followed.

---

[50] Muchapondwa, Nielson, Parks et al. (2016).

[51] We relied on AidData's Chinese Official Finance to Africa Dataset, 2000–2012, Version 1.1, to identify these projects.

[52] Given its higher level of economic development and relatively strong public sector institutions, we expected that in South Africa, open-source information about Chinese government-funded projects would be relatively easy to obtain. We chose Uganda because it represented a challenging case due to its lower baseline levels of economic development and institutional quality.

[53] Our enumerators in Uganda spent roughly eight hours per day on data-gathering efforts for two weeks each (roughly 1,500 researcher hours). All of the Ugandan enumerators were college graduates, and, on average, they had four years of experience performing social science research, mostly through in-person interviews. The same team had successfully worked on a previous project, interviewing 354 current and former members of the Ugandan parliament (see Findley, Harris, Milner, and Nielson 2017; Findley, Milner, and Nielson 2017). As such, they had significant experience contacting and meeting with government officials, indicating they had task-relevant skills. In South Africa, ground truthing was carried out by four professional researchers with educational backgrounds similar to those of the Ugandan enumerators.

## BOX 3.1 Ground-Truthing Chinese Development Projects

In collaboration with local researchers in South Africa and Uganda, we first asked each of the enumerators to review all of the TUFF-generated project records for a given country. We then provided training on how to conduct interviews with project stakeholders, collect photographic evidence, record the GPS coordinates of projects, and document all of the requisite evidence for a given project. During the training phase, we also worked with our team of enumerators to obtain the government authorizations and interview invitations needed for fieldwork.

Enumerators were assigned to a specific group of projects based on their mastery of the language used in that geographic location. Within each language group, projects were randomly assigned to enumerators for site visits. After project assignment, each enumerator assessed the feasibility of ground truthing by recording all publicly available sources of information, known physical locations, project personnel, required travel, and potential legal or administrative restrictions. After completing this "project pre-assessment" phase, the enumerators reviewed publicly available information about these projects and identified any additional project contacts beyond those in the TUFF-generated project records. Then, the enumerators sought to establish contact with these newly identified project contacts by phone and email. They also used snowball methods to identify additional project personnel or stakeholders who might be able to provide relevant information. Whenever possible, the enumerators secured in-person meetings with their interviewees and informants. If appointments could not be obtained, we asked enumerators to travel to project locations to take photographs, gather as much on-site information as possible, and make connections with people who were knowledgeable about the projects to secure interviews.

During these visits, the enumerators took photographs of the project sites, recorded GPS coordinates, and collected information from local project personnel and stakeholders. Each enumerator followed a set of scripted questions to ensure that they collected information in a standardized and comparable way. While each site visit followed the same interview protocol, certain visits required enumerators to ask additional questions. For instance, during visits to projects reportedly financed by a loan, enumerators prompted interviewed subjects to answer additional questions regarding specific loan terms. If the person being interviewed did not identify the Chinese government as the funder of the project in question, enumerators were instructed to ask: "Did the Chinese government provide assistance for this project?"[a]

[a] See Appendix 3.A for the list of site-visit questions.

Upon completion of the field research activities, we examined the data generated from these on-site observations and interviews alongside the data that we had previously collected through the TUFF methodology. The results revealed a high level of correspondence between the two datasets. In South Africa, only one of the projects revealed a conflict between information collected via local enumeration and information uncovered through AidData's TUFF methodology. While there were more projects with conflicting information in Uganda (seventeen projects), most of these discrepancies involved minor differences in project implementation details, all of which were easily corrected. The key characteristics of projects – their sectors, subnational locations, and monetary amounts – were for the most part accurate.[54] The ground-truthing process did not uncover substantially more projects than those detected through the TUFF methodology, as seen in Table 3.2.[55]

Table 3.2 *Ground-truthing Chinese government-financed projects in South Africa and Uganda*

| Location | Number of Projects in TUFF-Based Dataset | Number Successfully Ground-Truthed | Number of New Projects Uncovered |
|---|---|---|---|
| South Africa | 33 | 18 | 3 |
| Uganda | 61 | 42 | 0 |
| Total | 94 | 60 | 3 |

*Note:* These summary statistics are drawn from Muchapondwa, Nielson, Parks et al. (2016).

[54] When comparing the data generated from direct, on-site observations and the data generated from the TUFF methodology, we considered a single discrepancy in any one of the dataset fields to mean that the ground-truthing effort had uncovered "contradictory" information. For example, if a project entry listed 2006 as the official commitment year, but an enumerator determined during an on-site interview that the Chinese government committed funding for the project in 2001, we considered that discrepancy to be evidence of "contradictory" information. Similarly, if an on-site visit revealed that a project classified in the 1.1 version of the TUFF dataset as a "pipeline" project (i.e., a project that the Chinese government agreed to fund) had in fact reached the implementation stage, we treated this information as a contradiction.

[55] Ground truthing identified a small number of Chinese government-financed projects that were not uncovered through the TUFF methodology (see Table 3.2). For example, enumerators discovered a Chinese government-financed aquaculture demonstration center in South Africa that was not in the TUFF-based 1.1 version of our dataset. Enumerators discovered this project by uncovering a database, previously unknown to us, that was maintained by the South African Treasury's Department of International Development Cooperation; the database included a Project Status Report for the aquaculture demonstration center.

The work that our enumeration teams undertook in South Africa and Uganda also demonstrated that ground truthing is not a viable way to *comprehensively* track incoming aid and debt from the Chinese government. Not every cash or in-kind transfer from the Chinese government resulted in a physical project site – like a school, a hospital, or a stadium – where enumerators could conduct interviews and take photographs. When Beijing issued a grant or loan that the recipient government was allowed to deposit in a bank account and spend at its discretion, ground truthing had limited value.[56] When Beijing donated commodities like thousands of tons of rice that were broadly distributed to a wide variety of beneficiaries and locations, ground truthing was not very useful. Nor was ground truthing useful when the Chinese government funded training and technical assistance projects that did not leave a physical footprint. If a group of trainers rented a hotel ballroom for a week and then returned to China, there was not much value in having enumerators show up after the fact to quiz the hotel staff.

The TUFF methodology does a much better job of tracking these kinds of "intangible" financial flows. Table 3.2 demonstrates that in South Africa, the TUFF methodology uncovered fifteen Chinese government-funded projects that the enumeration team could not ground truth. In Uganda, the TUFF methodology captured nineteen Chinese government-funded projects that the enumeration team could not ground truth. In Appendix 3.B, we provide statistical evidence that ground truthing is subject to several important sources of detection bias. Whereas the method performed well in more observable sectors (like transportation infrastructure), it did not perform well in less observable sectors (like general budget support and debt forgiveness). We also found that ground truthing worked well when projects took place in specific localities, but it did not work well when projects were national in scope. These areas of weakness happen to be areas where remote and electronic methods of data collection (like the TUFF methodology) excel.

One shortcoming of the TUFF methodology – that we will discuss in subsequent chapters – is that it generates a significant number of project records that lack financial commitment amounts.[57] Therefore, we were interested to see if ground truthing might help fill some of these data gaps

---

[56] Similarly, when Beijing forgives an outstanding debt of a borrower, ground truthing is not a particularly useful method of data collection.

[57] In the TUFF-based dataset that we introduce in Chapter 4, the percentage of projects that are missing monetary amounts ranges from 20 percent in 2001 to 48 percent in 2014. Some types of flows are particularly likely to lack monetary amounts. Whereas 90 percent of projects that support technical assistance activities and scholarships lack monetary amounts, loans include monetary amounts 92 percent of the time.

and thereby correct downwardly biased estimates of the amounts of aid and debt that Beijing provides to countries. We found that ground truthing did not uncover many monetary values in cases where we had no preexisting information from the TUFF methodology. In South Africa, the enumeration team identified a single previously unreported monetary value for one project in the TUFF-based dataset. In Uganda, the enumeration team identified previously unreported monetary values for only two projects. Ground-truthing methods differed from the TUFF method's aggregate estimate of Chinese government financing to South Africa by only US$150,000. In Uganda, the absolute change was US$26,787,303, which only represented a 2.7 percent deviation from the TUFF-based aggregate estimate of Chinese government financing to that country.[58]

Ultimately, after analyzing the data that we collected in South Africa and Uganda and comparing it to the data generated by the TUFF methodology, we concluded that ground truthing is not a viable method for comprehensively tracking the wide array of financial transfers and in-kind contributions that developing countries receive from the Chinese government. It is still valuable because it reveals certain types of information that are more easily missed via remote and electronic methods of data collection. In Uganda and South Africa, we learned that the TUFF methodology (in its earlier form) had a tendency to overuse media sources and underuse official sources (which can lead to important errors of omission, such as the borrowing terms of a loan). We also learned that it did not consistently generate reliable information about the latest status of projects (i.e., whether they had been informally pledged, formally committed, implemented, or completed).[59] Therefore, after completing the ground-truthing exercise in South Africa and Uganda, we made a number of revisions to the TUFF methodology to address these and other sources of bias.[60] We published a first round of revisions in September 2015 (version 1.2) and a second round of revisions in October 2017 (version 1.3).

---

[58] We provide more information about the merits and shortcomings of ground truthing vis-à-vis remote and electronic methods of data collection in Appendix 3.B.

[59] See Figure B3.1 for illustrative examples of project status coding revisions that were made after ground truthing took place.

[60] In the combined sample of projects from Uganda and South Africa, we found a positive and statistically significant correlation between (a) whether the ground truthing uncovered new information that resulted in the recoding of one or more variables in the TUFF-based dataset and (b) the number of web-based sources for that project. This relationship suggests that the TUFF methodology performs best when it draws upon many sources. Therefore, we revised the 1.3 version of the TUFF methodology to increase the number and diversity of sources that underpin each project record.

## Lessons Learned: The Construction of the Dataset Used in This Book

The latest (1.3) version of the TUFF methodology

- uses a machine-learning algorithm to increase the efficiency with which media sources are processed, freeing up human expertise for the collection of official data and tasks that require more judgment;
- reduces the likelihood that any given project record will rely on a single source or only on media sources;
- gathers more information about the terms and conditions of grant and loan agreements (e.g., maturities, grace periods, interest rates) and about project implementation details (e.g., name of the contractor, project site locations, project implementation start and end dates); and
- exposes preliminary versions of the dataset to multiple rounds of scrutiny by subject matter experts.

We document the 1.3 version of the TUFF methodology in its entirety in our codebook, which is available online.[61] However, in the interest of helping readers understand the key features of this approach, we provide a brief summary of the data collection and quality assurance procedures here.

We divide the TUFF methodology into three stages: two stages of primary data collection (project identification and source triangulation) and a third stage of review and revision of individual project records (quality assurance). In the first stage of primary data collection, we use a standardized set of search criteria to query Factiva, a Dow Jones-owned media database that draws on approximately 33,000 media sources worldwide in twenty-eight languages, including newspapers and radio and television transcripts.[62] The queries generate a long list of media articles, but only a subset of these "candidate sources" contain information about Chinese government-financed projects. We therefore use a machine-learning algorithm[63] to identify the subset of articles that are most likely to contain the information about Chinese government-financed projects.[64] We refer to this machine-learning

---

[61] Strange, Ghose, Russell et al. (2017).

[62] All of these queries rely on a standardized set of keywords (such as grant, loan, and donate), but we run them independently for each host country. See Strange, Ghose, Russell et al. (2017) for more details.

[63] To classify the documents, the machine-learning software uses a linear support vector machine (SVM) classifier – with balanced TRUE/FALSE classes – and the term "frequency-inverse document frequency" (TFIDF) transformation from the Scikit-learn Python library classes. Classes were balanced by oversampling the TRUE class. For more information about the linear SVM classifier package, see Pedregosa, Varoquaux, Gramfort et al. (2011).

[64] To train the machine-learning tool, we use large amounts of training data (articles that we identified via Factiva and then classified as containing or not containing information

tool as the "TUFF Robot." It combs through millions of search results at a rate of approximately 15,000 results per hour – 475,000 results per week. It categorizes search results as either "relevant" or "irrelevant" based on whether they seem to contain information about Chinese government-financed projects. We then review each of the Factiva records that the machine-learning algorithm has classified as "relevant" and make case-by-case determinations about whether those sources do indeed contain information about Chinese government-financed projects.[65] In parallel to this primary data collection effort, we retrieve all of the official information about Chinese government-financed projects that is recorded in (a) the aid and debt information management systems of host countries, (b) IMF country reports, and (c) the websites of Chinese embassies and ECCOs.

Once a potential project has been identified during the first stage of data collection, we give it a unique identification number and enter it into a data management platform. We then assign it to a different researcher for a second stage of record review and augmentation. This researcher performs a set of targeted online searches to validate, invalidate, and/or enrich the project-level information that was retrieved in the first stage of data collection. Native speakers and trained language experts conducted these searches in English, Chinese, and host country languages to improve record accuracy and completeness. This second-stage researcher also sought to collect supplementary information from government sources (e.g., annual reports published by the lender or granting agency), field reports published by NGOs and implementing entities (e.g., private contractors), scholarly research (e.g., case studies of particular projects or doctoral dissertations on the development finance activities of a particular donor/lender in a particular country), and experts with information or knowledge about specific projects that is not in the public domain or is not easily identifiable (e.g., photographic evidence of a project's current status). This process of project-level investigation and triangulation is designed to reduce the risk of overreliance on individual sources (especially media reports) that might be inaccurate or incomplete.

The third stage of the TUFF methodology involves the systematic implementation of data quality assurance procedures to maximize the

---

about projects financed by the official donor/lender of interest) to "teach" the algorithm to accurately classify hundreds of thousands of articles into "relevant" and "irrelevant" categories. Use of this tool significantly reduces the amount of time that researchers would otherwise spend reviewing false positives – articles that contain no information about projects financed by the official donor/lender of interest.

[65] For ease of exposition, we use the pronoun "we" to describe the group of people responsible for undertaking these data collection procedures. That "we" includes a large team of full-time staff and part-time research assistants at AidData who have collaborated with us on this work.

accuracy and completeness of project records. First, we implemented a set of de-duplication procedures to minimize the risk of double counting. Second, to account for the fact that idiosyncratic coding decisions made by individual researchers could produce inconsistencies across project records, we undertook a set of automated data checks to identify and eliminate illogical and inconsistent codings. Third, a program manager overseeing the team of research assistants or a senior research assistant appointed by the program manager vetted each project record in the dataset to identify potential errors, missing data, or incorrect categorizations. Fourth, the dataset underwent another layer of review that focused specifically on projects with low "health of record" scores and on large-scale projects (as indicated by the monetary value of the transaction).[66] Finally, we subjected the dataset as a whole to several rounds of careful scrutiny by AidData staff and external peer reviewers.[67] Internal and external reviewers not only sought to identify errors of omission and commission but also flagged inconsistencies for us to address and additional sources that we should consult.[68]

The procedures that we have just described are substantially different from those used in the original (1.0) version of the TUFF methodology that we published in 2013. These methodological revisions have significantly improved data quality. The first dataset produced with the 1.0 version of the TUFF methodology relied on media reports for 89 percent of all sources. In the latest version of the dataset, produced with the 1.3 version of the TUFF methodology described here, only 56 percent of sources are from media, and the share of data that come from official and academic sources has increased: official government data and documentation from the Chinese, counterpart governments, and international organizations now constitute 27.6 percent of all sources. Peer-reviewed journal articles and other academic publications represent 6.8 percent of all sources. There has also been an increase in the average number of sources that underpin each project record – from 2.1 sources (in the first version of the dataset that was released in April 2013) to 3.7 sources (in

---

[66] "Health of record" scores are calculated to identify projects that might benefit from additional sourcing or investigation. More specifically, for all projects in the dataset, we calculated source triangulation and data completeness scores. The source triangulation indicator captures the number and diversity of information sources supporting a given project record; the data completeness indicator measures the extent to which fields/variables for a given project record are missing or populated with vague information.

[67] More than thirty external and internal reviewers were involved in this process for the version of the dataset used in this book.

[68] Among other things, these reviewers (a) generate descriptive statistics with the dataset and compare them with official and third-party estimates to identify anomalies or suspicious results and (b) review individual project records to suggest potential ways to address errors, biases, and gaps.

the version of the dataset that we use throughout this book). We have also seen an increase in the number of core fields (e.g., transaction amounts, flow types, and commitment years) that are populated for each project record in the dataset.

The 1.3 version of the TUFF methodology is the result of patient investment and careful refinement by five academics, nearly a dozen professional staff at AidData, and more than 150 research assistants based at William & Mary and the National University of Singapore over six years. To date, more than 240 working papers, policy reports, and journal publications have been published that rely upon datasets generated with the TUFF methodology.[69] These studies have led to major gains in our collective knowledge about the aims and impacts of China's overseas development program. In the next chapter, we describe some of this newly acquired knowledge. We outline broad empirical patterns in China's overseas spending, as revealed by the dataset, and compare the estimates of Chinese aid giving that emerge from our dataset with the estimates generated by others.

## Appendix 3.A
## Ground-Truthing Interview Questions

Project Name:
Project ID Number:
Project Location (Province, City, GPS Location):
Enumerator Name:
Person Interviewed:
Interview Contact Information (Phone, Email, Address):
1. Introduce yourself.
2. Learn about respondent.
3. What is your position?
4. How long have you been working in the post?
5. What has been your involvement in the project?
6. How is this project benefitting the community?
7. What is the closest trading center/local council (LC1)?
8. In what year was this project announced?
9. When did this project begin?
10. Is this project complete? If not, has work officially begun?

---

[69] We are grateful to Soren Patterson of AidData for collecting and generously sharing this information.

11. And when was the project originally planned to commence?
12. When was the project completely finished?
13. And when was the project originally planned to be finished?
14. Was this project financed by a grant or a loan?
15. What was the total project amount?
16. How much has already been disbursed?
17. Which donors or government agencies provided funding for this project?
    a. List them all
    b. For each funding source, ask:
    c. Which activities did funding source A finance?
    d. Which activities did funding source B finance?
    e. Etc.
18. What company or agency implemented this project?
19. What government agencies were also involved with this project?
20. How much money did each donor or funding agency provide for this project?
21. If China was not mentioned, ask: Did the Chinese government provide assistance for this project?
22. [IF LOAN] was this loan a line of credit?
23. [IF LOAN] Was this loan made at or below market rates?
24. [IF LOAN] What was the interest rate of the loan?
25. [IF LOAN] Are you familiar with any other details of the loan?
26. What individuals managed parts of the project during planning, funding, or implementing stages?
27. [End of interview, open-ended] What else can you say about this project?

*Source:* Muchapondwa, Nielson, Parks et al. (2016).


## Appendix 3.B
## Supplementary Analysis from Ground-Truthing Exercise in South Africa and Uganda


Despite repeated attempts to contact South African, Ugandan, or Chinese officials with knowledge about individual projects, our team of enumerators was unable to collect information for approximately 31 percent of the projects in Uganda and 45 percent of the projects in South Africa (see Table 3.2). Local officials either could not be reached or were not willing to share project details. The latter problem proved to be far more challenging than the former.

Knowing that the projects our enumeration teams failed to verify via ground truthing were probably not missing at random, we ran several statistical tests to identify potential sources of detection bias that may be inherent to this method of data collection. To explain why some projects were successfully ground truthed and others were not, we systematically tested for different potential sources of detection bias by performing logistic regressions where the dependent variable captures whether or not projects were successfully ground truthed and the independent variables capture project characteristics, including financial size, observability, the amount of time that had elapsed since project announcement, the specificity of the project's physical location, the distance of the project site from the capital city, and the availability of information about specific project personnel or stakeholders.[70]

The marginal effects from these logistic regressions suggest that whether or not a project is in an observable sector – as the binary variable shifts from zero to one – is associated with a 0.21 increase in the probability of successful ground truthing.[71] Given that the baseline probability of successful ground truthing is 0.64, this suggests some substantive significance. We also find that a project being local – that is to say, located at the village, municipality, or district level rather than being national in scope – is associated with a jump in the probability of successful ground truthing of 0.42. Having contacts listed in a TUFF project record is also associated with a 0.20 increase in the probability of ground-truthing success. We do not find that distance to the country's capital city or the financial size of a project is a good predictor of ground-truthing success.

In South Africa and Uganda, ground truthing did uncover new information about the status of nine projects; the TUFF methodology had incorrectly identified five of these projects as still being in the pipeline stage (rather than the implementation or completion stage).[72] We also learned that (as one might guess) field data collection is better able to uncover

---

[70] This work was undertaken in collaboration with Edwin Muchapondwa from the University of Cape Town and Daniel Nielson from the University of Texas. See Muchapondwa, Nielson, Parks et al. (2016).

[71] These marginal effects are reported in Muchapondwa, Nielson, Parks et al. (2016). To measure observability, we constructed a variable that takes a value of one for all projects assigned to the following OECD sector codes: Transport and Storage; Water Supply and Sanitation; Education; Industry, Mining, and Construction; Agriculture, Forestry, and Fishing; and Energy Generation and Supply. We assigned values of zero to projects with all other OECD sector codes (e.g., Banking and Financial Services, General Budget Support, Action Related to Debt, Support to NGOs and Government Organizations, Unallocated/Unspecified).

[72] Pipeline projects are those that have not yet reached implementation but that the Chinese government has informally pledged or formally committed to fund.

visual evidence of the current status of Chinese government-financed projects. Our enumeration teams visually confirmed the existence of eighteen projects in South Africa and Uganda through site visits (see Table 3.2). However, this apparent strength of ground truthing is also a weakness from a different vantage point: as reflected in Table B3.1, the ability to generate project data that are not plagued by high levels of detection

Table B3.1  *Logistic regression analysis of detection bias in ground-truthing success*

|  | Model 1 | Model 2 |
| --- | --- | --- |
| Observable Sector | 1.286** | 1.097** |
|  | (0.616) | (0.553) |
| Local | 2.457*** | 2.186*** |
|  | (0.615) | (0.548) |
| Contact Listed | 1.451* | 1.300* |
|  | (0.808) | (0.716) |
| Years Elapsed | −0.131 | −0.144* |
|  | (0.0862) | (0.0795) |
| Near Capital | 0.347 |  |
|  | (0.629) |  |
| Project Amount | 3.03e-10 |  |
|  | (1.36e-09) |  |
| Constant | −3.018** | −2.447*** |
|  | (1.211) | (0.930) |
| Observations | 92 | 94 |

*Notes:* These logistic regression results are drawn from Table 2 of Muchapondwa, Nielson, Parks et al. (2016). The dependent variable is a binary indicator of whether a TUFF-based project was successfully ground truthed. The independent variables include indicators of financial commitment amount (Project Amount), the observability of the project (Observable Sector), the amount of time that had elapsed since project announcement (Years Elapsed), the specificity of the physical location (Local), the availability of information about specific project personnel or stakeholders (Contact Listed), and the distance of the project site from the national capital (Near Capital). Standard errors in parentheses; *** $p<0.01$, ** $p<0.05$, * $p<0.1$.

Figure B3.1 Illustrative cases of ground truthing with visual evidence
*Notes:* This figure is drawn from Muchapondwa, Nielson, Parks et al. (2014). Our enumeration teams visually confirmed the physical implementation or completion of four projects in South Africa and fourteen projects in Uganda. In some cases, these on-site data collection efforts led to revisions to TUFF-based project status determinations (e.g., Projects #2517, #11357, #16469, and #15936). In other cases, they simply confirmed TUFF-based project status determinations (e.g., Project #14235). One project (an aquaculture demonstration center in South Africa) was not uncovered through the implementation of the TUFF methodology, but rather through the ground-truthing process itself.

bias. Our enumeration teams were significantly less likely to succeed in ground-truthing projects that reached completion several years before the site visits; each additional year of distance from the project's inception was associated with a 0.027 reduction in the probability of successful ground truthing.

# 4    Follow the Money

## Where Does Chinese Government Funding Go?

### Two Strategic Neighbors

Myanmar and Nepal, both located along China's vast inland frontier, share several basic features. They are among the poorest countries in Asia.[1] Their capitals – Naypyidaw and Kathmandu – are surrounded by rough terrain, which complicates transportation, agriculture, and other economic development efforts.[2] They both face major infrastructure deficits. They both have abundant energy resources that are not fully developed due to economic and political risks.[3] They have experienced violent civil wars in modern times, and these wars have triggered large-scale population movements and refugee crises in both countries.[4] Yet despite these similarities, the two countries have attracted very different types of financial support from Beijing: Myanmar has mostly attracted projects financed with loans priced at or near market rates, while Nepal has managed to secure more projects financed with grants and highly concessional loans.

As these differences show, understanding the nature, aims, and effects of Chinese development finance requires access to granular and comprehensive data on *individual projects*. As we discussed in Chapter 3, overall estimates of Chinese aid giving and lending help sell newspapers and magazines, but they are not particularly useful for understanding Beijing's behavior or underlying motivations. To measure both the

---

[1] Nepal has 30 million inhabitants and its per capita GDP is approximately US$1,000. Myanmar, somewhat larger at 50 million inhabitants, is slightly wealthier: its per capita GDP currently stands at around US$1,300.

[2] Asian Development Bank (2013).

[3] Sovacool, Dhakal, Gippner, and Bambawale (2011); Asian Development Bank (2017).

[4] While Nepal was never colonized, it was an important defense outpost and source of soldiers for the British Raj. It fell into a decade-long civil war in 1996 due to conflicts over ideology and resources between the incumbent monarchy and Maoist insurgents (Upreti 2004; Murshed and Gates 2005; Bohara, Mitchell, and Nepal 2006). Myanmar is a former British colony that has experienced internal turmoil since World War II, with government forces and rebel militias engaging in armed conflict for decades (Woods 2011; Jones 2014).

intended and the unintended impacts of Chinese development projects, researchers need data that can be broken down by sector, subnational location (the district or province where the project is sited), level of financial concessionality, timing of implementation, and other project-specific features. Chapter 3 introduced the methods that we use to produce such data. In this chapter, we describe the global patterns and trends that can be found in the data we have collected using those methods.

However, let's first return to the Nepal-Myanmar comparison. A casual observer might assume that China is bankrolling development projects in both countries for primarily geostrategic reasons. Nepal serves as a geographical buffer between China and India – specifically, between territory claimed by both Delhi and Beijing within the Indian state of Arunachal Pradesh.[5] It is currently the largest recipient of Indian development finance worldwide in terms of the number of projects, and since the 1960s, India and China have used their aid programs to compete for the allegiances of the country's leaders.[6] Nepal has taken advantage of this rivalry, playing the two superpowers against each other to make the most favorable deals it can.[7] A case in point is the Ithari-Dhalkewar road project, which the Nepalese government pitched to both Chinese and Indian authorities after the 1962 Sino-Indian war. China initially agreed to fund this project in April 1964. However, twelve months later, the Nepalese authorities asked Beijing to suspend work on the project and announced that the Indian government would instead finance the construction of the 170-kilometer road.[8] More recently, when Kathmandu experienced a 7.9-magnitude earthquake in April 2015, both Beijing and Delhi pledged large packages of relief and reconstruction assistance while looking for opportunities to outflank each other.[9]

---

[5] Often perceived as an important bargaining chip within this dispute, Nepal has recently pursued a foreign policy posture of neutrality, as its economy depends meaningfully on both regional giants (Wong 2017).

[6] Asmus, Eichenauer, Fuchs, and Parks (2021).

[7] Fuchs and Vadlamannati (2013); Stratfor (2018); Asmus, Eichenauer, Fuchs, and Parks (2021). Nepal was one of India's first aid recipients, and it became even more geopolitically significant for India when a newly unified China seized Tibet beginning in October 1950, effectively expanding its borders to Nepal's backyard (Khadka 1997).

[8] Ispahani (1989: 177).

[9] Malik (1994); Egreteau (2008); Zhao (2008); BBC (2015b); Rauhala (2015). See also Eichenauer, Fuchs, Kunze, and Strobl (2020) for a study of aid allocation after the 2015 Nepal earthquake. Both Nepal and Myanmar have a documented history of balancing between China and India. However, in 2016, Nepal noticeably increased cooperation with China in response to a months-long border blockade by India (Chowdhury 2018), and it eventually signed on to China's BRI. In late 2017, China discreetly facilitated deeper coordination between communist organizations in Nepal, which helped them earn critical

Like Nepal, Myanmar is geostrategically valuable to China and India and a source of competition between the Asian giants. It connects the Indian subcontinent to Western China and Southeast Asia, offering an alternative international shipping route that avoids the narrow and vulnerable Strait of Malacca. Analysts have linked China's efforts to develop a deep-water port in Sittwe, the capital of Myanmar's Rakhine State on the Bay of Bengal, to a broader "string of pearls" strategy, in which Beijing is purportedly developing a network of dual-use (civilian and naval) ports along the Indian Ocean.[10] Myanmar is also a potential ally for China in the Association of Southeast Asian Nations (ASEAN).[11]

Myanmar and Nepal have received similar levels of support from the Chinese government. Between 2000 and 2014, Beijing approved funding for seventy-one projects in Nepal (worth US$1.23 billion) and sixty-one projects in Myanmar (valued at US$2.02 billion). Nepal and Myanmar ranked seventeenth and twenty-first out of 138 developing countries, respectively, in terms of the total number of Chinese government-financed projects they received. However, these comparisons hide more than they reveal because of differences in the "color of the money" that Beijing has channeled to the two countries: 95 percent of this funding to Nepal was aid in the strict sense of the term (grants and low-interest loans), while much of the funding to Myanmar was less concessional and more commercial in nature.

This distinction is clearly visible in China's support for hydropower projects in each country. In Nepal, China Eximbank approved multiple loans for the 60-megawatt Upper Trishuli 3A hydroelectric power plant and for the transmission lines that evacuate electricity from the plant. These loans carried an interest rate of 1.75 percent, a maturity period of twenty-five years, and a grace period of five years. As such, they had grant elements above 60 percent, which far exceeds the OECD's long-standing threshold for official development assistance (ODA).[12]

provincial and federal seats in national elections. Nepalese Prime Minister K. P. Sharma Oli is notably closer to China than India (Pant 2017).
[10] Pehrson (2006); Brewster (2014); Yung, Rustici, Devary, and Lin (2014).
[11] Others view it as a "swing state" in the global balance of liberal and authoritarian politics (Fisher 2017).
[12] As noted in Chapter 3, the grant element is the difference between the nominal value of a loan and the present value of the loan repayments. When the interest rate of the loan is smaller than the market rate used to discount the loan, the grant element is positive. Here we assume a grace period of ten years and use the World Bank's grant element calculator. Recall that the OECD's grant element threshold for loan concessionality is 25 percent. In fact, the terms of this loan were even more generous because, after natural disasters delayed project implementation, China agreed to extend the grace period from 5 years to 9.5 years (The Nepalese Voice 2017). On the key distinction between measuring loan

In Myanmar, Beijing has channeled substantial amounts of funding to the hydropower sector, although it scaled back its engagement in this sector after the country's long-ruling military junta was replaced by a reformist government in 2011.[13] One of the projects that it bankrolled was the 140-megawatt Upper Paung Laung hydroelectric power plant. For this project, China Eximbank offered a US$160 million loan with a ten-year maturity and an interest rate of 2.75 percent. Not all of the terms and conditions of the loan are publicly known, but even with an exceptionally generous grace period (ten years), its grant element would not have exceeded 17 percent. These differences in borrowing terms reflect a broader pattern: Beijing has financed projects on more favorable terms in Nepal than in Myanmar.[14]

China's financial support for its two neighbors also differs in the economic sectors it prioritizes. In Nepal, Beijing has focused heavily on the "software" of development, including a diverse range of social sector projects in health, education, and public administration. For example, the Chinese government granted US$35 million for the construction of the Civil Service Hospital in Kathmandu, which opened for service in 2009, and has consistently provided Chinese medical teams to support the B. P. Koirala Memorial Cancer Hospital in Bharatpur. In the education sector, it has constructed the Banepa Polytechnic Institute, expanded the Shree Divya Deep Secondary School, and donated thousands of computers and books to various primary and secondary schools. Similarly, China has supported an array of public administration projects in Nepal: perhaps the most well known is a US$30 million grant for the construction of a National Armed Police Academy, which was completed in 2017.[15] In contrast, Beijing has not focused heavily on software projects in Myanmar. The lion's share of its funding to Myanmar has supported projects in the "hardware" of development: the energy, mining, industry, and construction sectors.

We provide this brief comparison to highlight the fact that China's overseas project portfolio is surprisingly diverse, and its aims and tactics

---

concessionality in ex ante terms and ex post terms, see Morris, Parks, and Gardner (2020).

[13] McDonald, Bosshard, and Brewer (2009); Sun (2013).

[14] This does not necessarily mean that Chinese loans have threatened Myanmar's debt sustainability, though roughly 30 percent of Myanmar's public debt was held by China in 2017, making Beijing the country's largest bilateral creditor. Like Myanmar, Nepal's sovereign debt is low and declining (2 percent of GDP in 2016); China is its fourth-largest bilateral creditor (IMF 2017).

[15] Chowdhury (2018). Nepalese police officers apparently have a running joke about this: the academy was promised by Delhi almost twenty years ago, but India never got around to building it.

vary considerably from country to country. Western politicians and journalists have a tendency to focus on the total amount of aid and credit that Beijing has provided to other countries, but these topline figures do not help us understand the nature, aims, and effects of Chinese development finance. Many of China's rivals and critics also argue that its "one-size-fits-all" approach to development finance does a disservice to recipient countries.[16] The comparison between Nepal and Myanmar suggests that the premise of this argument is simply wrong. To understand the nature, aims, and effects of China's overseas development program, you have to "follow the money" one project at a time. In the remainder of this chapter, we show that a project-level approach is essential to paint a more accurate picture of the nature and scope of Chinese development finance around the world.

## How Much and What Kinds of Financial Support Does Beijing Provide?

In the rest of this chapter, we revisit some foundational questions that earlier studies have struggled to accurately answer: How much financial support has Beijing provided to developing countries during the twenty-first century? How much of China's overseas development expenditure is aid, and how much of it is debt? How does China stack up relative to other large providers of development finance? Which countries receive the most development finance from China? Here, we use our dataset to map out the broad contours of Chinese development finance around the world.

As we mentioned in previous chapters, we have spent the last nine years working closely with AidData to develop and deploy the TUFF methodology to collect detailed financial, operational, and locational information about the overseas activities of Chinese government donors and lenders. All tables and figures in this chapter (and the rest of the book) are based on AidData's Global Chinese Official Finance Dataset (version 1.0).

The dataset reveals that over a fifteen-year period from 2000 to 2014, the Chinese government informally pledged or formally committed financial support for 5,466 projects in 138 countries. However, we do not include all of these projects in our analysis. First, we eliminate projects that did not advance beyond the informal pledge stage.[17] Pruning away these pledges is important since we cannot be sure that the corresponding projects ever reached the stage of a formal commitment (i.e., a formal,

---

[16] See the quotes in Chapter 1 from various Western politicians, but also Banik (2019: 2).
[17] A pledge can be a verbal, informal agreement or a written expression of interest in funding a project.

written, binding contract between a funder and a recipient). Second, we remove projects that were initially pledged or committed but then later canceled or suspended. We do so because we seek to measure the intended and unintended impacts of Chinese development finance (in Chapters 7 and 8), and it is very unlikely that these projects will affect our national and subnational outcomes of interest (e.g., economic growth, infant mortality, environmental degradation). Finally, we exclude all "umbrella" projects – such as master facility agreements and lines of credit – that fund multiple, subsidiary projects through a single umbrella pool of funding. To minimize the risk of double counting in our analysis, we only include the subsidiary projects that these umbrella projects supported.[18]

These adjustments leave us with a working dataset of 4,327 projects in 138 countries. The total monetary value of these official commitments from Chinese government institutions is US$351.7 billion (in constant 2014 US$). As we noted in Chapter 3, every project in the dataset is assigned to one of three government-funding categories:

- ODA-like projects, which are nominally intended to promote economic or social development and are provided at levels of concessionality that are consistent with the ODA criteria established by the Development Assistance Committee of the OECD (OECD-DAC);
- OOF-like (other official flows-like) projects, which are financed by the Chinese government and are consistent with the OOF criteria established by the OECD-DAC (see Box 1.1 ); and
- vague official finance projects, which are Chinese government-financed projects that we cannot categorize as ODA-like or OOF-like because of insufficiently detailed open-source information.[19]

In the interest of using as little technical jargon as possible, we will continue to refer to ODA-like projects as aid and OOF-like projects as debt. Figure 4.1 illustrates the importance of the aid-debt distinction. In monetary terms, only 23 percent of China's overall portfolio (US$80.66 billion) qualifies as aid; 61 percent of the portfolio

---

[18] Here, we include Chinese government-financed projects allocated to multiple recipients. These regional projects, where we lack a breakdown by country, are excluded in later chapters in the book that involve statistical analyses on Chinese development finance across or within individual countries.

[19] Typically, these vague official finance records are loans about which we lack the details (interest rates, grace periods, or maturity dates) needed to classify them as ODA, OOF, or projects about which we lack sufficient information to code the intent (developmental, commercial, or representational).

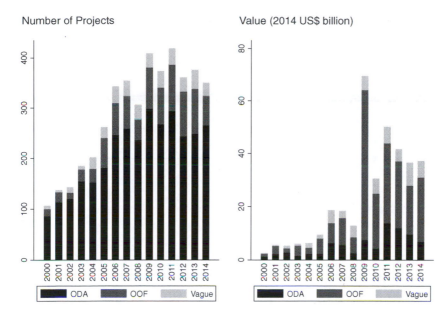

Figure 4.1 Chinese development finance commitments, 2000–2014
*Notes:* The number of Chinese aid-financed (ODA) and debt-financed (OOF) projects is shown on the left and their corresponding monetary amount on the right. "Vague" stands for vague official finance (Chinese government-financed projects that cannot be categorized into aid or debt because of insufficiently detailed open-source information).

(US$216.3 billion) qualifies as debt. The remaining projects in the portfolio (16 percent, or US$54.74 billion) cannot be easily categorized as aid or debt (vague official finance).[20] However, when the portfolio is broken down by project count, China's priorities look very different: 73 percent of its projects (3,159) are aid financed, 19 percent of its projects (811) are debt financed, and 8 percent of its projects (357) cannot be reliably categorized as either aid or debt.

These patterns raise a basic but important question: if most Chinese government-funded projects are financed with aid, why do debt-financed projects account for the lion's share of the funding? The short answer is that grants and highly concessional loans are far

---

[20] The observable attributes of these vague official finance projects are more similar to debt-financed projects than aid-financed projects (e.g., sector, project size, funding institution).

smaller than the big-ticket loans that China prices at or near market rates. To better understand this distinction, we assigned OECD-DAC sector classifications (three-digit purpose codes) to all projects in the dataset and analyzed how Chinese government-financed projects are distributed across sectors. Our findings indicate that the Chinese government invests far more *money* in the energy, transportation, industry, mining, and construction sectors than it does in the education, health, and governance sectors, but it funds many more *projects* in the health, education, and governance sectors.[21] These small and inexpensive projects are disproportionately funded with aid; the large and costly projects in the economic infrastructure and production sectors tend to be funded via debt (i.e., non-concessional and semi-concessional loans and export credits). In numerical terms, the median monetary value of a Chinese aid-financed project is only US$4.6 million, while the median monetary value of a Chinese debt-financed project is *twenty-five times larger* (US$125.2 million).[22]

Two Chinese government-funded projects in Nepal and Myanmar from our dataset help illustrate this dynamic. In Nepal, Beijing agreed to build a customs inspection station in Tatopani, a village with just over 3,000 inhabitants along the country's border with Tibet.[23] It supported this public administration sector project with a US$3.9 million grant – a figure similar to the median value (US$4.6 million) of all Chinese aid-financed projects in our dataset. In Myanmar, Beijing financed a project in the industry, mining, and construction sector – a paper mill in the town of Yedashe – with US$149.9 million of semi-concessional debt;[24] this figure is similar to the median monetary value (US$125.2 million) of all Chinese debt-financed projects in our dataset.

---

[21] Indeed, approximately 55 percent of all the projects in our dataset were classified as social sector and emergency response activities, with only 30 percent of the dataset consisting of economic and productive sector projects. We assigned each project in our dataset one of twenty-four OECD sector codes based on its primary purpose. To simplify things, we have also combined these twenty-four categories into five categories: social infrastructure and services ("social"), economic infrastructure and services ("economic"), production sectors ("production"), humanitarian aid ("humanitarian"), and a residual category ("other").

[22] The average aid-financed project is worth US$43.22 million, which reflects the fact that we are missing monetary values for many aid-financed projects. The average debt-financed project is worth US$436.1 million, which is partially inflated by a significant number of outlier projects worth several billion dollars each.

[23] The station, closed after Nepal's earthquake in 2015, reportedly received additional assistance from China and closed and reopened multiple times (New Spotlight 2018; Xinhua 2020).

[24] The mill was completed in 2009 by China Chengda Engineering Co. Ltd. It primarily processes newspaper pulp and packing paper.

## From Benefactor to Banker

This book is primarily about the importance of understanding China's evolution from benefactor to banker. In Chapter 2, we explained how Beijing's economic reforms during the 1980s and 1990s laid the initial groundwork for this transition, but the adoption of the Going Out strategy supercharged it. In Figure 4.1, the precise timing of the transition is visible: less concessional and more commercially oriented lending begins to dominate China's global development finance portfolio in monetary terms right around the 2008 global financial crisis. Between 2000 and 2007, Beijing's global portfolio of development projects was financed according to an aid-to-debt ratio of 0.61:1, meaning that it committed 61 cents of aid for every dollar of debt that it issued. However, after 2007, it shifted gears and focused substantially more effort on foreign currency-denominated lending for overseas development projects. This transition brought about a sharp decline in the aid-to-debt ratio – to 0.27:1 – between 2008 and 2014.[25] Over our entire fifteen-year period of study (2000–2014), the average annual rate of growth in the provision of Chinese debt was 2.5 times higher than that of Chinese aid.[26] By the first full year of implementation under the BRI (2014), Beijing was issuing nearly four dollars of debt for every dollar of aid it committed.

This focus on debt sets Beijing apart from its peers. Figure 4.2 compares China's overseas spending patterns with those of other major powers during the same period. The figure demonstrates that Beijing effectively became the bilateral "lender of first resort" during the twenty-first century. In terms of aggregate international development finance commitments, from 2000 to 2014 China trailed only the United States. However, the composition of Beijing's spending looks very different from that of its peers. Whereas during the twenty-first century, the members of the OECD-DAC provided the overwhelming majority of their development finance via aid, China provided most of its development finance via debt – semi-concessional and non-concessional loans and export credits.

To be clear, China did not abandon its foreign aid program. Quite the opposite: Figure 4.1 demonstrates that its program expanded significantly between 2000 and 2014. In monetary terms, Beijing committed approximately US$1.96 billion each year between 2000 and 2003 for new aid projects in low-income and middle-income countries,[27] and this figure jumped to US$10.51 billion during the 2011–2014 period. New project

---

[25] These ratios represent the arithmetic means over all yearly aid-to-debt ratios for each period, calculated using current US$.

[26] Dreher, Fuchs, Parks et al. (2021).

[27] This figure represents the average annual value of all Chinese aid commitments between 2000 and 2003.

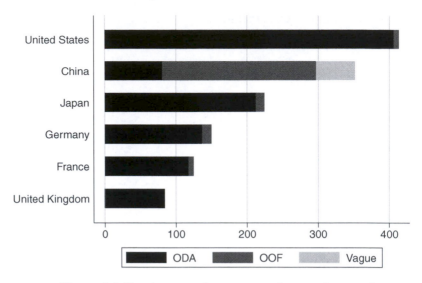

Figure 4.2 Development finance commitments from major powers,
2000–2014
*Notes:* The figure shows the total monetary amount of development
finance commitments of six major donors in billions of constant 2014
US dollars. Data from Authors and OECD.

approvals tell a similar story: on average, China supported 118 new aid-
financed projects in each year between 2000 and 2003 and 262 new aid-
financed projects in each year during the 2011–2014 period. These figures
reflect the shift from net recipient to net donor that we first described in
Chapter 2. This transition happened right around the same time as the
transition from benefactor to banker that we saw in Figure 4.1.

Due to the rebalancing of the aid-to-debt ratio that occurred during this
period, it is important not to exaggerate China's heft as an aid provider
during the twenty-first century. On average, it allocated US$5.37 billion
a year for aid-financed projects during our fifteen-year period of study
(2000–2014) – a level of spending that puts China roughly on par with the
Netherlands and Norway.[28] Beijing's commitment to foreign aid spending is also relatively volatile. In 2011, its aid commitments soared to

---

[28] Our global estimates of Chinese aid are quite similar to those produced by other careful
research efforts, including that of Kitano (2016), as well as to official statements by the
Chinese government itself. China's 2014 White Paper (State Council 2014) puts total
annual foreign aid from China at about US$4.8 billion. Kitano (2016) arrives at a slightly
higher estimate of US$5.2 billion (in 2012). For data on the Netherlands and Norway,

US$13.77 billion, making it one of the world's largest donors (behind only three OECD-DAC donors – the United States, the United Kingdom, and Germany).[29] However, this rise was short lived. China's foreign aid program shrank significantly between 2011 and 2014. This contraction may reflect the fragility of domestic political support for foreign aid (as discussed in Chapter 3), or it may be due to Beijing's decision to ramp up lending for overseas projects at or near market rates (as discussed in Chapter 2).[30]

Another way to think about China's position in the international development finance market is to consider the size of its aid budget related to the size of its economy – in other words, the percentage of gross national income (GNI) made up by aid. This percentage is often used to compare the relative significance of aid contributions from different donors. Since 1970, the United Nations has encouraged all donor countries to devote at least 0.7 percent of their GNI to development aid. Figure 4.3 presents China's aid-to-GNI ratio over our entire study period. It shows that China's level of aid spending is quite small relative to the size of its economy, with its aid-to-GNI ratio varying between 0.04 and 0.13 percent from 2000 to 2014 (with a general trend upward). China's performance on this metric was consistently lower than that of the United States and Japan, and considerably lower than that of France, the United Kingdom, and Germany. Its average aid-to-GNI ratio was also three to five times lower than the average aid-to-GNI ratio of OECD-DAC donors. This is not especially surprising, of course, given that China was a net recipient of development aid as recently as 2005, but its contemporary aid-to-GNI ratio is at a very low level by historical standards: as we showed in Chapter 2, China's aid spending as a percentage of total government spending peaked in the late 1960s and early 1970s. However, it does offer important context for thinking about China's shift from donor to banker.

---

see www.oecd.org/dac/stats/documentupload/ODA%202014%20Tables%20and%20C harts.pdf, last accessed November 18, 2020.

[29] We draw all data on donors other than China from www.stats.oecd.org.

[30] As we discussed in Chapter 3, it is also possible that our data collection method may undercount Chinese government financing in recent years since it relies on publicly disclosed information that may not be available for newer projects. However, it is unlikely that this potential bias toward undercounting in recent years is sufficiently large to account for a decline in Chinese ODA from US$13.77 billion in 2011 to US$6.84 billion in 2014.

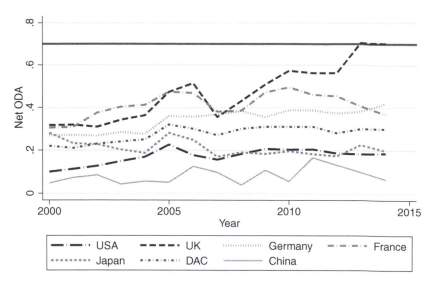

Figure 4.3 Aid effort of major powers: Aid as percentage of GNI, 2000–2014
Source: OECD; World Bank WDI; Authors' data
*Notes:* The figure shows the total monetary amount of aid (official development assistance, ODA) commitments of six major powers and the OECD-DAC in percentage of their GNI.

## What Factors Shape the Overall Size of China's Overseas Development Program?

Next, we shed some light on the factors that the Chinese authorities consider when they set the overall size of the country's overseas development program in any given year. As readers will recall from Chapters 1 and 2, Beijing adopted the Going Out strategy in part because of a domestic industrial input overproduction problem. Chinese state-owned companies produce industrial inputs – like aluminum, cement, glass, iron, steel, and timber – at levels that substantially exceed domestic demand, and the authorities fear that if they stop subsidizing these inefficient, over-leveraged, and unproductive firms, massive layoffs will take place and potentially trigger social unrest or political instability. To address this challenge, Beijing decided to stimulate external demand for its industrial inputs. It did so by increasing the provision of foreign aid and credit for development projects that involve physical construction and rely on imported Chinese construction materials (e.g., roads, railways, hospitals, schools, convention centers, government buildings, and stadiums). Therefore, in years when domestic industrial overproduction is high, one would expect the overall size of China's overseas development program to expand; in years when domestic industrial overproduction is low, one would expect the overall size of China's overseas development program to shrink. In previous work with Richard Bluhm from Leibniz University Hannover, we tested the hypothesis by first constructing a variable that measures China's overall production of six physical project inputs – aluminum, cement, glass, iron, steel, and timber – in a given year and then evaluating whether it was a good predictor of the overall size of China's overseas development program.[31] Figure 4.4 demonstrates that it is indeed a powerful predictor: a one-standard-deviation increase in industrial inputs leads to an increase in the overall size of China's overseas development program of somewhere between 176 percent and 461 percent.[32]

Beijing has also used foreign aid and credit to address another domestic oversupply problem. When the Chinese government adopted its Going Out strategy in 1999, it did so with the expectation that it would soon face strong macroeconomic headwinds. The country's foreign exchange reserves were continually growing due to annual trade surpluses, but the authorities knew that if they allowed these reserves to enter the domestic economy, they would increase the risk of inflation and currency

---

[31] Bluhm, Dreher, Fuchs et al. (2020). Specifically, we use factor analysis to construct the (logged and detrended) first factor of the six materials, drawing on data from the National Bureau of Statistics of China (NBSC) and the United States Geological Survey (USGS). We use USGS data on China's annual production of aluminum in 10,000 tons (www.usgs.gov/centers/nmic/aluminum-statistics-and-information, last accessed October 12, 2019). The annual production volumes of cement, pig iron, steel (all in 10,000 tons), timber (in 10,000 cubic meters), and glass (in 10,000 weight cases) have been retrieved via Quandl and complemented with information from the NBSC website (www.stats.gov.cn/english/statisticaldata/yearlydata/YB1999e/m12e .htm, last accessed October 12, 2019).

[32] The results are based on country-fixed-effects regressions with (log) Chinese official finance commitments to a particular developing country as dependent variable. We focus here on the 90 percent confidence interval and a one-standard-deviation increase in physical project inputs. Given that the first factor that we have derived for production materials with factor analysis has no natural scale, we consider this most intuitive. In our testing for the effect of production inputs on financing, we use a one-year lag. There is no reason to expect a longer delay between industrial input production and the approval of new Chinese development projects, for during our entire period of study, the Chinese government had well-established mechanisms that allowed it to provide foreign aid and debt quickly. Indeed, the main players in China's aid bureaucracy – MOFCOM and now CIDCA – formulate aid budgets annually, unlike most Western donors; see, for example, Zhao and Jing (2019). Therefore, in years when the authorities considered industrial input overproduction to be a sufficiently large problem to justify the use of international development finance as a remedy, they could quickly secure new loan- and grant-financed project approvals.

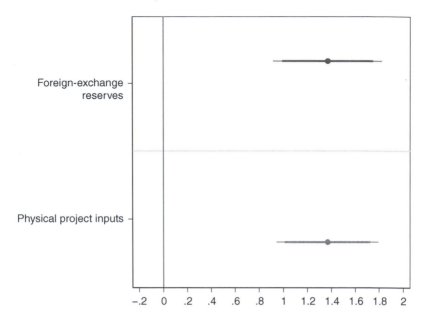

Figure 4.4  Physical and financial project inputs and China's allocation of development projects (aid vs. debt, 2000–2014)
*Notes:* Regression results are based on two country-fixed-effects regressions with (log) Chinese official financing (OF) commitments to a particular developing country as dependent variable. Our variables of interest are (lagged) measures of physical and financial project inputs. Each panel displays the effect of a one-standard-deviation change of the respective explanatory variable in tandem with 90 percent and 95 percent confidence intervals.

revaluation.[33] Therefore, to create favorable conditions for continued economic growth at home, they sharply increased foreign exchange-denominated loans to overseas borrowers on commercial and semi-commercial terms rather than highly concessional ones.[34] Figure 4.4 demonstrates the magnitude of this relationship: a one-standard-deviation increase in China's foreign exchange reserves increases the overall size of China's overseas development program by between 170 and 476 percent.[35] We will return to these input factors when we discuss how to estimate causal effects of Chinese development finance on various

[33] Zhang (2011a).    [34] Dreher, Fuchs, Parks et al. (2021).
[35] Specifically, we use the net change in a country's holdings of international reserves resulting from transactions on the current, capital, and financial accounts (in trillions of constant 2010 US$), as collected by the World Bank's World Development Indicators.

developmental outcomes in Chapters 7 and 8. But first, in the chapter that immediately follows, Chapter 5, we turn to the question of which countries receive which kinds of financing from China's government.

## Other Important Features of China's Overseas Development Program

**Sectoral Diversity.** An important but frequently ignored point about China's overseas development program is the sectoral diversity of its portfolio. Everyone knows that China is heavily engaged in economic sectors like transportation and energy, and our dataset confirms this. But the data also show that China's funding is not limited to these sectors; it is active in other sectors such as health, education, emergency response, and governance, as we show in Figure 4.5.[36] Of course, as noted earlier, China spends much more *money* on economic and productive sector projects – mostly via loans and export credits – than it does on social sector and emergency response projects.[37]

**Project Status.** The data that we have collected also reinforce one of the key points from Chapter 3: to know what the Chinese government is actually funding, you have to follow the *status* of every project over its life cycle from inception to completion. Previous studies of Chinese development finance have ignored this variable, which has led to artificially inflated estimates of the financial size of China's international development finance program. This approach assumes that all initial financial pledges are honored and every project that Beijing agrees to fund is eventually implemented. But Chinese development projects are frequently scaled back, renegotiated, suspended, or even canceled after their initial announcement. (Project cancelations often occur because the project is backed by another financier, as with Nepal's 1960s Ithari-Dhalkewar road project, which was originally funded by China but eventually implemented with Indian funding.) We have therefore taken special care to track the status of each project in our dataset. In the remainder of

---

[36] Although the "government and civil society" OECD sector classification is designed to capture projects that support government institutions or civil society institutions, the vast majority of China's support to this sector focuses on the construction of government buildings (including presidential palaces) and government institutions (i.e., public governance activities).

[37] The mean grant size in our dataset is US$9.2 million and the median grant size is US$1.9 million; the mean and median sizes of technical assistance projects in our dataset are US$8.2 million and US$3.0 million, respectively. By contrast, the average loan in our dataset is worth US$306.4 million, and the median loan size is US$96.5 million. In these calculations, we (for obvious reasons) do not include projects for which we are missing data on the monetary amount.

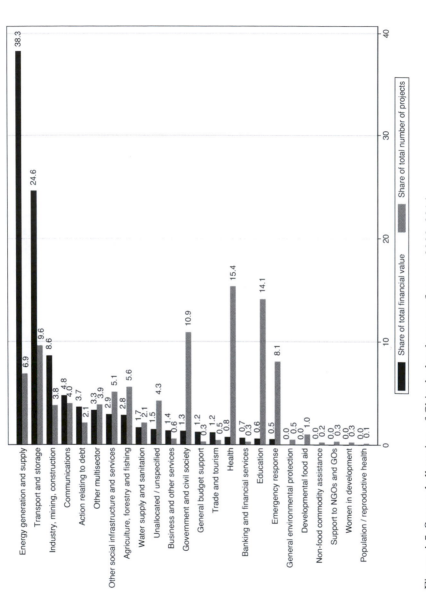

Figure 4.5 Sectoral allocation of China's development finance, 2000–2014

*Notes:* The figure shows the share of each development finance sector (according to the definitions of the OECD's Creditor Reporting System) in China's development finance, both in percentage of total monetary value (in black) and in percentage of total number of projects (in gray). Data from Authors.

this book, we use this status variable for two reasons: first, to reduce the likelihood of inflating or mischaracterizing the scale and scope of China's international development finance program and, second, to isolate the subset of projects that plausibly affects important outcomes, such as economic growth, infant mortality, violent conflict, and environmental degradation.[38]

Figure 4.6 breaks downs the number of Chinese development projects each year by status. From the 4,327 projects that reached at least the official commitment stage, we found evidence that 2,805 projects – 65 percent of all officially committed projects – reached completion. We also found evidence that another 625 projects (15 percent of all officially committed projects) had entered implementation but not yet reached completion. For the final 875 projects – roughly 20 percent of all officially committed projects – we found no evidence that these projects moved beyond the formal commitment stage (i.e., entered implementation). (As one might expect, Figure 4.6 indicates that projects committed to in recent years are less likely to have reached the completion stage than those committed to in earlier years.)

**Limitations.** We had originally hoped to incorporate some additional data into our analysis, but we ultimately could not due to the limitations of the public sources that we used to construct our dataset. We wanted to measure the size and the timing of financial *disbursements* through Chinese government grants and loans to precisely capture levels of subnational and national exposure to Chinese development projects. These disbursement data would have been especially useful for our analysis of the intended and unintended impacts of development projects (see Chapters 7 and 8).[39] However, during the construction of our dataset, we found that reliable disbursement data were rarely recorded in any public sources. Therefore, in subsequent chapters we instead use the status variable and two variables that measure project implementation start and end dates to estimate the timing of local exposure to Chinese development finance.

In addition, our variable identifying which Chinese government institutions financed specific projects is substantially less complete than other variables in the dataset. Nevertheless, a basic division of labor is clearly evident: most overseas projects supported by China's policy banks and state-owned commercial banks receive debt financing (mostly loans and export credits priced at or near market rates), while most aid projects are

[38] Other potential uses of the project status variable include analysis of the causes and consequences of financial pledges and project suspensions and cancelations.
[39] In Chapters 5 and 6, we seek to measure the underlying motivations that guide the allocation of Chinese development finance. Given that we are trying to understand the *intentions* of the Chinese government, financial commitments are arguably more relevant than actual disbursements.

financed by China's MOFCOM, MFA, and their respective networks of overseas embassies and economic and commercial coun-
sellor offices (ECCOs). Our dataset includes 630 projects supported
by China Eximbank, 110 projects supported by China Development
Bank, and several dozen projects supported by China's "Big-4"
state-owned commercial banks (Bank of China, Industrial and
Commercial Bank of China, China Construction Bank, and
Agricultural Bank of China). It also includes thousands of projects
supported by MOFCOM, MFA, and their local affiliates, though
our current dataset does not enable us to cleanly isolate the specific
agencies involved with each project.

### Which Countries Get What Types of Chinese Development Finance?

By the mid-2000s, Beijing was acting more as a banker than a benefactor.
However, developing countries have experienced this transition in the aid-
to-debt ratio unevenly. Which countries have received which types of
Chinese development projects? Africa experienced this transition less so
than other regions. Table 4.1 indicates that African countries received
more than half of all Chinese aid – in terms of numbers of projects and
dollars – between 2000 and 2014. This finding is consistent with Beijing's
own white papers on foreign aid, which report that the majority of Chinese
aid has gone to Africa.[40] Our dataset also indicates that over the same 15-
year period, Asia was the second largest regional recipient of Chinese aid.
But the gap between aid to the two continents was large: for every aid dollar
that China spent on Asia during this time period, it spent approximately
two-and-a-half dollars on Africa, and for every aid project that China green-
lit in Asia between 2000 and 2014, it green-lit more than two aid projects in
Africa.[41]

China's provision of semi-concessional and commercial debt reflects
a different set of regional priorities. In terms of numbers of debt-financed
projects, Africa and Asia received nearly identical levels of support from
China between 2000 and 2014. However, in monetary terms, the bulk of
China's lending went to Asian borrowers.[42] For every dollar that China

---

[40] State Council (2011, 2014).

[41] To be more precise, the ratio is 2.4 aid projects in Africa for every aid project in Asia. Of
course, Africa contains more countries than Asia, and so these continent-level trends do
not necessarily hold true for individual countries.

[42] Note that this pattern is not evidence of China's shift in focus to the BRI; the vast majority
of the loans in our dataset were issued well before this initiative got underway.

Number of Projects

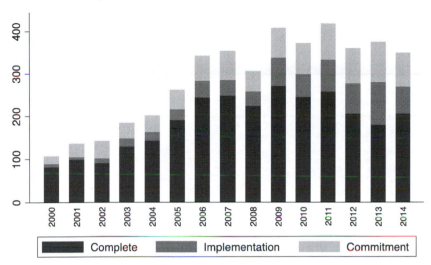

Figure 4.6 Number of China's development projects by status, 2000–2014

*Notes:* The figure shows the number of projects for each commitment year. Projects that reached the completion stage are in black, those at the implementation stage are in dark gray, and those at the commitment stage are in light gray. This does not necessarily mean that a project has not reached the next stage in the lifecycle of a project; it only means that we did not find any information in open-source materials that one of the subsequent stages had been reached. We excluded canceled, suspended, and pledged projects. Data from Authors.

lent to Africa between 2000 and 2014 at or near market rates, it lent US$1.70 to Asia. Similarly, in Latin America, the Caribbean, and Eastern and Central Europe, the provision of debt far exceeds the provision of aid. Between 2000 and 2014, every aid dollar that Beijing spent on development projects in Latin America and the Caribbean was matched by roughly four dollars of lending for development projects at or near market rates. The aid-to-debt ratio was even starker in Eastern and Central Europe: for every aid dollar that China committed to the region, it lent nearly US$19 at semi-concessional or commercial rates.[43]

---

[43] The Chinese government committed very little funding to the Middle East and the Pacific, but most of it was in the form of aid rather than debt.

Table 4.1 *Regional distribution of Chinese development finance commitments, 2000–2014*

| Region | Total Number of Projects | Total Value of Projects (US $ billion) | Total Number of Aid-Financed Projects | Total Value of Aid-Financed Projects (US $ billion) | Total Number of Debt-Financed Projects | Total Value of Debt-Financed Projects (US $ billion) |
|---|---|---|---|---|---|---|
| Africa | 2,345 | 118.1 | 1,855 | 46.1 | 273 | 45.4 |
| Asia | 1,113 | 116.5 | 765 | 18.3 | 262 | 77.5 |
| Eastern and Central Europe | 171 | 56.7 | 62 | 2.8 | 103 | 52.7 |
| Latin America | 317 | 53.4 | 165 | 9.9 | 127 | 40.5 |
| Middle East | 103 | 3.1 | 76 | 0.5 | 16 | 0.03 |
| Pacific | 265 | 2.8 | 227 | 2.2 | 28 | 0.9 |
| **Total** | 4,314 | 350.6 | 3,150 | 79.8 | 809 | 217.03 |

*Notes:* The table presents a breakdown by world region of the number and monetary value of China's total development finance projects, the number and monetary value of Chinese aid-financed projects (ODA), and the number and monetary value of Chinese debt-financed projects (OOF). Monetary values are in constant 2014 billions of US$.

Some countries, like Myanmar, have mostly attracted projects financed with semi-concessional and commercial debt, while others – particularly poorer countries and those with close political relations with China (see Chapter 5) – have received more aid. Tables 4.2 and 4.3, which show the top recipients of aid and debt from Beijing between 2000 and 2014, present starkly different pictures. As Table 4.2 shows, China's top aid recipient was Cuba, thanks to an extraordinarily large debt cancelation that took place in 2011. African nations claimed seven out of the top ten spots, and Cambodia and Sri Lanka made up the remaining two. Several other countries with close political and historical ties to China – such as Zimbabwe, Tanzania, and Pakistan – received very large numbers of Chinese aid projects between 2000 and 2014. As Table 4.3 shows, Russia was the leading recipient in monetary terms of Chinese debt during our fifteen-year period of study, which (prior to the publication of this book) led one popular media outlet to misleadingly identify China's northern neighbor as the "biggest recipient of Chinese foreign aid."[44]

[44] Allen-Ebrahimian (2017).

Table 4.2 *Top twenty recipients of Chinese aid-financed projects, 2000–2014*

| | Country | Number of Aid-Financed Projects | Country | Monetary Value of Aid-Financed Projects (US $ billion) |
|---|---|---|---|---|
| 1 | Cambodia | 132 | Cuba | 6.68 |
| 2 | Zimbabwe | 101 | Côte d'Ivoire | 3.97 |
| 3 | Tanzania | 86 | Ethiopia | 3.66 |
| 4 | Pakistan | 80 | Zimbabwe | 3.61 |
| 5 | Liberia | 76 | Cameroon | 3.40 |
| 6 | Uganda | 75 | Nigeria | 3.08 |
| 7 | Ghana | 74 | Tanzania | 3.02 |
| 8 | Ethiopia | 67 | Cambodia | 3.01 |
| 9 | Zambia | 66 | Sri Lanka | 2.79 |
| 10 | Kenya | 66 | Ghana | 2.53 |
| 11 | Papua New Guinea | 65 | Mozambique | 2.43 |
| 12 | Cameroon | 60 | Pakistan | 2.41 |
| 13 | Nepal | 59 | Congo, Rep. | 2.10 |
| 14 | Niger | 56 | Kenya | 1.60 |
| 15 | Congo, Rep. | 56 | Kyrgyz Republic | 1.55 |
| 16 | Rwanda | 53 | Sudan | 1.49 |
| 17 | Namibia | 53 | Bangladesh | 1.44 |
| 18 | Sudan | 53 | Zambia | 1.42 |
| 19 | Sierra Leone | 52 | Niger | 1.41 |
| 20 | Indonesia | 49 | Uganda | 1.29 |

*Notes:* The table presents the top twenty recipients of China's aid-financed projects (ODA) by project number and monetary value (in constant 2014 billions of US$). Data from Authors.

But Russia has received hardly any aid from China, either before or after 2000; in fact, it was for many years a crucial *supplier* of aid and technical expertise to China.[45] The funding that Russia has received from China is nearly all debt financing – large-scale loans and export credits with high interest rates and short repayment profiles that China's state-owned banks issued to Rosneft and Transneft, two Russian state-owned oil and gas companies. During our period of study, Pakistan, Angola, Laos, Venezuela, Ethiopia, and Turkmenistan were also major recipients of loans and export credits priced at or near market rates. They all received more than US$10 billion of development finance from China between 2000 and 2014.

In other words, our data show that China provides aid and debt to two very different groups of countries. As we will explain in the next chapter,

---

[45] Asmus, Fuchs, and Müller (2018).

Table 4.3 *Top twenty recipients of Chinese debt-financed projects, 2000–2014*

|   | Country | Number of Debt-Financed Projects | Country | Monetary Value of Debt-Financed Projects (US $ billion) |
|---|---|---|---|---|
| 1 | Angola | 76 | Russia | 36.62 |
| 2 | Sudan | 55 | Pakistan | 21.91 |
| 3 | Sri Lanka | 42 | Angola | 15.64 |
| 4 | Pakistan | 41 | Laos | 11.35 |
| 5 | Cambodia | 36 | Venezuela | 11.22 |
| 6 | Laos | 25 | Ethiopia | 11.17 |
| 7 | Venezuela | 24 | Turkmenistan | 10.05 |
| 8 | Kenya | 23 | Ecuador | 9.94 |
| 9 | Indonesia | 23 | Sri Lanka | 9.89 |
| 10 | Uzbekistan | 22 | Sudan | 8.75 |
| 11 | Belarus | 21 | Brazil | 8.53 |
| 12 | Ethiopia | 21 | Indonesia | 8.47 |
| 13 | Ghana | 21 | Kazakhstan | 8.27 |
| 14 | Nigeria | 20 | Belarus | 7.51 |
| 15 | Zimbabwe | 19 | Cambodia | 5.70 |
| 16 | Bangladesh | 17 | India | 5.57 |
| 17 | Myanmar | 16 | Argentina | 4.64 |
| 18 | Cameroon | 16 | South Africa | 4.32 |
| 19 | Vietnam | 16 | Nigeria | 4.16 |
| 20 | Tanzania | 15 | Kenya | 4.10 |

*Notes:* The table presents the top twenty recipients of China's debt-financed projects (including OOF-like and vague official finance) by project number and monetary value (in constant 2014 billions of US$). As explained earlier in this chapter, vague official finance projects are typically more similar to debt-financed projects than aid-financed projects.

China's aid-financed projects and its debt-financed projects are guided by fundamentally different allocation criteria. However, some seemingly exceptional countries receive substantial amounts of Chinese aid *and* debt, such as Ethiopia, Nigeria, Pakistan, Sri Lanka, Zimbabwe, and Cambodia. Cambodia is a striking example. As one of Beijing's closest political partners and a crucial pro-China broker in ASEAN, it was the eighth-largest Chinese aid recipient during our period of study, securing approximately US$200 million a year (on average) between 2000 and 2014. However, it also secured many Chinese loans (collectively worth about US$5 billion) that were priced at or near commercial rates. In total, it secured 168 development projects from Beijing (including 132 aid projects, 34 debt projects, and two vague projects) – higher numbers than for any other country in the world, which is especially remarkable given that Cambodia has a population of only 16 million people.

Our dataset also reveals which countries rely most heavily on Chinese development finance – a concern that Beijing's critics and rivals often raise. Table 4.4, which lists countries according to their levels of economic dependence upon Chinese aid and debt during our study period, demonstrates that Beijing is now a crucial source of financing for a diverse group of developing countries (and small island states in particular). On average, Chinese aid commitments represented at least 1 percent of GNI for twenty-five developing countries. However, when we consider levels of

Table 4.4 *Countries most economically dependent on Chinese development finance, 2000–2014*

|  | Recipient | Aid (percent GNI) | Recipient | Aid and Debt (percent GNI) |
|---|---|---|---|---|
| 1 | Montenegro | 6.54 | Laos | 9.42 |
| 2 | Tonga | 5.22 | Montenegro | 7.30 |
| 3 | Vanuatu | 3.23 | Bahamas | 6.74 |
| 4 | Dominica | 3.21 | Turkmenistan | 5.85 |
| 5 | Samoa | 3.07 | Tonga | 5.22 |
| 6 | Cuba | 2.95 | Dominica | 4.10 |
| 7 | Mauritania | 2.13 | Cambodia | 4.37 |
| 8 | Liberia | 1.96 | Samoa | 4.29 |
| 9 | Kyrgyz Republic | 1.94 | Kyrgyz Republic | 3.55 |
| 10 | Zimbabwe | 1.94 | Zimbabwe | 3.53 |
| 11 | Grenada | 1.92 | Vanuatu | 3.39 |
| 12 | Antigua & Barbuda | 1.82 | Cuba | 2.99 |
| 13 | Eritrea | 1.71 | Tajikistan | 2.85 |
| 14 | Congo, Rep. | 1.68 | Ethiopia | 2.84 |
| 15 | Cambodia | 1.61 | Liberia | 2.78 |
| 16 | Guyana | 1.58 | Congo, Rep. | 2.39 |
| 17 | Niger | 1.46 | Mauritania | 2.15 |
| 18 | Tajikistan | 1.29 | Eritrea | 2.12 |
| 19 | Côte d'Ivoire | 1.17 | Fiji | 1.98 |
| 20 | Fiji | 1.12 | Grenada | 1.92 |
| 21 | Mozambique | 1.10 | Bosnia-Herzegovina | 1.85 |
| 22 | Rwanda | 1.07 | Guyana | 1.83 |
| 23 | Comoros | 1.06 | Antigua & Barbuda | 1.82 |
| 24 | Micronesia | 1.06 | Niger | 1.59 |
| 25 | Guinea-Bissau | 1.03 | Sri Lanka | 1.58 |

*Notes:* The table presents the twenty-five countries that received most of China's aid-financed projects and the twenty-five countries that received the most Chinese total development finance, based on the monetary value of project commitments relative to the countries' economic size. We report the fifteen-year average in percentages of their GNI. Data from Authors and WDI.

dependence on development finance (aid *and* debt) from China, this picture changes. Some countries – like Laos, Montenegro, Bahamas, Turkmenistan, and Tonga – are more heavily reliant on Chinese development finance. These lists are worth keeping in mind when we use a range of statistical tests in Chapters 7 and 8 to measure the potential effects of Chinese development finance on economic and noneconomic outcomes.

Our dataset can also be used to compare the proportion of development finance provided by China with that provided by other financiers in the same country. Table 4.5 identifies countries that rely heavily upon

Table 4.5 *Countries with the highest levels of Chinese aid as a percentage of all bilateral aid, 2000–2014*

| Rank | Recipient | Chinese Aid (as percentage of all aid) |
| --- | --- | --- |
| 1 | Nauru | 92.69 |
| 2 | Antigua & Barbuda | 49.01 |
| 3 | Cuba | 36.54 |
| 4 | Trinidad & Tobago | 32.37 |
| 5 | Costa Rica | 30.76 |
| 6 | Montenegro | 28.34 |
| 7 | Dominica | 27.83 |
| 8 | Cook Islands | 25.24 |
| 9 | Grenada | 24.90 |
| 10 | Congo, Rep. | 23.77 |
| 11 | Turkmenistan | 22.46 |
| 12 | Mauritius | 21.68 |
| 13 | Jamaica | 19.41 |
| 14 | Tonga | 19.09 |
| 15 | Gabon | 18.00 |
| 16 | Fiji | 17.99 |
| 17 | Equatorial Guinea | 17.45 |
| 18 | Zimbabwe | 16.41 |
| 19 | Samoa | 16.40 |
| 20 | Seychelles | 15.63 |

*Notes:* The table shows the share of Chinese aid as a percentage of total ODA to each country over the 2000–2014 period. This statistic is calculated by dividing the sum of China's aid commitments by the sum of China's aid commitments plus the total commitments of ODA received from of OECD-DAC members, multilateral institutions, non-OECD-DAC donors, and private donors (in current US$). Data from Authors and OECD.stat.

Chinese aid, expressed as a percentage of the total amount of aid that they receive from all donors (averaged over our fifteen-year study period). For each of the twenty countries listed in Table 4.5, Chinese aid accounts for at least 15 percent of all aid inflows. These countries are geographically diverse; Beijing does not appear to be concerned with establishing itself as a lead donor in any one region, such as East or Southeast Asia. However, Chinese aid does account for a disproportionate share of total aid inflows to a number of small island states. It also accounts for more than 15 percent of total aid to several larger developing countries, such as Indonesia, Sri Lanka, and Zimbabwe. These results suggest that China's relative heft as a donor is highly uneven across countries and regions.

## Conclusion: A Glimpse of the Universe of China's Development Finance

The granular data on Chinese development projects that we have collected clearly illustrate the shift from benefactor to banker. At the turn of the century, China mostly offered Renminbi-denominated grants and interest-free loans to low-income and middle-income countries. However, over time, it dramatically ramped up foreign currency-denominated lending for projects around the globe, pricing these loans at or near market rates. However, Beijing's benefactor-to-banker transition has had dramatically different effects on different countries and regions around the world. Decomposing China's overseas development finance program into its constituent parts is an important first step toward understanding its "split personality" as a donor and creditor. Contrary to the conventional wisdom that China is now a leading foreign aid donor, we find that its aid giving is on par with European countries like Norway and the Netherlands in absolute amounts, and significantly lower than what the average OECD-DAC donor gives relative to GNI. However, China's overseas lending program is truly vast, and its reputation as a lender of first resort is supported by empirical evidence. Equipped with this context, we will proceed using statistical analysis in the next four chapters to shed light on the aims and impacts of China's overseas development program.

# 5  Apples and Dragon Fruits
## How Does China Allocate Aid and Credit across Countries?

### Is China a "Rogue" Donor?

In the spring of 2007, Moisés Naím, then editor-in-chief of the Washington, DC-based magazine *Foreign Policy*, penned an op-ed that would shape public debate on China's overseas development program for the following decade. He argued that "rogue" donors like China had no intention of supporting the economic development efforts of other countries. They were instead "motivated by a desire to further their own national interests, advance an ideological agenda, or sometimes line their own pockets."[1] He warned that if left unchecked, China and other illiberal donors would destabilize the international development finance regime established by Western powers after World War II: "What we have here – in states like China, Iran, Saudi Arabia, and Venezuela – are regimes that collectively represent a threat to healthy, sustainable development.... If they continue to succeed in pushing their alternative development model, they will succeed in underwriting a world that is more corrupt, chaotic, and authoritarian."[2]

This characterization quickly became the conventional wisdom among think tank researchers, public intellectuals, and newspaper editorial boards in Western capitals. Consider this description of China's overseas development program by the *New York Times* editorial board:

Misspent your country's wealth? Waged war against an ethnic minority? Or just tired of those pesky good governance requirements attached to foreign aid by most Western governments and multilateral institutions? If you run an African country and have some natural resources to put in long-term hock, you've got a friend in Beijing ready to write big checks with no embarrassing questions. That's nice for governments, but not so nice for their misgoverned people.[3]

---

This chapter draws selectively upon empirical approaches, prose, and arguments from two prior studies: Dreher and Fuchs (2015) and Dreher, Fuchs, Parks et al. (2018). These articles include more detailed links to previous research than we reference here.
[1] Naím (2007: 95).   [2] Ibid.
[3] New York Times (2007). See also The Economist (2009, 2016, and 2017b).

The notion that China is undermining the existing international development finance regime also gained currency among Western policymakers. Heidemarie Wieczorek-Zeul, then Germany's development minister, issued the following warning in 2006: "Beijing's government completely ignores local political realities when pursuing its own interests on the African continent.... [It] pressures African countries that just received Western debt relief to use loans provided by China to repair lavish presidential or other government ministry and commission buildings."[4] More recently in 2018, Australian International Development Minister Concetta Fierravanti-Wells questioned whether developing countries were getting good value for money from Chinese development projects: "You've got the Pacific full of these useless buildings which no [one] maintains, which are basically white elephants."[5]

The rogue donor narrative has had especially strong staying power within the US government. During her 2012 trip to Africa, then-US Secretary of State Hillary Clinton criticized China's overseas development program, contrasting it with "a model of sustainable partnership that adds value, rather than extracts it."[6] She indicated that, unlike other countries, "America will stand up for democracy and universal human rights even when it might be easier to look the other way and keep the resources flowing."[7] After stepping down from her position as the country's top diplomat, Clinton more explicitly criticized China. In her book *Hard Choices*, she wrote that during her tenure at the State Department, China "paid little attention to the health and development challenges that Western nations and international organizations worried about" and "turned a blind eye to human rights abuses and antidemocratic behavior."[8] She also questioned China's motivations, noting that in Africa, "Chinese companies would enter a market and sign lucrative contracts to extract resources and ship them back to Asia. In return they built eye-catching infrastructure projects like soccer stadiums and superhighways (often leading from a Chinese-owned mine to a Chinese-owned port)."[9] A similar criticism was levied by US President Barack Obama in a 2015 interview with the BBC: "[China has] been able to funnel an awful lot of money into Africa, basically in exchange for raw materials that are being extracted from Africa." He added that "economic relationships can't simply be about building countries' infrastructure with foreign labor or extracting Africa's natural resources."[10]

---

[4] Deutsche Welle (2006).     [5] Cited in McGuirk (2018).     [6] Cited in French (2014).
[7] Cited in French (2014).     [8] Clinton (2014: 271).     [9] Ibid.
[10] Baker (2015); BBC (2015a).

The administration of US President Donald Trump went even further, asserting that China's reckless and predatory lending practices work against the long-term development objectives of low-income and middle-income countries. In a 2018 speech, then-US Vice President Mike Pence made a thinly veiled reference to China, noting that "as we're all aware, some are offering infrastructure loans to governments across the Indo-Pacific and the wider world. Yet the terms of those loans are often opaque at best. [The] projects they support are often unsustainable and of poor quality. And too often, they come with strings attached and lead to staggering debt."[11] John Bolton, at the time the US national security advisor, was even more direct: "the predatory practices pursued by China ... stunt economic growth in Africa."[12]

Multilateral institutions have joined the chorus of criticism. One of their concerns is that Chinese state-owned banks have promoted a "race to the bottom" in the infrastructure finance market by offering to finance roads, railways, dams, and nuclear power plants without the environmental, social, and fiduciary safeguards that are required by other aid agencies and development banks.[13] In 2006, the president of the European Investment Bank (EIB), Philippe Maystadt, warned a group of EU finance ministers that Chinese banks "do not bother about social or human rights conditions."[14] In the same year, then-president of the World Bank, Paul Wolfowitz, slammed China for fast-tracking risky infrastructure projects without appropriate environmental safeguards; he also warned that "[t]here is a real risk of seeing countries which have benefited from debt relief become heavily indebted once more."[15]

The Chinese government paints a more flattering self-portrait. The State Council – the country's highest-level policymaking body – emphasizes the needs-based orientation and demand-driven nature of China's development finance. In 2011, it released a White Paper on foreign aid that asserted its government "makes great efforts to ensure its aid benefits as many needy people as possible."[16] Beijing has also promoted a counternarrative of "South-South cooperation" that emphasizes its solidarity with the Global South and the opportunity to pursue an alternative

---

[11] Pence (2018).    [12] Bolton (2019).

[13] This is also a concern among bilateral development finance institutions (e.g., Laurance, Peletier-Jellema, and Geenen 2015: R261–R262).

[14] Cited in Parker and Beattie (2006).

[15] Cited in Crouigneau and Hiault (2006). Around the same time, G-7 finance ministers and Central Bank governors expressed similar concerns, noting that "it is imperative that all donors share information and take account of debt sustainability issues in their lending practices" (G-7 2006).

[16] State Council (2011: 6).

development model with Chinese financial backing that is domestically led and free from the policy dictates of Western powers. During the Chinese Communist Party's 19th National Congress, President Xi Jinping made the case that China had "blaz[ed] a new trail for other developing countries to achieve modernization" and that "[i]t offers a new option for other countries ... who want to speed up their development while preserving their independence."[17]

Beijing has found that this narrative resonates with many of its overseas counterparts.[18] Leaders of the developing world frequently lavish praise on the Chinese government for its willingness to bank-roll the "hardware" of economic development – roads, railways, power plants, electricity grids, and telecommunication systems – and address local needs that traditional donors and creditors have neglected for decades.[19] Cambodian Prime Minister Hun Sen has described his country's relationship with China as less cumbersome and intrusive than its relationship with Western donors: "China talks less but does a lot" and "[t]hey build bridges and roads and there are no complicated conditions."[20] Another senior government official from Cambodia's Council of Ministers has argued that "[w]ithout Chinese aid, we go nowhere."[21]

Yet these views are difficult to reconcile with Naím's claim that China "couldn't care less about the long-term well-being of the population of the countries they 'aid.'"[22] Is China a rogue donor or a benevolent development partner? In this chapter, we present new empirical evidence that directly addresses this question.

However, before we try to identify the factors that guide China's aid and credit allocation decisions, it is important to consider what we know about the motivations of traditional donors and creditors. Dozens of empirical studies have established that the foreign policy interests of OECD-DAC donors influence their aid allocation decisions.[23] Western powers use aid to reward allies, punish enemies, build coalitions, and influence public opinion in recipient

---

[17] Cited in Xinhua (2017).

[18] For example, Rafael Correa, who was stridently critical of the conditionality practices of Western aid agencies during his tenure as Ecuador's president from 2007 to 2017, made fast friends with China. He argued that "China ... could pull Ecuador out of underdevel-opment" because of the arms-length, transactional nature of the bilateral relationship: they have a "surplus of liquidity and a shortage of hydrocarbons while we have a surplus of hydrocarbons and a shortage of liquidity" (cited in Morley 2017: 435).

[19] Wade (2008); Bräutigam (2009); Swedlund (2017a).

[20] Barta (2012); Strangio (2014: 215).    [21] The Economist (2017b).

[22] Naím (2007: 95).

[23] Rai (1980); Schraeder, Hook, and Taylor (1998); Kuziemko and Werker (2006); Vreeland and Dreher (2014).

countries.[24] We also know from previous research that official creditors from the OECD-DAC lend to other governments to safeguard their own economic interests, help their firms do business in overseas markets, and encourage other countries to buy their goods and services.[25] So, as an initial point of departure, it is important to keep in mind that Western donors and lenders are not motivated purely by humanitarian or development interests.

As Gerda Asmus and her colleagues from Heidelberg University have explained, there are several reasons why Beijing's aid and credit allocation practices might diverge from those followed by Western donors and lenders.[26] First, China never agreed to follow the behavioral rules and norms of the OECD-DAC (or similar international bodies), so there is no particular reason for it to be constrained in its pursuit of national interests. OECD-DAC donors must undergo a regular peer review process, which exposes the degree to which they are in or out of compliance with international rules and norms.[27] China, which has not subscribed to these rules and norms, does not. This means that the authorities in Beijing enjoy "a certain level of freedom to pursue their own short-term national interests through their aid activities."[28]

Second, although China has both a large population and a large economy, it remains less economically developed than OECD-DAC member countries (like Australia, France, Germany, Japan, and the United States). As we explained in Chapter 3, China's low level of per capita income creates a domestic political challenge: with large segments of its population still living in poverty, the Chinese government must justify using tax revenue to address economic development challenges outside the country's borders.[29] For China (and other "needy" donors like India),

---

[24] Morgenthau (1962); Bueno de Mesquita and Smith (2007); Berman, Shapiro, and Felter (2011); Dietrich, Winters, and Mahmud (2018).

[25] Alesina and Dollar (2000); Jensen (2003); Evrensel (2004); Manova (2013).

[26] Asmus, Fuchs, and Müller (2020) explain that these three reasons apply in most cases to the other so-called BRICS (Brazil, Russia, India, and South Africa). Also see Dreher, Fuchs, and Nunnenkamp (2013).

[27] Ben-Artzi (2017). The OECD-DAC has established a lengthy set of principles, standards, and procedures that govern member donors' relations with recipient countries. Most notably, the 2005 Paris Declaration on Aid Effectiveness lays out principles for how to make aid more effective. Although the BRICS donors have signed the Paris Declaration, it is commonly understood that they did so as recipients and not as donors of aid (e.g., Chaturvedi 2008; Bräutigam 2009). Evidence in Minasyan, Nunnenkamp, and Richert (2017) suggests that aid effectiveness improved for those donors that enhanced their quality of aid giving after the Paris Declaration.

[28] Sato, Shiga, Kobayashi, and Kondoh (2011: 2097).

[29] This problem also exists in OECD-DAC countries (Paxton and Knack 2012), but it is likely less acute, because these countries have substantially higher levels of per capita income.

altruism is a more difficult "sell" to taxpayers than direct political or commercial benefits. It therefore makes sense for needy donors to emphasize the domestic benefits of foreign aid.[30]

Third, China sees its overseas development activities as guided by a set of South-South cooperation principles, which diverge from those followed by members of the OECD-DAC. These principles include prioritizing cost competitiveness and speed of project implementation over due diligence procedures and safeguards, the pursuit of mutual benefits rather than an exclusive focus on benefits to recipient countries, a commitment to noninterference in the internal affairs of recipient countries rather than policy conditionality, and a focus on the profitability and economic viability of individual projects rather than the overall sustainability of sovereign debt.[31]

These are all plausible reasons why Chinese aid and credit allocation practices might diverge from those followed by OECD-DAC donor countries. However, the question of whether China is more self-interested and less altruistic than its Western peers is ultimately an empirical one, and our ambition in this chapter is to provide a convincing answer. In previous work, we have analyzed the cross-country allocation of Chinese aid from 1956 to 2005, and the cross-country allocation of Chinese aid and credit to African countries during the twenty-first century. In those studies, we identified strong correlations with various measures of the country's foreign policy and commercial interests.[32] However, at the time, we did not have global data on twenty-first-century Chinese development finance. In this chapter, we leverage the dataset introduced in Chapter 4 to identify the factors that motivate the contemporary provision of Chinese aid and debt. To test the claim that Beijing is a rogue actor, we benchmark China against its OECD-DAC peers and the World Bank over the same time period (2000–2014).

We hypothesize that aid and debt are different policy tools that serve fundamentally different purposes. If a government wants to buy foreign policy favors from another government, our expectation is that it will provide financing on favorable terms – through grants and low-interest loans. However, if a government's objective is to turn a profit or expand into a new market, our expectation is that it will use commercial financing instruments, such as a loan or an export credit that is priced at or near market rates. We think of these two hypotheses as two sides of the same

---

[30] Fuchs and Vadlamannati (2013); Budjan and Fuchs (forthcoming).
[31] Mwase and Yang (2012). See also Mawdsley (2013).
[32] Dreher and Fuchs (2015); Dreher, Fuchs, Parks et al. (2018). See also Box 2.1.

coin. If Chinese aid and debt are different tools that Beijing uses for different purposes, we would need to find evidence that supports both of these expectations.

Previous attempts to determine if China allocates development finance in ways that are less altruistic and more self-interested than its Western peers and competitors have been hobbled by definitional issues and measurement challenges.[33] By conflating Chinese aid and debt, many studies have promoted misleading conclusions about Beijing's motivations and fueled the rogue donor narrative that is now widely accepted by pundits and policymakers.[34] Therefore, we take special efforts in this chapter to avoid making "apples to oranges" comparisons – or, perhaps more appropriately in the case of China, "apples to dragon fruits" comparisons. Recall that in Chapter 4, we described a painstaking effort to classify each project in our dataset according to whether its observable attributes are consistent with the OECD's criteria for official development assistance (ODA or "aid") or other financial flows (OOF or "debt"). We now put these project-level data to use.

We test our two core hypotheses by running one set of statistical models to account for the cross-country allocation of Chinese aid and another set of statistical models to account for the cross-country allocation of Chinese debt. Our results confirm that Chinese aid and debt are indeed means to different ends. Beijing allocates aid in ways that closely resemble the practices of Western donors. Like Western donors, it allocates aid in response to levels of poverty and other indicators of recipient need, and like Western donors, it uses aid to reward countries that adopt its foreign policy positions and punish those that do not. We also find that contrary to the conventional wisdom, Beijing is no more likely than major Western donors to provide aid to corrupt or authoritarian regimes. None of these findings is consistent with the notion that China is a rogue donor compared with its Western peers. If anything, China seems to be

---

[33] For instance, one study commissioned by the US Congressional Research Service developed a measure of "PRC foreign assistance and related activities," which it defined as "pledges of aid or loans and government-sponsored investment projects." The study analyzes cross-country variation in this measure and concludes that "China's foreign aid is driven primarily by the need for natural resources" (Lum, Fischer, Gomez-Granger, and Leland 2009: 5). Similarly, Foster, Butterfield, Chen, and Pushak (2008: 64) conclude that "most Chinese government-funded projects in Sub-Saharan Africa are ultimately aimed at securing a flow of Sub-Saharan Africa's natural resources for export to China."

[34] Likewise, the absence of common definitions and consistent measurements across OECD-DAC and non-OECD-DAC suppliers of international development finance has led to flawed comparisons between the allocations of such donors and lenders.

a donor that has taken a page out of the playbook of the OECD-DAC.

However, one of our other core findings may help explain why the rogue donor narrative has had so much staying power: China's *lending practices* are substantially different from those followed by official creditors from the OECD-DAC. We find that Beijing's loans issued at or near market rates are more likely to go to corrupt and authoritarian countries. These are not practices followed or encouraged by official creditors from OECD-DAC countries. Therefore, the conflation of aid and credit seems to be at the heart of the confusion: Western politicians and journalists use rogue donor as a shorthand term for *all* of China's overseas development projects. The fact that Beijing is increasingly acting as a lender rather than a donor makes it more difficult to dislodge this popular misperception.

In the next section of this chapter, we will evaluate whether China allocates aid and credit according to its own political and economic interests. We will then consider these findings based on what we know about allocation decisions made by OECD-DAC donors and creditors.

### Aid for Policy Concessions: The Role of Political Interests

At the heart of the rogue donor narrative is the notion that Beijing – more than Western donors – uses foreign aid to further its own geostrategic interests. While the Chinese government acknowledges that its aid is related to its foreign policy interests, it rejects the notion that these interests exert undue influence or outweigh considerations related to the needs of recipient countries.[35] According to the State Council, "China never uses foreign aid as a means to ... seek political privileges for itself" and it "does its utmost to tailor its aid to the actual needs of recipient countries."[36]

Previous studies have noted that China has a track record of using aid strategically: to attract political support at high-level diplomatic events, to influence the voting behavior of recipient governments in various international fora, and to secure diplomatic recognition for the People's Republic of China at the expense of Taiwan.[37] However, China's use of aid as a foreign policy instrument does not necessarily

---

[35] MOFCOM (1996: 70) notes that it uses its grants to coordinate diplomatic work and that the construction of "some public institutions ... produced great political influences."

[36] State Council (2011: 3).

[37] Taylor (1998); Tull (2006); Lammers (2007); Dreher and Fuchs (2015). Along similar lines, Cheung, de Haan, Qian, and Yu (2014) show that significantly more of China's contracted engineering projects go to China's political allies.

mean that it is any more self-interested than Western donors, which have used foreign aid to reward allies, punish enemies, build coalitions, buy votes, and shape public sentiment in recipient countries since the end of World War II.[38]

Beyond these empirical results, most theories of political bargaining suggest that China will behave like any other great power. We hypothesize that any government's ability to "buy" policy concessions from another government will increase with the favorability (or financial concessionality) of its offer.[39] Stated differently, when a government provides a financial transfer to another government on favorable terms, it can expect a favor in return; but when a government provides a financial transfer to another government on non-preferential (i.e., commercial) terms, it cannot expect a favor in return.[40] This line of reasoning suggests that China would likely use aid rather than debt to achieve its foreign policy goals.

In fact, China's line ministries in charge of foreign policy play a direct role in the allocation of highly concessional funds like grants and interest-free loans. During our period of study (2000–2014), China did not have an independent foreign aid agency. China's MOFCOM and MFA oversaw the country's aid program. Therefore, the same government institutions that were responsible for securing diplomatic recognition, building international coalitions, and casting votes at the United Nations were directly involved in allocating foreign aid. Decision-making authority for debt-financed projects lies elsewhere. The central government has tasked its policy banks, China Eximbank and the China Development Bank, with the pursuit of a different set of goals. These are profit-seeking institutions that primarily (and increasingly) issue foreign currency-denominated loans at or near market rates. So, for both theoretical and organizational reasons, we expect that China's foreign policy interests will guide its allocation of aid but will play a less prominent role in its allocation of credit.

---

[38] Morgenthau (1962); Bueno de Mesquita and Smith (2007); Berman, Shapiro, and Felter (2011); Dietrich, Winters, and Mahmud (2018).

[39] Although Asmus, Fuchs, and Müller (2020) identify some reasons why aid from non-Western donors might be less altruistic compared with their Western counterparts, the broader aid allocation literature suggests that all aid providers are guided by a common set of motivational factors (Alesina and Dollar 2000; Berthélemy and Tichit 2004; Dreher, Nunnenkamp, and Thiele 2011).

[40] Dreher, Nunnenkamp, and Thiele (2008) explain why donors commonly use grants to obtain political favors. For an alternative theory on aid as exchange, see Bueno de Mesquita and Smith (2007).

We use statistical analysis to investigate the factors that influence Beijing's allocation of aid and credit.[41] To test whether China uses either of these financial instruments to pursue its foreign policy objectives, we analyze the sensitivity of the Chinese aid and Chinese debt to several variables. The first measure accounts for the recipient country's stance on the One-China policy, that is, the presence or absence of a recipient country's formal diplomatic relationship with China. Specifically, we test whether countries that maintain diplomatic relations with the government in Taiwan rather than (mainland) China receive significantly less aid or debt from Beijing.[42]

The second measure is how closely a recipient country aligns its voting behavior with China in the UNGA, an indicator that is frequently used by social scientists to measure levels of foreign policy alignment between states.[43] The third measure we examine is the strength of a country's historical aid relationship with China; we test whether countries that have received funding from the Chinese government over longer stretches during earlier decades receive more funding from China today, which may indicate that funding is more likely to go to long-standing political allies.[44] On this "old friends" metric, we observe that Nepal, a country that we discussed in Chapter 4, had the highest likelihood of receiving aid between 1970

---

[41] For those interested in the statistical details, we use a time-series cross-national dataset that integrates our data on Chinese government-financed projects, estimating a random-effects model with binary variables for each year in our dataset. We focus on random-effects regressions to exploit variation across recipient countries. While we report results from fixed-effects regressions for comparison, we do not expect our explanatory variables to hold much power in explaining year-to-year changes in development finance; rather, we stress the importance of retaining the between-recipient country variation for testing our expectations. Note that we lag the time-varying explanatory variables by one year to mitigate endogeneity concerns. The only exception is the variable measuring the number of people killed by disasters, as disasters are largely exogenous to development finance, and disaster relief is disbursed quickly. The binary oil indicator refers to the year 1999, prior to the start of our time series.

[42] We use a binary indicator variable that takes a value of one if a recipient country maintains diplomatic relations with the government in Taiwan rather than (mainland) China. Data are our own update of the dataset in Rich (2009).

[43] See Alesina and Dollar (2000); Kilby (2009, 2011); Vreeland and Dreher (2014), among many others. In our baseline model, we use the share of observations in which China and the recipient government vote the same. We employ the variable "agree2un" from Voeten, Strezhnev, and Bailey (2009), which is based on two-category vote data (1 = "yes" or approval for an issue; 2 = "no" or disapproval for an issue).

[44] To measure this, we use the share of years in which a recipient country received Chinese aid from 1970 to 1999 using data that we collected in earlier work (Dreher and Fuchs 2015). More precisely, we define this variable as $h_{CHN,i} = \frac{1}{30}\sum_{y=1}^{30} h_{CHN,i,y}$, where $h_{CHN,i,y}$ is a binary variable that equals one when recipient $i$ received at least one project from China in year $y$.

and 1999 (80 percent), followed by Mauritania and Tanzania (both 71 percent).

Figure 5.1 presents the results of our analysis, showing the relationship of each one of these measures to the amount of Chinese development finance received by the developing countries in our dataset.[45] We plot the effects of a typical change in each explanatory variable in tandem with its respective range of plausible values, the confidence interval. Our results are reported both in terms of dollar amounts (in dark gray) and numbers

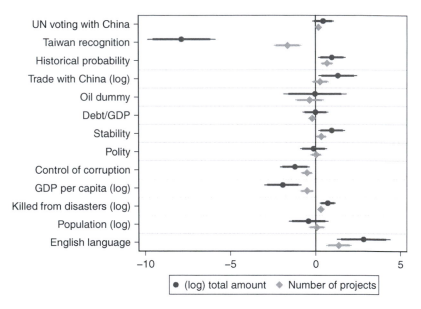

Figure 5.1 China's allocation of development finance, 2000–2014
*Notes:* Regression results are based on a random-effects regression with (log) Chinese development finance (ODA + OOF + vague official finance) commitments (in dark gray) or the number of projects committed (in light gray) to a particular developing country as dependent variable. All regressions control for binary variables for each year. Each panel displays the effect of a binary variable that switches from zero to one or of a one-standard-deviation change of a non-binary variable in tandem with 90 percent and 95 percent confidence intervals. We provide full regression results in Table B5.1 of Appendix 5.B.

---

[45] Table B5.3 in the chapter appendix reports descriptive statistics for our key variables.

of projects (in light gray).[46] To test whether aid or debt drives these aggregate results, Figure 5.2 splits Chinese development finance into its aid and debt components. In addition to political self-interest, we examine several other measures, including levels of economic need, political stability, and natural resource availability in recipient countries. We will discuss all of these factors in detail.

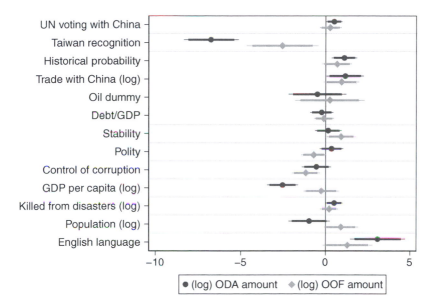

Figure 5.2 China's allocation of aid and debt, 2000–2014
*Notes:* Regression results are based on a random-effects regression with (log) Chinese aid (ODA) commitments (in dark gray) or (log) Chinese debt (OOF) commitments (in light gray) to a particular developing country as dependent variable. All regressions control for binary variables for each year. Each panel displays the effect of a binary variable that switches from zero to one or of a one-standard-deviation change of a nonbinary variable in tandem with 90 percent and 95 percent confidence intervals. We provide full regression results in Table B5.1 of Appendix 5.B.

---

[46] The "typical" changes that we discuss correspond to a switch from zero to one for binary variables or a one-standard-deviation change in all other cases. Effects that do not include the value of zero in the 90 percent confidence intervals are statistically significant. When we talk of "positive" or "negative" effects in our discussion of results, we refer to coefficients that are significant at least at the 10 percent level. Note that aid amounts are logged.

The results provide evidence that foreign policy interests guide Beijing's development finance: politically aligned countries receive more financial support from China. Specifically, we find that countries that do not recognize Taiwan receive 1.6 additional projects from China per year, on average (Figure 5.1). This large effect is not surprising, given that diplomatic recognition of Taiwan makes countries ineligible for Chinese aid.[47] Diplomatic recognition, as we expected, appears to be relatively more consequential for aid than for debt (Figure 5.2).

We also find a strong positive correlation between voting in the UNGA and the receipt of Chinese development finance. A 10 percent increase in voting similarity with China increases the number of Chinese development projects by 0.3 – a sizable effect compared with the average number of new development projects committed in a given year (2.3 projects) – and the monetary value of Chinese aid projects. However, UNGA voting has no detectable effect on the amount of credit that countries receive from Beijing. Finally, we find that countries that were prominent Chinese aid recipients during the 1970–1999 period receive more Chinese aid today, but these historical aid relationships have no bearing on the amount of debt finance. Taken together, these results demonstrate that foreign policy considerations guide Chinese aid more so than Chinese debt.[48]

## Debt for Profit: The Role of Economic Interests

If China uses aid for political purposes, why does it provide debt? According to critics, China uses its overseas development program to

---

[47] See also Kersting and Kilby (2014). Of course, there are exceptions to this rule. In our dataset, for example, China supported a bridge construction in Senegal in 2004, that is, before the West African country ceased diplomatic relations with Taiwan. See also the historic examples listed in Dreher and Fuchs (2015). However, none of the African "Taiwan recognizers" in the 2000–2011 period – Burkina Faso, the Gambia, São Tomé and Príncipe, and Swaziland – received official financing from China during that period. African states that have shifted their positions vis-à-vis the One-China policy in Beijing's favor have witnessed major changes in inflows of official finance from China. For example, Chad received no Chinese official finance from 2000 to 2005, receiving its first inflows only after China and Chad reestablished diplomatic relations on August 5, 2006.

[48] We also estimated all models with fixed effects for countries. Recall that we estimate random-effects models in our main analyses, as China's development finance is rather volatile from one year to the next. The variables that we employ here cannot reasonably account for much of this volatility. When we nevertheless run models with country-fixed effects for comparison, significance levels are generally lower, but our core conclusions continue to hold. We again find that Chinese aid is lower if countries recognize Taiwan and demonstrate relatively low levels of voting alignment with China at the United Nations. We show these results in Figure A5.1 of Appendix 5.A.

help Chinese firms gain a foothold in overseas markets where they can export goods and services and secure future contracts.[49] A related criticism is that China blends non-concessional and semi-concessional trade finance with concessional development finance, which undermines the OECD's "Gentlemen's Agreement" on officially supported export credits.[50] According to this agreement, which OECD-DAC countries informally put in place in 1999, "buyers [should] choose to purchase products and services based on price and quality of the goods rather than financing terms alone."[51] The agreement introduced a set of rules to prevent official export credit providers from engaging in a race to the bottom, with every provider motivated to provide its domestic exporters with ever more generous financing terms to retain an advantage over their competitors in other countries. Beijing's critics insist that its use of "blended finance" instruments – or so-called mixed credits that combine commercial lending and concessional lending – give Chinese firms an unfair commercial advantage over firms from OECD-DAC countries.

A case in point is Kenya's standard gauge railway (SGR) project, which we first introduced in Box 2.2. To finance this project, China Eximbank gave the Kenyan government a US$2 billion export credit at commercial borrowing rates (LIBOR plus a 3.6 percent margin and a fifteen-year maturity) *and* a US$1.6 billion loan on highly concessional terms (a 2 percent interest rate and a twenty-year maturity). In response, the Export-Import Bank of the United States publicly dressed down China Eximbank in a high-profile report that used the SGR as an example of China Eximbank's bad behavior.[52]

The fact that MOFCOM has overseen China's bilateral aid program for several decades does suggest that commercial considerations may influence the way that the Chinese government allocates grants and interest-free loans as well.[53] MOFCOM has itself acknowledged that due to the country's overseas aid program, "[Chinese] enterprises entered the markets of the developing countries very quickly and were welcomed

[49] See, for example, Davies (2007) and Dou (2017). Shinn (2006: 15) refers to Chinese medical aid as "a clever and low cost way to introduce Chinese-made medications to the African market."

[50] Parks (2019).    [51] Export-Import Bank of the United States (2017: 8).

[52] In its *Report to the U.S. Congress on Global Credit Competition*, the Export-Import Bank of the United States argued that China Eximbank's practice of blended finance "brings both financial costs and near-prohibitive competitive advantages into the dealings of commercial transactions ... [and] seeing its return is a particularly concerning development" (Export-Import Bank of the United States 2017: 20).

[53] Lammers (2007).

by the governments and enterprises of these countries."[54] As we noted in Chapter 4, China Eximbank's concessional lending window requires a financial subsidy from the central government to cover the price difference between commercial interest rates and the lower concessional interest rates that the policy bank offers. This subsidy comes from MOFCOM's Department of Foreign Aid, so it is certainly not implausible that MOFCOM's policy objectives could influence China Eximbank's concessional lending practices.[55]

Another point of controversy is whether Beijing uses aid to secure access to natural resources in other countries. China's critics claim that its top priority is to sustain high levels of domestic economic growth, which it cannot do without stable access to natural resources – in particular, oil, natural gas, copper, and cobalt, which it lacks in sufficient quantities at home. According to these critics, China uses aid as a "deal-sweetener" to gain access to natural resource contracts and concessions.[56] However, the Chinese government flatly rejects the claim that its aid program is designed to secure access to natural resources in other countries.[57]

A close cousin of this argument is that Chinese state-owned banks are more aggressive than other official creditors because they demand that resource-rich borrowers securitize their loans by offering natural resource assets as collateral, which can be seized in the event of default.[58] This criticism reflects a basic misunderstanding of China's commodity-backed loans. These loans are usually secured (i.e., collateralized) not through direct access to commodities but through commodity export sales. In other words, the proceeds from the sale of commodity exports are deposited in an escrow account; these funds can be used by borrowers either as a source of collateral or as funds for direct loan repayment.[59] There is no evidence that Chinese banks ask

---

[54] MOFCOM (1999: 75). The vast majority of projects financed via Chinese aid and debt are tied to the purchase of goods and services from Chinese firms (Pehnelt 2007; Mattlin and Nojonen 2015; Ghossein, Hoekman, and Shingal 2018). However, many Western donors and lenders engage in the same practice, despite decades of pressure to institutionalize the principle of international competitive bidding and a considerable reduction in the overall percentage of tied OECD-DAC aid (Easterly and Pfutze 2008; Nowak-Lehmann, Martínez-Zarzoso, Klasen, and Herzer 2009; Tarnoff and Lawson 2011; Hühne, Meyer, and Nunnenkamp 2014).

[55] Corkin (2011).

[56] Tull (2006); Foster, Butterfield, Chen, and Pushak (2008: 64); Lum, Fischer, Gomez-Granger and Leland (2009: 5); Halper (2010).

[57] State Council (2011).     [58] Lusaka Times (2018); Straits Times (2018); Okoth (2019).

[59] Corkin (2013); Bräutigam and Gallagher (2014). A case in point is the China Eximbank-financed Bui Dam project in Ghana. One of the loans that the Ghanaian government contracted with China Eximbank for this project was secured by a contract to sell approximately 30,000 tons of cocoa to China each year at international spot prices until five years after Bui Dam became operational, with the proceeds used to repay

that commodities themselves be used as a source of collateral or a method of loan repayment.[60]

However, there are still reasons to believe that natural resource endowments could influence the way that Chinese state-owned banks allocate international credit. After the adoption of the Going Out strategy in 1999, the Chinese authorities tasked the country's "policy banks" – state-owned banks that pursue both profits and national policy objectives – with using loans and export credits to facilitate the acquisition of natural resources that were in short domestic supply.[61] Then, after the 2008 global financial crisis, the Chinese authorities specified that the policy banks seek profitable investments in the natural resource sector.[62] Chen Yuan, the former Chairman of the China Development Bank, noted at the time that "[e]veryone is saying we should go to the western markets to scoop up [underpriced assets].... I think we should not go to America's Wall Street, but should look more to places with natural and energy resources."[63]

Our hypothesis is that commercial interests will predominate in the way that China allocates debt but not in the way that it allocates aid. Specifically, we expect that when Beijing issues loans at or near market rates, it will favor countries with good credit, high levels of political stability, and abundant natural resources. As we noted in Chapter 2, China's policy banks – China Eximbank and the China Development Bank – have an official mandate to invest the country's surplus foreign

China Eximbank; any outstanding debts were to be repaid via electricity sales (Chin and Gallagher 2019; Tang and Shen 2020).

[60] Bräutigam and Gallagher (2014); Gelpern, Horn, Morris et al. (2021).

[61] Downs (2011).

[62] Dreher, Fuchs, Parks et al. (2021). China's State Administration of Foreign Exchange (SAFE) invested the lion's share of China's foreign exchange reserves in US Treasury bonds prior to 2008. However, it changed course in response to the 2008 global financial crisis. As Kong and Gallagher (2017) explain, SAFE turned to CDB to generate higher investment returns. Under the so-called "entrust loan" agreement of 2008, SAFE deposited foreign exchange reserves in the CDB and directed it to engage in international on-lending (borrowing from an external creditor and then lending to another party) activities on its behalf. CDB, in exchange, collected a commission. CDB's foreign currency-denominated loans sharply increased in volume from US\$64.5 billion in 2008 to US\$260 billion in 2014. CDB was also directed by SAFE to focus its international on-lending activities in the natural resource and energy sector – a shift that is clearly evident in our dataset. Nine of the ten largest CDB loans in our dataset are in the natural resource and energy sector; all of these loans were committed between 2008 and 2014; and all of these loans are priced at commercial rates (i.e., 5.5 percent–7 percent interest rate or London Interbank Offered Rate plus a margin), which is consistent with SAFE's interest in maximizing investment returns.

[63] Cited in Anderlini (2009).

exchange reserves in economic sectors and commercial activities that will deliver strong returns.[64]

We also predict that China's allocation of debt-financed projects across countries will favor its trading partners. Official export credits, which are generally provided on less concessional terms than aid, are explicitly designed to advance the lender's national economic objectives – by helping firms from exporting countries do business in overseas markets and encouraging firms from importing countries to buy goods and services from firms in exporting countries.[65] In fact, when Beijing adopted the Going Out strategy, which was aimed at promoting national exports and stimulating business for Chinese firms overseas, it identified official export credit as an instrument that could facilitate the implementation of this strategy.[66]

In our statistical analysis, we use several measures to capture the potential influence of commercial considerations. As a measure for China's trade interests, we consider the volume of China's trade with each country.[67] To capture China's potential interest in securing access to natural resources, we include a variable that captures if a country is an oil producer.[68] To account for the creditworthiness of borrower countries, we use a public debt-to-GDP ratio and a political stability index.[69] The intuition here is that highly indebted countries and politically unstable countries pose higher levels of repayment risk and should therefore be less appealing to commercially oriented creditors.

---

[64] These banks are the largest sources of outbound credit from China to the developing world; they claim to prioritize "bankable" projects and screen loans on commercial viability grounds (Bräutigam 2009; Corkin 2011; Yu 2013; Sun 2014).

[65] Moravcsik (1989).

[66] Kobayashi (2008); Chen and Orr (2009); Bräutigam (2011). Chinese government loans are "tied" in the sense that borrowers must purchase Chinese goods and services on a preferential basis (Huang 2015). This subsidy from Beijing helps Chinese enterprises compete for market share with foreign firms. According to one study, 85 percent of Chinese firms that performed work for foreign government loan projects between 1995 and 2010 ended up carrying out follow-up projects or new projects in the same countries (Huang 2015).

[67] We obtained data from the IMF Direction of Trade Statistics database, available at https://data.imf.org/?sk=9D6028D4-F14A-464C-A2F2-59B2CD424B85, last accessed May 23, 2017. We use logged trade volumes in constant 2009 US$.

[68] Specifically, we use a binary variable that takes a value of one if a country produced oil in 1999, just before our study period begins. This measure follows the reasoning in Easterly and Levine (2003), who discuss the benefits of using a measure that is exogenous to aid. Data are from the British Geological Survey (2016).

[69] Debt data are from Abbas, Belhocine, Elganainy, and Horton (2010). Political stability data are from the Worldwide Governance Indicators project and range from −2.5 to 2.5 (Kaufmann, Kraay, and Mastruzzi 2004). The Political Stability and Absence of Violence/Terrorism index "measures perceptions of the likelihood of political instability and/or politically motivated violence, including terrorism." See WGI website at https://info.worldbank.org/governance/wgi/, last accessed August 14, 2020.

We present our results in Figures 5.1 and 5.2. Our findings indicate that China provides more development finance (in both total monetary terms and project numbers) to politically stable countries. However, the nature of this relationship is easier to understand when we disaggregate Chinese development finance into aid and debt (Figure 5.2): Beijing prefers to issue debt to politically stable countries, which is not surprising since political stability reduces the likelihood of default and facilitates loan repayment.[70] This finding is consistent with an argument that Huang Meibo from Shanghai University of International Business and Economics has previously made: "recipient countries' political stability and good credit standing are emphasized" when Chinese state-owned banks make loan approval decisions for overseas development projects.[71] It is also consistent with Johanna Jansson's claim that the "principal concern [of China Eximbank and China Development Bank] is the perceived profitability of the project in question. They need to be confident that their investment will be repaid."[72] We are also reminded of an interview that we conducted in Beijing, in which a MOFCOM official told us point-blank that "China Eximbank is mostly motivated by profit."[73]

As Figures 5.1 and 5.2 show, China favors its trading partners when it allocates credit *and* aid. The credit finding is not surprising, but the strength of the aid finding runs contrary to our expectations. It is also difficult to reconcile with one of the interviews that we conducted with officials from MOFCOM's Department of Foreign Aid in August 2015, in which we were informed that "economic concerns are not considered at all" when the Chinese government allocates grants and interest-free loans to other countries.[74] However, as we noted earlier in this chapter,

---

[70] Specifically, we find that a one-point increase in political stability on the −2.5 to 2.5 scale almost triples the amount of Chinese debt. This average effect can be computed as exp $(1.082347)-1 = 195$ percent. However, we do not find that countries with low levels of public indebtedness – countries that would also presumably have low rates of default – receive more Chinese development finance in total monetary terms. Given that countries with similar levels of political stability are also similar in terms of their levels of indebtedness, we ran statistical models that do not net out the effect of political stability. In these models, we find that while a country's debt-to-GDP ratio does not help explain the allocation of Chinese aid or development finance writ large, it *does* help explain the allocation of credit. These additional results are not included in the figures, but they are available on request.

[71] Huang (2015: 17).

[72] Jansson (2013: 157). Similarly, Corkin (2011: 72) provides this description of how China Eximbank prices its commercial loans: "the base [interest] rate is London Interbank Offered Rate (LIBOR), with an additional percentage added according to the country's sovereign credit rating (if it exists), the political situation, and its economic and financial stability."

[73] Authors' interview, August 2015.    [74] Ibid.

China is special among its aid-giving peers in that it entrusted a *commerce* ministry with oversight of a foreign aid program.[75] So perhaps we should not be so surprised that there is evidence of a link between Chinese aid and trade.

Finally, Figures 5.1 and 5.2 demonstrate that oil-producing countries do not receive more aid- or debt-financed projects from China. Since oil is not the only natural resource that might motivate China, we also ran statistical models with six alternative indicators of natural resource endowments. As we show in Figure A5.2 (in the chapter appendix), there is no evidence that China provides more aid or more credit to countries abundant in natural resources.[76] This finding contradicts one of the core claims of those who have popularized the rogue donor narrative: Chinese aid does *not* flow disproportionately to countries with abundant oil and other extractable resources. Neither do Chinese loans issued at or near market rates favor resource-rich countries in most regions – a surprising finding, since under the Going Out strategy, Beijing's policy banks were given a formal mandate to secure access to natural resources that China lacks in sufficient quantities at home. However, in one region of the world (Africa), we find that Chinese state-owned banks *do* favor countries that are rich in natural resources when they issue loans.[77]

### The Economic Limits of China's Noninterference Principle

Another key feature of the rogue donor narrative is the idea that Chinese aid favors corrupt and authoritarian regimes and that Chinese aid makes it easier for these governments to delay much-needed governance reforms, thereby prolonging the longevity of such regimes.[78] While issues of democracy, human rights, and rule-based governance in recipient countries are increasingly central to the way that OECD-DAC donors allocate and disburse aid, the Chinese government maintains its historic commitment to the principle of noninterference in internal affairs of recipient countries.[79] As we noted in Chapter 2, this principle goes all the way back to the Five Principles for Peaceful Coexistence that

---

[75] Budjan and Fuchs (forthcoming).

[76] This also holds when we remove the trade variable from our regressions.

[77] See Dreher, Fuchs, Parks et al. (2018). This also holds in our sample for the energy depletion variable in a regression with African countries and logged loan amounts.

[78] Davies (2007); Kurlantzick (2007); Doig (2019).

[79] MOFCOM (1990: 63) claims that it has "full respect for the recipient's sovereignty, without attaching any conditions and not asking for any special privileges, which displayed the true spirit of sincere cooperation." However, there is some evidence that

China adopted in 1954 and the Eight Principles of Foreign Economic and Technological Assistance adopted in 1964.

Scholars are divided on the question of how Beijing puts these principles into practice. Some argue that it distributes funding to countries without considering political regime type, corruption, human rights, or the rule of law. Others maintain that China uses the noninterference principle to rhetorically justify extensive engagement with poorly governed countries.[80] According to Gernot Pehnelt from the University of Jena, China has ventured into resource-rich and poorly governed countries – like Angola, the Democratic Republic of the Congo, Equatorial Guinea, and Sudan – because it entered international commodity markets later than OECD-DAC donors and creditors; consequently, it faces "higher opportunity costs of morality and governance and human rights-oriented policies."[81]

Critics and rivals agree that China's noninterference principle is a convenient excuse for its disregard of issues of democracy, human rights, and rule-based governance. They also agree that China's value-neutral funding policies will undermine the effectiveness of conditional aid policies and programs administered by the OECD-DAC and multilateral donors and creditors. In 2007, Hilary Benn, the head of the United Kingdom's Department for International Development (DFID) now the Foreign, Commonwealth and Development Office (FCDO) since September 2020, admonished Beijing for its apparent disinterest in seeing African countries pursue good governance, arguing that "China's failure to match the conditions placed on aid by countries such as Britain – including evidence of good governance, respect for human rights and spending directed to alleviate poverty – could set back progress."[82] Paul Collier, the former director of the World Bank's Research Department, wrote around the same time that "[governance] in the bottom billion is already unusually bad, and the Chinese are making it worse, for they are none too sensitive when it comes to matters of governance."[83] More recently, the US government has taken a special interest in this issue. In 2018, US Vice President Mike Pence gave a high-profile speech in which he argued that "Beijing has extended a lifeline to the corrupt and incompetent Maduro regime in Venezuela that's been oppressing its own people."[84] Shortly thereafter, a member of the US State

China seeks to influence economic policies in host countries when those policies impinge upon the viability of its own investments. For example, China reportedly demanded that Zimbabwe "raise electricity tariffs to cost-efficient levels as a pre-condition for its investment" (Bräutigam 2009: 150). In Venezuela, it reportedly sought to influence macroeconomic policies to increase the probability of its own loans being repaid (Downs 2011).
[80] Halper (2010).     [81] Pehnelt (2007: 8).     [82] McGreal (2007).     [83] Collier (2007: 86).
[84] Office of the White House (2018).

Department warned governments in the Western hemisphere to "avoid the temptation to use easy Chinese financing to liberate themselves from inconvenient requirements of oversight and good governance by Western institutions."[85]

There are theoretical and empirical reasons to take these criticisms seriously. Both democratic and autocratic governments use incoming aid and debt to stay in power,[86] but autocratic governments are particularly effective at doing so.[87] This is one reason that OECD-DAC and multilateral donors increasingly deny aid to autocratic and corrupt regimes, instead granting financial favor to those governments that protect human rights, fight corruption, and promote free and fair elections.[88] Several studies suggest that these efforts to promote political liberalization, human rights, and rule-based governance in the developing world have proven successful.[89]

However, as Deborah Bräutigam noted in 2009, "China's rise has clearly given dictators additional financing options."[90] If corrupt or authoritarian governments consider the assistance of OECD-DAC and multilateral suppliers of development finance to be overly intrusive or otherwise unwelcome, they now have the option of simply rejecting these sources of funding and accepting no-strings-attached funding from Beijing.[91] Diego Hernandez from Heidelberg University has provided evidence that recipients of Chinese aid receive World Bank loans with fewer policy conditions; his statistical model predicts 15 percent fewer World Bank policy conditions for every 1 percent increase in Chinese aid.[92] Three additional studies, by Sarah Bermeo, Erasmus Kersting and Christopher Kilby, and Xiaojun Li, show that receiving aid from China

---

[85] Ellis (2019). Reform-minded developing country officials have expressed similar concerns. Papa Kwesi Nduom, Ghana's former minister of public sector reform in Ghana, has warned that "some governments in Africa may use Chinese money in the wrong way to avoid pressure from the West for good governance" (Swann and McQuillen 2006).

[86] Bueno de Mesquita and Smith (2009a, 2009b, 2010); Jablonski (2014); Cruz and Schneider (2017); Findley, Harris, Milner, and Nielson (2017).

[87] Licht (2010); Wright (2010); Ahmed (2012); Bermeo (2016).

[88] Dollar and Levin (2006); Molenaers, Gagiano, and Smets (2017); Parks and Davis (2019); Annen and Knack (2020).

[89] Dunning (2004); Finkel, Pérez-Liñán, and Seligson (2007); Carnegie and Marinov (2017); Parks and Davis (2019); Parks and Strange (2019).

[90] Bräutigam (2009: 285).

[91] Bräutigam (2009). Apart from the fact that Chinese aid has created alternative financing options for autocratic leaders, Bräutigam (2009: 21) argues that "China's aid does not seem to be particularly toxic" and "the Chinese do not seem to make governance worse."

[92] Hernandez (2017). Brazys and Vadlamannati (2021) also provide evidence that the receipt of Chinese development finance reduces the likelihood that host countries will implement market-liberalizing reforms. Watkins (2021) shows that Chinese funding reduces compliance with World Bank conditions. Also see Annen and Knack (2020).

and other autocratic sources erodes democratic governance and reduces the probability of democratic transition.[93]

Yet none of these studies speaks directly to the question of whether Chinese aid and debt are allocated based on different criteria. Given that a long-standing principle of China's foreign aid program is respect for national sovereignty and noninterference in the internal affairs of recipient countries, our expectation runs contrary to the rogue donor narrative: we hypothesize that China allocates aid without regard to political regime type or the quality of institutions (governance) in recipient countries. But our expectation for China's provision of official credit cuts in the opposite direction: Chinese state-owned banks that issue loans on market or close-to-market terms should have a stronger interest in backing financially viable and economically productive projects, so we predict that Chinese debt will favor borrower countries with higher levels of institutional quality – a factor that strongly influences public investment efficiency and loan repayment rates.[94]

In our statistical analysis, we measure institutional quality using a twenty-one-point indicator of democracy, where the highest value corresponds to a fully institutionalized democracy.[95] We also use a Control of Corruption index from the Worldwide Governance Indicators (WGI) project to test whether Chinese aid or debt favors more (or less) corrupt countries.[96] We predict that Chinese debt will favor less corrupt countries and Chinese aid will be allocated without consideration of corruption levels.

Figures 5.1 and 5.2 include these statistical results. We find no evidence that Chinese aid is tied to recipient country political institutions as measured by the level of democracy or control of corruption.[97] This finding is consistent with China's principle of noninterference in the

---

[93] Bermeo (2011); Kersting and Kilby (2014); Li (2017).

[94] Isham, Kaufmann, and Pritchett (1997); Isham and Kaufmann (1999); Reinhart and Rogoff (2004); Faria and Mauro (2009); Denizer, Kaufmann, and Kraay (2013); Presbitero (2016).

[95] We use the twenty-one-point "polity2" variable from the Polity IV Project (Marshall, Gurr, and Jaggers 2013). Svensson (1999), Kosack (2003), and Montinola (2010) provide evidence that democracies put aid resources to better use than non-democracies. However, others disagree. See Dreher, Lang, and Ziaja (2018) or Doucouliagos (2019) for recent surveys.

[96] We take the Control of Corruption index from the Worldwide Governance Indicators project (Kaufmann, Kraay, and Mastruzzi 2004). The index, which "captures perceptions of the extent to which public power is exercised for private gain, including both petty and grand forms of corruption, as well as 'capture' of the state by elites and private interests," ranges from −2.5 to 2.5. See WGI website at https://info.worldbank.org/gov ernance/wgi/</int_u>, last accessed August 14, 2020.

[97] See also Broich (2017) for similar results.

internal affairs of partner countries. It also belies the popular claim that Chinese aid favors corrupt or authoritarian regimes.

However, the picture changes when we focus on Chinese debt-financed projects: less democratic and more corrupt countries do receive more money from Beijing. When a country transitions from being fully democratic to fully autocratic (on our regime type measures), it can expect to secure an almost tenfold increase in Chinese debt. Likewise, our statistical model predicts that a country with a corruption level that is one typical change lower (a 0.51-point change on a −2.5 to 2.5 scale) will see a 69 percent reduction in access to Chinese credit on average. The starkly contrasting nature of our statistical findings for aid and credit may explain how the popular notion that "China uses its largesse to prop up poorly governed countries" has taken hold. The lion's share of Chinese development finance is backed by debt, and Beijing's portfolio is becoming more focused on debt than aid. Therefore, when no distinction is made between aid and debt, it may seem as though Beijing favors corrupt and autocratic countries across the board.

Given that this finding runs contrary to our initial hypothesis, it is worth explaining in more detail. There are several potential explanations for why Chinese debt-financed projects are disproportionately located in corrupt countries. Corruption may "grease the wheels" of commerce,[98] facilitating more profit-oriented financial transactions between China and its partner countries. As we explain at greater length in Chapters 6 and 9, some of China's biggest banks invite political leaders from borrower countries to formulate and submit project proposals. Chinese contractors with a significant in-country presence thus have an incentive to "game the system" by colluding with the specific political leaders who submit project proposals. Anecdotal evidence suggests that they do so by first identifying a project that they are uniquely well-positioned to implement and that will benefit the leader with whom they are colluding and then inflating the cost of the project to increase their profit and cover the cost of illicit payment(s) to the leader and/or relatives and allies of the leader. The political leader is then expected to present the candidate project to Beijing as an official priority of the borrowing government, leaving no "contractor fingerprints" on the proposal submission.[99]

Another possible explanation is that Chinese state-owned banks are better positioned than official creditors from the OECD-DAC to

---

[98] See, for example, Dutt and Traca (2010) and Dreher and Gassebner (2013).
[99] Parks (2019).

work with countries that suffer from high levels of corruption. Chinese state-owned banks use a special set of tools – which are generally not used by Western lenders – to reduce the risks of financial misappropriation and repayment delinquency.[100] Two of these tools are commodity-backed loans and escrow accounts; we explain how China Eximbank has used these tools to manage fiduciary risk in the Republic of Congo in Box 5.1.[101] Another uniquely Chinese practice is "circular lending": rather than depositing the proceeds of a loan in an account that is controlled by a high-risk borrower, Beijing's state-owned banks will disburse project funds to a specific Chinese contractor that is identified in the loan agreement as the party responsible for project implementation. The purpose of this "ring-fencing" strategy is to minimize the risk of funds being misappropriated by borrower countries that suffer from high levels of corruption.[102]

---

**BOX 5.1   How China Became the Lender of First Resort in Congo-Brazzaville**

The Republic of Congo (ROC) possesses many of the characteristics that should increase a country's probability of receiving Chinese debt-financed development projects: China is one of its most important trading partners; it is rich in natural resources (and located in Africa); it suffers from high levels of public sector corruption; and there are few institutional checks and balances to constrain the behavior of the country's president.[a] As our statistical models predicted, the Chinese government approved many semi-concessional loans for development projects in the ROC.

On June 19, 2006, China Eximbank and the ROC signed a US-$1.6 billion "strategic partnership" that allowed the Congolese authorities to obtain loans for big-ticket infrastructure projects. More than a dozen projects were quickly approved and implemented through this mechanism, and after the ROC exhausted the first line of credit, China Eximbank extended another US$1.6 billion line of credit in 2013.

This dramatic expansion in China Eximbank's lending to Congo-Brazzaville came at a time when traditional bilateral and multilateral lenders had effectively stopped extending credit to the country. In March 2006, Paris Club creditors had agreed to join forces with the World Bank and the IMF and provide US$3 billion of debt relief to the

---

[100] Gelpern, Horn, Morris et al. (2021).     [101] Yarbrough and Yarbrough (2014).
[102] Bräutigam (2011); Horn, Reinhart, and Trebesch (2019); Gelpern, Horn, Morris et al. (2021); Parks, Morris, Lin, and Gardner (2020).

## BOX 5.1 Cont

Republic of Congo.[b] With few exceptions, they also stopped issuing new loans to the ROC at this time, so when China Eximbank entered into the June 2006 strategic partnership, Beijing became the country's largest official creditor.[c] The only other major creditors that stuck with Congo-Brazzaville were three private oil traders: Glencore (a London-based company), Orion (a Paris-based company), and Trafigura (a Singapore-based company).[d]

Knowing that its borrower posed a significant risk of delinquency and default, China Eximbank collateralized all of the loans that Congo-Brazzaville contracted through the strategic partnership mechanism. This practice of collateralization is not followed or encouraged by official creditors outside of China, but it is more common among commercial creditors – including Glencore, Orion, and Trafigura – that operate in high-risk markets.[e] China Eximbank required Société Nationales des Pétroles Congolais (SNPC) – the ROC's state-owned oil company – to deposit a portion of the cash proceeds from its oil exports into an escrow account (controlled by the lender).[f] China Eximbank was therefore in a position to seize a fully liquid asset in the event that the borrower stopped meeting its repayment obligations.

Despite its efforts to manage repayment risk, China Eximbank found itself in a difficult position by the end of the fifteen-year period that we study in this book. Global oil prices plummeted from more than US$100 a barrel in 2013 to just over US$40 a barrel in 2016, which made it significantly more difficult for the ROC to service its debts to the Chinese lender. The Congolese authorities approached the IMF for a bailout, but their initial request was rejected. Public debt had reached a level that the IMF considered to be "unsustainable" (nearly 90 percent of the country's GDP), and the IMF told the Congolese authorities that any bailout package would be contingent upon a debt rescheduling deal with China Eximbank. A deal was ultimately reached in April 2019, but the borrower actually ended up *worse off* after its debts were rescheduled. Although China Eximbank agreed to lengthen the repayment periods on eight loans that Congo-Brazzaville previously contracted, it insisted that the borrower repay its loans at higher levels of interest, which resulted in China Eximbank securing a larger lifetime repayment of principal and interest (in net present value terms) than it would have under the original borrowing terms.[g]

An earlier version of this case study was published in Gardner, Lin, Morris, and Parks (2020).

[a] Carter (2016).

[b] The Republic of Congo signed the first US$1.6 billion strategic partnership with China Eximbank just three months after the Paris Club and the Bretton Woods institutions agreed to provide US$3 billion of debt relief.

BOX 5.1  Cont

[c] See https://datatopics.worldbank.org/dssitables/annual/COG, last accessed December 1, 2020.

[d] These companies were willing to extend oil-backed (i.e., collateralized) loans on commercial terms. See www.imf.org/en/Publications/CR/Issues/2020/01/27/Republic-of-Congo-2019-Article-IV-Consultation-Press-Release-Staff-Report-and-Statement-by-48984</int_u> and https://datatopics.worldbank.org/debt/ids/DSSIMTables/M-DSSI-COG.htm, last accessed January 31, 2020.

[e] Gelpern, Horn, Morris et al. (2021).

[f] The borrower was required to keep a minimum deposit balance of 20 percent of total outstanding loans in an escrow account.

[g] After the restructuring in 2019, the net present value of the ROC's total repayments to China Eximbank rose from US$1.3 billion (before restructuring) to US$1.6 billion (after restructuring). See Gardner, Lin, Morris, and Parks (2020).

As Figure A5.3 in Appendix 5.A demonstrates, we also explored whether Chinese aid might be sensitive to other political and institutional features of recipient countries, such as levels of democratic voice and accountability, institutional constraints on the behavior of the country's political leader, whether or not a government has a right-wing political orientation, and whether a country has a communist or socialist legacy. When we replace our democracy measure with any one of these six indicators (and still account for levels of corruption), we find no evidence that Beijing takes any of the political or institutional characteristics of countries into account when it allocates aid. This is only the case when it allocates credit: countries that impose fewer constraints on the executive receive more Chinese debt.

## What about Poverty?

In our statistical analysis, we also test whether levels of need in recipient countries influence the allocation of Chinese aid and debt. To do so, we use measures of average per capita income and population size.[103] In addition to measuring levels of need, these variables provide an indication of the "price" that the Chinese government would need to pay to purchase foreign policy alignment from recipient governments: the support of poorer and smaller nations should be cheaper to buy than that from richer and larger countries.[104] We also include a variable that measures the total number of casualties of disasters in the recipient country, because we expect Chinese aid

[103] We log both variables; data are from the World Bank (2016).
[104] Bueno de Mesquita and Smith (2007, 2009a).

flows – and particularly humanitarian assistance – to increase follow-ing natural disasters.[105]

As Figure 5.1 shows, poorer countries receive more Chinese development finance in terms of both projects and monetary amounts. Our statistical results show that when GDP per capita increases by 10 percent, Chinese development finance drops by 17 percent. Aid rather than debt seems to drive this effect. We also find that countries with larger numbers of casualties from disasters, one of our measures of need, receive more development finance from China (in terms of monetary amounts and project counts).[106] This effect is also driven by aid rather than debt. Taken together, these findings suggest that Beijing responds to humanitarian and socioeconomic needs when it allocates aid. However, the findings could also be read as evidence that Beijing thinks it is easier to buy policy concessions from low-income governments and governments that require support in catastrophic times.

While China gives larger commercial loans to more populous countries, we do not find that these larger recipient countries receive systematically more Chinese aid. If anything, China supports less populous countries more – the so-called small-country bias. Again, the (supposedly) cheaper price of policy support from smaller countries might drive this effect.[107] The results again highlight the fact that aid and debt are means to different ends.

## How Does China Compare to Its Peers?

Proponents of the rogue donor narrative assert that China's motivations for providing foreign aid and debt are fundamentally different from those of traditional donors and creditors. Here, we discuss the results of our comparison between China and traditional donors: the World Bank and China's Western peers. Specifically, we analyze official financial flows from the United States, all OECD-DAC donors combined, the International Development Association (IDA), and the International Band for Reconstruction and Development (IBRD).[108]

---

[105] The data are on a log scale. We have retrieved them from the International Disaster Database EM-DAT at www.emdat.be/, last accessed January 31, 2020. Note that we add a value of one before taking logarithms to avoid taking the log of zero.

[106] This also holds when we control for fixed effects for countries (see Figure A5.1 of Appendix 5.A).

[107] See Bueno de Mesquita and Smith (2009a) for a discussion. Note that the negative coefficient should be interpreted with caution as it is imprecisely estimated (p-value: 0.12).

[108] We use data from the World Development Indicators. Since bilateral data on OOF commitments from OECD-DAC donors are unavailable, we restrict our comparison to

Figure 5.3 replicates the aid analysis in Figure 5.2 for each of these peers and peer groups. In these tests, we replace (a) our measure of UN voting with China with a measure of voting alignment with the United States and (b) our measure of trade with China with a measure of trade with the United States when we focus on development finance from the United

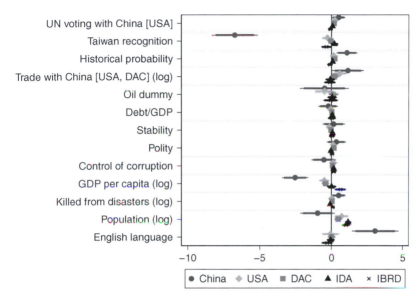

Figure 5.3 Comparison with established donors, 2000–2014

*Notes:* Regression results are based on a random-effects regression with (log) Chinese aid (ODA) commitments, (log) US ODA commitments, (log) OECD-DAC ODA commitments, (log) IDA commitments, or (log) IBRD commitments to a particular developing country as dependent variable. All regressions control for binary variables for each year. Each panel displays the effect of a binary variable that switches from zero to one or of a one-standard-deviation change of a nonbinary variable in tandem with 90 percent and 95 percent confidence intervals. We provide full regression results in Table B5.2 of Appendix 5.B.

ODA flows. The World Bank has two funding windows. Its IDA offers poor countries access to grants and highly concessional loans (ODA), while its IBRD offers loans on non-concessional terms (OOF). Between 2000 and 2014, 64 percent of official finance flows from the World Bank were channeled through the IBRD (OOF) and the remaining 36 percent were channeled through the IDA (ODA). World Bank data were retrieved from https://data.worldbank.org/ on September 12, 2017.

States and with all OECD-DAC donor countries in all other tests. The results show that the association between development finance and a recipient country's voting in the UNGA is not specific to China. Countries that vote with the United States receive larger funds from both the United States and all OECD-DAC donors combined. We make the obvious inference: China is not distinctive in this respect when it links the allocation of its aid to political interests.[109] We uncover similar results for commercial interests: recipient countries that trade more with the United States also receive more development finance from the United States – again, quite in line with the results for China given earlier. Overall, the evidence suggests that China, the United States, and the broader group of OECD-DAC countries *all* tie their provision of finance to foreign policy and commercial considerations.

However, there are some notable differences between the ways that Beijing and Western donors allocate their aid. While China is apparently agnostic about the importance of recipient political institutions, OECD-DAC countries (as a group) give more development finance to more democratic countries; similarly, less corrupt countries benefit disproportionally from IDA and IBRD commitments. This is in line with the stated policies of many Western donors and multilateral lenders, which they design to reward countries with higher-quality institutions. We also find that Chinese development finance is more sensitive than that of all other donors to the per capita GDP levels of recipient countries; in other words, China is more responsive to poverty.[110] Finally, China is the only donor in our analysis that appears to not allocate more aid to more populous countries. The United States, the OECD-DAC donors, and the World Bank provide significantly more aid to countries with larger populations.

---

[109] Kuziemko and Werker (2006), Kilby (2011), Vreeland and Dreher (2014), and many others have demonstrated that traditional donors also allocate aid based on political considerations.

[110] This corroborates earlier findings by Dreher and Fuchs (2015) for project shares during the 1996–2005 period: China showed the strongest concern for recipient income among the sample of donors, which also included the United States, the three largest EU donors, Japan, Korea, and two Arab donors. Note that the significantly positive coefficient on per capita income in the IBRD regression is not surprising given that its target group consists of middle-income and creditworthy low-income countries only. However, a recent paper analyzing Chinese aid at the *subnational* level presents findings that appear to be in tension with these cross-national results on poverty orientation (Briggs 2020). We return to this question in Chapter 6.

### Conclusion: Let's Put the Rogue Donor Narrative
### Where It Belongs – in the Trash Can

The portrayal of China as a rogue donor has helped media outlets generate clicks and Western politicians stir up nationalist sentiment. But there is little evidence to support it. We find no evidence that Chinese aid disproportionately benefits countries with abundant natural resources. Nor do we find evidence Chinese aid favors autocratic or corrupt regimes. Beijing has simply taken a page out of the Western donors' playbook; the United States and other OECD-DAC donors have a long track record of using aid to purchase foreign policy favors from other countries, and we find that Beijing is simply playing the same game. Among Western donors, it is taboo to openly discuss their use of aid as a foreign policy tool. Beijing, on the other hand, is more comfortable talking about the fact that aid should be mutually beneficial.

We also provide evidence that Chinese aid is responsive to the economic needs of recipient countries. It favors countries with lower levels of per capita income – in fact, it favors them *more* than OECD-DAC donors do. We find little support overall for the notion that China's motivations are substantially different from those that guide traditional donors. China is simply not a rogue donor.

What, then, explains the popularity and durability of the rogue donor narrative? We think that the root of the problem is that politicians and journalists have muddled the distinction between aid and debt. This chapter demonstrates that China uses aid and debt as means to different ends. Beijing uses *aid* to promote its foreign policy interests, and it uses *debt* to promote its commercial interests. So, if we want to understand Beijing's aims, we need to understand its "split personality" as both a benefactor and a banker.

China's lending practices do in fact diverge sharply from the practices of other official creditors. When its state-owned banks issue loans at or near market rates, they favor corrupt and autocratic countries; since a large and growing percentage of Chinese development finance is backed by debt rather than aid, *Beijing is effectively becoming a lender of first resort for poorly governed countries.* Therefore, it might be more appropriate to think of China as a "rogue lender." This would certainly be true if Beijing's overseas lending fueled corruption and autocratic behavior in borrower countries, which is a possibility we explore in Chapter 8.

To determine if China is a rogue lender, one also has to grapple with the question of how to benchmark Beijing's state-owned banks: should they be compared with official creditors or commercial creditors from market-led OECD-DAC countries?[111] This is a major, unresolved issue, and it will likely be hotly contested by China and other major players in the global development finance market in the years to come. Indeed, it is already in dispute. In the spring of 2020, the COVID-19 pandemic dramatically reduced levels of economic activity around the globe, severely compromising low-income and middle-income countries' ability to generate revenue and make loan repayments. The G-20 called upon all bilateral creditors to issue a moratorium on loan repayments from the world's poorest countries. The members of the Paris Club immediately agreed to participate in the so-called Debt Service Suspension Initiative (DSSI), but Beijing's initial response was less enthusiastic.[112] It announced that China Development Bank would not participate in the DSSI, arguing that it lends at commercial rates and should therefore be treated as a commercial, rather than an official, creditor. Paris Club creditors were incredulous, asking how Beijing could possibly take the position that one of its most important state-owned banks is not an official creditor. If this conflict is not resolved, it could bring major misfortune to developing countries. We will revisit this issue in Chapter 9 when we consider the future of the BRI and the likelihood that Beijing will work with other lenders to rewrite international development finance rules and norms in ways that are mutually beneficial (i.e., to ensure that all lenders are adequately protected from repayment risk and borrowers are engaging in responsible debt management practices).

Finally, since a key finding of this chapter is that Chinese and Western development finance is guided by some of the very same motivational factors, readers might wonder how Chinese development projects stack up against those financed by Western donors and creditors.[113] Are they more or less effective? The effectiveness of development finance depends on many factors, most of which have little to do with why the money was provided.[114] In

---

[111] As we noted in Chapter 1, in market-led economies, where the government expects a decentralized set of actors in the private sector to pursue profit and lend with the objective of maximizing investment returns, there is no strong rationale for government involvement in commercial lending activities. However, in China, the government is a major economic actor that seeks to maximize profit, so the country's state-owned banks are extensively engaged in lending activities that resemble the activities of commercial creditors from OECD-DAC countries.

[112] Gardner, Lin, Morris, and Parks (2020).

[113] Headey (2008); Bearce and Tirone (2010); Minoiu and Reddy (2010); Dreher, Fuchs, Parks et al. (2018).

[114] For example, different mechanisms of project design, delivery, and supervision might make Chinese development finance more or less effective than development finance from traditional sources.

Chapter 7, we benchmark the socioeconomic impacts of Chinese development projects against those achieved via multilateral and OECD-DAC development projects.

## Appendix 5.A
## Additional Figures

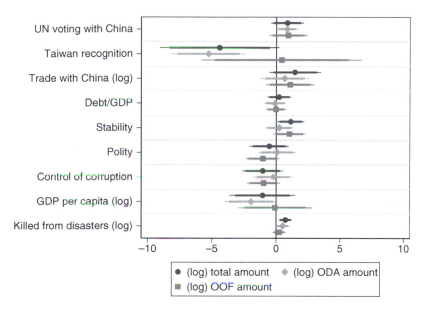

Figure A5.1  China's allocation of aid and debt (fixed-effects regressions, 2000–2014)

*Notes:* Regression results are based on a fixed-effects regression with (log) Chinese aid (ODA) commitments or (log) Chinese debt (OOF) commitments to a particular developing country as dependent variable. All regressions control for binary variables for each year. Each panel displays the effect of a binary variable that switches from zero to one or of a one-standard-deviation change of a nonbinary variable in tandem with 90 percent and 95 percent confidence intervals. We removed population size as it does not vary much over time.

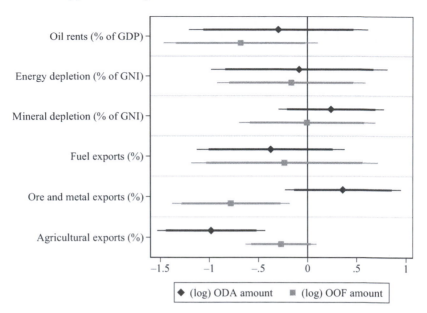

Figure A5.2 Natural resources and China's allocation of aid and debt, 2000–2014

*Notes:* Regression results are based on six random-effects regressions with (log) Chinese aid (ODA) commitments or (log) Chinese debt (OOF) commitments to a particular developing country as dependent variable. Specifically, we estimate variants of the regressions in Figure 5.2 where we replace "Oil dummy" with one of six indicators of natural resource endowments. All regressions control for binary variables for each year. Each panel displays the effect of a binary variable that switches from zero to one or of a one-standard-deviation change of a nonbinary variable in tandem with 90 percent and 95 percent confidence intervals.

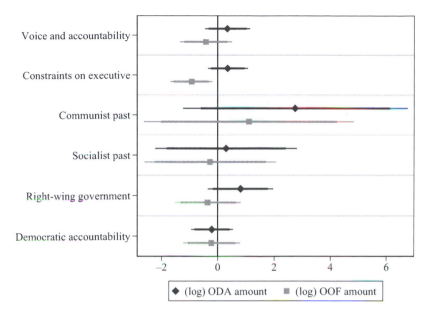

Figure A5.3 Institutions and China's allocation of aid and debt, 2000–2014

*Notes:* Regression results are based on six random-effects regressions with (log) Chinese aid (ODA) commitments or (log) Chinese debt (OOF) commitments to a particular developing country as dependent variable. Specifically, we estimate variants of the regressions in Figure 5.2 where we replace the Polity variable with one of six indicators of institutional quality. All regressions control for binary variables for each year. Each panel displays the effect of a binary variable that switches from zero to one or of a one-standard-deviation change of a nonbinary variable in tandem with 90 percent and 95 percent confidence intervals.

**Appendix 5.B**
**Additional Tables**

Table B5.1 *China's allocation of development finance*

|  | (1) | (2) | (3) | (4) |
|---|---|---|---|---|
| UN voting with China | 0.456 | 0.190** | 0.497** | 0.271 |
|  | (0.154) | (0.040) | (0.040) | (0.405) |
| Taiwan recognition | −7.855*** | −1.629*** | −6.722*** | −2.564** |
|  | (0.000) | (0.000) | (0.000) | (0.017) |
| Historical probability | 0.967** | 0.679*** | 1.098*** | 0.669 |
|  | (0.019) | (0.000) | (0.004) | (0.138) |
| Trade with China (log) | 1.322** | 0.283 | 1.161** | 0.940* |
|  | (0.023) | (0.252) | (0.041) | (0.079) |
| Oil dummy | −0.025 | −0.339 | −0.490 | 0.243 |
|  | (0.979) | (0.428) | (0.576) | (0.817) |
| Debt/GDP | −0.001 | −0.201* | −0.228 | −0.104 |
|  | (0.999) | (0.096) | (0.514) | (0.727) |
| Stability | 0.951** | 0.349** | 0.155 | 0.918** |
|  | (0.017) | (0.030) | (0.699) | (0.037) |
| Polity | −0.110 | 0.027 | 0.345 | −0.703* |
|  | (0.785) | (0.871) | (0.326) | (0.059) |
| Control of corruption | −1.211*** | −0.505*** | −0.542 | −1.178*** |
|  | (0.007) | (0.003) | (0.218) | (0.005) |
| GDP per capita (log) | −1.926*** | −0.496** | −2.536*** | −0.266 |
|  | (0.001) | (0.016) | (0.000) | (0.619) |
| Killed from disasters (log) | 0.716*** | 0.312*** | 0.503** | 0.207 |
|  | (0.003) | (0.005) | (0.047) | (0.421) |
| Population (log) | −0.414 | 0.076 | −0.966 | 0.917* |
|  | (0.487) | (0.757) | (0.120) | (0.077) |
| English language | 2.831*** | 1.368*** | 3.088*** | 1.296* |
|  | (0.000) | (0.000) | (0.000) | (0.083) |
| Number of countries | 110 | 110 | 110 | 110 |
| Number of observations | 1,561 | 1,561 | 1,561 | 1,561 |

*Notes:* Regression results are based on a random-effects regression with (log) Chinese development finance (ODA + OOF + vague official finance) commitments (column 1), number of projects committed (column 2), (log) Chinese aid (ODA) commitments (column 3), or (log) Chinese debt (OOF) commitments (column 4) to a particular developing country as dependent variable. All regressions control for binary variables for each year. Coefficients of nonbinary variables are standardized. The corresponding marginal effects are illustrated in Figures 5.1 and 5.2. p-values in parentheses. * significant at the 10%-level, ** significant at the 5%-level, *** significant at the 1%-level.

Table B5.2 *Comparison with established donors, 2000–2014*

|  | (1) | (2) | (3) | (4) | (5) |
|---|---|---|---|---|---|
| UN voting with China [USA] | 0.497** | 0.250*** | 0.185*** | 0.074 | −0.077 |
|  | (0.040) | (0.002) | (0.000) | (0.313) | (0.412) |
| Taiwan recognition | −6.722*** | −0.298 | −0.036 | 0.21 | −0.357* |
|  | (0.000) | (0.119) | (0.760) | (0.136) | (0.056) |
| Historical probability | 1.098*** | 0.159 | 0.235*** | 0.085 | −0.107 |
|  | (0.004) | (0.305) | (0.001) | (0.242) | (0.293) |
| Trade with China [USA, DAC] (log) | 1.161** | 0.578** | 0.212 | −0.092 | −0.114 |
|  | (0.041) | (0.028) | (0.170) | (0.608) | (0.592) |
| Oil dummy | −0.49 | −0.489 | 0.135 | 0.047 | −0.055 |
|  | (0.576) | (0.164) | (0.451) | (0.786) | (0.838) |
| Debt/GDP | −0.228 | −0.049 | 0.033 | 0.059 | 0.028 |
|  | (0.514) | (0.484) | (0.457) | (0.364) | (0.852) |
| Stability | 0.155 | −0.154* | −0.027 | 0.077 | 0.033 |
|  | (0.699) | (0.059) | (0.652) | (0.398) | (0.763) |
| Polity | 0.345 | 0.126 | 0.176*** | −0.036 | 0.036 |
|  | (0.326) | (0.118) | (0.000) | (0.685) | (0.679) |
| Control of corruption | −0.542 | 0.13 | 0.078 | 0.163* | 0.171* |
|  | (0.218) | (0.385) | (0.233) | (0.072) | (0.058) |
| GDP per capita (log) | −2.536*** | −0.507*** | −0.425*** | 0.014 | 0.638*** |
|  | (0.000) | (0.005) | (0.001) | (0.937) | (0.002) |
| Killed from disasters (log) | 0.503** | 0.021 | 0.045* | −0.092 | 0.1 |
|  | (0.047) | (0.596) | (0.098) | (0.177) | (0.201) |
| Population (log) | −0.966 | 0.723*** | 0.477*** | 1.188*** | 1.036*** |
|  | (0.120) | (0.007) | (0.001) | (0.000) | (0.000) |
| English language | 3.088*** | −0.067 | 0.019 | −0.048 | −0.298 |
|  | (0.000) | (0.834) | (0.897) | (0.743) | (0.146) |
| Number of countries | 110 | 110 | 110 | 67 | 48 |
| Number of observations | 1,561 | 1,337 | 1,416 | 583 | 362 |

*Notes:* Regression results are based on a random-effects regression with (log) Chinese aid (ODA) commitments (column 1), (log) US ODA commitments (column 2), (log) OECD-DAC ODA commitments (column 3), (log) IDA commitments (column 4), or (log) IBRD commitments (column 5) to a particular developing country as dependent variable. All regressions control for binary variables for each year. Coefficients of nonbinary variables are standardized. The corresponding marginal effects are illustrated in Figure 5.3. p-values in parentheses. * significant at the 10 percent level, ** significant at the 5 percent level, *** significant at the 1 percent level.

Table B5.3 *Descriptive statistics*

|  | count | mean | sd | min | max |
|---|---|---|---|---|---|
| **Explained variables** | | | | | |
| (log) Chinese OF | 1,561 | 9.278 | 8.921 | 0 | 23.21 |
| (log) Chinese aid (ODA) | 1,561 | 7.274 | 8.306 | 0 | 21.69 |
| (log) Chinese debt (OOF) | 1,561 | 4.615 | 8.107 | 0 | 23.17 |
| (log) Chinese social OF | 1,561 | 4.467 | 7.087 | 0 | 22.21 |
| (log) Chinese economic OF | 1,561 | 4.625 | 8.116 | 0 | 23.21 |
| (log) Chinese production OF | 1,561 | 2.072 | 5.624 | 0 | 22.41 |
| (log) Chinese humanitarian OF | 1,561 | 1.229 | 3.971 | 0 | 20.29 |
| Chinese OF project count | 1,561 | 2.318 | 3.253 | 0 | 35 |
| (log) DAC ODA | 1,415 | 19.27 | 1.227 | 14.81 | 23.17 |
| (log) US ODA | 1,342 | 17.17 | 2.015 | 9.210 | 21.21 |
| (log) IBRD | 362 | 19.17 | 1.444 | 14.92 | 22.48 |
| (log) IDA | 583 | 18.25 | 1.401 | 14.38 | 21.92 |
| **Explanatory variables** | | | | | |
| UN voting with China | 1,561 | 0.965 | 0.0658 | 0.542 | 1 |
| UN voting with USA | 1,561 | 0.198 | 0.123 | 0 | 1 |
| Taiwan recognition | 1,561 | 0.132 | 0.339 | 0 | 1 |
| Historic probability | 1,561 | 0.207 | 0.217 | 0 | 0.800 |
| Trade with China (log) | 1,561 | 19.98 | 2.321 | 12.04 | 25.32 |
| Trade with DAC (log) | 1,561 | 22.12 | 1.944 | 16.82 | 27.10 |
| Trade with USA (log) | 1,550 | 20.22 | 2.414 | 13.59 | 26.79 |
| Oil dummy | 1,561 | 0.495 | 0.500 | 0 | 1 |
| Debt/GDP | 1,561 | 57.59 | 45.95 | 1.978 | 487.4 |
| Stability | 1,561 | −0.540 | 0.796 | −2.812 | 1.308 |
| Oil rents (% of GDP) | 1,395 | 6.200 | 13.05 | 0 | 73.33 |
| Mineral depletion (% of GNI) | 1,440 | 1.154 | 2.888 | 0 | 23.84 |
| Energy depletion (% of GNI) | 1,430 | 5.143 | 10.73 | 0 | 83.01 |
| Fuel exports (%) | 1,151 | 17.74 | 27.59 | 0 | 99.79 |
| Ore and metal exports (%) | 1,192 | 10.13 | 16.40 | 0 | 85.97 |
| Agricultural exports (%) | 1,191 | 5.589 | 11.35 | 0 | 90.76 |
| Polity | 1,561 | 12.67 | 5.733 | 0 | 20 |
| Control of corruption | 1,561 | −0.575 | 0.510 | −1.816 | 1.250 |
| Voice and accountability | 1,561 | −0.513 | 0.704 | −2.210 | 1.160 |
| Constraints on executive | 1,509 | 4.540 | 1.886 | 1 | 7 |
| Communist past | 1,561 | 0.0474 | 0.213 | 0 | 1 |
| Socialist past | 1,561 | 0.102 | 0.303 | 0 | 1 |
| Right-wing government | 1,561 | 0.133 | 0.340 | 0 | 1 |
| Democratic accountability | 1,189 | 3.666 | 1.396 | 0 | 6 |
| GDP per capita (log) | 1,561 | 7.300 | 1.085 | 4.806 | 9.571 |
| Killed from disasters (log) | 1,561 | 3.247 | 2.389 | 0 | 12.34 |
| Population (log) | 1,561 | 16.18 | 1.510 | 12.90 | 20.97 |
| English language | 1,561 | 0.270 | 0.444 | 0 | 1 |

# 6    Aid *à la Carte*
## The Subnational Distribution of Chinese Development Finance

Visitors to the village of Yoni, located in Sierra Leone's Bombali district, will find "a wonderful school in the middle of what Africans call 'the bush.'"[1] In 2010, when the school was built with Chinese aid, Yoni was the hometown of Sierra Leone's president, Ernest Bai Koroma. A fancy new school in the president's hometown could be a simple coincidence, of course. But previous research suggests that government officials may actively discriminate in favor of their home provinces and districts.[2] When Koroma first came to power in 2007, Bombali was one of the country's poorest districts. However, it experienced a reversal of fortune during his presidency.[3] By the end of Koroma's second term in office, the district's capital, Makeni, was one of the few places in the country that enjoyed twenty-four-hour access to electricity.[4] Bombali, one of the country's four most populous districts, was a political stronghold during Koroma's 2012 reelection campaign. Across the country's other thirteen districts, he received an average vote share of only 51.2 percent; in Bombali, he received 93.2 percent of the vote.

As this example suggests, development finance is not allocated solely according to the motivations of donors and lenders: it is also influenced by the motivations of actors in recipient countries. This is particularly true when development projects are geographically distributed *within* countries. It may also be particularly true of Chinese development projects. Recall from Chapters 1 and 2 that the Chinese government prides itself on the demand-driven nature of its aid and credit allocation processes. Its 2014 White Paper on Foreign Aid explains that "[w]hen providing

---

This chapter draws selectively upon empirical results, prose, and argumentation from our joint work with Roland Hodler and Paul Raschky in Dreher, Fuchs, Hodler et al. (2019). The article focuses on Africa exclusively and includes more technical empirical analysis and additional links to previous research.

[1] Acemoglu and Robinson (2012).

[2] See, for example, Barkan and Chege (1989); Moser (2008); Hodler and Raschky (2014); Mu and Zhang (2014); Burgess, Jedwab, Miguel et al. (2015); Do, Nguyen, and Tran (2017); Bommer, Dreher, and Perez-Alvarez (2019).

[3] World Bank (2013).    [4] Inveen (2017).

foreign assistance, China adheres to the principles of not imposing any political conditions, not interfering in the internal affairs of the recipient countries and *fully respecting their right to independently choose their own paths and models of development.*"[5] However, this approach of only providing development finance when (and for what) counterpart governments request is risky. Without oversight, political leaders in host countries may seek to allocate funds to subnational jurisdictions based on their political self-interests rather than local socioeconomic needs.

In this chapter, we look at the motivations of recipient governments, examining how they shape the ways that Chinese development finance is allocated across subnational jurisdictions. First, we evaluate whether China's allocation of aid and debt within countries flows to areas with higher levels of socioeconomic need. Second, we explore whether political leaders manipulate incoming financial flows from China to advance their own political interests. We do so by examining whether and when funds from Beijing favor the home provinces of political leaders. Finally, we compare and contrast the ways in which Chinese and World Bank development projects are subnationally distributed.

We build upon a rapidly expanding literature that exploits georeferenced data on development finance and socioeconomic conditions to better understand why particular project sites are selected and what effects those decisions have on local outcomes.[6] In one of these previous studies, Ryan Briggs from the University of Guelph analyzes the subnational allocation of development finance from the World Bank.[7] His findings demonstrate that World Bank funds are generally targeted to areas that have a disproportionate number of rich people rather than those with mostly poor people,[8] and a companion study shows that China does even worse at targeting poverty.[9] In this chapter, we revisit

---

[5] State Council (2014, emphasis added). As we note in Chapter 2, the principle of noninterference in the internal affairs of recipient countries and respect for sovereignty can be traced back to the Final Communiqué of the 1955 Asian-African Conference in Bandung.

[6] See, for example, Findley, Powell, Strandow, and Tanner (2011); Francken, Minten, and Swinnen (2012); Briggs (2014); Jablonski (2014); Nunnenkamp, Öhler, and Sosa Andrés (2017); Eichenauer, Fuchs, Kunze, and Strobl (2020).

[7] Briggs (2017).

[8] The evidence presented in Briggs (2017) is cross-sectional in nature. However, BenYishay, DiLorenzo, and Dolan (2019) present causally identified evidence from a sixteen-year panel that arrives at the same basic conclusion about the sensitivity of World Bank development projects to levels of socioeconomic need. Briggs (2018a, 2018b) has also demonstrated that the same core finding – that aid favors relatively wealthy subnational localities and wealthier people within subnational localities – applies to a broad set of bilateral and multilateral donors and creditors.

[9] Briggs (2016).

this question with our substantially larger dataset of Chinese development projects worldwide. In doing so, we build upon our previous work with Richard Bluhm from Leibniz University Hannover, Roland Hodler from the University of St. Gallen, and Paul Raschky from Monash University.[10] Using the dataset that we introduced in Chapter 4, we assigned latitude and longitude coordinates to the specific locations where China implemented its development projects. This allows us to study the role of socioeconomic need and domestic political interests in the subnational allocation of incoming aid- and debt-financed development projects.

## China's "On Demand" Approach and Political Capture

In June 2013, we traveled to Beijing to present the first version of our dataset to Chinese government officials and other stakeholders. As part of our trip, we visited the Chinese Academy of International Trade and Economic Cooperation (CAITEC) of MOFCOM and inquired about China's approach to aid allocation. One MOFCOM official informed us that China "treats every country the same [way]" and that "the initiative generally comes from the recipient side."[11] Likewise, Ministry of Health officials told us in October 2014 that they "send medical teams to the [geographical] areas of the country that are selected by the recipient government." The fact that the Chinese project selection system is demand driven made us wonder if politicians in host countries might be able to "game the system," using Chinese government-financed development projects to advance their own political goals. We also wondered if this type of political manipulation would make Chinese development projects any less effective at achieving their objectives: accelerating economic growth, reducing inequality, and improving the health and well-being of local populations.[12]

We were not alone in wondering if this might be the case. Denis Tull of the German Institute for International and Security Affairs had previously written that "Chinese aid tends to benefit the governments of receiving countries more directly than the policies of Western donors, who are

---

[10] Dreher, Fuchs, Hodler et al. (2019); Bluhm, Dreher, Fuchs et al. (2020).

[11] Authors' interview, June 2013.

[12] Previous research suggests that leaders may direct development finance not to the projects where developmental returns can be maximized but to those projects that serve their political interests (Cohen 1995; Moss, Pettersson, and van de Walle 2007; Wright 2010; Briggs 2014).

preoccupied with the reduction of poverty."[13] Similarly, Deborah Bräutigam had argued that China's unique way of enacting the country ownership principle might "lead to 'prestige' projects that do not appear to be poverty-reducing."[14]

In principle, any aid agency or development bank that uses a request-based system to identify and define projects could be vulnerable to internal political manipulation by recipient governments, with politicians steering funds to politically consequential jurisdictions.[15] But there are also reasons to believe that Chinese state-owned banks and aid agencies might be more responsive – and thus more vulnerable to this type of manipulation – than their OECD-DAC and multilateral peers.

Consider, for example, how the Chinese government sources project proposals and vets them prior to approval. The process typically begins when a recipient government proposes a project to the Economic and Commercial Counselor Office (ECCO) attached to China's in-country diplomatic mission.[16] If the application meets a minimum viability standard, this office submits it to MOFCOM and MFA in Beijing. A team of technical experts from MOFCOM then travels to the country to perform a project and budget feasibility assessment in consultation with the domestic authorities. Upon their return to Beijing, the technical team prepares a final project proposal for the State Council's consideration. If the State Council authorizes the project, the Ministry of Finance transfers funds to MOFCOM and the procurement process begins.[17] Despite these formal procedures, two Australian scholars, Matthew Dornan and Philippa Brant, note that project appraisal processes remain weak: technical teams do not conduct rigorous economic analyses of potential projects.[18]

A key vulnerability in this process – where political favoritism can easily creep in – is at the proposal development stage. Whereas the World Bank typically negotiates projects with government technocrats in the line ministries of recipient countries, the Chinese government usually asks the Office of the President or the Prime Minister to prepare and submit

---

[13] Tull (2006: 467).    [14] Bräutigam (2011: 761).

[15] In fact, whenever donors grant recipient governments a high level of discretion over project site selection decisions, those projects are vulnerable to this type of domestic political manipulation (Masaki 2018).

[16] Our description of this process relies heavily upon Davies, Edinger, Tay, and Naidu (2008) and Corkin (2011).

[17] There is a different procedure for recipient governments seeking a concessional loan worth more than 20 million Renminbi, which, at today's exchange rate, makes the threshold just under US$3 million.

[18] Dornan and Brant (2014).

project proposals.[19] This approach effectively cuts technocrats in line ministries, opposition politicians, civil society organizations, and journalists out of the process, making it more difficult to sound the alarm when politically motivated projects are proposed.[20] Political leaders therefore have substantial leeway to steer projects toward politically consequential jurisdictions if they wish to do so.[21]

The Chinese government almost certainly knows that this is the case. In fact, it seems to encourage this behavior to build and cement alliances with political leaders in host countries. As Matthew DiLorenzo of Old Dominion University and Mengfan Cheng of New York University have shown, Beijing strategically increases aid to new leaders and governments shortly after they come to power.[22] Recall from Chapter 1 that as soon as Maithripala Sirisena came to power in Sri Lanka, the Chinese government green-lit a US$100 million grant for a new hospital in his home district. Then, according to President Sirisena, "[w]hen the Chinese ambassador visited my house to fix the date for [the opening of the hospital], he said that ... Xi Jinping sent me another gift.... He has gifted 2 billion yuan [US$295 million] *to be utilized for any project [that I] wish.*"[23]

Of course, China is not the only powerful government whose funds are vulnerable to manipulation by recipient government leaders. Their interests and demands can also reroute development finance from OECD-DAC and multilateral development agencies.[24] As economists Michael Faye and Paul Niehaus have shown, Western donors use aid to help politically aligned recipient governments get reelected.[25] And as Ryan Jablonski, a political scientist at the London School of Economics and Political Science, has demonstrated, there is strong evidence of bias in the subnational allocation of World Bank development funds in Kenya; such funds are preferentially awarded to the strongholds of the incumbent and in constituencies where voters share the incumbent's ethnicity.[26]

However, there are fundamental differences in the way that China and its peers operationalize the principle of "country ownership." In contrast to China's flexible and demand-driven project approval process, most

---

[19] AfDB, OECD, UNDP, and UNECA (2011).     [20] Jansson (2013).

[21] Engelsma, Milner, and Shi (2017).

[22] DiLorenzo and Cheng (2019). According to Bräutigam (2012: 23), the Chinese government sees no reason to fend off these behaviors: "[t]hose designing China's aid program see nothing wrong with fulfilling a host president or key minister's desire to have a fancy Chinese school built in his or her hometown."

[23] Reuters (2018), emphasis added.

[24] Cohen (1995); Briggs (2012, 2014); Masaki (2018).     [25] Faye and Niehaus (2012).

[26] Jablonski (2014).

OECD-DAC aid agencies and multilateral development banks have due diligence standards and procedures to ensure that economic viability criteria guide the process of designing projects and allocating scarce resources across subnational jurisdictions.[27] For example, the World Bank, the Asian Development Bank, the Inter-American Development Bank, the European Union, and the US Government's Millennium Challenge Corporation all use some form of cost-benefit analysis to vet candidate projects.[28]

A brief comparison of the project appraisal procedures followed by China and the World Bank helps illustrate the unique nature of Beijing's approach.[29] In principle, the World Bank subjects every project that it considers funding to cost-benefit analysis prior to approval. A simple rule for project acceptability was codified in 1994, with the adoption of Operational Policy (OP) 10.04 ("Economic Evaluation of Investment Operations").[30] The policy mandates that to be approved for World Bank financing, projects should "[create] more net benefits to the economy than other mutually exclusive options for the use of the resources in question."[31] OP 10.04 further stipulates that World Bank staff should evaluate "the project's consistency with the Bank's poverty reduction strategy" and "[consider] mechanisms for targeting the poor."[32] According to the World Bank's Independent Evaluation Group, one of the main motivations for the adoption of OP 10.04 was to create "a safeguard against project choices being captured by narrow

---

[27] Jenkins (1997); Deininger, Squire, and Basu (1998); Warner (2010); OECD (2015).

[28] Warner (2010: 57).

[29] Like China, the World Bank officially follows the principle of political noninterference in the affairs of recipient countries. Section 10 of Article IV in the World Bank's Articles of Agreement makes clear that the organization should make investment decisions based on economic, not political, criteria: "[t]he Bank and its officers shall not interfere in the political affairs of any member; nor shall they be influenced in their decisions by the political character of the member or members concerned. Only economic considerations shall be relevant to their decisions, and these considerations shall be weighed impartially in order to achieve the purposes stated in Article I." However, China and the World Bank put the principle of noninterference into practice in very different ways. A case in point is the World Bank's use and China's disuse of cost-benefit analysis for screening, selecting, and siting projects.

[30] In practice, not all World Bank development projects are subjected to cost-benefit analysis (Warner 2010). However, its project appraisal procedures are still far more robust than those used to vet prospective Chinese development projects.

[31] Specifically, OP 10.04 states that "[t]o be acceptable on economic grounds, a [World Bank-financed] project must meet two conditions: (a) the expected present value of the project's net benefits must not be negative; and (b) the expected present value of the project's net benefits must be higher than or equal to the expected net present value of mutually exclusive project alternatives."

[32] World Bank (1994).

political or sectional interests."[33] The same report notes that "[e]fficiency considerations always compete with other motives in project selection, and the policy is designed to give efficiency the upper hand in this competition."[34]

We consulted with two former employees of the Department of Foreign Aid (DFA) within MOFCOM; both informed us that there is no comparable set of economic analysis procedures in place to screen candidate projects.[35] China uses a demand-driven approach to source, select, and site development projects.

There are also reasons to believe that the risks inherent in China's "on demand" approach – particularly the risk that there will be fewer projects in areas that need them the most – are most relevant to its *aid-financed* projects. The project design and approval procedures that we have just described pertain most directly to projects financed with grants and highly concessional loans. When Beijing's state-owned banks issue loans at or near market rates, they follow some but not all of these processes; in general, they subject candidate projects to a more stringent set of due diligence procedures.[36] In Chapter 5, we showed that Chinese debt-financed development projects are more heavily concentrated in less democratic and more corrupt countries. However, since these projects are primarily guided by commercial criteria (rather than political criteria), they may be less vulnerable to host government manipulation. Chinese state-owned banks issue foreign currency-denominated loans to overseas borrowers to achieve economic returns that are superior to those that they would achieve elsewhere (e.g., by parking their excess dollars in US Treasury bills). Therefore, they may be more careful about insulating projects from political biases that could put their commercial interests at risk.

By pinpointing the specific locations where Chinese development projects take place, we can investigate how Beijing's on demand approach affects the geographic allocation of aid and credit *within* recipient countries. In this chapter, we carry out our statistical analyses not at the

---

[33] Warner (2010: 2).    [34] Warner (2010: 2).

[35] Authors' email correspondence with DFA officials in January 2019.

[36] For example, according to China Development Bank, "[t]he major factors that [it] take[s] into consideration when evaluating and approving a loan for a project include: repayment capacity of the borrower; level of capitalisation of the borrower; significance of the project to the PRC national or regional economy; overall technical and financial feasibility of the project; reliability and stability of the project's other sources of funding; quality of security and guarantees; availability of other credit enhancement measures; compliance by the borrower with national industrial policies; and compliance by the borrower with environmental laws and regulations." See www.rns-pdf.londonstockexchange.com/rns/5729Q_-2 016-11-30.pdf, last accessed December 1, 2020.

country level but at the province level.[37] To do so, we use a geocoded dataset that we first introduced in a study with Richard Bluhm as part of a multiyear collaboration with AidData.[38] It consists of all officially committed projects (from the dataset described in Chapter 4) worldwide *that entered implementation or reached completion*. In total, this dataset captures 3,485 projects (worth US$273.6 billion in constant 2014 US$) spread across 6,184 discrete locations in 138 countries from 2000 to 2014. Figure 6.1 shows the locations of these projects over the 2000–2014 period.

We focus on the relationship between the amount of Chinese development finance a province receives and several potentially important characteristics including its level of socioeconomic need, its natural resource endowments, and its political connection to the national leader who is in power.[39] We present the results of our statistical analyses graphically.

Consistent with our approach in Chapter 5, we also benchmark the subnational allocation of Chinese development projects against development projects financed by the World Bank.[40] As we previously noted, this comparison is particularly relevant because the World Bank, unlike China, is well known for screening and selecting loan proposals based on strict project appraisal policies and procedures. As such, its projects might be less vulnerable to domestic political capture in developing countries.

### Does Chinese Development Finance Favor Needy Provinces?

We start by analyzing the distribution of Chinese development projects within countries in relation to levels of socioeconomic need. We use

---

[37] To be precise, we run aid allocation regressions at the first-order administrative unit (ADM1) level. In most countries, ADM1s are provinces, so for ease of exposition we will refer to these units of observation as provinces in the remainder of this chapter. Alternatively, in some countries, ADM1s refer to states or governorates. We rely on the Database of Global Administrative Areas (GADM) to define subnational administrative regions and their boundaries.

[38] Bluhm, Dreher, Fuchs et al. (2020).

[39] More specifically, we measure the total amount of official development assistance (ODA) and other official flows (OOF) from China to a particular province in a given year (on a logarithmic scale). We take the logarithm of the total amount of Chinese official finance commitments to estimate (semi)elasticities. Note that we add a value of US$1 before taking logarithms to avoid taking the log of zero.

[40] With data from AidData (2017), we compute the total amount of World Bank financial commitments to a particular province in a given year, including highly concessional ("aid") projects from the IDA and less concessional ("debt") projects from the IBRD. We then log this variable. Given that no comprehensive global dataset exists for the development finance of any bilateral Western donor over a longer period, we cannot compare our findings with the United States or the OECD-DAC more broadly.

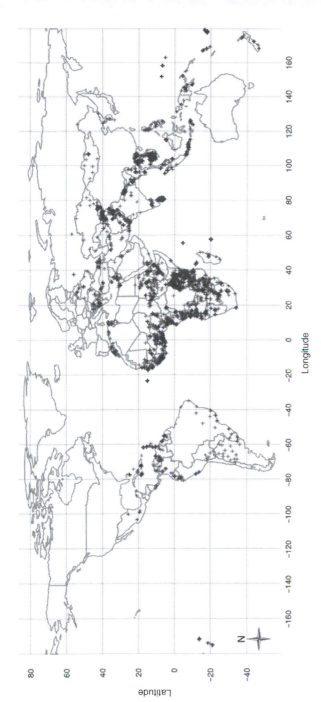

Figure 6.1 Locations of Chinese government-financed projects, 2000–2014
*Notes:* The figure shows all geo-referenced Chinese government-financed projects that reached the implementation or completion stage over the period 2000 to 2014. We have taken it from Bluhm, Dreher, Fuchs et al. (2020).

several measures to capture recipient need for each province in a given year. First, since province-level GDP data are not available for many developing countries, we proxy for local levels of economic development using remotely sensed data on nighttime light output. These data come from the US Defense Meteorological Satellite Program. Its Operation Line Scan satellites circle the earth in sun-synchronous orbit and record evening lights between 8:30 p.m. and 9:30 p.m. on a 6-bit scale ranging from zero (completely unlit) to 63 (fully lit). The National Oceanic and Atmospheric Administration then processes these data, creates annual composites of the daily images at a resolution of 30 arc seconds (or roughly 926 meters at the equator), and makes them available to the general public.[41] Given that unlit and dimly lit areas of countries tend to be poorer, they should receive more Chinese development finance if aid (or credit) follows need. As a second measure of need, we use the population size of a province.[42] If Chinese development finance is sensitive to local levels of need, we would expect to see more funding go to more populous provinces. Our third proxy for need is drought exposure. More specifically, we test whether areas that have experienced droughts (and are likely suffering from increased food prices and reduced food supply) receive more funding from Beijing.[43] Fourth, following Ryan Briggs's work on poverty targeting in Africa, we use the estimated travel time (in minutes, on a logarithmic scale) to the nearest city of 50,000 or more people in the year 2000 to study whether rural and remote parts of a country receive more or less Chinese development finance.[44]

The left panel of Figure 6.2 examines which factors influence the subnational allocation of Chinese development finance in the global sample and in four world regions.[45] The results demonstrate that Chinese development finance does not favor jurisdictions with high

---

[41] We use the so-called stable lights product, which filters out most background noise, forest fires, gas flares, and stray lights. Nighttime lights have been measured in a consistent manner around the globe since 1992. While there are some well-known deficiencies, for example, with respect to bottom and top coding (Jean, Burke, Xie et al. 2016; Bluhm and Krause 2018), researchers have shown that they are a good proxy variable for local human development outcomes (Weidmann and Schutte 2017; Bruederle and Hodler 2018).

[42] These data come from the Global Human Settlement Layer (GHSL) of the Joint Research Centre (JRC) at the European Commission. We transform them to a logarithmic scale. We thank Richard Bluhm for sharing the data with us.

[43] The indicator takes a value of one if the annual average precipitation in millimeters is more than two standard deviations lower in a given province and year than the province-specific average. Data are from Willmott and Masura (2001). We retrieved these and the following datasets from AidData's GeoQuery tool (Goodman, BenYishay, and Runfola 2019).

[44] Briggs (2018a).    [45] Table B6.5 reports descriptive statistics for our key variables.

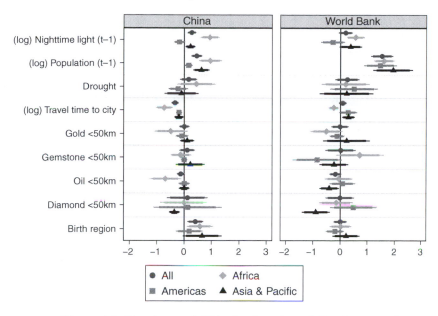

Figure 6.2 Correlates of China's allocation of development finance across provinces, 2000–2013

*Notes:* Each panel of the figure summarizes the results of four regressions. Regression results are based on least-squares regressions with (log) Chinese official finance commitments (left panel) or (log) World Bank official finance commitments (right panel) to a particular province of a developing country as dependent variable. Country-year fixed effects are included. Each panel displays the effect of a one-standard-deviation change of the respective explanatory variable (or the effect of switching from zero to one in the case of binary variables) in tandem with 90 percent and 95 percent confidence intervals. We cluster standard errors at the country level. We provide full regression results in Table B6.1 of Appendix 6.B.

levels of socioeconomic need.[46] Using nighttime light output to proxy for economic development, we find that, if anything, *richer* provinces receive more funding from Beijing than poorer ones. This is true in the global sample and in two regional subsamples: Africa

---

[46] As we employ country-year fixed effects in our regression analysis, we net out the amounts of funding countries receive in total in a year (this ensures that we compare countries that receive equal amounts of overall finance). We report results using project numbers rather than logged monetary values in Figure A6.1, which we provide in the chapter appendix for comparison.

and Asia.[47] A province that is twice as developed according to its nighttime light emissions receives 18.9 percent more Chinese development finance.[48] Similarly, we do not find that Chinese development finance favors geographically remote areas (as measured by travel time to cities). If the travel time to the next city is twice as long for one province than for another, this province's development finance receipts are 233.3 percent *lower* on average, all else being equal. This neglect of remote areas is most pronounced for Chinese *aid* and social sector projects (see Figure A6.2 in the chapter appendix).[49] We find that provinces with larger populations receive more funding from China, but provinces with drought exposure do not.[50] For the sake of comparison, we present these results alongside those for the World Bank in the right panel of Figure 6.2. While World Bank development finance also does not favor poor areas, relatively more of it reaches remote areas when compared with Chinese development finance.[51]

With data on the subnational distribution of Chinese development finance and natural resource endowments, we can also explore whether Beijing is using aid or credit to secure access to specific commodities. While Chinese development finance at the national level does not appear to be driven by natural resources – as we discussed in the previous chapter – it might be driven by local natural resource endowments within developing countries. To account for this possibility, we use data on the locations of onshore petroleum, gold, gemstone, and diamond deposits. For each province and each natural resource, we create a binary variable that measures whether there are deposits of the resource in question within a radius of 50 kilometers.[52]

---

[47] Latin America is the exception. Overall, these findings are consistent with those reported in research by Briggs (2016) and our own earlier work (Dreher, Fuchs, Hodler et al. 2019). Tang and Shen (2020) use difference-in-differences and difference-in-difference-in-differences approaches to estimate the socioeconomic impacts of the China Eximbank-financed Bui hydroelectric dam project in Ghana. They find that urban and rich households benefited more than other households from the project.

[48] ln(2)*0.273 = 18.9 percent. We provide full regression results in Table B6.1 of Appendix 6.B.

[49] Indeed, we find that overall, Chinese development projects in the social sector are *less* sensitive to local levels of socioeconomic need than Chinese development projects in any other sector.

[50] Populous provinces are likely more politically "valuable" to political leaders.

[51] To be able to test whether the coefficients in the World Bank regression are significantly different from the ones in the China regression, we re-estimate both regressions with non-standardized variables as seemingly unrelated estimations. Indeed, the difference is statistically significant for remoteness (p-value of 0.000) but not for nighttime light (p-value of 0.437).

[52] We obtain data on gold deposit locations from GOLDATA (Balestri and Maggioni 2014), data on gemstone deposit locations from GEMDATA (Lujala 2009), and data

In Figure 6.2, we present our results at the subnational level, which are similar to those at the cross-country level. Provinces with petroleum, gold, gemstone, and diamond deposits do not receive more Chinese development finance.[53] To make sure that resource-seeking motives do not remain hidden in our aggregate measure of development finance, we rerun this analysis for Chinese aid and debt and we disaggregate our analysis by sector. One might expect resource-seeking motives to be most pronounced in projects financed with debt rather than aid, and in the economic infrastructure (which includes energy) and production sectors (which includes mining). However, even in these "most likely" cases, we do not find positive effects from any of the natural resource endowment variables (see Figure A6.2 for details). When we compare the subnational allocation of Chinese development projects and World Bank development projects, the results are similar. Taken together, these results and those at the cross-country level (Chapter 5) seem to contradict the notion that China primarily uses its overseas development program to access and exploit the natural resources of host countries.

### Does Chinese Development Finance Favor Politically Privileged Provinces?

To account for the political interests of the recipient government, we follow an approach that we took in previous work with Roland Hodler and Paul Raschky. Our main empirical tests investigate whether presidents and prime ministers in recipient countries manipulate Chinese development projects for their own political gain. Specifically, we use a variable that measures whether the political leader of a country in a given year was born in a given province.[54] We created this variable using data that two of us coded in collaboration with Andreas Kammerlander, Lennart Kaplan, Charlotte Robert, and Kerstin Unfried, researchers from the Universities of Freiburg, Göttingen, and Heidelberg.[55] Using these data, we can successfully attribute leaders to 92 percent of the country-year observations in our analysis.[56]

---

on onshore petroleum and diamond deposit locations from the Peace Research Institute Oslo (Gilmore, Gleditsch, Lujala, and Rød 2005; Lujala, Rød, and Thieme 2007).

[53] On the contrary, in some specifications, provinces with oil and diamonds receive even less finance.

[54] Dreher, Fuchs, Hodler et al. (2019).

[55] Dreher, Fuchs, Kammerlander et al. (2021). Their Political Leaders' Affiliation Database (PLAD) is based in part on our coding of the birthplaces of African political leaders (Dreher, Fuchs, Hodler et al. 2019, 2021).

[56] The gap results from the lack of sufficiently precise subnational information on leader birthplaces and the fact that some leaders were born outside the countries that they

The left panel of Figure 6.2 – specifically, the "birth region" variable – examines whether or not provinces where the country's current political leader was born received more funding from China. In short, the answer is yes. In the average country, Beijing provides 52 percent more funding to the province in which the political leader was born than to other provinces.[57] The effect is particularly strong in Africa. We also find some evidence that it exists in Asia and the Pacific region, but this result is estimated with a lower level of statistical precision. By contrast, we find no evidence that World Bank development finance favors the home provinces of political leaders in any region of the world (right panel, Figure 6.2).[58] This pattern of evidence suggests that China's on-demand approach is particularly vulnerable to domestic political manipulation.[59]

These tests compare provinces within the same country and year. A skeptical reader might wonder if these results are spurious because of the influence of confounding factors. Perhaps leaders' home provinces differ from other provinces in other ways that make them more likely to receive more funding from China. For example, many leaders are born in capital cities, and provinces with capital cities might receive more Chinese development finance for reasons that are unrelated to the fact that a leader was born there.[60] We address this potential problem in some depth in a previously published study with Roland Hodler and Paul Raschky.[61] Our basic strategy is to study the same provinces over time, testing whether a province receives more funding from China when one of its natives is in power than at other times.[62] The left panel of Figure 6.3 shows the results of these analyses for the global sample. It also breaks down results for three

---

governed. Despite this gap, we were able to study 394 changes in the "home province" variable over time in our sample.

[57] We computed the average effect as $\exp(0.417)-1$. The corresponding 90 percent confidence interval ranges from 19 percent [$=\exp(0.170)-1$] to 93 percent [$=\exp(0.658)-1$].

[58] This contrasts with findings in Öhler and Nunnenkamp (2014), who – among others – also investigate whether more World Bank projects are sited in leader birth regions in Africa. However, their results are based on data from just seventeen African countries.

[59] The finding of statistically significant differences in the home province effects between China and the World Bank in seemingly unrelated estimations completes the picture (p-value of 0.022).

[60] Our simple linear regressions with country-year fixed effects also have advantages. They allow us to highlight the between-province variation in our sample, which enables us to study relationships between the subnational allocation of development finance from China and variables that show no or almost no variation over time. It also helps us identify the relationship between leaders' birthplaces and the receipt of Chinese funds, despite the relatively small variation in the leaders' home provinces over time (271 provinces are a "birth province" at least once during the sample period).

[61] Dreher, Fuchs, Hodler et al. (2019).

[62] That is, we control for province fixed effects. The "birthplace effect" could also be driven by underlying province-specific trends over time. We run three "placebo" regressions to test this: we first control for the immediate years before and after a political leader's term

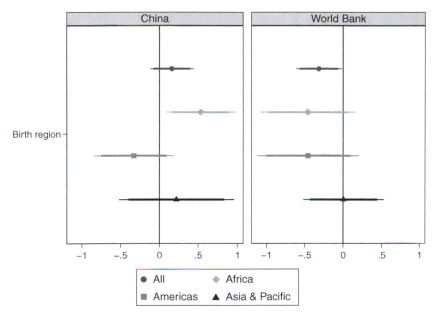

Figure 6.3 Effect of leader birth region on China's and the World Bank's allocation of development finance across provinces, 2000–2013
*Notes:* Each panel of the figure summarizes the results of four regressions. Regression results are based on least-squares regressions with (log) Chinese official finance commitments (left panel) or (log) World Bank official finance commitments (right panel) to a particular province of a developing country as dependent variable. Country-year fixed effects and province fixed effects are included. Each panel displays the effect when birth region is switched from zero to one, in tandem with 90 percent and 95 percent confidence intervals. We cluster standard errors at the country level. We provide full regression results in Table B6.2 of Appendix 6.B.

major regions of the developing world. While there is no effect of birth regions in the global sample, in the Americas, or in Asia and the Pacific, we find that the home provinces of African political leaders receive substantially more funding from China. On average, provinces in African countries

in office, then for the second years before and after the term, then for the third years before and after. We focus on Africa because this is the only world region where we identified a positive significant home-province effect in our province fixed effects specification. We find significant positive birthplace effects only during the leaders' term in office. We show this in Figure A6.3 of Appendix 6.A.

receive 70 percent more funding from China when a leader from that province is in power than the same regions do at other times.[63]

The World Bank results – shown in the right panel of Figure 6.3 – do not indicate similar home-province favoritism. It appears that the more stringent rules and procedures that guide World Bank project approval decisions help shield it from the political interests of African leaders. This finding complements new research undertaken by Ryan Briggs.[64] He has shown that World Bank staff members responsible for project design and implementation are acutely aware of efforts by recipient governments to manipulate their projects for domestic political purposes, and their awareness of this risk may help explain why World Bank projects favor wealthier and less remote subnational jurisdictions (see Box 6.1).[65]

---

### BOX 6.1  Why Does Aid Not Target the Poorest? Experimental Evidence from the World Bank

Ryan Briggs from the University of Guelph recently conducted a conjoint experiment involving 115 World Bank task team leaders (TTLs) to better understand why the World Bank – a multilateral institution that defines its mission as "ending extreme poverty by 2030 and boosting prosperity among the poorest 40 percent in low- and middle-income countries" – does not favor subnational jurisdictions that are primarily populated by poor people.[a] As he explains,

> The conjoint experiment asked respondents to choose one of a pair of hypothetical aid projects that were in the sector and region of the world where they had previously stated that they had the most experience. Each project varied on five dimensions, all of which were independently randomly assigned. Projects could have an *average income of the project location* value of above national average, at national average, or below national average. Projects could be *located* in the capital city, an urban area, on the outskirts of a city, a rural area, or a remote area. Projects had a *political affiliation* of the president's hometown, an area where residents favor the party in power, an area where residents favor an opposition party, an area where residents have weak partisan affiliations, or an area with no political affiliation. Each project had a *budget* that was larger than

---

[63] We computed the average effect as exp(0.531)−1. The corresponding 90 percent confidence interval ranges from 17 percent to 146 percent.

[64] Briggs (2021).

[65] Marx (2018) provides evidence that local politicians implement highly visible World Bank projects right before elections. Doing so allows leaders to claim credit for the projects, which helps them maximize voter turnout and influence results (Cruz and Schneider 2017; Cruz, Keefer, and Labonne 2018; Cruz, Keefer, Labonne, and Trebbi 2018).

**BOX 6.1 Cont**

typical, typical, or smaller than typical. Finally, the *implementing partner* for each project was either the client government or an NGO. This setup yields 450 possible kinds of projects.[b]

Briggs then identified five reasons why aid might not effectively target geographical areas with a disproportionate number of poor people and mapped each of these reasons to a different outcome variable in the experiment. For each pair of projects (with randomly assigned features), he asked participants in the study to identify the project that would (a) more likely be favored by the borrowing government, (b) more likely be approved by the World Bank's Board of Directors, (c) be easier to implement, (d) receive a higher [ex post] outcome rating, and (e) have a larger positive impact on development. Since each pair of projects corresponded to a different outcome variable, every participant in the study made five binary choices for five pairs of projects.

Briggs's analysis of the survey data demonstrates that World Bank staff members responsible for the design and implementation of projects believe that aid has a greater development impact in poor and remote areas, but they are also concerned that project implementation is more difficult in these areas and that client governments will seek to use aid for their own domestic political purposes. Notably, he also finds participants in the experiment believed that client governments would "be most interested in projects that are placed in the president's hometown. When shown a project located in the president's hometown, [World Bank] TTLs select[ed] that project to be of greater interest to the client government more than 70 percent of the time."[c]

[a] A "conjoint experiment" is an experiment carried out to estimate respondents' preferences based on their evaluations of a set of alternatives.
[b] Briggs (2021: 7–8).
[c] Briggs (2021: 8).

The results in Figure 6.3 suggest that the home-province bias in Chinese development finance is only robust for Africa. Should we therefore conclude that Sri Lanka's "airport in the jungle" (see Chapter 1) does not reflect a systematic global pattern? Not necessarily. These results include both aid- and debt-financed Chinese development projects, so we dug deeper to understand which specific types of Chinese development projects drive the birthplace effect in developing countries.

To do so, we reproduced the analyses presented in Figure 6.3 for two subsamples: projects financed with Chinese aid and projects

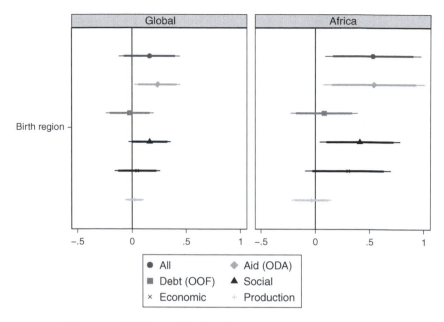

Figure 6.4 Effect of leader birth region on China's allocation of development finance across provinces by flow class and sector, 2000–2013

*Notes:* Each panel of the figure summarizes the results of five regressions. The left panel shows results for the global sample; the right panel shows results for the Africa subsample. Regression results are based on least-squares regressions with (log) Chinese official finance commitments to a particular province of a developing country as dependent variable. The five regressions correspond to the following flow classes and sectors: aid (ODA), debt (OOF), Social Infrastructure & Services ("Social"), Economic Infrastructure & Services ("Economic"), Production Sectors ("Production"). Country-year fixed effects and province fixed effects are included. Each panel displays the effect of birth region switching from zero to one in tandem with 90 percent and 95 percent confidence intervals. We cluster standard errors at the country level. We provide full regression results in Table B6.3 of Appendix 6.B.

financed with Chinese debt.[66] We also reproduced the analyses for different sectors. Figure 6.4 summarizes our results for both the global sample and for Africa. We find that China gives more *aid* to

[66] We include projects categorized as vague official finance in the "debt" subsample since the observable attributes of these projects more closely resemble OOF than ODA.

a province when it is the birthplace of the country's leader than it does to the same province at other times (when other leaders are in power). In contrast, we find no evidence that Chinese *debt* follows the same pattern. This finding is consistent with a core finding from Chapter 5: Chinese aid is generally guided by political criteria and Chinese debt is generally guided by economic and commercial criteria.

Looking at variation across sectors might also help clarify which types of aid projects leaders are most likely to capture. We find strong and positive effects in the social sector, especially in Africa.[67] This suggests that political leaders steer Chinese-supported social infrastructure projects, such as schools, hospitals, and soccer stadiums (projects that typically provide visible benefits to residents) toward their home provinces. By contrast, productive sector projects – like factories, mines, and agricultural demonstration centers – are not more likely to be located in a leader's home province. The same finding holds for economic infrastructure (e.g., roads, bridges, and electricity grids).

Finally, also building upon our earlier work with Roland Holder and Paul Raschky, we investigate whether the birthplace effect is driven by a clientelistic logic of political survival.[68] In Africa, in particular, the logic of political survival is generally governed by clientelism, whereby politicians provide particularistic rewards to their core constituents (or "clients") in exchange for votes.[69] African leaders who must compete in nationwide elections have strong incentives to provide rewards that are targeted to the specific geographic areas where they can best influence election outcomes (see Box 6.2 for an example). A leader should have especially strong incentives to target rewards to geographic areas that are more likely to engage in clientelistic voting than to base their vote on the overall performance of the economy.[70] African politicians' home provinces are likely to have high concentrations of co-partisans and co-ethnics; therefore, they are arguably more likely to participate in clientelistic

---

[67] While this result is similar in the global sample, the coefficient is marginally insignificant. Our results for Africa are broadly in line with those of Dolan and McDade (2020), who tested sectoral effects of Chinese development finance there. They find that regions where the current leader of a country was born have a higher probability than other regions to receive projects in the sectors of education, social infrastructure and services, and energy, but not in agriculture, communication, emergency relief, government, health, or transportation.

[68] Dreher, Fuchs, Hodler et al. (2019).

[69] Wantchekon (2003); van de Walle (2007); Casey (2015).

[70] Engelsma, Milner, and Shi (2017).

voting.[71] They are also less likely to vote based on the overall performance of the economy for several reasons. First, voters in these provinces are more likely to receive and believe misleading information about the political leader (as they are more trusting of the local messengers who transmit such information). Second, even if rational voters from the political leader's home province are disappointed with the performance of the incumbent, they may still support the incumbent if they expect that their co-partisans from the same province will do the same or if they expect worse treatment from a new political leader from another region.

---

### BOX 6.2 The Politics of Chinese Project Sites in Sudan

Sudan provides a useful illustration of how Chinese aid can be used by host government leaders to increase their odds of remaining in power. Since 2000, Sudan has received billions of dollars of Chinese development finance. Many of the projects financed with this money were located within the so-called Hamdi Triangle, an area in the Nile River Valley between the cities of Dongola, Sennar, and El Obeid (in North Kordofan). This area is the heartland of the Arab Riverine tribes and the political base of the ruling National Conference Party (NCP).[a] President Bashir's hometown of Shendi lies squarely within the Hamdi Triangle, along the bank of the Nile River.[b] This area of the country assumed special political significance after 2005, when the authorities in Khartoum signed a Comprehensive Peace Agreement with the Sudan People's Liberation Army (SPLA) that called for presidential and legislative elections in 2010 and a referendum on South Sudan's independence in 2011.

The presidential election and the referendum posed political threats to the incumbent; in response, Abdel Rahim Hamdi – a political strategist for the NCP and former minister of finance – laid out a "grand strategy" for domestic political survival at a 2005 NCP conference.[c] He argued that the ruling party's electoral fortunes would hinge on its ability to deliver job opportunities and public services to the core constituents in the area between Dongola, Sennar, and El Obeid; therefore, he called for concentrated investment in this area. He argued that Sudan would have to seek non-Western funding to target particularistic rewards to local residents.[d] In the years following the adoption of this strategy, Sudan solicited and secured approval for many Chinese development projects to be sited in these areas and in other pro-NCP constituencies.[e] Hamdi may have been on to something; President Bashir was easily reelected in 2010 with 68 percent of the vote.

[a] Roessler (2013).

---

[71] Wahman and Boone (2018).

> **BOX 6.2  Cont**
>
> [b] Verhoeven (2015).
>
> [c] Hamdi (2005).
>
> [d] Specifically, Hamdi (2005) wrote: "Financial flows . . . from [Western] institutions will be characterized by the following: they will be late; will be far less than promised; they will be surrounded by rules and bureaucracy. . . . Investment funds will go to areas that are already predetermined in the [Comprehensive Peace Agreement]; this is, to the [G]eographical [S]outh with its defined borders, Nuba Mountains, Southern Blue Nile. Moreover, these investment funds will be supervised by certain Commissions which ensure that they go to the specified zones only. Due to these facts, foreign investment will remain out of our hands and will not benefit the North much. In a sharp contrast to that, [non-Western] investment, both official and private will go to the Geographical North."
>
> [e] Roessler (2013).

This logic implies that the bias toward the home provinces of political incumbents should become more pronounced in political systems with competitive elections. We first tested this hypothesis for Africa in joint work with Roland Hodler and Paul Raschky by leveraging an index that measures the electoral competitiveness of executive elections (with higher values indicating higher competitiveness).[72] Now, we test this hypothesis with a global sample. As shown in the left panel of Figure 6.5, more Chinese development finance is channeled to the home provinces of political leaders in countries that have highly competitive executive elections (where the index reaches its highest value on the 0–6 scale, which is the case for 71 percent of the observations in our global sample). This effect is observable not only when we focus on all world regions combined but also when we analyze Africa separately.

Building again on our past work with Hodler and Raschky, we examine whether the *timing* of executive elections also matters. Our expectation is that political leaders will be especially interested in providing particularistic rewards (in the form of Chinese development projects) immediately prior to executive elections. We account for election timing in an additional set of statistical models, which we also summarize in Figure 6.5.

---

[72] Dreher, Fuchs, Hodler et al. (2019). We take these data from the Database of Political Institutions (Beck, Clarke, Groff et al. 2001). For ease of interpretation, we rescale the index so that it ranges from zero to six.

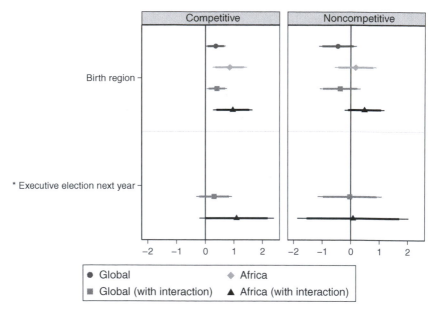

Figure 6.5 Effect of leader birthplace on China's allocation of development finance across provinces by competitiveness of executive elections, 2000–2013

*Notes:* Each panel shows the results from four regressions. The left panel shows results for the subsample of countries with competitive elections; the right panel shows results for the subsample of countries without competitive elections. Regression results are based on least-squares regressions with (log) Chinese official finance commitments to a particular province of a developing country as dependent variable. Country-year fixed effects and province fixed effects are included. Each panel displays the effect of birth region switching from zero to one in tandem with 90 percent and 95 percent confidence intervals. The specifications "with interaction" show the additional effect of birth region if an executive election takes place in the following year. We cluster standard errors at the country level. We provide full regression results in Table B6.4 of Appendix 6.B.

We find that the home-province effect in Africa is stronger in the year prior to an executive election.[73] On average, in African countries with competitive elections, Chinese development finance increases by 134 percent in the home province of the current political leader. Funding from China triples

---

[73] The coefficient for the global sample is also positive but imprecisely estimated.

in addition if elections are scheduled to take place in the following year.[74] These results suggest that the clientelistic logic of political survival does in fact help explain why the home provinces of incumbent leaders disproportionately benefit from the receipt of Chinese development finance.

In Africa, clientelism and presidential political systems are widespread. Therefore, China's demand-driven project selection system is particularly vulnerable to African leaders using aid for clientelistic purposes. But this is only part of the problem. Equally troubling is that Chinese government institutions do not have robust institutional safeguards in place to detect and discourage politicians from using their projects for domestic political purposes. China administers a flexible and responsive project identification system, and it invites politicians rather than technocrats to participate in this system, so the candidate projects that it considers for approval usually reflect the political motivations of the leaders who submit the proposals in the first place.[75] While we have focused in this chapter on the home provinces of political leaders to detect one source of political bias, this is certainly not the only way that political motivations can influence the subnational distribution of Chinese development projects. Chinese development finance could also be allocated to politically competitive jurisdictions (to swing election outcomes), areas with ethnic ties to government leaders, or territorial enclaves where the state does not yet enjoy a monopoly on the use of force.[76] We hope that other social scientists will take up this research agenda.

---

[74] Using the results in column 4 of Table B6.4, these marginal effects are calculated as exp (0.852)−1 and exp(1.096)−1, respectively.

[75] China's demand-driven project selection system also encourages collusion between host country politicians and Chinese contractors. As Denghua Zhang and Graeme Smith explain, "[i]n some circumstances, Chinese firms and host governments enter into an informal alliance in which China's companies persuade host governments to raise new aid projects with China while the contractors promise to help behind the scenes to secure financing. The projects are reverse-engineered to suit the political needs of local politicians and the commercial strategies of Chinese contractors. Recipient governments propose to the Chinese government that they want these companies to do the aid projects, in line with the principle of local ownership. One government official [from Papua New Guinea] explained: 'All of these projects look like well-thought-out technical solutions, but each of them arise from contractors knocking on politicians' doors, giving them bright ideas, and then they become the owners of those ideas'" (Zhang and Smith 2017: 2335). Similarly, Deborah Bräutigam has argued that "[t]he Achilles Heel of China's bank financing model is that it relies heavily on Chinese companies to develop projects together with host country officials. This creates strong incentives for kickbacks and inflated project costs. Particularly in election years, companies and public works ministers may collude to get projects approved" (Bräutigam 2019).

[76] Engelsma, Milner, and Shi (2017); Dreher, Fuchs, Hodler et al. (2019); Gehring, Kaplan, and Wong (2019); Anaxagorou, Efthyvoulou, and Sarantides (2020).

## Conclusion: The President's Wish List Trumps Socioeconomic Need

Our findings in this chapter indicate that Chinese development finance does not go to the geographic areas within recipient countries where it is most needed: much of it ends up in wealthier provinces. Chinese development projects also favor politically privileged jurisdictions: the home provinces of political leaders receive substantially more Chinese development finance in countries with competitive elections, and even more at election time. This is a problem from a development perspective because, even before the receipt of Chinese development finance, the average home province of a political leader is significantly wealthier than the rest of the country. Therefore, if Chinese development finance improves local socioeconomic outcomes (an issue we explore in Chapter 7), it may cement or widen inequalities between politically privileged and politically marginalized jurisdictions.

This pattern of resource allocation also highlights the fact that in many countries, the subnational allocation of Chinese government funding is a product – and a reflection – of the recipient country's political system and culture.[77] If Chinese government institutions had institutional safeguards designed to privilege economic considerations over political considerations during the project identification and design phase, this type of bias would probably be less acute. This notion is borne out by the fact that the World Bank, which uses ex ante cost-benefit analysis to vet project proposals based on economic viability rather than their political value, does not disproportionately site its development projects in the home provinces of political leaders (in any region of the world).

However, there is a silver lining: projects financed with Chinese aid are more vulnerable to political manipulation than projects financed with Chinese debt; therefore, as Beijing continues its transition from benefactor to banker, the percentage of its overseas portfolio that is plagued by home region bias should shrink.

In the next chapter, we turn to the empirical question of whether Chinese development finance improves development outcomes. We also test whether Chinese development projects are less effective when they are subject to the political motivations that we document in this and the previous chapter.

---

[77] Recent research by Cervellati, Esposito, Sunde, and Yuan (2020) shows that the disease environment in recipient countries can also play an important role: regions with a high malaria risk have a lower density of Chinese development projects and host fewer Chinese workers.

## Appendix 6.A
## Additional Figures

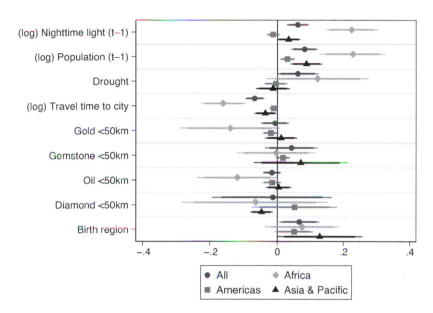

Figure A6.1 Correlates of China's allocation of development finance across provinces (project count, 2000–2013)

*Notes:* The figure summarizes the results of four regressions. Regression results are based on least-squares regressions with the number of Chinese development projects to a particular province of a developing country as dependent variable. Country-year fixed effects are included. Each panel displays the effect of a one-standard-deviation change of the respective explanatory variable (or the effect of switching from zero to one in the case of binary variables) in tandem with 90 percent and 95 percent confidence intervals. We cluster standard errors at the country level.

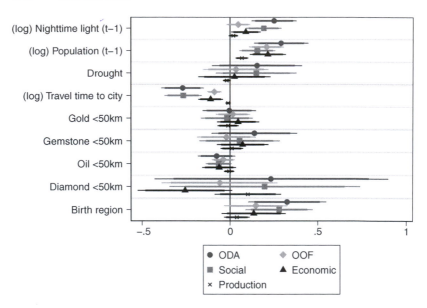

Figure A6.2 Correlates of China's allocation of development finance across provinces by flow class and sector, 2000–2013

*Notes:* The figure summarizes the results of five regressions. Regression results are based on least-squares regressions with (log) Chinese official finance commitments to a particular province of a developing country as dependent variable. The five regressions correspond to the following flow classes and sectors: aid (ODA), debt (OOF), Social Infrastructure & Services ("Social"), Economic Infrastructure & Services ("Economic"), Production Sectors ("Production"). Country-year fixed effects are included. Each panel displays the effect of a one-standard-deviation change of the respective explanatory variable (or the effect of switching from zero to one in the case of binary variables) in tandem with 90 percent and 95 percent confidence intervals. We cluster standard errors at the country level.

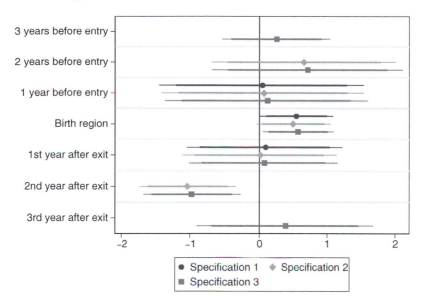

Figure A6.3 Effect of leader birth region on China's allocation of development finance across provinces (Africa, 2000–2013, with "placebo test")

*Notes:* The figure summarizes the results of three regressions. Regression results are based on least-squares regressions with (log) Chinese official finance commitments to a particular province of a developing country as dependent variable. Country-year fixed effects and province fixed effects are included. Each panel displays the effect of "birth region" switching from zero to one in tandem with 90 percent and 95 percent confidence intervals. Specifications 1–3 include a binary indicator equal to one in the year before a region becomes the birth region of the (new) political leader and a binary indicator equal to one in the year in which a region is no longer the birth region of the (old) political leader. Specifications 2–3 include a binary indicator equal to one in the second year before a region becomes the birth region of the (new) political leader and a binary indicator equal to one in the second year in which a region is no longer the birth region of the (old) political leader. Specification 3 includes a binary indicator equal to one in the third year before a region becomes the birth region of the (new) political leader and a binary indicator equal to one in the third year in which a region is no longer the birth region of the (old) political leader. A statistically significant coefficient on variables that indicate that a region will become the birth region in the future would imply that the political leaders' birth regions received more Chinese funding before political leaders assumed power, which would cast doubt on our interpretation that these regions receive more Chinese funding because political leaders favor them. By contrast, a statistically significant coefficient on variables that indicate that a region was the birth region in the past would not necessarily invalidate a causal interpretation. It might well be that part of the funding pledged for a birth region is formally committed right after the leader left office. We cluster standard errors at the country level.

Table B6.1 *Correlates of China's allocation of development finance within countries, 2000–2013*

| | China | | | | World Bank | | | |
|---|---|---|---|---|---|---|---|---|
| | (1) | (2) | (3) | (4) | (5) | (6) | (7) | (8) |
| (log) Nighttime light | 0.273*** | 0.945*** | -0.178* | 0.227** | 0.189 | 0.568*** | -0.278 | 0.378* |
| | (0.001) | (0.000) | (0.083) | (0.015) | (0.147) | (0.001) | (0.198) | (0.077) |
| (log) Population | 0.456*** | 0.960*** | 0.159** | 0.629*** | 1.543*** | 1.618*** | 1.479*** | 1.951*** |
| | (0.000) | (0.000) | (0.030) | (0.000) | (0.000) | (0.000) | (0.000) | (0.000) |
| Drought | 0.161 | 0.446 | -0.222 | -0.099 | 0.256 | 0.199 | 0.509 | 0.233 |
| | (0.304) | (0.200) | (0.205) | (0.747) | (0.260) | (0.654) | (0.243) | (0.637) |
| (log) Travel time to city | -0.336*** | -0.730*** | -0.191*** | -0.197** | 0.082 | -0.246*** | 0.287* | 0.299** |
| | (0.000) | (0.000) | (0.001) | (0.023) | (0.259) | (0.009) | (0.086) | (0.015) |
| Gold <50 km | 0.003 | -0.486 | -0.080 | 0.108 | -0.014 | -0.515* | -0.124 | 0.232 |
| | (0.973) | (0.112) | (0.477) | (0.402) | (0.934) | (0.077) | (0.345) | (0.588) |
| Gemstone <50 km | 0.109 | -0.125 | -0.002 | 0.225 | 0.013 | 0.722 | -0.846* | -0.233 |
| | (0.449) | (0.518) | (0.972) | (0.393) | (0.964) | (0.104) | (0.065) | (0.375) |
| Oil <50 km | -0.126* | -0.685** | 0.005 | 0.003 | -0.182* | -0.052 | 0.084 | -0.407** |
| | (0.065) | (0.019) | (0.962) | (0.975) | (0.099) | (0.836) | (0.717) | (0.025) |
| Diamond <50 km | 0.120 | -0.011 | 0.130 | -0.356*** | -0.011 | -0.146 | 0.488 | -0.893*** |
| | (0.750) | (0.979) | (0.831) | (0.001) | (0.966) | (0.639) | (0.250) | (0.001) |
| Birth region | 0.417*** | 0.580** | 0.187 | 0.673* | -0.004 | 0.017 | -0.193 | 0.210 |
| | (0.005) | (0.018) | (0.435) | (0.063) | (0.975) | (0.933) | (0.242) | (0.406) |

| | (1) | (2) | (3) | (4) | (5) | (6) | (7) | (8) |
|---|---|---|---|---|---|---|---|---|
| R-Squared | 0.31 | 0.34 | 0.17 | 0.29 | 0.57 | 0.59 | 0.60 | 0.59 |
| Number of countries | 132 | 51 | 24 | 38 | 132 | 51 | 24 | 38 |
| Number of observations | 33,808 | 10,780 | 6,036 | 11,134 | 33,808 | 10,780 | 6,036 | 11,134 |

*Notes*: Regression results are based on least-squares regressions with (log) official finance commitments by China (columns 1–4) or the World Bank (columns 5–8) to a particular province of a developing country in one of four regions as dependent variable. Country-year fixed effects are included. The four regions are Global (columns 1 and 5), Africa (columns 2 and 6), Americas (columns 3 and 7), or Asia (columns 4 and 8). We cluster standard errors at the country level. The corresponding marginal effects are illustrated in Figure 6.2. p-values in parentheses. * significant at the 10% level, ** significant at the 5% level, *** significant at the 1% level.

Table B6.2 *Effect of leader birth region on China's and the World Bank's allocation of development finance within countries, 2000–2013*

| | China | | | | World Bank | | | |
|---|---|---|---|---|---|---|---|---|
| | (1) | (2) | (3) | (4) | (5) | (6) | (7) | (8) |
| Birth region | 0.174 | 0.531** | -0.330 | 0.268 | −0.299** | −0.461 | −0.456 | 0.075 |
| | (0.223) | (0.020) | (0.195) | (0.465) | (0.049) | (0.140) | (0.168) | (0.768) |
| R-Squared | 0.41 | 0.44 | 0.26 | 0.38 | 0.63 | 0.64 | 0.64 | 0.64 |
| Number of countries | 136 | 53 | 25 | 38 | 136 | 53 | 25 | 38 |
| Number of observations | 34,845 | 11,347 | 6,156 | 11,427 | 34,845 | 11,347 | 6,156 | 11,427 |

*Notes:* Regression results are based on least-squares regressions with (log) official finance commitments by China (columns 1–4) or the World Bank (columns 5–8) to a particular province of a developing country in one of four regions as dependent variable. Country-year-fixed effects and province-fixed effects are included. The four regions are Global (columns 1 and 5), Africa (columns 2 and 6), Americas (columns 3 and 7), or Asia (columns 4 and 8). We cluster standard errors at the country level. The corresponding marginal effects are illustrated in Figure 6.3. p-values in parentheses. * significant at the 10% level, ** significant at the 5% level, *** significant at the 1% level.

Table B6.3 *Effect of leader birth region on China's allocation of development finance within countries by flow class and sector, 2000–2013*

| | Global | | | | | Africa | | | | |
|---|---|---|---|---|---|---|---|---|---|---|
| | (1) | (2) | (3) | (4) | (5) | (6) | (7) | (8) | (9) | (10) |
| Birth region | 0.231** | −0.006 | 0.162 | 0.058 | 0.021 | 0.540** | 0.080 | 0.410** | 0.303 | −0.035 |
| | (0.034) | (0.956) | (0.103) | (0.583) | (0.620) | (0.024) | (0.606) | (0.031) | (0.131) | (0.700) |
| R-Squared | 0.38 | 0.35 | 0.39 | 0.36 | 0.26 | 0.39 | 0.41 | 0.43 | 0.35 | 0.36 |
| Number of countries | 136 | 136 | 136 | 136 | 136 | 53 | 53 | 53 | 53 | 53 |
| Number of observations | 34,845 | 34,845 | 34,845 | 34,845 | 34,845 | 11,347 | 11,347 | 11,347 | 11,347 | 11,347 |

*Notes:* Regression results are based on least-squares regressions with one of five flow classes and sectors of Chinese development finance commitments to a particular province of a developing country worldwide ("Global," columns 1–5), or in Africa (columns 6–10) as dependent variable. Country-year-fixed effects and province-fixed effects are included. The five flow classes and sectors are ODA (columns 1 and 6), OOF (columns 2 and 7), Social Infrastructure & Services (columns 3 and 8), Economic Infrastructure & Services (columns 4 and 9), and Production Sectors (columns 5 and 10). We cluster standard errors at the country level. The corresponding marginal effects are illustrated in Figure 6.4. p-values in parentheses. * significant at the 10% level, ** significant at the 5% level, *** significant at the 1% level.

Table B6.4 *Effect of leader birth region on China's allocation of development finance within countries by competitiveness of executive elections, 2000–2013*

|  | Competitive | | | | Noncompetitive | | | |
|---|---|---|---|---|---|---|---|---|
|  | (1) | (2) | (3) | (4) | (5) | (6) | (7) | (8) |
| Birth region | 0.361** | 0.852*** | 0.403** | 0.962*** | −0.454 | 0.172 | −0.374 | 0.479 |
|  | (0.042) | (0.007) | (0.026) | (0.008) | (0.174) | (0.637) | (0.295) | (0.171) |
| Birth region * executive election |  |  | 0.302 | 1.096* |  |  | −0.034 | 0.082 |
|  |  |  | (0.342) | (0.097) |  |  | (0.952) | (0.932) |
| R-Squared | 0.42 | 0.45 | 0.42 | 0.45 | 0.42 | 0.46 | 0.42 | 0.46 |
| Number of countries | 95 | 35 | 95 | 35 | 69 | 35 | 69 | 35 |
| Number of observations | 24,025 | 6,638 | 23,930 | 6,607 | 9,541 | 4,138 | 9,494 | 4,114 |

*Notes:* Regression results are based on least-squares regressions with (log) Chinese OF commitments to a particular province of a developing country with competitive executive elections (columns 1–4) or noncompetitive executive elections (columns 5–8) in one of two world regions as dependent variable. Country-year-fixed effects and province-fixed effects are included. The two world regions are "Global" (columns 1, 3, 5, and 7) and Africa (columns 2, 4, 6, and 8). We cluster standard errors at the country level. The corresponding marginal effects are illustrated in Figure 6.5. p-values in parentheses. * significant at the 10% level, ** significant at the 5% level, *** significant at the 1% level.

Table B6.5  *Descriptive statistics*

|  | count | mean | sd | min | max |
|---|---|---|---|---|---|
| (log) Chinese official finance (OF) | 34,867 | .6510326 | 3.221126 | 0 | 23.73667 |
| (log) Chinese aid (ODA) | 34,867 | .4129948 | 2.501776 | 0 | 20.79561 |
| (log) Chinese debt (OOF) | 34,867 | .286621 | 2.246398 | 0 | 23.73667 |
| (log) Chinese social OF | 34,867 | .2243593 | 1.840269 | 0 | 21.52076 |
| (log) Chinese economic OF | 34,867 | .3421152 | 2.436061 | 0 | 23.73667 |
| (log) Chinese production OF | 34,867 | .0751794 | 1.120363 | 0 | 21.07329 |
| (log) World Bank official OF | 34,867 | 3.207227 | 6.208263 | 0 | 21.11421 |
| (log) Night time light ($t-1$) | 53,163 | −3.406375 | .9589268 | −4.60517 | 3.64593 |
| (log) Population ($t-1$) | 53,184 | 12.9259 | 1.721617 | −4.60517 | 19.15912 |
| Drought | 54,121 | .0114558 | .106418 | 0 | 1 |
| (log) Travel time to city | 55,909 | 5.411484 | .9632204 | 1.501657 | 8.514017 |
| Gold <50 km | 55,931 | .0792763 | .2701719 | 0 | 1 |
| Gemstone <50 km | 55,931 | .0435179 | .2040217 | 0 | 1 |
| Oil <50 km | 55,931 | .232018 | .4221242 | 0 | 1 |
| Diamond <50 km | 55,931 | .016127 | .1259651 | 0 | 1 |
| Birth region | 55,931 | .0543348 | .2266792 | 0 | 1 |
| Executive election | 41,243 | .700725 | .457946 | 0 | 1 |

# 7 Paving the Way to Growth and Development?
## The Socioeconomic Impacts of Chinese Development Projects

In 2009, China Eximbank approved a loan to the government of Kenya to widen and upgrade a 50.4-kilometer highway from Nairobi City Center to the town of Thika in Kiambu County. The project was designed to reduce congestion and travel times between Nairobi and a set of satellite towns along a critically important transportation corridor.[1] Kenyans increasingly rely on employment, education, and services in Nairobi, but they prefer to live in less crowded and less expensive peri-urban and suburban areas within commuting distance of the country's capital. Consequently, these areas have experienced high levels of population growth, which has placed a strain on the roads to and from Nairobi. Before the project began, one study analyzing the severity of this problem along the Nairobi-Thika Highway found that "[t]raffic demand ... [was] almost twice the existing capacity."[2]

The project was implemented by three Chinese contractors between 2009 and 2012, and by nearly all accounts it was well executed.[3] Upon completion, traffic flows increased from 85,000 vehicles per day to 123,000 vehicles per day and journey speeds rose from 8 kilometers per hour to at least 45 kilometers per hour in sections with the highest levels of traffic. Average commuting times from Thika to Nairobi fell from

---

This chapter draws selectively upon empirical results, prose, and arguments from four prior studies: Bluhm, Dreher, Fuchs et al. (2021), Cruzatti, Dreher, and Matzat (2020), Dreher, Fuchs, Parks et al. (2021), and Dreher, Fuchs, Hodler et al. (2021). These articles include more technical empirical analysis and additional links to previous research.

[1] Details on this case can be found in African Development Fund (ADF) (2007); KARA and CSUD (2012); African Development Bank (AfDB) (2014a, 2014b).

[2] African Development Bank (2016: 9). The purpose of the project was to accommodate higher levels of vehicular traffic, increase time savings for passengers and cargo, and reduce the costs of motorized vehicle operation and road maintenance.

[3] Based on a set of field and laboratory test results that the AfDB commissioned externally after project completion, the Nairobi-Thika Highway achieved an overall quality rating of good (African Development Bank 2014a: 294). An ex post evaluation of the project also revealed that the quality of the work performed by AfDB-financed contractors and China Eximbank-financed contractors was comparable (African Development Bank 2014a: 121). However, the AfDB-funded road work experienced larger cost overruns than the China Eximbank-funded road work (African Development Bank (2014a: 294).

2–3 hours to 30–45 minutes.[4] Prior to the start of the project, the African Development Bank (AfDB) conducted a cost-benefit analysis that projected a 30 percent economic rate of return. At project closure, the AfDB updated its cost-benefit analysis and found that the project's actual economic rate of return was closer to 25 percent – still much higher than the 12 percent opportunity cost of capital in Kenya.

Figure 7.1 shows the route of the highway and the crossroads and interchanges that were constructed or rehabilitated as part of the project. It uses remotely sensed nighttime light data to visualize changes in economic activity that took place between 2008 and 2013.[5] Economic activity became substantially less concentrated in the core of Nairobi during and after the implementation of the project. It spread out along the transport corridor; many of the largest increases in economic activity took place near the crossroads and interchanges that were constructed or rehabilitated to better connect satellite towns to the highway. Between 2008 and 2013, the geographical areas within a 4-kilometer buffer around the Nairobi-Thika Highway experienced an approximately 53 percent increase in average nighttime light output.[6] The project also substantially reduced the concentration of economic activity as people and businesses moved to new locations that became economically viable: the areas within a 4-kilometer buffer of the highway experienced a 27 percent reduction in the spatial concentration of nighttime light output.[7] At the same time, land values doubled in Thika and rose even faster in areas closer to Nairobi (like Kasarani, where land values increased from US$46,000 per acre to US$500,000 per acre); farmgate prices (the market value of a product minus selling costs) for dairy products and

---

[4] See, for example, KARA and CSUD (2012). According to African Development Bank (2014b), "[t]he road has … spurred the establishment of new manufacturing, food processing, and small and medium enterprises" and "brought employment opportunities to the people along the road corridor."

[5] "NTL Change" on the map refers to the change in nighttime light output measured in the year 2013 compared with 2008.

[6] Critics of the project noted that the highway improvements would make it easier for residents of President Kibaki's home district (Othaya) to travel to and from Nairobi (Cummings and Obwocha 2018). While this would be consistent with our result from Chapter 6 that leaders' birthplaces are more likely to receive aid, Othaya is located nearly 100 kilometers north of the end point (Thika) of the highway; in addition, Figure 7.1 suggests that the economic benefits generated by the project primarily went to satellite towns along the 50-kilometer corridor, not to locations far beyond the project area.

[7] In this chapter, we use the terms "spatial concentration," "spatial inequality," and "spatial decentralization" of economic activity interchangeably, as they all refer to changes in the distribution of people and output across geographic space. Spatial concentration, as measured by the Gini coefficient introduced later in this chapter, fell from 0.425 in 2008 to 0.31 in 2013 in the 4-kilometer buffer.

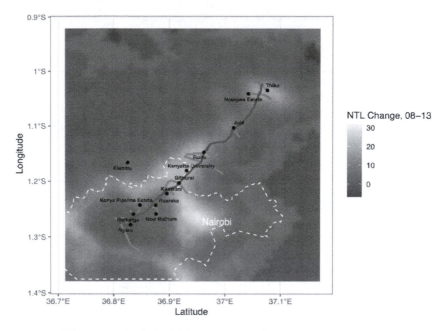

Figure 7.1 Nairobi-Thika Highway: Change in nighttime light (NTL)
output from 2008 to 2013
Source: Bluhm, Dreher, Fuchs et al. (2020)

horticulture rose due to increased access to markets; and trade and
investment alongside the road corridor expanded.

These are impressive results, but we could have just as easily
turned a spotlight on a Chinese government-financed road that had
fallen into a state of disrepair, an airport in a rural outpost that sits
unused, or a seaport with almost no container traffic. As just one
example of a "white elephant" project (that resulted from the type of
political capture that we describe in Chapter 6), consider this firsthand
account by a World Bank official stationed in Equatorial Guinea:

During the reign of [President Francisco] Macias, the Chinese had been big in
Equatorial Guinea and still had a significant presence. Their aid projects were
highly visible.... They laid a modern beautiful road on the continent from beyond
Niefang through the hinterland to Mongomo, the hometown of [former
President] Macias and of the current president and his clan. This road, probably
the best in the country, was used by only a few vehicles every day.[8]

---

[8] We draw this description of the Nkue-Mongomo road project from Klitgaard (1990: 96).

Individual case studies like that of the Nairobi-Thika highway in Kenya and the Nkue-Mongomo road in Equatorial Guinea are not generalizable; for that reason, they are ultimately unsatisfying as explanations for the effects of Chinese development finance. Unfortunately, politicians, journalists, and researchers who offer cherry-picked cases rather than systematically gathered evidence that is broadly generalizable dominate much of the existing debate about the effectiveness of Chinese development projects. Beijing's critics point out that its government agencies and state-owned banks have relatively weak internal systems for appraising the economic viability of potential projects, making it easy for politically motivated projects to get approved. This assertion is borne out by our analyses in Chapter 6. However, another popular criticism – that Chinese development projects generate few economic benefits – remains largely untested.

Beijing's critics claim that in its zeal to help partner countries efficiently install the "hardware" of economic development (e.g., highways, railroads, dams, and bridges), it has prioritized speed over quality during project implementation.[9] A separate but related argument is that Chinese state-owned banks do not adequately account for repayment capacity, thereby saddling developing country governments – and their taxpayers – with unsustainable debt burdens.[10] These critiques have quickly become the conventional wisdom outside of China. Ricardo Hausmann, director of the Growth Lab at Harvard's Center for International Development, argues that "Chinese development finance ... delivers a corruption-filled sugar high to the economy, followed by a nasty financial (and sometimes political) hangover."[11] According to *The Economist*, "China seems to be repeating many of the mistakes made by Western donors and investors in the 1970s, when money flowed into big ... infrastructure projects that never produced the expected economic gains."[12]

The OECD-DAC aid agencies and multilateral development banks insist that they have learned from mistakes of the past – and developed robust standards and safeguards to ensure that their projects are

---

[9] See, for example, Shepard (2016); Doig (2019).

[10] See, for example, Hurley, Morris, and Portelance (2019); Kapstein and Shapiro (2019). In August 2018, fifteen US senators wrote a letter to US Treasury Secretary Steve Mnuchin and US Secretary of State Mike Pompeo to express grave concern about this issue (Perdue, Blunt, Cornyn et al. 2018).

[11] Hausmann (2019). Hausmann previously served as the chief economist of the Inter-American Development Bank and the minister of planning for Venezuela. He is certainly not the only social scientist who is skeptical of the economic value of the BRI and other Chinese government-financed development projects (e.g., Ansar, Flyvbjerg, Budzier, and Lunn 2016).

[12] The Economist (2017a). For an early version of this thesis that gained traction in the West, see Naím (2007).

implemented in careful and sustainable ways – but Beijing has not. They claim that China does not mitigate social and environmental risks or adhere to international competitive bidding rules, does not blacklist contractors that engage in fraudulent or corrupt behavior, and does not subject projects to rigorous monitoring and evaluation procedures.[13]

Leaders of developing countries, on the other hand, lavish praise on the Chinese government for its willingness to bankroll and expeditiously implement large-scale infrastructure projects that Western and multilateral donors and creditors will not. Abdoulaye Wade, during his tenure as the president of Senegal, admonished Western donors for their cumbersome bureaucratic procedures, noting that "a contract that would take five years to discuss, negotiate and sign with the World Bank takes three months when we have dealt with the Chinese authorities."[14] Some developing country leaders have gone further, singling out China as a major driver of economic growth in their countries. Meles Zenawi, the former prime minister of Ethiopia, insisted that "one of the main reasons for [the] turnaround in the economic fate of Africa is the emergence of the emerging nations in general and China in particular."[15]

In this chapter, we move beyond cherry-picked cases and test these competing claims using data on China's entire development finance portfolio. To do so, we evaluate the effects of Chinese development projects on a core set of national and subnational development outcomes: economic development, population health, and the spatial concentration of economic activity. We use the World Bank as a benchmark for testing whether the effects of Chinese development projects are superior or inferior to those funded by traditional donors and creditors. China and the World Bank are peers – and competitors – in that their project portfolios are roughly comparable in size and

---

[13] Parks (2019). In 2018, the president of the Asian Infrastructure Investment Bank (AIIB) said that "[f]or Belt and Road projects … broad consultation is really the key … to prevent … white elephants.… [We] are very careful before we put our resources in any project. Working with us you're safe" (Ge 2018).

[14] Wade (2008).

[15] See interview excerpts from 2012 at http://et.china-embassy.org/eng/zagx/t899134.htm (accessed October 12, 2019). A 2012 *Christian Science Monitor* profile of the late prime minister suggests that he purposefully used Chinese aid and debt to fund "growth sector" projects that Western donors and creditors would not fund: "[r]egarded as shrewd even by his most vitriolic critics, Meles positioned the country expertly, allowing it to develop according to his unique [policy] prescriptions, while being supported by diverse allies.… [US]$3 billion of Western aid poured in for food aid, health facilities, and schools every year, while Chinese loans paid for infrastructure such as hydropower dams and a railway network" (Davison 2012).

geographical scope.[16] Also, like China, the World Bank manages a significant portfolio of aid-financed projects (through a concessional window called the IDA) and debt-financed projects (through a semi-concessional and non-concessional window called the IBRD).[17] These similarities make the World Bank an especially useful comparator.

### Why Chinese Development Projects Might Be More – or Less – Effective Than Western Bilateral and Multilateral Development Projects

There are several reasons why Chinese development projects might be equally effective as – or even more effective than – development projects from OECD-DAC aid agencies and multilateral development banks. First, unlike Western donors and creditors, China prefers to fund an integrated package of projects that is aligned with a host country's national development strategy.[18] It will often colocate a set of complementary projects in specific geographic areas to nurture local markets, create clusters of interdependent firms, spur additional investment, or catalyze economic agglomeration processes.[19] Ethiopia is a case in point. To establish this East African nation as a hub for light manufacturing, the Ethiopian authorities adopted a "Growth and Transformation Plan II" that prioritized the creation of eight industrial parks where, by 2020,

---

[16] Morris, Parks, and Gardner (2020) and Zeitz (2021).

[17] For the three core development outcomes that we analyze in this chapter, we can also generate results for the World Bank using data and methods of analysis that are comparable to those we use for China. We have access to geocoded World Bank and Chinese project data for the same five world regions (Africa, Asia and Pacific, Latin America and the Caribbean, and the Middle East) over the same period of time (2000–2014), which allows us to measure the effects of Chinese and World Bank development projects over a consistent set of spatial and temporal scales.

[18] Chin and Gallagher (2019: 256) note that "[w]hereas Western-backed [development finance institutions] and [multilateral development banks] conduct individual project financing, China's policy banks, at home and abroad, take a ... portfolio approach and finance what they refer to as 'strategic credit spaces' where bundles of loans or lines of credit are issued for an array of coordinated and corresponding projects." They also point out that after China negotiates a *package* of projects with a host country's political leader, it evaluates risk across the package as a whole, rather than on a project-by-project basis (Chin and Gallagher 2019: 254). Coordinated public investment strategies have a rich intellectual history related to "big push" theory (Rosenstein-Rodan 1943: 1961) and "growth pole" theory (Perroux 1950; Hirschman 1958), and Chin and Gallagher (2019: 251) note that "[s]ome in the senior ranks of the Chinese state policy banks have drawn inspiration from ['big push' theory], including the former chief economist at the China Development Bank [CDB], Lixing Zou, who saw CDB as having played such a coordinating role within the Chinese growth miracle."

[19] Li, Newenham-Kahindi, Shapiro, and Chen (2013: 306–307); Bunte, Desai, Gbala et al. (2018).

foreign investors would benefit from high-quality infrastructure, tax breaks, and special regulations. China agreed to build one of these industrial parks in the city of Hawassa; in an effort to maximize exports from this special economic zone, it agreed to reduce the cost of transportation by financing the construction of two expressways (the Addis-Adama expressway and the Mojo-Hawassa expressway) linking the industrial park in Hawassa to a dry port in Mojo. Beijing also financed the construction of the Addis Ababa-Djibouti railway to connect the dry port in Mojo to a seaport in Djibouti. Indeed, Figure 7.2 suggests that the placement of the railway in close proximity to eight industrial parks (all of which produce goods for export) was designed to maximize the economic multiplier effect of the infrastructure investment.[20]

Second, China and its Western peers often prioritize different sectors of the economy when they provide development finance. OECD-DAC and multilateral suppliers of development finance have a variety of interests and objectives that are only loosely related to the goal of promoting economic development – for example, providing relief to refugees and internally displaced persons, combatting climate change and biodiversity loss, removing land mines, and promoting human rights. China, by comparison, focuses the vast majority of its funding on economic and social infrastructure (see Chapter 4), which can directly address some of the key constraints to economic development in ways that other cross-border financial flows cannot.[21] For example, roads and railways can make it easier for firms to get products to market and improve access to public services; dams can increase irrigated land for agricultural production; and electrification programs can reduce the amount of time that households spend collecting firewood for cooking and lighting, thereby increasing employment and improving human health (via reduced exposure to indoor air pollution).[22]

[20] World Bank (2019).

[21] Western suppliers of development finance have dramatically scaled back their funding to the infrastructure sector (Hicks, Parks, Roberts, and Tierney 2008; Tierney, Nielson, Hawkins et al. 2011). David Dollar, who previously served as the World Bank's country director for China (2004–2009) and the US Treasury Department's economic and financial emissary to China (2009–2013), has argued that this gap exists because "Western donors have by and large gotten out of hard infrastructure sectors ... and [t]hey [instead] channel their assistance overwhelmingly to social sectors or to infrastructure sectors such as water supply and sanitation that have direct effects on household health" (Dollar 2008).

[22] See, for example, Dinkelman (2011); Grimm, Sparrow, and Tasciotti (2015). The differences in sectors that are funded by China and other donors and lenders may be particularly important since the developing world has large unmet infrastructure needs (Fay, Toman, Benitez, and Csordas 2011).

Figure 7.2 The clustering of industrial parks alongside the China Eximbank-financed Addis Ababa-Djibouti Railway
*Notes:* We are grateful to Weng Lingfei of Chongqing University and Jeffrey Sayer of the University of British Columbia for sharing this map and giving us permission to republish it. See Weng and Sayer (2019).

Third, China has a reputation for implementing large-scale infrastructure projects quickly and efficiently.[23] In 2008, the Senegalese president explained why his administration preferred Chinese government-financed infrastructure projects over those from Western sources:

China's approach to our needs is simply better adapted than the slow and sometimes patronising post-colonial approach of European investors, donor organisations and nongovernmental organisations.... China has helped African nations build infrastructure projects in record time – bridges, roads, schools, hospitals, dams, legislative buildings, stadiums and airports.... I am a firm believer in good governance and the rule of law. But when bureaucracy and senseless red tape impede our ability to act – and when poverty persists while international functionaries drag their feet – African leaders have an obligation to opt for swifter solutions.[24]

Surveys of leaders in low-income and middle-income countries suggest that this sentiment is increasingly widespread.[25]

However, other features of Chinese development finance might make it less economically effective than Western sources of development finance. Earlier in this book, we demonstrated that both international and domestic politics influence projects financed by the Chinese government. In Chapter 5, we provided evidence that recipient governments get substantially more Chinese aid when they vote with Beijing in the UNGA and do not establish diplomatic relations with the government in Taipei. Then, in Chapter 6, we showed that Chinese development projects are disproportionately located in the home areas of political leaders, and that this source of political bias is particularly strong in the run-up to competitive executive elections.

The fact that World Bank development projects do not favor the home areas of political leaders suggests that traditional bilateral and multilateral sources of development finance may be less vulnerable to this type of political capture than Chinese development finance. In fact, the World Bank explicitly justifies its use of ex ante, cost-benefit analysis to screen candidate projects as "a safeguard against project choices being captured by narrow political or sectional interests."[26] Many other Western-style suppliers of international development finance – such as the Asian Development Bank, the Inter-American Development Bank, the

---

[23] See, for example, Swedlund (2017a, 2017b); Bunte (2018).    [24] Wade (2008).
[25] Custer, DiLorenzo, Masaki et al. (2018: 34).
[26] Warner (2010: 2). As we have pointed out before, when the World Bank vets incoming project proposals, it employs a simple rule: "the expected present value of the project's net benefits must be higher than or equal to the expected net present value of mutually exclusive project alternatives" (Warner 2010: 2).

European Union, and the US Government's Millennium Challenge Corporation – use similar procedures to vet project proposals.[27]

To the best of our knowledge, Chinese development finance institutions do not have an analogous set of institutional safeguards in place. They typically request project proposals from and negotiate project agreements with political leaders in recipient countries, which create significant scope for leaders to exploit Chinese-funded projects for political gain. Indeed, the Chinese government itself acknowledges that its project appraisal standards are in need of revision. The chief economist of China Export and Credit Insurance Corporation (Sinosure) has characterized the due diligence procedures China's policy banks use to assess the economic viability of projects as "downright inadequate."[28]

The fact that Chinese development finance is subject to multiple sources of political bias has prompted speculation that it could be less economically effective. Western politicians and journalists have popularized the idea that China bankrolls white elephant projects because they have political value to the leaders of recipient countries, which in turn allows Beijing to secure foreign policy favors from these leaders. Similarly, some economists and political scientists argue that any form of public expenditure allocated according to political criteria will be less effective at improving economic development outcomes than public expenditure allocated according to need and efficiency considerations. Previous research demonstrates that political pressures can result in the approval of low-quality projects and higher rates of project non-completion.[29] Also, while politically motivated public expenditure can improve short-run economic outcomes in politically consequential jurisdictions (around the time of elections), it can undermine longer-run economic outcomes in the very same localities.[30] Therefore, if political capture reduces the effectiveness of development finance and Chinese development finance is more vulnerable to political capture than Western sources of development finance, one might expect Chinese development projects to have smaller socioeconomic impacts than development projects financed by Western sources such as the World Bank.

At the same time, there are reasons to believe that politically motivated development projects may be just as effective as other development projects.[31] If many unfunded investment projects offer similar potential economic returns, choosing among these projects according to political

[27] Warner (2010: 57).     [28] Pilling and Feng (2018).
[29] Kilby (2013); Williams (2017); Dreher, Eichenauer, and Gehring (2018).
[30] Kilby and Dreher (2010); Labonne (2016); Dreher, Eichenauer, and Gehring (2018).
[31] Rajan and Subramanian (2008: 655); Dreher, Klasen, Vreeland, and Werker (2013).

criteria may not reduce their levels of economic impact.[32] Also, regardless of the motivations of those who allocate aid and debt, development finance institutions and their contractors may still seek to implement high-quality projects. The impact of political bias on the effectiveness of international development finance is ultimately an empirical question.[33]

As discussed in earlier chapters, social scientists often measure the political motivations of foreign financiers and their recipients by using levels of voting alignment between donor countries and recipient countries in the UNGA or temporary membership on the UN Security Council (UNSC).[34] In this chapter, we focus on the alignment of UNGA voting between China and its potential funding recipients, since we know from Chapter 5 that UNGA voting is an important determinant of how Chinese development finance (and aid in particular) gets allocated. For each year in our study period, we identify all of the UNGA votes that were taken and measure the percentage of cases in which China and a given country cast identical votes. We then use this measure to test whether Chinese development projects are any less effective in countries that have aligned their UNGA votes with China.[35] The logic of this argument is that China will be more lenient in providing funds to foreign policy allies, approving lower-quality projects that are primarily designed to benefit the political leaders of these countries.

We also test whether politically biased Chinese development projects are less effective than other types of Chinese development projects at subnational scales. To do so, we rely on Chapter 6's finding that the home region of a recipient country's chief executive – a key indicator of political privilege – often receives more Chinese funding than other regions. Given that some of the funds going to leaders' birth places are being allocated according to political criteria, one might expect these funds to have smaller impacts on development outcomes.

---

[32] Mehmood and Seror (2019: 14).

[33] Mehmood and Seror (2019) show that a country's income increases with aid when the size of the shadow economy is sufficiently large. They test their model with data for Pakistan and find that aid increases growth in leaders' home regions there.

[34] Thacker (1999); Alesina and Dollar (2000); Kuziemko and Werker (2006); Dreher, Klasen, Vreeland, and Werker (2013); Dreher, Lang, and Richert (2019).

[35] An obvious alternative would be to focus on whether countries recognize the government of Taiwan instead of the People's Republic of China. However, variation over time is much lower, so this indicator is less useful for the short period under study in this chapter.

## How Chinese Aid and Debt Can Affect Outcomes: Economic Development, Population Health, and Spatial Inequality

To evaluate the effectiveness of Chinese development projects across and within countries, we focus on three outcomes: economic development, population health, and the concentration of economic activity in the geographic areas where projects are located. We refer to the latter as spatial inequality for short.

Our first measure is economic development, which captures both levels of economic output (i.e., the production of goods and services) and levels of income. Many studies have investigated if and when aid from Western bilateral and multilateral sources affects economic development; in general, however, the evidence from these studies is inconclusive, finding either no effects or small effects.[36] There have been almost no studies on the economic effects of Chinese development finance.[37]

In principle, Chinese development finance could drive economic development in both the short and the long term. It could directly increase short-run consumption, which contributes to a recipient country's GDP, and it could increase productive investment, which not only directly enters GDP calculations but can also enhance the recipient's long-term production capacity, thereby indirectly increasing growth in later years (we do not capture that here). On the other hand, Chinese development finance might have no effect on economic development at all, if it supports projects that would have been financed by the recipient government

---

[36] As we have pointed out before, evidence on the effects of Western aid on economic growth and other development outcomes is decidedly mixed (Werker 2012; Dreher, Lang, and Ziaja 2018; Doucouliagos 2019). At national and subnational scales, some studies present evidence of positive impacts (Clemens, Radelet, Bhavnani, and Bazzi 2012; Galiani, Knack, Xu, and Zou 2017; Bitzer and Gören 2018; Civelli, Horowitz, and Teixeira 2018), while others find no effects (Rajan and Subramanian 2008; Doucouliagos and Paldam 2009; Dreher and Lohmann 2015; Dreher and Langlotz 2020). Still others show that aid promotes development only under specific conditions (Burnside and Dollar 2000; Dreher, Minasyan, and Nunnenkamp 2015; Minasyan, Nunnenkamp, and Richert 2017). One such condition is whether the motive for granting aid is benevolent or selfish, as discussed in the first section of this chapter.

[37] Using data on economic cooperation as a proxy for Chinese development finance, Busse, Erdogan, and Mühlen (2016) report a positive correlation between (lagged) Chinese funding and economic growth in African recipient countries. However, this correlation is not robust, and no attempts are made to test the causal effect of development finance in an (external) instrumental-variables framework. They instead rely on internal instruments and estimate their regressions with a system generalized methods of moments (GMM) estimator. These instruments cannot plausibly be exogenous to growth. Building upon the empirical strategy that we introduce in this chapter, Li (2019) finds that Chinese aid increases growth in sub-Saharan African countries – in particular, when it is given to countries with medium levels of democracy and countries that receive little aid from the United States.

anyway, thereby allowing the recipient government to spend its own funds on less productive activities like patronage and graft. Economists refer to this funding displacement phenomenon as "fungibility." In 1947, Paul Rosenstein-Rodin, then deputy director of the World Bank's Economics Department, wrote that "[w]hen the World Bank thinks it is financing an electric power station, it is really financing a brothel."[38] Nearly fifty years later, the World Bank published a flagship policy report on aid effectiveness that was equally blunt. After completing a battery of statistical tests to estimate the economic growth effects of development finance, the authors of the report delivered the following message to policymakers: "what you see is *not* what you get" and "[you] should take it for granted that [your] financing is fungible because that is reality."[39]

It is also possible for development finance – from China or any other source – to hurt economic development if it weakens a recipient country's currency or disincentivizes the pursuit of growth-promoting policies and institutions (see Chapter 8 for a more detailed discussion of this topic). However, these effects are especially hard to measure, given that the net effect of (Chinese) development finance on economic development captures both positive and negative effects of many intermediate variables. This problem is even more acute when we measure development finance and development outcomes at the country level; even projects that promote economic development in the subnational localities where they are implemented may not affect it at the national level. Analyzing project impacts at the district and province levels may therefore help us more effectively isolate and understand causal relationships between development finance and economic development. However, if fungibility is more prevalent at subnational scales than national scales, these local-scale analyses might be less likely to detect project impacts than country-level analyses.[40] Therefore, to understand the impact of Chinese government financing at both the micro and macro levels, we analyze both district-level data and country-level data.

At the country level, we proxy economic development with the growth rate of per capita GDP; on subnational scales, we use a proxy that

---

[38] Cited in Devarajan, Rajkumar, and Swaroop (1999: 1).

[39] Dollar and Pritchett (1998: 60, 91).

[40] For example, this might be the case if China finances projects in localities that would have received the projects anyway and the recipient government funding that is freed up produces a successful project elsewhere within the country (Cruzatti, Dreher, and Matzat 2020). The existing literature on fungibility at subnational scales is more encouraging than the literature on fungibility at national levels (e.g., van de Walle and Mu 2007; Wagstaff 2011).

economists widely use and that we already employed in Chapter 6: night-time light output per capita.[41] Nighttime light output was initially pro-posed as way of proxying levels of GDP in countries with weak statistical capacity; eventually it was adopted as a measure of subnational economic output everywhere. It is strongly and positively correlated with GDP at both provincial (ADM1) and district (ADM2) levels.[42] Also, unlike administratively collected GDP data, it is measured consistently and reliably at high levels of spatial resolution via satellites, making it easy to compare across regions and making it impossible for incompetent or politically motivated government statistical agencies to skew the num-bers. According to Christopher Magee and John Doces of Bucknell University, who have analyzed administratively collected GDP data and satellite-generated data on nighttime light output for countries around the world, the official economic growth rates reported by authoritarian regimes overstate true economic growth rates by approximately 0.5–1.5 percentage points.[43] As Ho Fai Chan, an economist at Queensland University of Technology, and his colleagues show, democracies inflate their GDP statistics too. Indeed, they have a very strong incentive to do so: a 1 percent over-statement of a country's economic growth rate correlates with a 0.5 percent increase in public support for the democrat-ically elected government in power.[44] All of these studies reinforce the

[41] See, for example, Elvidge, Baugh, Kihn et al. (1997); Henderson, Storeygard, and Weil (2012); Dreher and Lohmann (2015).

[42] Hodler and Raschky (2014: 1028–1031) estimate the relationship between nighttime light output and subnational GDP using subnational GDP estimates that cover 1,503 subnational regions within eighty-two countries. They estimate that an increase in nighttime light output by 1 percent is associated with an increase in GDP at national and subnational levels of approximately 0.3 percent. Subsequent studies have demon-strated that nighttime light output correlates strongly with traditional measures of eco-nomic welfare and human development all the way down to the village level (Khomba and Trew 2017; Bruederle and Hodler 2018). For example, Weidmann and Schutte (2017) demonstrate that nighttime light output correlates strongly (0.73) with survey-based measures of asset wealth at the local level (Demographic and Health Survey enumeration areas with 2km–5km buffers), and Khomba and Trew (2017) find a strong, positive correlation (0.53) between nighttime light growth and household consumption gains.

[43] Magee and Doces (2015). Martinez (2021) has corroborated this finding with a different set of empirical tests. Evidently, the Chinese government is also aware of the unreliable nature of administratively generated GDP data. A leaked cable dispatch from the US Embassy in Beijing summarizes a 2007 meeting between Clark T. Randt Jr. (the US ambassador to China) and Li Keqiang (then a senior party official who eventually became the premier of the country's State Council). Li Keqiang reportedly told the US ambassa-dor to China that "GDP figures are 'man-made' and therefore unreliable," and that he considered electricity consumption to be a more useful gauge of economic output. The cable dispatch also notes that, with a "knowing smile," Li Keqiang noted that GDP statistics were "for reference only" (Randt 2007).

[44] Chan, Frey, Skali, and Torgler (2019).

same key point: governments lie, but satellites don't. Therefore, the evidence in this chapter that relies on remotely sensed nighttime light output per capita is particularly important.

Our second outcome of interest is population health, which we also measure at both national and subnational levels. Although it is a less popular measure than economic development in the aid effectiveness literature, an increasing number of studies estimate the population health impacts of development finance.[45] National-level studies typically find either no effects or small effects; as we previously noted, however, development projects are often implemented at subnational scales, so their impacts might be difficult to capture with country-level measures.[46] In this chapter, we follow the approach used in our joint work on infant mortality with John Cruzatti and Johannes Matzat from Heidelberg University.[47] Infant mortality – defined as the proportion of children born who die before they are twelve months old – is a measure that is available at both national and subnational scales. It is commonly used to gauge whether vulnerable populations are experiencing human welfare gains. It is seen as complementary to GDP per capita, since the benefits of economic development may not be evenly distributed.

Development projects can affect infant mortality in many ways. When hospitals and health clinics are constructed or rehabilitated, parents and their children may be able to access faster, less expensive, and/or higher-quality health services. When road and rail networks are improved, families may more easily access health care, enabling them to vaccinate their children, monitor their wellness and growth, and treat their illnesses. When a foreign power or multilateral institution bankrolls a rural electrification program, it may reduce household use of firewood for cooking and lighting, thereby curbing indoor air pollution – a human health hazard that claims an estimated 2 million lives each year.[48]

---

[45] See, for example, Williamson (2008); Sonntag (2010); Nunnenkamp and Öhler (2011); Chauvet, Gubert, and Mesplé-Somps (2013).

[46] Another strand of empirical research attempts to measure the local effects of health aid. These studies have focused on infant mortality outcomes within Nigeria, Côte d'Ivoire, and Cambodia; health outcomes and perceived health care quality in Malawi; disease burden and severity in Uganda; child mortality in the Democratic Republic of the Congo; and health outcomes across a sample of thirty countries around the world. See De and Becker (2015); Marty, Dolan, Leu, and Runfola (2017); Kotsadam, Østby, Rustad et al. (2018); Odokonyero, Marty, Muhumuza et al. (2018); BenYishay, Parks, Trichler et al. (2019); Dolan, BenYishay, Grépin et al. (2019); Greßer and Stadelmann (2021); Wayoro and Ndikumana (2019).

[47] Cruzatti, Dreher, and Matzat (2020).    [48] Barron and Torero (2014).

However, as with any other measure of development impact, the net effect of development finance on infant mortality could be zero if recipient country governments reduce or change the composition of their own spending in response to higher levels of external support. Other factors can also reduce impact – for example, if foreign funders poach scarce providers of public services from local institutions,[49] or foreign-financed infrastructure and services are underutilized because local residents prefer traditional infrastructure and services.[50]

Finally, in addition to measuring economic growth and population health outcomes, we measure the spatial concentration of economic activity – or spatial inequality. In a recent study that we co-authored with Richard Bluhm, we developed a measure of how concentrated nighttime light output is across small geographic units within larger areas, such as districts, provinces, and countries.[51] We then calculated a measure of statistical dispersion, the Gini coefficient, based on the distribution of nighttime light output (our proxy for total GDP). This produces a measure of spatial inequality that varies between zero and one (for details see Box 7.1). This measure is useful because it tells us how widely or narrowly the benefits of economic growth and development are being shared. A value of one represents complete economic inequality – for example, a province in which a single 9.3-kilometer by 9.3-kilometer area contains all economic activity in that province. A value of zero represents complete economic equality – for example, a province in which every single 9.3-kilometer by 9.3-kilometer area has the same level of economic activity. This satellite-generated outcome variable is measured consistently and reliably over time for more than 32,000 subnational localities around the world. Again, governments lie, but satellites don't.

---

[49] For example, if a doctor leaves a local health clinic and moves to a nearby Chinese government-funded hospital, this will likely produce no net gain in expert medical personnel in the area.

[50] For example, a recipient government might choose not to build a hospital in an area with donor-financed HIV/AIDS or malaria programs. In this situation, malaria- and HIV/AIDS-related outcomes might improve while other health-related measures deteriorate.

[51] See Bluhm, Dreher, Fuchs et al. (2020). Our analyses include all recipient countries that are not classified by the World Bank as high-income countries in a given year (see https://datahelpdesk.worldbank.org/knowledgebase/articles/906519-world-bank-country-and-lendinggroups, last accessed September 13, 2017).

## BOX 7.1 Measuring Spatial Inequality

We again draw on data on nighttime light output, introduced in Chapter 6. Recall that these data are from the Defense Meteorological Satellite Program, recorded from evening lights between 8:30 and 9:30 p.m., on a 6-bit scale ranging from zero (totally unlit areas) to 63 (brightly lit areas). We calculate our measure of spatial inequality across four steps. First, we divide the entire world into a grid of six arc minute cells (an area of about 9.3 kilometers by 9.3 kilometers at the equator) and align the grid with the nighttime light output data. Second, we intersect this grid with the global second-order administrative boundaries, which creates "squiggly" cells along the district (ADM2) borders. Third, we compute three variables for each squiggly cell in this grid in every year: the sum of nighttime light output ($s_i$), the land area of each cell in $km^2$ ($a_i$), and the light intensity in the cell ($x_i = s_i/a_i$).[a] Finally, we compute the Gini coefficient of nighttime light intensities over all lit cells within a particular district in the following way:

$$Gini = \frac{\sum_{i=1}^{n} w_i \sum_{j=1}^{n} w_j |x_i - x_j|}{2 \sum_{i=1}^{n} w_i \sum_{i=1}^{n} w_i x_i},$$

where $w_i = a_i / \sum_{i=1}^{n} a_i$ is an area-based weight and $n$ is the total number of lit cells in a district.

This spatial Gini coefficient that we introduced in Bluhm, Dreher, Fuchs et al. (2020) can then be interpreted as the average (weighted) difference between the light intensities of all possible pairs of cells within an administrative region. Alternatively, we may think of it geometrically as the area under the Lorenz curve plotting the cumulative distribution of weighted light intensities against the cumulative distribution of cell areas (in $km^2$). Note that our index captures the overall dispersion of economic activity, which is a product of the population distribution and the distribution of nighttime light per capita. At the country-year level, we construct the Gini coefficient for inequality between first-order administrative units (ADM1s) in analogy, based on the average nighttime light intensity and land area of each ADM1 region (e.g., province).

*Notes:* We take this description and all data we use here from Bluhm, Dreher, Fuchs et al. (2020). We thank Richard Bluhm for sharing the datasets with us.

[a] Before aggregating the lights to the grid level, we turn off all pixels that do not fall on land and average the light intensities whenever data from more than one satellite are available.

When economic activity is unequally distributed across geographic space, it does not necessarily harm economic development; sometimes it simply reflects the comparative advantages of subnational jurisdictions within countries. However, in other cases, there are grounds for concern. Economic activity may be concentrated in major cities because rural and remote populations have suffered from decades or centuries of neglect and discrimination,[52] or the geographical distribution of economic activity may be skewed because of ethnic favoritism and discrimination.[53] International development organizations claim that they are making special efforts to address economic disparities that exist within and across subnational localities.[54] However, empirical research demonstrates a yawning gap between rhetoric and action. Aid agencies and development banks generally do a poor job of targeting economically disadvantaged jurisdictions within countries;[55] if anything, they seem to prefer to site their projects in *wealthier* localities within host countries.[56]

China, however, is a potentially special case because of the emphasis it places on "connective infrastructure" projects – roads, railways, bridges, and tunnels – that can open up rural areas to economic development. Transportation investments can increase the mobility of people, goods, and capital – by reducing the costs of trade and migration, making it easier for firms to reach more distant markets, and allowing workers to commute or relocate to places of work that are farther afield. Connective infrastructure can also spread economic activity to rural, remote, and

[52] Colonial-era investments were highly localized in many developing countries; this set in motion powerful forces of economic agglomeration and created spatial inequalities that have persisted over long periods of time (Bonfatti and Poelhekke 2017; Roessler, Pengl, Marty et al. 2020). In Ghana, for example, the British invested heavily in two railroad lines in the early 1900s: a Western line that connected the mines of Tarkwa and Obuasi to the coast and an Eastern line that connected Accra with gold mines and cocoa-growing areas in the rural hinterlands. Over time, villages, towns, and economic activity clustered alongside these transportation corridors. This spatial equilibrium has proven to be remarkably stable; colonial investments created increasing local returns to scale and served as anchors for future rounds of public investment during the postcolonial era, further centralizing rather than decentralizing economic activity (Jedwab and Moradi 2016).

[53] See, for example, De Luca, Hodler, Raschky, and Valsecchi (2018). Ethiopia – where some ethnic groups (the Tigray, Oromo, Amhara) have significant representation in the central government, and others (Somalis and Afars) face high levels of political discrimination – provides a good example of the former. Public resources and economic activity are concentrated in the geographical areas dominated by the Tigray, Oromo, and Amhara rather than in the ethnic homelands of the Somalis and Afars (Argaw 2017).

[54] Van de Walle and Mu (2007); Chen, Mu, and Ravallion (2009); Wagstaff (2011).

[55] Öhler and Nunnenkamp (2014); Nunnenkamp, Öhler, and Sosa (2017).

[56] Zhang (2004); Briggs (2017, 2018a, 2018b); Nunnenkamp, Öhler, and Sosa (2017); BenYishay, DiLorenzo, and Dolan (2019); Öhler, Negre, Smets et al. (2019). Our findings in Chapter 6 demonstrate that Chinese development projects also favor the wealthier areas within countries.

economically disadvantaged areas by nurturing the development of local markets, increasing access to larger (urban) markets where (rural) firms can sell their goods and services, reducing price differences and volatility across locations, promoting the entry of new firms, lowering the cost of inputs and consumer goods, increasing land values and agricultural production, facilitating knowledge and technology spillovers, and enabling commuters to travel longer distances to places of employment.[57] The fact that China spends far more money on connective infrastructure than its peers in the global development finance market makes its funding particularly relevant to spatial inequality.

There are also some reasons to believe that China might be more effective than other donors and creditors at using connective infrastructure investments to reduce excessive concentration of economic activity in a small number of cities, districts, or provinces. When China opened up its own economy to foreign investment during the 1980s, it experienced rapid economic growth and sharp increases in spatial inequality.[58] The government responded with a set of spatial inclusion policies and programs – including the "Develop the West Campaign" – that redirected private and public investment to less economically developed areas in the central and western parts of the country. The development of interior-to-coast transportation networks played an important role in helping China reverse growing inequality within and across its own provinces.[59] Now, as a foreign donor and creditor, China focuses many of its connective infrastructure projects on interior-to-coast transportation networks.[60] This approach sets it apart from its peers in the development finance market; most of the OECD-DAC aid agencies and multilateral development banks that are engaged in the transportation sector prefer to invest in overland (interior-to-interior) transportation networks between countries.[61]

Do the connective infrastructure projects that China finances abroad more effectively diffuse economic activity than similar projects funded by Western donors and creditors? We seek to address this question by first

---

[57] See the references given in Bluhm, Dreher, Fuchs et al. (2020). Another important feature of transportation infrastructure projects is that they are public goods. Roads, bridges, railways, and ports are typically non-rival in consumption and non-excludable, meaning that their benefits generally accrue to a wide range of individuals and segments of the economy. Many other types of infrastructure investments (e.g., electricity lines, water pipes, sewerage connections, schools, hospitals, and public housing) are rival in consumption, providing benefits from which specific groups can be – and in developing countries often are – excluded (Burgess, Jedwab, Miguel et al. 2015; De Luca, Hodler, Raschky, and Valsecchi 2018; Ejdemyr, Kramon, and Robinson 2018).

[58] Fleisher, Li, and Zhao (2010).

[59] Lessmann (2013); Huang and Wei (2016); Wu, Yang, Dong et al. (2018).

[60] Bonfatti and Poelhekke (2017).    [61] Bonfatti and Poelhekke (2017).

testing if Chinese government-financed transportation projects are effective at reducing spatial inequalities within and between subnational jurisdictions. We then compare the impacts of these projects with those of World Bank projects in the same sector and jurisdiction. Although we use World Bank development projects as a way to benchmark the effectiveness of Chinese development projects against an objective standard, our findings for the World Bank are interesting on their own since the Bretton Woods institution recently redefined its mission "as ending extreme poverty by 2030 and boosting prosperity among the poorest 40 percent in low- and middle-income countries."[62]

### How We Measure the Development Impacts of Chinese Development Projects

Our statistical analyses investigate how Chinese development finance that is committed in a given year affects three types of development outcomes – economic development, population health, and spatial inequality – two years later. For the analysis of economic development and population health impacts, we focus on the number of Chinese development projects (of any type).[63] For the analysis of spatial inequality impacts, we investigate how the presence of at least one transportation project affects the geographic concentration of economic activity.[64]

In our statistical analysis at the country level, we net out the effect of different population sizes across countries. We also net out other factors that do not vary, either across countries or across time within a specific country.[65] We measure economic growth using the growth rate of real per

---

[62] The UN Sustainable Development Goals also identify targets for the growth rate of the bottom 40 percent of the population and for the inclusion (social, economic, and political) of different ethnicities and social groups; these targets serve the broad goal of "reducing inequalities."

[63] Note that Cruzatti, Dreher, and Matzat (2020) primarily investigate the effects of health projects, while we focus on all development projects. Because development finance is also fungible between sectors, we see our broader focus as a valuable test of robustness and addition to the literature.

[64] We focus on transportation projects because theory and previous empirical research suggest that these types of projects can have particularly large effects on the geographic concentration of economic activity. We use a binary indicator of "treatment" because the transportation projects in our dataset are often assigned multiple geocodes to capture different segments of linear infrastructure (e.g., multiple sections of a single highway). However, a project location count variable would not capture the intensive margin of infrastructure investments as much as it would the way in which the projects were geocoded.

[65] In other words, we run ordinary least squares (OLS) regressions with country and year fixed effects, where we control for a recipient country's (logged) population size. We cluster standard errors at the recipient-country level.

capita GDP, population health using the infant mortality rate, and spatial inequality between provinces (ADM1) using the Gini coefficient measure described in Box 7.1.

We then perform an analogous set of tests at the district (ADM2) level in each country and year. We net out the effects of all variables that equally affect all districts in the same country and year. We also net out the effects of any factor that does not vary within a district over time.[66] To measure economic development at the subnational level, we again draw upon remotely sensed nighttime light output data and use (logged) night-time light output per capita as a proxy for GDP per capita. We measure the spatial concentration of economic activity using the within-district Gini coefficient described in Box 7.1. And finally, to test the effect of development finance on infant mortality at the subnational level, we draw on geo-referenced data from seventy-one Demographic and Health Surveys (DHS) in forty-eight countries.[67] The census enumeration areas in these surveys are villages (in rural areas) or blocks of a city (in urban areas). The center of each enumeration area is geo-referenced. One key advantage of these surveys is that they include information about children born in any year prior to the survey. Although DHS data are not available for each year in each country, we can still extract information about the health status of children in other years, which means that we can derive infant mortality estimates for all of the years in our study period (in geographic areas where development projects took place).[68]

We expect the health impacts of Chinese development finance to be more easily detectable when we focus on small geographic areas in close proximity to project sites. Funds are often highly concentrated in certain localities within a country, and the number of projects that seek to improve health outcomes is usually small, so treatment effects might not be easily detectable at the country, province, or even district levels. We therefore focus on small geographic areas around the center of each DHS enumeration area – within a radius of 55 km. The decision to focus on these small geographic areas, however, has one important drawback: it

---

[66] That is to say, our regressions control for country-year fixed effects and district fixed effects. We cluster standard errors at the country-year level.

[67] We take these data from Cruzatti, Dreher, and Matzat (2020). We thank John Cruzatti and Johannes Matzat for sharing them with us.

[68] The dataset includes yearly information on child mortality for 103,008 children per year, on average; the total number of children included in the sample is 1.3 million, and the average infant mortality rate is 55. We make use of 55,946 enumeration areas, with an average of 3.7 children covered per enumeration area and year. There are 2,161 Chinese development project locations in the sample; 1,507 of these locations are within a radius of 55 kilometers of at least one enumeration area, and 217 of these are health-related projects.

is unlikely that within-country fungibility would be detected on such a fine scale.[69]

Looming large over all of these cause-and-effect questions is the so-called selection problem. In Chapter 5, we demonstrated that Beijing provides more aid to countries with higher levels of need (i.e., lower levels of per capita income), but the picture changed when we focused on provinces in Chapter 6: aid-financed Chinese development projects actually favor subnational localities with lower levels of need. As such, a simple correlation between a development outcome and the receipt of Chinese development finance will not necessarily tell us anything about impact. It may simply be that China provides more funding to places that are predisposed to perform well – or poorly – on that outcome of interest.

We must therefore address the possibility that jurisdictions with different levels of exposure to Chinese development finance are qualitatively different from one another in ways that may undermine our ability to identify cause-and-effect relationships. To address this, we adopt a causal inference strategy that we developed in previous work.[70] Specifically, we employ a statistical technique that does not explain our various outcome variables using the actual number of Chinese development projects but rather the number of projects that our model predicts a country or subnational locality will likely receive. The reason that this prediction is crucial for causal inference is that it is based on explanatory variables *that are not directly related to our outcomes of interest*. It therefore provides something that social scientists refer to as a "plausibly exogenous source of variation," which is essential for expunging the effects of selection bias and isolating the effects on economic development, population health, and spatial inequality that can only be explained by the receipt of Chinese development projects.

The challenge of this approach is finding variables that can predict the number of Chinese development projects in a country or subnational location and year that do not correlate with our outcome variables of interest for any reason other than the receipt of Chinese development finance. We focus on two proxy variables that we know from Chapter 4 affect China's annual provision of development finance worldwide but that have no direct effect on other countries' levels of economic

---

[69] Variation in the availability of Chinese development projects within DHS clusters over time is insufficient to allow including cluster fixed effects. However, just as in the regressions focusing on the other two outcomes, we include fixed effects for country-years and (ADM2) districts. We cluster standard errors at the level of district-years.

[70] We describe this "shift-share" instrumental variable strategy at greater length in Bluhm, Dreher, Fuchs et al. (2020); Dreher, Fuchs, Parks et al. (2021); Dreher, Fuchs, Hodler et al. (2021).

development, population health, or spatial inequality. These variables capture two of the key reasons why China experienced a benefactor-to-banker transition during the twenty-first century (after its adoption of the Going Out strategy in 1999): its industrial input overproduction problem and its foreign currency oversupply problem. Both of these factors account for year-to-year changes in China's aggregate provision of development finance, but they are otherwise unrelated to country- and locality-specific outcomes of interest.

Our first proxy variable measures the production of six industrial inputs – aluminum, cement, glass, iron, steel, and timber – in China. Our second proxy variable is the size of China's foreign currency reserves. As we demonstrated in Chapter 4, these variables explain interannual changes in the overall size of China's overseas development program. In years when China suffers from high levels of industrial input overproduction, it increases its provision of funding for overseas development projects that require such inputs. Likewise, in years when foreign currency reserves are plentiful, China seeks to maximize profit by expanding its foreign currency-denominated lending to overseas borrowers. However, these two measures alone do not allow us to predict how much of the interannual change in total Chinese development finance will go to different countries and subnational jurisdictions, so we draw upon the "old friends" metric from Chapter 5, which measures the number of years a country or province has received funds from China over the 1970–1999 period. To predict the number of Chinese development projects committed to a given jurisdiction, we combine our predictors for the overall (global) supply of Chinese development finance (which varies over time) with a contemporaneous variant of the old friends measure, calculated over the 2000–2014 period (which varies across countries). Intuitively, we expect that when industrial production and foreign currency reserves increase, China will increase the overall supply of development finance, and this increase will disproportionately benefit countries and districts that are friends of China. In years when foreign currency reserves run low and domestic industrial input production falls, we expect that Beijing will reduce its funding to those countries with a newer or weaker relationship with China before they reduce funding to friends. We explain the technical details of this approach in Appendix 7.B.[71]

---

[71] In short, we estimate a two-stage least squares (2SLS) regression, where we instrument the number of Chinese development projects with two instrumental variables – the interaction of the "probability to receive financial support from China" with an indicator

We also test whether political motivations that influence the allocation of development finance hinder the effectiveness of the projects that
are ultimately undertaken. To do so, we investigate whether Chinese
development projects differentially affect outcomes in jurisdictions that
enjoy varying levels of "political privilege."[72] At the country level, our
proxy for political privilege is the degree to which a recipient country
voted in line with China in the UNGA (at the time the project was
committed). At the district level, our proxy for political privilege is
a binary variable indicating whether or not the recipient district was
the home district of the country's political leader (again, at the time the
project was committed). The funding that China commits to
a recipient in years when it is politically privileged comes in two flavors:
"extraordinary" – and potentially less effective – projects that the
recipient gets because of political privilege and "ordinary" projects
that the recipient would get even during normal times.

## What the Data Say

We summarize our main results with partial leverage plots. These plots
use lines of best fit to summarize the key relationships between Chinese
development projects and the outcomes of interest while accounting for
the other explanatory variables in our models. They also provide information on the statistical significance of the key relationships and make it
easier to identify the potential influence of outlying observations. In
Appendix 7.A, we report the full results of our statistical analyses in
Tables A7.1–A7.4.[73]

---

that measures (a) how available industrial input materials are in a year (based on factor
analysis) and (b) changes in China's foreign currency reserves.

[72] We measure our dependent variable using project counts rather than dollars for this
analysis.

[73] In these tables, panel A shows simple OLS regressions, reflecting correlations that are
likely biased due to endogeneity; panel B presents reduced-form estimates, replacing the
respective official financing variables with our instrumental variables; panel C shows
the second stage of the regressions estimated with 2SLS; and panel D shows the corresponding first-stage results. In the first-stage regressions, both instrumental variables
show the expected positive sign in all specifications: as Chinese development project
inputs (both material and financial) increase, they generate disproportionately large
increases in projects for countries that are regular recipients of official financial support
from China. In other words, as China has more materials on hand, it puts more of them
into development projects, and mostly in countries that it is already friends with. As
illustrated by the Kleibergen-Paap F-test statistics reported at the bottom of the table, our
instrumental variables are strong. Table A7.5 reports descriptive statistics for our key
variables.

*Economic Development*

The left panel of Figure 7.3 shows the estimated effect of Chinese development finance on GDP per capita growth in countries around the world.[74] As highlighted by the upward-sloping line of best fit, the average effect of Chinese development projects on economic growth is positive. On average, we find that one additional project increases GDP per capita growth by almost a full percentage point.[75] This is a substantial effect, given that between 2002 and 2016, the average level of per capita GDP growth among the recipient countries in our sample was 2.85 percent.[76]

To better understand *how* Chinese development projects have achieved these impacts, we re-estimate our models with outcome variables that capture the constituent parts of GDP per capita growth, including investment, consumption, savings, imports, and exports. If Chinese development projects only increase consumption (short-term growth), there would be little reason to expect future growth to increase. To the contrary, strong impacts on investment might promote longer-run effects on growth if these investments are productive. Our statistical findings indicate that Chinese development projects increased investment (gross capital formation) and, to a lesser extent, consumption. When we disaggregate Chinese development finance by sector, we see that economic infrastructure, social infrastructure, and production sector projects all register positive growth effects.[77]

We also tested whether, as previous studies suggest, Chinese development projects are more effective in recipient countries with strong domestic institutions and "good government." We tested for differential effectiveness in countries with (a) better economic policies, (b) lower levels of corruption, (c) higher levels of democratic accountability, (d) fewer ethnic tensions, or (e) higher levels of press freedom. We found no evidence to support the notion that the economic effects of Chinese

---

[74] Again, this is based on the statistical analysis described earlier, which takes account of endogeneity by focusing on predicted projects rather than actual Chinese projects (see column 1 of Table A7.1).

[75] This finding also holds if we measure by monetary value rather than number of projects; in the average recipient country, a doubling of Chinese development finance in monetary terms leads to a 0.07–1.28 percentage point increase in GDP per capita growth within two years (Dreher, Fuchs, Parks et al. 2021).

[76] We also find that Chinese development projects increase GDP per capita growth between one and three years after they are approved (Dreher, Fuchs, Parks et al. 2021). These effects begin to shrink around year four.

[77] We also find that Chinese development projects increase imports, which could be the result of more construction materials for development projects being imported. We provide more details in Dreher, Fuchs, Parks et al. (2021).

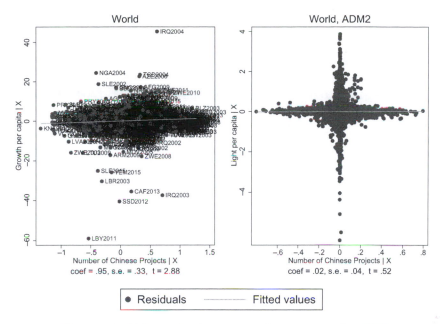

Figure 7.3 Chinese development projects, per capita GDP growth at the country level, and nighttime light per capita at the district level
*Notes:* The figure shows partial leverage plots corresponding to columns 1 and 2 in Table A7.1. See the notes for this table for details on data and methods.

development finance vary along any of these dimensions.[78] Nor did we find any evidence that Chinese development projects are any more – or less – effective based on the political orientation of the host government.

Turning to the right panel of Figure 7.3, we find that, on average, there is no effect of Chinese development projects on our subnational measure of economic development – nighttime light per capita at the district (ADM2) level. Interpreted in concert with our results at the country level, this might be due to the aid being fungible, so that projects benefit

---

[78] See Dreher, Fuchs, Parks et al. (2021) for details. We implement these regressions with a control function (CF) approach (based on the residuals from the first-stage regressions, using bootstrapped standard errors with 500 replications) under the assumption that the extent of the bias does not depend on the variable we interact with aid. An alternative to this approach is 2SLS, which interacts the instrument with the variable we interact projects with as the second instrument; however, this approach treats the interaction with the endogenous variable as a separate endogenous variable and thus "can be quite inefficient relative to the more parsimonious CF approach" (Wooldridge 2015: 429).

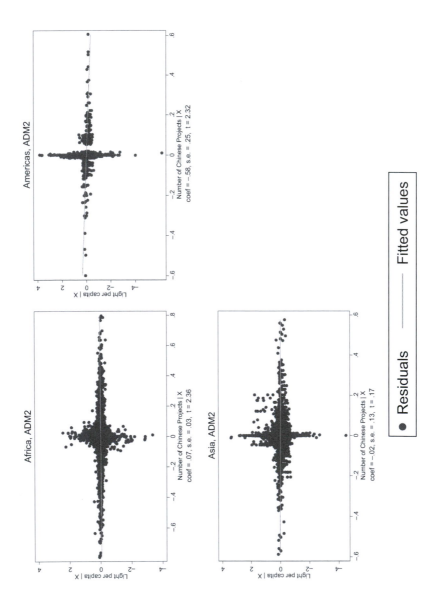

Figure 7.4 Chinese development projects and nighttime light per capita at the district level by world region
*Notes:* The figure shows partial leverage plots corresponding to columns 3–5 in Table A7.1. See the notes for this table for details on data and methods.

places different from the ones they are officially given to. However, as Figure 7.4 (and Table A7.1) demonstrate, this average result hides important variation across different regions of the world.[79] In Africa, we find that one additional Chinese development project increases nighttime light per capita by almost 8 percent. We also find that a 10 percent increase in the monetary amount of financial support from the Chinese government leads to a 1.3 percent increase in per capita nighttime light output in Africa; the size of this effect corresponds to an increase in district-level GDP per capita of approximately 0.39 percent.[80] This result does not hold in Asia, where we find no evidence that Chinese development projects increase per capita nighttime light at the district level. Nor does it hold in the Americas, where Chinese development projects seem to actually reduce per capita luminosity.

### Spatial Concentration of Economic Activity

Figure 7.5 (and Table A7.2) summarize our findings for the second outcome measure: the spatial concentration of economic activity.[81] Our findings are consistent with our previous work with Richard Bluhm; as the right panel of Figure 7.5 shows, we find that Chinese infrastructure projects disperse economic activity within the districts (ADM2s) where they take place. The magnitude of this effect is substantial: the implementation of a Chinese government-financed transportation infrastructure project generates a 10 percentage point reduction in the concentration of economic activity in the average district. The size of this effect is broadly similar across Africa and Asia, but not in the Americas (see Figure 7.6).[82] We obtain similar results at the country level when we focus on inequality between provinces (ADM1s).[83]

In previous work, we have also tried to pinpoint *where* exactly this diffusion of economic activity is taking place.[84] Here is what we found. First, Chinese connective infrastructure projects are especially effective at reducing spatial concentration in two types of subnational

---

[79] We do not provide a regional analysis at the country level due to the resulting small number of observations. For the same reason, we exclude Europe from the regional analysis.

[80] We report these additional results in Dreher, Fuchs, Hodler et al. (2021). The effect size exceeds the amount of funding in magnitude, indicating that Chinese development projects have an effect on the local economy that exceeds the initial investment (e.g., infrastructure installation) phase.

[81] The model specifications that we use are similar but not identical to those we report in Bluhm, Dreher, Fuchs et al. (2020).

[82] However, the effect only reaches conventional levels of statistical significance in Asia.

[83] See the left panel of Figure 7.5.      [84] See Bluhm, Dreher, Fuchs et al. (2020).

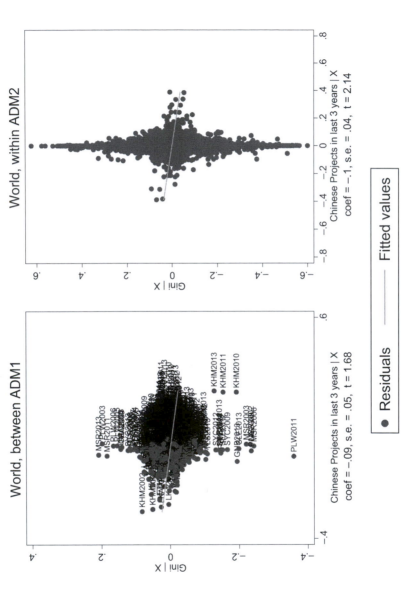

Figure 7.5 Chinese development projects and spatial concentration (between provinces and within districts)
*Notes:* The figure shows partial leverage plots corresponding to columns 1 and 2 in Table A7.2. See the notes for this table for details on data and methods.

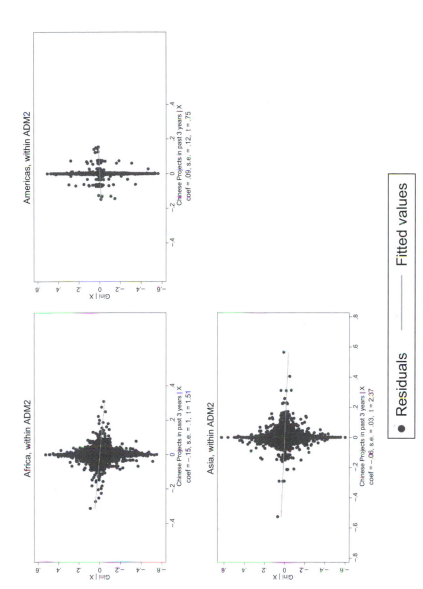

Figure 7.6 Chinese development projects and spatial concentration at the district level

*Notes:* The figure shows partial leverage plots corresponding to columns 3–5 in Table A7.2. See the notes for this table for details on data and methods.

jurisdictions: urban areas and areas that are located near the coast. Second, these types of projects reduce the share of economic activity taking place in the highest quintile of the nighttime light distribution and increase the share of activity that takes place in the second, third, and fourth quintiles. These two patterns suggest that economic output is relocating from dense areas like city centers to their immediate peripheries (i.e., peri-urban and suburban areas). These effects appear to be strongest in African countries, and also in less developed subnational jurisdictions within developing countries worldwide – where there are high baseline levels of demand for transportation infrastructure. All of these findings broadly comport with where we began this chapter: the case of the Nairobi-Thika Highway project.

### Population Health

Figure 7.7 (and Table A7.2) summarizes our results for our third and final outcome measure: infant mortality. At the country level (see the left panel of Figure 7.7), we find that exposure to Chinese development projects reduces infant mortality: one additional project reduces the number of children who die by 2 (out of every 1,000 live births). However, when we focus on a radius of 55 kilometers around interviewed households (the right panel of Figure 7.7), we find that infant mortality actually *increases* with levels of local exposure to Chinese development projects: on average, the implementation of an additional Chinese development project increases the number of children dying by almost 4 out of every 1,000 live births.

These seemingly contradictory results deserve some discussion. Why might Chinese development projects reduce infant mortality at the national level but increase it in its neighborhoods?[85] We think that fungibility is the most likely explanation, where a Chinese development project in one locality effectively displaces development projects from non-Chinese sources to other localities. The project would then still add value at the country level. At the local level, to the extent that the replaced project is more effective in fighting child mortality than the Chinese project, mortality increases.

---

[85] The results at national and subnational scales are not directly comparable. Our country-level results refer to a relatively large set of countries, but subnational results come from a different and substantially smaller set of countries. Also, a substantial share of the projects for which we have data at the country level are not included in the subnational analysis due to insufficiently precise locational information. However, when we limit the country-level analysis to the same countries and projects that we include in the subnational analysis, the results at the country level barely change. The results from these different levels of analysis therefore seem to differ in substantive ways.

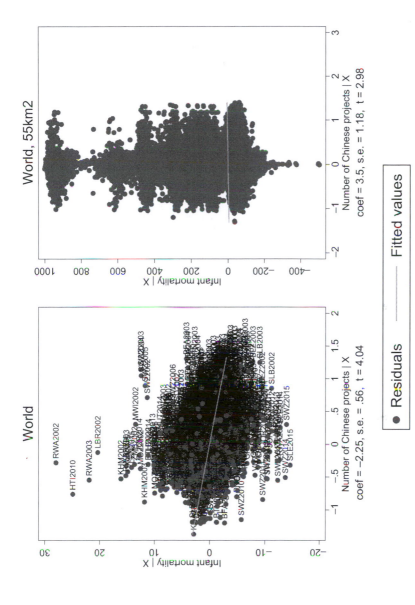

Figure 7.7 Chinese development projects and infant mortality at the country level and 55 kilometers square grid cell level

*Notes:* The figure shows partial leverage plots corresponding to columns 6 and 7 in Table A7.2. See the notes for this table for details on data and methods.

Table 7.1 *Summary of key results*

|  | China | | | World Bank |
|---|---|---|---|---|
|  | Development Finance | Aid | Debt | Development Finance |
| Economic Growth (Country) | + | + | + | 0 |
| Nighttime Light per Capita (ADM2) | 0 | 0 | 0 | + |
| Spatial Concentration (Country) | − | − | − | 0 |
| Spatial Concentration (ADM2) | − | − | − | 0 |
| Infant Mortality (Country) | − | − | − | + |
| Infant Mortality (Local) | + | + | + | + |

*Notes:* "+"/"−" indicates that development finance increases/decreases an outcome at least at the 10 percent level of statistical significance. "0" indicates the effect is not statistically significant at least at the 10 percent level.

Fungibility may also help explain another counterintuitive result: that local exposure to Chinese development projects appears to undermine local health outcomes. In previous work with John Cruzatti and Johannes Matzat, we tried to get to the bottom of this question.[86] We learned that when a locality benefits from a Chinese health project, it becomes less likely that the World Bank will approve a health project in the same area. We also found that when a recipient government is already allocating a relatively high percentage of domestic public expenditure on health, it becomes more likely that exposure to Chinese development projects will undermine local health outcomes. These two patterns suggest that Chinese development projects may be substituting for projects that would have been financed by other sources (thus freeing up funds for projects elsewhere), which would explain why Chinese development finance reduces infant mortality at national scales but increases it within geographical areas that are proximate to Chinese development project sites.[87]

### Disaggregating the Effects of Development Finance

Finally, we summarize a set of statistical tests that we undertook to gauge (a) whether Chinese aid-financed projects and debt-financed projects

---

[86] Cruzatti, Dreher, and Matzat (2020).
[87] In Cruzatti, Dreher, and Matzat (2020), we provide several additional pieces of evidence that may help explain why Chinese health-sector projects undermine local health outcomes.

produce similar or different results, (b) whether Chinese and World Bank development projects produce similar or different results, and (c) whether Chinese development finance is differentially effective when it is provided to foreign policy allies and politically privileged jurisdictions within recipient countries. Table 7.1 provides a summary of key results.

First, we sought to determine whether aid- and debt-financed Chinese development projects produce similar effects. We did so by replicating the analyses of Tables A7.1 and A7.2 with data for the two subsamples.[88] Several findings stand out. Beijing's debt-financed development projects register stronger country-level economic growth effects than its aid-financed projects, which may prove consequential in the medium to long run if China's development finance portfolio continues to shift away from aid and toward debt.[89] However, for our other outcomes beyond growth (luminosity, the spatial concentration of economic activity, and infant mortality), aid and debt seem to generate comparable results. Another interesting empirical pattern relates to variation across different regions of the world. In general, Beijing's aid- and debt-financed projects produce heterogeneous results in most world regions, but in Africa, its aid-financed *and* debt-financed projects seem to consistently increase economic growth and reduce the spatial concentration of economic activity.

Next, we sought to determine if Chinese development projects are more or less impactful than World Bank development projects (see Table A7.3).[90] We found no effect of World Bank development finance on per capita GDP growth at the country level; at the district level, however, we did find a positive effect on per capita nighttime light output. Recall that, on average, there is no effect of Chinese development projects on nighttime light per capita at the district (ADM2) level. However, in

[88] We do not report these additional results in tables, but they are available on request.

[89] Recall that debt-financed projects are substantially larger than aid-financed projects. The effects of these two types of financing are not statistically different from each other when we measure them in monetary terms.

[90] To compare the effects of Chinese and World Bank development projects, we run similar analyses for World Bank development finance. While we describe our detailed identification strategy in the appendix to this chapter, the intuition is similar to the one we have introduced for China earlier. Rather than focusing on the effect of actual World Bank development finance, we predict funding with variables that are not related to outcomes by other means than World Bank funding. We proxy the bank's capacity for loans in any given year with its available resources and introduce variation between countries or subnational regions, as we do with China – using the number of years a country or district has received funds as a share of all years in the sample period. We then use the joint variation in these variables to predict World Bank funding. More specifically, our two instrumental variables are the IBRD's equity-to-loans ratio and the IDA's "funding position," each interacted with the share of years in the 2000–2014 period a country or district received funding from these institutions.

Africa, an additional Chinese development project increases luminosity by almost 8 percent;[91] the World Bank effect in Africa is roughly two-thirds smaller than the average effect of Chinese development projects.[92] Unlike Chinese development projects in the transportation infrastructure sector, World Bank projects in this sector have no effect on the spatial concentration of economic activity (within districts or across provinces). Recall that Beijing's support for projects in the same sector has facilitated major reductions in the spatial concentration of economic activity. Finally, with respect to our third outcome of interest, we find that World Bank development projects actually increase infant mortality on *both* national and subnational scales, while Chinese development projects reduce infant mortality at the country level and increase it only at the district level. What can we conclude from this comparison? These results provide no evidence to support the rogue donor hypothesis, which implies that Chinese development finance is less effective than World Bank development finance. If anything, our results suggest that, at least on the three core development outcomes that we use in this chapter, World Bank development projects underperform Chinese development projects.

As we previously noted, the funding that China commits to a recipient in years when it is politically privileged comes in two flavors: extraordinary – and potentially less effective – projects that the recipient gets because of political privilege, and ordinary projects that the recipient would have received during normal times. If the effectiveness of political funding is sufficiently low to reduce average project effectiveness in years of political privilege, the effect of all development finance received in such years should be smaller than the effect of funding received at other times. In Table A7.4, we report the results of our test of whether Chinese development projects given for political reasons are less effective.[93] First, we test whether Chinese development finance is less effective at the country level when it is given to political allies (which we measure via UNGA voting alignment). We find no evidence that politically motivated projects underperform on any of our development outcome measures. Second, given that the home districts of political leaders in recipient countries are

---

[91] This finding is in line with our previous results in Dreher, Fuchs, Hodler et al. (2021).

[92] While the effect of Chinese projects in Africa is significant at the 5 percent level, recall that the coefficient for the global sample is imprecisely estimated. Our results suggest that a 10 percent increase in World Bank disbursements increases per capita nighttime light output by 0.2 percent at the district level.

[93] To identify the effect of the interaction of development finance and the variables measuring political importance in our instrumental variables regressions, we include interactions of our previous instruments with the respective political privilege variable as additional instruments.

areas of political privilege, we test whether Chinese development projects in these districts are any less effective. Our results indicate that Chinese development projects in the home districts of leaders are equally effective at promoting per capita nighttime light output when the leaders from those districts are in power and out of power.[94] We obtain similar results when we use levels of infant mortality within a 55-kilometer radius of project locations as an alternative outcome measure: in general, Chinese development projects that might have been influenced by political motivations are no less effective than those that are less likely to be politically influenced. Our results for the spatial inequality outcome measure are slightly more uneven: there is evidence that politically motivated Chinese development projects are less effective in one particular region of the world; overall, though, we find no clear evidence that political bias substantially reduces the effectiveness of Chinese development projects at either national or subnational scales.[95]

## Conclusion: Real Development Benefits ... with Caveats

As China continues its transition from benefactor to banker, it increasingly funds big-ticket, infrastructure projects with loans that are priced at or near market rates. The evidence that we have presented in this chapter suggests that these projects generate large socioeconomic impacts in the countries where they take place, at both local and national scales.

These results provide grounds for measured optimism. They suggest that if executed well, the BRI – a global infrastructure initiative that is primarily being financed with Chinese debt – could help spur global growth in highly impoverished regions.[96] However, China's global spending spree has set off alarm bells in Western capitals. BRI critics claim that China is more interested in purchasing the loyalty of foreign leaders than in promoting the wealth and well-being of developing countries, or that governing elites in recipient countries use Chinese government financing to support projects that advance their own prospects, not those of the people. Beijing's allies and clients argue that these criticisms are wrong-

---

[94] This is consistent with the Africa-specific results that we reported in previous work (Dreher, Fuchs, Hodler et al. 2021).

[95] When we focus on Asia exclusively, we find that Chinese development projects undertaken in the home districts of political leaders (when they are in power) increase the spatial concentration of economic activity. However, this result is not surprising since, at baseline, leaders' home districts are among the wealthier districts within their countries (Briggs 2017; Dreher, Fuchs, Hodler et al. 2019). Since we do not find any statistically significant effects in other world regions, we do not report results for these regions in a table.

[96] Freund and Ruta (2018).

headed; they point out that Chinese state-owned banks and government institutions finance and implement large-scale, high-impact infrastructure projects far more efficiently than their Western and multilateral counterparts, and that China supports geographically clustered projects that create "growth poles" and set in motion powerful economic agglomeration processes.

The empirical evidence presented here shows that irrespective of political bias, Chinese development projects improve socioeconomic outcomes at both national and subnational scales. However, these impacts vary significantly across jurisdictions, and more research is needed to understand why. We also show that socioeconomic impacts of Chinese development projects are comparable with, if not superior to, those generated by the World Bank. However, Chinese development projects may also have negative externalities, such as corruption, political instability, and environmental degradation; we turn our attention to these questions in the next chapter.

## Appendix 7.A

## Tables and Figures

Table A7.1 *Chinese development finance and economic development*

|  | (1) | (2) | (3) | (4) | (5) |
|---|---|---|---|---|---|
|  | Growth p.c. | (Log) Light p.c. | (Log) Light p.c. | (Log) Light p.c. | (Log) Light p.c. |
|  | World | World | Africa | Americas | Asia |
| **Panel A: OLS estimates – Dependent variable: GDP p.c. growth/(Log) light p.c.** | | | | | |
| Chinese OF | 0.147*** | 0.0004 | −0.0003 | −0.0370 | 0.0061 |
|  | (0.05) | (0.0026) | (0.0022) | (0.0230) | (0.0054) |
| (log) Population (t−1) | 5.824** | −0.5190*** | −0.3940*** | −0.6573*** | −0.3821** |
|  | (2.89) | (0.0649) | (0.1256) | (0.0729) | (0.1515) |
| **Panel B: Reduced form – Dependent variable: GDP p.c. growth/(Log) light p.c.** | | | | | |
| Reserves*probability (t−3) | 0.086 | −0.2085 | −0.0060 | −4.7074*** | −0.1938 |
|  | (2.905) | (0.1903) | (0.1369) | (1.4339) | (0.5914) |
| Input*probability (t−3) | 1.285*** | 0.0487** | 0.0504** | 0.2781** | 0.0208 |
|  | (0.453) | (0.0189) | (0.0200) | (0.1003) | (0.0507) |

Table A7.1 (cont.)

| | | | | | |
|---|---|---|---|---|---|
| (log) Population (t−1) | 5.123* | −0.5190*** | −0.3955*** | −0.6563*** | −0.3821** |
| | (3.020) | (0.0649) | (0.1250) | (0.0728) | (0.1514) |
| **Panel C: 2SLS estimates – Dependent variable: GDP p.c. growth/(Log) light p.c.** | | | | | |
| Chinese OF | 0.948*** | 0.0218 | 0.0750** | −0.5808** | −0.0219 |
| | (0.329) | (0.0417) | (0.0318) | (0.2505) | (0.1304) |
| (log) Population (t−1) | 2.137 | −0.5190*** | −0.3950*** | −0.6553*** | −0.3822** |
| | (3.391) | (0.0649) | (0.1254) | (0.0728) | (0.1517) |
| **Panel D: First-stage estimates – Dependent variable: Chinese financing (t−2)** | | | | | |
| Reserves*probability (t−3) | 2.476 | 2.0973 | 0.7946 | 8.2745* | 4.6198 |
| | (1.810) | (1.5105) | (1.7246) | (4.8306) | (3.4648) |
| Input*probability (t−3) | 0.968*** | 0.2869 | 0.5329** | −0.5113 | −0.1694 |
| | (0.327) | (0.2286) | (0.2539) | (0.7830) | (0.5385) |
| (log) Population (t−1) | 3.045** | −0.0017 | −0.0068 | 0.0018 | −0.0066 |
| | (1.377) | (0.0041) | (0.0103) | (0.0019) | (0.0113) |
| Number of countries | 150 | 129 | 49 | 25 | 32 |
| Number of districts | | 35,420 | 6,048 | 12,046 | 8,827 |
| Number of observations | 2,061 | 409,507 | 72,359 | 144,040 | 105,581 |
| Kleibergen-Paap F | 39.38 | 53.75 | 40.45 | 20.31 | 14.51 |
| Hansen J statistic (p-value) | 0.426 | 0.0327 | 0.700 | 0.960 | 0.771 |

*Notes*: The dependent variables are measured per capita (p.c.). The sources for the dependent variables are (1) World Bank WDI, taken from Dreher, Fuchs, Parks et al. (2021), (2)–(5) National Oceanic and Atmospheric Administration, taken from Bluhm, Dreher, Fuchs et al. (2020). "Chinese OF" denotes the number of Chinese government-financed projects. The instrumental variables are interactions of the first factor of China's production of aluminum, cement, glass, iron, steel, and timber, and China's net change in international reserves with a recipient's probability to receive official finance. The probability to receive official finance is defined as the share of years in the sample period a country or ADM2 region has received at least one project. Column 1 includes fixed effects for countries and years, and columns 2–5 for ADM2 regions and country-years. Sample periods are (1) 2002–2016 and (2)–(5) 2002–2013. Standard errors are clustered at the country level and reported in parentheses. *, **, ***: significant at the 10, 5, 1 percent levels, respectively.

Table A7.2 *Chinese development finance, spatial concentration, and health*

| | (1) | (2) | (3) | (4) | (5) | (6) | (7) |
|---|---|---|---|---|---|---|---|
| | Gini | Gini | Gini | Gini | Gini | Mortality | Mortality |
| | World | World, ADM2 | Africa, ADM2 | Americas, ADM2 | Asia, ADM2 | World | World, 55km$^2$ |
| **Panel A: OLS estimates – Dependent variable indicated in column header** | | | | | | | |
| Chinese OF (t−2) | −0.005 | −0.0070 | −0.0072 | 0.0161 | −0.0069 | −0.228** | 0.118 |
| | (0.004) | (0.0043) | (0.0068) | (0.0160) | (0.0058) | (0.096) | (0.298) |
| (log) Population (t−1) | −0.140*** | −0.0057 | −0.0173 | 0.0048 | −0.0182** | −50.454*** | |
| | (0.051) | (0.0042) | (0.0109) | (0.0059) | (0.0076) | (6.519) | |
| **Panel B: Reduced-form estimates – Dependent variable indicated in column header** | | | | | | | |
| Reserves*probability (t−3) | −0.3656* | −0.5064*** | −0.6054* | 0.7658 | −0.4829*** | −6.981*** | 68.5125*** |
| | (0.2067) | (0.1851) | (0.3554) | (1.4453) | (0.1221) | (1.776) | (22.0031) |
| Input*probability (t−3) | 0.0312 | 0.0379 | 0.0290 | −0.0225 | 0.0453* | −2.046*** | −5.5717* |
| | (0.0188) | (0.0256) | (0.0430) | (0.2644) | (0.0242) | (0.499) | (3.3733) |
| (log) Population (t−1) | −0.1183** | −0.0057 | −0.0175 | 0.0046 | −0.0183** | −47.380*** | |
| | (0.0503) | (0.0043) | (0.0111) | (0.0059) | (0.0076) | (6.332) | |
| **Panel C: 2SLS estimates – Dependent variable indicated in column header** | | | | | | | |
| Chinese OF (t−2) | −0.0867* | −0.0950** | −0.1523 | 0.0884 | −0.0644** | −2.247*** | 3.5018*** |
| | (0.0516) | (0.0445) | (0.1010) | (0.1171) | (0.0272) | (0.557) | (1.1756) |

Table A7.2 (cont.)

| | (1) | (2) | (3) | (4) | (5) | (6) | (7) |
|---|---|---|---|---|---|---|---|
| (log) Population (t−1) | −0.1161** (0.0512) | −0.0058 (0.0043) | −0.0180 (0.0111) | 0.0047 (0.0059) | −0.0186** (0.0075) | −41.444*** (6.919) | |
| **Panel D: First-stage estimates – Dependent variable: Chinese financing (t−2)** | | | | | | | |
| Reserves*probability (t−3) | 2.3600* (1.2080) | 4.5824* (2.5116) | 2.0298 (2.5022) | −5.7190* (2.8639) | 8.0163** (3.4601) | 0.632 (2.321) | 1.7285* (0.9243) |
| Input*probability (t−3) | −0.0272 (0.2091) | −0.2560 (0.4112) | 0.1420 (0.4828) | 1.5373*** (0.4573) | −0.8175 (0.5298) | 1.303*** (0.385) | 0.9125*** (0.1363) |
| (log) Population (t−1) | 0.0314 (0.0978) | −0.0013 (0.0022) | −0.0037 (0.0024) | 0.0004 (0.0006) | −0.0033 (0.0075) | 2.663* (1.402) | |
| Number of countries | 157 | 129 | 49 | 25 | 32 | 151 | 53 |
| Number of districts | | 32,551 | 5,120 | 11,701 | 7,701 | | 61,165 |
| Number of observations | 1,781 | 355,535 | 55,712 | 135,657 | 84,111 | 1,983 | 409,374 |
| Kleibergen-Paap F | 20.86 | 10.74 | 15.54 | 9.590 | 3.958 | 42.40 | 166.2 |
| Hansen J statistic (p-value) | 0.190 | 0.733 | 0.512 | 0.290 | 0.724 | 0.303 | 0.00509 |

*Notes:* The dependent variables and sources are (1)–(5) Gini coefficients measuring the spatial concentration of economic activity based on data from the National Oceanic and Atmospheric Administration, taken from Bluhm, Dreher, Fuchs et al. (2020), (6) infant mortality from World Bank WDI, and (7) infant mortality from the Demographic and Health Surveys, various countries and years, taken from Cruzatti, Dreher, and Matzat (2020). "Chinese OF" denotes (1)–(5) a binary indicator that is one when at least one Chinese transport project is committed, and (6)–(7) the number of Chinese government-financed projects. The instrumental variables are interactions of the first factor of China's production of aluminum, cement, glass, iron, steel, and timber, and China's net change in international reserves with a recipient's probability to receive official finance. The probability to receive official finance is defined as the share of years in the sample period a country or region has received at least one project. Columns 1 and 6 include fixed effects for countries and years, columns 2–5 and 7 for ADM2 regions and country-years. Sample periods are (1)–(5) 2002–2013, (6) 2002–2015, and (7) 2002–2014. Standard errors are clustered at the (1)–(6) country level or (7) ADM2-year level and reported in parentheses. *, **, ***: significant at the 10, 5, 1 percent levels, respectively.

Table A7.3 *World Bank development finance, economic development, spatial concentration, and health*

| | (1) Growth p.c. World | (2) (Log) Light p.c. World, ADM2 | (3) Mortality World | (4) Mortality World, 55km$^2$ | (5) Gini World | (6) Gini World, ADM2 |
|---|---|---|---|---|---|---|
| **Panel A: OLS estimates – Dependent variable indicated in column header** | | | | | | |
| World Bank OF (t−2) | 0.004 | −0.0002 | −0.012 | 0.000 | −0.002 | −0.0004 |
| | (0.017) | (0.0002) | (0.025) | (0.039) | (0.002) | (0.0012) |
| (log) Population (t−1) | 6.287*** | −0.5185*** | −53.369*** | | −0.109** | −0.0062 |
| | (2.287) | (0.0647) | (6.830) | | (0.048) | (0.0043) |
| **Panel B: Reduced-form estimates – Dependent variable indicated in column header** | | | | | | |
| IBRD liquidity*prob. | −0.040 | −0.0108** | 0.273*** | −1.2383* | 0.001 | 0.0001 |
| | (0.060) | (0.0053) | (0.085) | (0.6959) | (0.001) | (0.0000) |
| IDA liquidity*prob. | 0.008 | −0.0012 | 0.240*** | −0.5948*** | 0.001 | 0.0001** |
| | (0.026) | (0.0014) | (0.056) | (0.1386) | (0.000) | (0.0000) |
| (log) Population (t−1) | 6.166** | −0.5178*** | −44.433*** | | −0.079 | −0.0062 |
| | (2.426) | (0.0644) | (6.415) | | (0.052) | (0.0043) |
| **Panel C: 2SLS estimates – Dependent variable indicated in column header** | | | | | | |
| World Bank OF (t−2) | −0.125 | 0.0200* | 1.150** | 5.7987*** | −0.046 | −0.1443 |
| | (0.189) | (0.0106) | (0.449) | (2.0050) | (0.051) | (0.1814) |

Table A7.3  (cont.)

| | (1) | (2) | (3) | (4) | (5) | (6) |
|---|---|---|---|---|---|---|
| (log) Population (t–1) | 5.593** | −0.5191*** | −47.335*** | | −0.091* | −0.0065 |
| | (2.707) | (0.0658) | (8.930) | | (0.054) | (0.0045) |
| **Panel D: First-stage estimates – Dependent variable: World Bank financing (t–2)** | | | | | | |
| IBRD liquidity*prob. | −5.037 | −0.6146*** | −4.360 | 0.0529 | 0.162 | 0.0003* |
| | (3.955) | (0.1755) | (3.843) | (0.1954) | (0.493) | (0.0002) |
| IDA liquidity*prob. | 1.897 | −0.1260 | −1.184 | −0.0985*** | 0.029 | 0.0000 |
| | (4.063) | (0.1185) | (4.897) | (0.0246) | (0.077) | (0.0001) |
| (log) Population (t–1) | −1.387** | 0.0630 | −0.866 | | 0.307 | −0.0020 |
| | (0.629) | (0.0902) | (0.698) | | (0.222) | (0.0044) |
| Number of countries | 152 | 130 | 153 | 54 | 147 | 130 |
| Number of districts | | 35,764 | | 81,470 | | 32,895 |
| Number of observations | 2,370 | 413,635 | 2,303 | 624,738 | 1,674 | 359,831 |
| Kleibergen-Paap F | 9.261 | 13.97 | 8.306 | 8.113 | 7.469 | 1.880 |
| Hansen J statistic (p-value) | 0.917 | 0.674 | 0.000459 | 0.246 | 0.175 | 0.0306 |

*Notes:* See Tables A7.1 and A7.2. World Bank Official Finance (OF) is measured as (1)–(4) (log) commitments from the IDA and IBRD (constant 2010 US\$, with a value of one added before taking logs), and (5)–(6) a binary indicator that is one when at least one World Bank transport projects is committed. The instrumental variables are the IBRD's equity-to-loans ratio and the IDA's "funding position," both interacted with the share of years in the 2000–2014 period a country or district received funding from these institutions.

Table A7.4 *Chinese development finance, interactions with political privilege*

| | (1) | (2) | (3) | (4) | (5) | (6) | (7) |
|---|---|---|---|---|---|---|---|
| | Growth p.c. World | Mortality World | Gini World | Light p.c. World, ADM2 | Mortality World, 55km² | Gini World, ADM2 | Gini Asia, ADM2 |
| | **2SLS estimates – Dependent variable indicated in column header** | | | | | | |
| Chinese OF (t−2) | −0.845 | −2.762 | 0.6241 | 0.0216 | 3.2700** | −0.0957** | −0.0646** |
| | (1.235) | (1.839) | (0.5570) | (0.0425) | (1.3661) | (0.0457) | (0.0271) |
| UNGA voting (t−2) | 2.137 | 0.685 | −0.0906* | | | | |
| | (1.472) | (1.984) | (0.0521) | | | | |
| Chinese OF*UNGA voting | 2.278 | −3.767 | −0.7457 | | | | |
| | (2.179) | (2.795) | (0.6659) | | | | |
| Leader district (t−2) | | | | 0.0081 | 1.4216 | −0.0077** | −0.0081 |
| | | | | (0.0142) | (1.3240) | (0.0032) | (0.0055) |
| Chinese OF*Leader district | | | | −0.0375 | −0.0856 | 0.0678 | 0.0877*** |
| | | | | (0.0455) | (1.6115) | (0.0483) | (0.0259) |
| (log) Population (t−1) | 1.543 | −41.040*** | −0.0971 | −0.5190*** | | −0.0058 | −0.0185** |
| | (3.332) | (7.189) | (0.0650) | (0.0649) | | (0.0043) | (0.0076) |
| Number of countries | 148 | 150 | 145 | 129 | 53 | 129 | 32 |
| Number of districts | 2,010 | 1,938 | 1,577 | 35,420 | 61,165 | 32,551 | 7,701 |
| Number of observations | | | | 409,507 | 409,374 | 355,509 | 84,111 |
| Kleibergen–Paap F | 19.31 | 20.81 | 4.883 | 32.59 | 73.44 | 5.779 | 873.9 |
| Hansen J statistic (p-value) | 0.480 | 0.435 | 0.391 | 0.00848 | 0.00801 | 0.642 | 0.435 |

*Notes:* See Tables A7.1 and A7.2. "UNGA voting" is the share a country voted in line with China in the United Nations General Assembly in a year; "Leader district" is a binary variable indicating whether or not the recipient district was the home district of the country's leader at the time the project was committed.

Table A7.5 *Descriptive statistics*

|  | Count | Mean | SD | Min | Max |
|---|---|---|---|---|---|
| Sample of Table A7.1, column 1 |  |  |  |  |  |
| Chinese OF projects | 2,061 | 1.97 | 3.04 | 0.00 | 35.00 |
| OOF/vague projects | 2,061 | 0.51 | 1.35 | 0.00 | 31.00 |
| Chinese ODA projects | 2,061 | 1.47 | 2.33 | 0.00 | 24.00 |
| GDP per capita growth (annual %) | 2,061 | 2.85 | 5.15 | −62.23 | 50.12 |
| Population | 2,061 | 3.12E+07 | 1.09E+08 | 9,635 | 1.32E+09 |
| Sample of Table A7.1, columns 2–5 |  |  |  |  |  |
| (Log) Light p.c. World | 409,507 | −3.05 | 1.10 | −4.61 | 8.11 |
| (Log) Light p.c. Africa | 72,359 | −3.74 | 0.99 | −4.61 | 5.43 |
| (Log) Light p.c. Americas | 144,040 | −2.77 | 0.82 | −4.61 | 7.39 |
| (Log) Light p.c. Asia | 105,581 | −3.64 | 0.94 | −4.61 | 5.43 |
| Sample of Table A7.2 |  |  |  |  |  |
| Chinese transport project, binary | 1,781 | 0.08 | 0.27 | 0.00 | 1.00 |
| Gini World | 1,781 | 0.53 | 0.21 | 0.02 | 0.94 |
| Gini World, ADM2 | 355,535 | 0.36 | 0.20 | 0.00 | 0.91 |
| Gini World, Africa | 55,712 | 0.34 | 0.20 | 0.00 | 0.91 |
| Gini World, Americas | 135,657 | 0.37 | 0.20 | 0.00 | 0.90 |
| Gini World, Asia | 84,111 | 0.37 | 0.19 | 0.00 | 0.89 |
| Mortality World | 1,983 | 38.27 | 27.02 | 3.40 | 137.70 |
| Mortality World, 55km2 | 409,374 | 47.72 | 134.08 | 0.00 | 1,000.00 |
| Sample of Table A7.3 |  |  |  |  |  |
| World Bank OF | 2,370 | 10.06 | 9.31 | 0.00 | 22.66 |
| Sample of Table A7.4 |  |  |  |  |  |
| UNGA voting with China | 2,009 | 0.77 | 0.14 | 0.07 | 1.00 |
| Leader district | 364,851 | 0.00 | 0.06 | 0.00 | 1.00 |

## Appendix 7.B
## Regression and Identification Strategy

This appendix describes our statistical analyses more formally. At the country-year level, we estimate the following regressions:

$$Y_{k,i,t} = \beta_1 Projects_{CHN,i,t-2} + \beta_2 pop_{i,t-1} + \beta_3 \eta_i + \beta_4 \mu_t + \varepsilon_{i,t}, \qquad (1)$$

where $Y_{k,i,t}$ is one of our $k$ indicators of development in recipient country $i$ in year $t$. Our first indicator is yearly real GDP per capita growth, the second is the infant mortality rate, and the third is spatial concentration. While the first and second indicators are straightforward, the third requires explanation. Based on our work in Bluhm, Dreher, Fuchs et al. (2020), we measure concentration with a spatial Gini coefficient that uses nighttime light output at the grid-cell level as a measure of aggregate economic activity – that is, the product of population and light output per capita – and then calculate the Gini coefficient based on the distribution of this proxy variable for total GDP. The resulting measure ranges between zero and one, with higher values indicating higher levels of spatial concentration (as detailed in Box 7.1).

$Projects_{CHN,i,t-2}$ in equation (1) is the number of Chinese development projects committed two years before we observe an outcome $k$, $pop_{i,t-1}$ stands for the recipient country's (logged) population size, $\eta_i$ and $\mu_t$ represent country and year fixed effects, respectively, and $\varepsilon$ is the error term. Standard errors are clustered at the recipient-country level.

We estimate the following first-stage regression, at the country-year level:

$$Projects_{CHN,i,t-2} = \gamma_1 Material_{t-3} * p_{CHN,i} + \gamma_2 Reserves_{t-3}$$
$$* p_{CHN,i} + \gamma_3 pop_{i,t-1} + \gamma_4 \eta_i + \gamma_5 \mu_t + u_{i,t-2} \qquad (2)$$

Our instruments for $Projects_{CHN,i,t-2}$ are the interactions of (lagged) Chinese project input materials $Material_{t-3}$ and $Reserves_{t-3}$ that vary over time, and the probability of receiving Chinese development projects $p_{CHN,i}$, which varies across recipient countries. $Material$ is the first factor of China's production of six project input materials and $Reserves$ is measured as the changes in China's net foreign exchange reserves (in trillions of constant 2010 US$). We calculate the probability of receiving Chinese development finance as the share of years in the 2000–2014 period a country has received at least one Chinese development project, $p_{CHN,i}$.

More precisely, we measure the "shock" to China's year-to-year supply as China's production of six physical inputs in development projects – aluminum (in 10,000 tons), cement (in 10,000 tons), glass (in 10,000 weight cases), iron (in 10,000 tons), steel (in 10,000 tons), and timber (in 10,000 cubic meters). Rather than using these construction materials to form six different instrumental variables, we employ factor analysis to derive the de-trended first factor – deriving one new variable from the variety of input factors, using weights for the individual variables in a way that maximizes variation of the combined one. Our second shock captures de-trended net changes in China's foreign currency reserves. We then combine each of these shocks with a variable that captures variation across different recipient countries: the probability to receive Chinese development projects. We define the probability of receiving projects from China as $p_{CHN,i} = \frac{1}{15} \sum_{t=1}^{15} p_{CHN,i,t}$, where $p_{CHN,i,y}$ is a binary variable that equals one when recipient $i$ received at least one project from China in year $y$.

Readers might be concerned that these instruments violate the exclusion restriction because the probability of receiving projects may directly affect development. However, our regressions control for the direct effect of the probability of receiving projects as well as of input materials and reserves through the inclusion of fixed effects. Given that we thereby control for the effects of the (time-invariant) probability of receiving projects, the interaction of this probability with the (conditionally) exogenous variables results in an exogenous instrument under mild assumptions (Nizalova and Murtazashvili 2016; Bun and Harrison 2019). The intuition of this approach is that of a difference-in-differences regression, where we investigate a differential effect of Chinese production of construction materials and the availability of currency reserves on the number of projects in countries with a high compared to a low probability of receiving such projects. The identifying assumption is that development outcomes in countries with differing probabilities of receiving Chinese development finance will not be affected differently by changes in China's yearly production of potential project inputs and changes in reserves, other than via the impact of projects and controlling for the set of fixed effects. In other words, as in any difference-in-differences setting, we rely on an (continuous) exogenous treatment and the presence of parallel trends across groups. Controlled for year fixed effects, Chinese production of project inputs and changes in currency reserves cannot be correlated with the error term and are thus conditionally exogenous to development projects. For different trends to exist, these trends across countries with a high compared with a low probability of receiving projects from China would have to vary in tandem with year-to-year changes in the production of construction materials and changes in reserves.

The exogeneity of our interacted instruments would be violated if changes in the production of project inputs or changes in reserves affected development differentially in countries with a high probability to receive projects compared with those with a low probability to receive projects for reasons unrelated to projects. As we discuss in Bluhm, Dreher, Fuchs et al. (2020), Chinese project inputs might be correlated with a number of other variables. Some of those might differentially affect development in these groups of countries via development projects exclusively. For example, yearly production of the six inputs we consider here is likely to be correlated with other inputs in development projects. The effect of projects that we estimate would then capture the combined effects of these project inputs, which would not threaten our identification strategy.

The production of potential physical project inputs or changes in reserves could also be correlated with overall export volumes or foreign direct investments. Frequent recipients of Chinese development projects are also likely to be host countries for Chinese investment projects. Similarly, they may also have stronger trade ties with China. As such, any differential effects of development finance on outcomes that we detect could result from trade and investment rather than development finance. To address this concern, the research papers this chapter builds on hold trade and investment constant in some specifications. We do not only control for their volumes but also for their interactions with the probability to receive official finance to allow for differential effects in the two groups of countries or subnational localities. Our findings are robust for accounting for FDI and trade. While this does not definitively prove that there are no other omitted variables that bias our estimates, the fact that controlling for the two most obvious confounds does not affect our results should enhance our confidence in the findings. The same holds for a number of placebo tests that we perform, such as using future values of the instrument to predict current values of development finance, which, as expected, turns out to have low power. We also run specifications where we instrument Chinese exports and FDI with our instrument based on physical construction materials (controlling for Chinese financing; see Dreher, Fuchs, Parks et al. 2021). Results for these placebo regressions show very weak first-stage F-statistics, as one would expect if official financing (rather than exports and investments that are unrelated to development projects) is the key method to transfer surplus material abroad. As a further placebo test, we rerun our model including only projects that should be unrelated to the availability of physical inputs. This subset of projects primarily includes budget support, support to nongovernmental organizations, and debt relief agreements. If our instrument captures the availability of physical project inputs, then it should not be a strong predictor of less tangible projects that do not rely on these inputs. Again, the first-stage F-statistic is very low in this placebo regression.

Following Christian and Barrett (2017), we plot the variation in the first factor of Chinese (de-trended) project inputs and changes in net reserves in concert with the variation in project numbers and growth at the country level for two different groups that are defined according to the median of the probability to receive projects (we report similar graphs for the alternative outcome variables at the subnational locality and country level in the research papers we base this chapter on).

Figure A7.1 shows there is little reason to believe that the parallel-trends assumption is violated. More precisely, the probability-specific trends in project numbers and growth, respectively, seem rather parallel across the regular recipients (those with a probability of receiving projects that is above the median) and the irregular recipients (those with a probability of receiving projects that is below the median). There is also no obvious nonlinear trend in regular compared with irregular recipients that is similar for project numbers and growth.

Our specification is distinct from the extant literature on aid and growth in a number of ways (e.g., Clemens, Radelet, Bhavnani, and Bazzi 2012; Galiani, Knack, Xu, and Zou 2017; Dreher and Langlotz 2020). First, we rely on commitments rather than disbursements of aid and credit. Given that development projects should only affect development after its disbursement, the latter are preferable over the former. However, comprehensive data on disbursements of Chinese development finance are not available and are virtually impossible to measure with open-source data collection methods. In our main specification, we thus lag commitments by two years to allow for sufficient time for projects to progress beyond the commitment stage. We base our lag duration on a subset of 300 projects in the dataset for which there is information on the actual project start and end dates.[97] The observed average project duration amounts to 664 days, and thus we apply a two-year lag in our baseline regressions.[98]

---

[97] In subsetting the data, we exclude projects with a project length of zero days, which is typically the case for monetary grants. However, even in these cases, the *recipient* government will need considerable time to implement these projects, which makes a time lag necessary.

[98] Historical Chinese aid data also reveal a median of two years between project start and completion (data from Bartke 1989). While these data suggest two years may be an

Second, most previous studies focus on amounts of funding rather than project numbers. In our case, using commitment amounts comes with the disadvantage that we do not have data on amounts for a substantial number of projects, as we discussed in detail in Chapter 3. In the research articles that we base this chapter on, we therefore provide results for amounts in concert with results for numbers. Here, we focus on the number of projects to reduce clutter but discuss our results for monetary amounts (from our related research) in parallel.

Third, we utilize annual data rather than data averaged over three-, four-, or five-year periods (e.g., Clemens, Radelet, Bhavnani, and Bazzi 2012; Dreher and Lohmann 2015; Galiani, Knack, Xu, and Zou 2017; Dreher and Langlotz 2020). For our tests to show a potential effect of projects that actually exists with an 80 percent probability, we would require several thousand observations rather than the sample of roughly 420 observations that we would have if we averaged our data over five-year-periods.[99] This is an empirical challenge within the aid effectiveness literature at large (Ioannidis, Stanley, and Doucouliagos 2017).[100] However, while much of the literature focusing on Western donors makes use of samples starting in the 1970s, the first year we have comprehensive, global, data on Chinese development finance is 2000.[101] Our results should therefore be interpreted differently from those of most of the related aid effectiveness literature: we primarily test whether Chinese projects affect outcomes in the short run. That is, we can test whether the funds received are spent in the receiving country (rather than redirected elsewhere) and whether they create spillover effects in the local economy.

Fourth, we differ from much of the extant literature in our choice of control variables. In keeping with Dreher, Fuchs, Hodler et al. (2021), our main regressions are parsimonious. They control for fixed effects for years $\tau$ and countries $\eta$ and the (logged) population size of recipient countries $pop_i$. Typical regressions in the aid effectiveness literature

---

appropriate lag period, they are not necessarily a representative sample of projects (and potentially suffer from selection effects). In Dreher, Fuchs, Parks et al. (2020), we perform analyses using various lag lengths.

[99] This high number of required observations is driven by our fixed effects setting, as country and time fixed effects capture most of the variation in the dependent variable so that the variation caused by development finance conditional on these fixed effects is rather small.

[100] According to Ioannidis, Stanley, and Doucouliagos (2017), only about 1 percent of the 1,779 estimates in the aid-and-growth literature surveyed have adequate power (see also Doucouliagos 2019; Dreher and Langlotz 2020).

[101] As we have discussed in Chapter 3, Chinese volumes of development finance are also available for earlier years (Dreher and Fuchs 2015), but these values are not necessarily comparable to post-2000 amounts as they are gathered based on different data collection procedures.

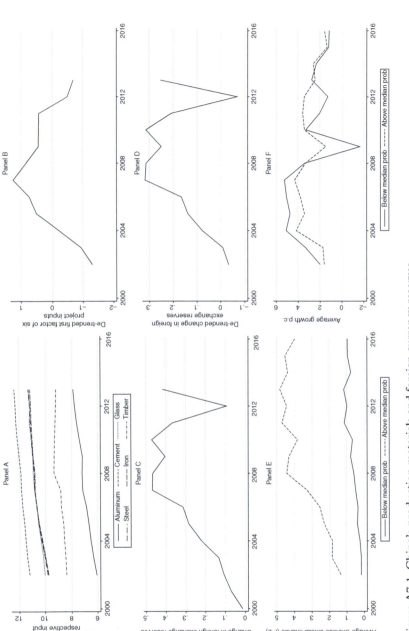

Figure A7.1  China's production materials and foreign currency reserves

*Notes:* Panel A shows China's (logged) production of aluminum (in 10,000 tons), cement (in 10,000 tons), glass (in 10,000 weight cases), iron (in 10,000 tons), steel (in 10,000 tons), and timber (in 10,000 cubic meters) over time. Panel B shows the de-trended first factor of the six input materials derived with factor analysis. Panel C reports the change in net foreign exchange reserves (in trillions of constant 2010 US$). Panel D reports the de-trended values of the latter. Panel E shows official finance in terms of project numbers within the group that is below the median of the probability of receiving it and the group that is above the median over time. Panel F shows the average real GDP per capita growth rate

include additional control variables such as initial-period per capita GDP, ethnic fractionalization, assassinations, proxies for institutional and economic policies, and proxies for financial development (e.g., Burnside and Dollar 2000). All of these variables are arguably endogenous and introduce bias even if aid is instrumented using a perfectly excludable instrumental variable. Given that our exclusion restriction holds absent the inclusion of these control variables, their omission reduces the efficiency of the estimator but does not bias our estimates.[102]

We then turn to the ADM2 level[103] and estimate analogous regressions at the level of district $j$ in country $i$ and year $t$, where $\eta_j$ are fixed effects for regions, and $\mu_{i,t}$ are fixed effects for country-years:

$$Y_{k,i,j,t} = \beta_1 Projects_{CHN,i,j,t-2} + \beta_2 pop_{i,j,t-1} + \beta_3 \eta_j + \beta_4 \mu_{i,t} + \varepsilon_{i,j,t}, \quad (3)$$

$$Projects_{CHN,i,j,t-2} = \gamma_1 Material_{t-3} * p_{CHN,i,j} + \gamma_2 Reserves_{t-3} * p_{CHN,i,j}$$

$$+ \gamma_3 pop_{i,j,t-1} + \gamma_4 \eta_j + \gamma_5 \mu_{i,t} + u_{i,j,t-2}. \quad (4)$$

Our final set of regressions tests, at the country and district level, whether political motives for allocating the projects reduce their effectiveness:

$$Y_{k,i,t} = \beta_1 Projects_{CHN,i,t-2} + \beta_2 Projects_{CHN,i,t-2} * UNGA_{i,t-2}$$

$$+ \beta_3 UNGA_{i,t-2} + \beta_4 pop_{i,t-1} + \beta_5 \eta_i + \beta_6 \mu_t + \varepsilon_{i,t}, \quad (5)$$

$$Y_{k,i,j,t} = \beta_1 Projects_{CHN,i,j,t-2} + \beta_2 Projects_{CHN,i,j,t-2} * BIRTH_{i,j,t-2}$$

$$+ \beta_3 BIRTH_{i,j,t-2} + \beta_4 pop_{i,j,t-1} + \beta_5 \eta_j + \beta_6 \mu_{i,t} + \varepsilon_{i,j,t}. \quad (6)$$

To this end, we interact $Projects_{CHN}$ with proxies for a recipient's political privilege vis-à-vis China or the national government at the time it received the financial commitment. At the country level, we interact the provision of financial support from the Chinese government with the degree to which the recipient country votes in line with China in the UNGA. At the district level, our proxy for political privilege is a binary variable indicating whether or not the recipient district was the home district of the country's leader at the time the project was committed. The funding that China commits to a recipient in years when the

---

[102] One might object that population size should not be included in fixed-effects regressions, given that it hardly varies over time. As we show in Dreher, Fuchs, Parks et al. (2020), omitting population barely changes our results; if anything, the effect of development finance cannot be rejected at higher levels of significance in some regressions.

[103] Our subnational analysis of infant mortality rather uses a finer local scale. We adjust our identification strategy accordingly.

recipient is politically privileged is a combination of two types: extraordinary – and potentially less effective – projects that the recipient gets because of political privilege and projects that the recipient would get even during normal times. To the extent that the effectiveness of the former is sufficiently low to reduce average project effectiveness in years of political privilege, the interaction in equation (5) would show a negative coefficient. The same holds true for the interaction in equation (6) at the district level. To identify the effect of the interaction in our instrumental variables regressions, we include interactions of our previous instruments with the respective political privilege variables as additional instruments.

To compare the effects of Chinese projects with those from the World Bank, we run similar regressions for aid and debt from the World Bank. Following Lang (2021), we calculate the World Bank's "budget" to proxy the availability of funding with measures of its financial resources: the IBRD's equity-to-loans ratio and the IDA's "funding position." Lang suggests the IMF's liquidity ratio interacted with the probability of a country to be under an IMF program as an instrument for IMF loans. We use similar proxies for the World Bank. To measure the availability of IBRD resources, we rely on the IBRD's equity-to-loans ratio, which the IBRD has consistently reported in its annual financial statements since 1994. The equity-to-loans ratio is a measure of the IBRD's "ability to issue loans without calling its callable capital" (Bulow 2002: 245). To measure the availability of IDA resources, we rely on a measure of IDA's funding position, which the World Bank defines as "the extent to which IDA can commit to new financing of loans, grants and guarantees given its financial position at any point in time and whether there are sufficient resources to meet undisbursed commitments of loans and grants" (IDA 2015: 24). This indicator is publicly disclosed by the bank every year in its annual financial statement. However, it only began this practice in 2008, so we reconstruct data for earlier years by using the bank's method for calculating this indicator. We first sum the bank's net investment portfolio and its nonnegotiable, non-interest-bearing demand obligations (on account of members' subscriptions and contributions) and then divide this figure by the sum of the bank's undisbursed commitments of development credits and grants.

Our instrumental variables are thus the IDA- and IBRD-liquidity ratios interacted with the share of years in the 2000–2014 period a country or district received funding from these institutions. The exclusion restriction relies on the assumption that changes in the bank's liquidity over time do not differentially affect outcomes in countries with a low probability to receive funding from the bank compared with outcomes in countries with a high probability to receive development finance, other than via the development finance.

As illustrated in Table A7.3, the first-stage F-statistics are reasonably high. The interactions of IDA and IBRD liquidity with the probability to receive funding – where significant – point in the opposite direction compared with the first-stage results for China noted earlier. This is in line with Dreher and Langlotz (2020) and Lang (2021) who show that bilateral donors tend to focus temporary increases in aid on frequent recipients, while international organizations (the IMF, specifically) extend their range beyond their traditional customer base.

Finally, we briefly report results from a large number of robustness tests that we have conducted across several earlier research efforts. The tests we cover here can be categorized into four groups. The first includes variants of our instrumental variables. We have used China's steel production, the first factor of six input materials, China's overall development finance budget; and changes in the availability of international reserves, one at a time and in various combinations, and interacted each of these measures with the probability of receiving funding. We measure this both contemporaneously and with the old friends measure introduced in Chapter 5. While contemporaneous probabilities are clearly exogenous conditional on fixed effects, historic probabilities are more likely to be exogenous ex ante (i.e., without controlling for fixed effects); historic probabilities are therefore less likely to be correlated with omitted variables that differentially affect countries or subnational localities with a high or low probability to receive support in years with varying exposure to a China shock. While the power of the instruments is typically lower when we use historic probabilities, results are consistent.

Our second group of tests for robustness applies varying definitions of Chinese development finance. We have investigated receipt of Chinese support (a binary indicator), the number of project commitments at a point in time, and project amounts (which we investigated in logs, absolute numbers, or per capita terms). In most of our papers, we have separately investigated effects in three broad sectors: economic infrastructure and services, social infrastructure and services, and production sectors. In previous work, we also constructed a measure of "early impact" projects. While the specific results vary depending on the outcome measures we employ, they are generally consistent across these different definitions.

Our results are qualitatively unchanged in a third group of tests where we replicate the analyses netting out the effect of the most common determinants of growth employed in the aid effectiveness literature.

These include the average number of assassinations in a recipient country, its government surplus as a share of GDP, its rate of inflation, money as a share of GDP, and trade openness.

The fourth and final set of robustness checks includes variants of our regression models where we change the spatial or temporal unit of analysis. We focus on provinces (ADM1s) rather than districts (ADM2) or use three-year averages rather than yearly observations. Again, results are broadly consistent.

# 8 Poisonous Dragon Fruits?
## The Side Effects of Chinese Development Finance

### Raising the Stakes: Kenya's Standard Gauge Railway

In the spring of 2013, a total of 12.3 million Kenyan voters went to the polls to choose their next president. Raila Odinga, the incumbent prime minister, ran against Uhuru Kenyatta, his deputy prime minister. Kenyatta – who is a member of the Kikuyu ethnic group – forged an unusual political alliance to defeat his rival. He ran on a unity ticket with William Ruto, who is from the Kalenjin ethnic group. The alliance stunned political analysts: Ruto and Kenyatta had previously accused each other of organizing election and post-election violence that destabilized Kenya in 2008. But politics makes for strange bedfellows, and Kenyatta's unity ticket strategy worked. He and Ruto garnered strong support from their co-ethnic voters and won 50.03 percent of the popular vote, defeating Odinga.[1]

On the campaign trail, Kenyatta distinguished himself from his rival by emphasizing the importance of economic growth.[2] When he assumed the presidency, he sought to deliver on his campaign promise by prioritizing several flagship infrastructure projects. Chief among these was the 475-kilometer standard gauge railway (SGR), a project that would transport passengers and cargo from Nairobi to the southeastern port city of Mombasa at 120 kilometers per hour and reduce travel times and transport costs by as much as 60 percent. This project, which we discussed in Chapters 2 and 5, was the largest infrastructure project to be undertaken in Kenya since its independence in 1963. The Kenyan government

---

This chapter draws selectively upon empirical results, prose, and arguments from four prior studies: BenYishay, Parks, Runfola, and Trichler (2016), Strange, Dreher, Fuchs et al. (2017), Parks and Strange (2019), and Dreher, Fuchs, Parks et al. (2021). These articles include more detailed links to previous research than we reference here.

[1] See Ferree, Gibson, and Long (2014).

[2] Ferree, Gibson, and Long (2014: 157) note that whereas "Odinga emphasized fighting corruption, land reform, and social issues ... Kenyatta was better known on the campaign trail for championing economic growth."

estimated that upon completion, the railway would increase the country's annual rate of economic growth by 1.5 percentage points.[3]

Mega-transport projects like this one are notoriously difficult to implement and are often beset by delays and cost overruns, so President Kenyatta did not take any chances.[4] He became personally involved in the design and execution of the SGR. He made clear that his overriding goal was to ensure completion of the project by the time he stood for reelection in August 2017.[5] The first sign of Kenyatta's special interest in the project came on May 11, 2014, when he exempted the SGR from competitive bidding requirements and authorized a no-bid contract to the China Road and Bridge Corporation (CRBC).[6] Then, on July 21, his administration contracted two loans from China Eximbank worth approximately US$3.5 billion to facilitate payment to the CRBC for the implementation of the project.[7]

This decision provoked intense criticism and controversy. Members of parliament questioned the wisdom of contracting one of the two loans on commercial borrowing terms and agreeing to levy a new tax on imported goods to facilitate loan repayment. The absence of competitive bidding also prompted speculation about artificially inflated project costs and illicit payments between the CRBC and Kenyan politicians.[8] However, Kenyatta pressed forward, and the project broke ground on December 12, 2014.

By all accounts, the SGR project was implemented at an astonishingly fast pace. The CRBC quickly identified President Kenyatta as the "project owner," which meant that it would execute the project in a manner that was consistent with his priorities and rely on him to

---

[3] According to Wissenbach (2019: 346), "[t]he project was originally turned down by traditional lenders (the World Bank) based on a narrow cost-benefit analysis."

[4] Dimitriou, Low, Sturup et al. (2014) define mega-transport projects as "land-based transport infrastructure investments in the form of bridges, tunnels, road and rail links or combinations of these, that entail a construction cost of over US$1 billion." There is a substantial body of literature on the difficulty of implementing these types of projects on time and on budget (e.g., Flyvbjerg, Holm, and Buhl 2002).

[5] Wissenbach (2019).

[6] The decision to issue the contract with the CRBC was also controversial because the World Bank had recently debarred the CRBC's parent company – the China Communications Construction Company (CCCC) Limited – from contracting for World Bank-funded projects because of its involvement in a fraudulent scheme related to the World Bank-financed Philippines National Roads Improvement and Management Project.

[7] Kenya National Assembly (2014).

[8] According to the *New York Times*, on one television show, "a politician who had switched allegiances from the opposition to Mr. Kenyatta's party and who extolled the railway's virtues was quickly overwhelmed by calls from viewers. 'You are lying,' one person said. 'You were bribed'" (de Freytas-Tamura 2017).

resolve politically contentious matters that could delay or derail the project.[9] Environmental and land valuation concerns were the two primary threats to timely project completion. Conservationists sounded the alarm when they learned that the railway would run through the Tsavo National Park wildlife sanctuary. But the CRBC moved quickly to mitigate the risk of biodiversity loss, undertaking a variety of in situ conservation activities. They created access corridors for wildlife migration, building some bridges as high as seven meters tall to ensure the safe passage of giraffes and elephants from one side of the park to the other.[10] Alongside the railway, they also installed dust-suppressing sprinklers, noise screens, and drinking water facilities for wildlife to mitigate concerns about health hazards during the construction phase and water scarcity during dry seasons.[11]

Another major challenge was that the construction of the 475-kilometer railway would require the displacement of nearby residents. Kenyatta needed a fair way to value and compensate these people, so he set aside US$290 million for compensation purposes and helped resolve contentious disputes with local politicians who lobbied for special factors like "ancestral interests."[12] The CRBC also hired local people who were trusted by local residents, such as pastors from nearby churches, to serve as community liaison officers. These officers helped the Chinese firm and the president understand and respond to local grievances – a tactic that previous research has called "an effective strategy for gaining greater [local] acceptance of the SGR."[13]

The SGR project was completed on June 1, 2017, eighteen months ahead of schedule. Kenyatta scheduled the completion ceremony just two months before voters would go to the polls, on Madaraka Day – a national holiday that commemorates the day when colonial Britain granted Kenya the right to internal self-rule.[14] Yuan Wang of Columbia University and Uwe Wissenbach of the European External Action Service note that the SGR (which was "the only mega project to be finished on time during the first term [2013–17] of President Kenyatta") was "presented [to the electorate] as a flagship project of a government committed to economic development and as a result of Kenyan agency,

---

[9] Wang and Wissenbach (2019).     [10] Wang and Wissenbach (2019).     [11] Liu (2017).
[12] Wang and Wissenbach (2019).     [13] Wissenbach and Wang (2017: 14).
[14] At the project completion ceremony, Kenyatta gave a speech and said that our "history … was first started 122 years ago when the British, who had colonised this nation, kicked off the train to nowhere … it was then dubbed the 'Lunatic Express.' Today … despite again a lot of criticism we now celebrate not the 'Lunatic Express' but the Madaraka Express that will begin to reshape the story of Kenya for the next 100 years" (BBC News 2017).

symbolically closing a 110-year chapter of reliance on colonial infrastructure."[15]

With the SGR in hand, Kenyatta pursued a different electoral strategy than he had in 2013. Rather than appealing to co-ethnics, he adopted a slogan of "45-million-strong" – a reference to his platform of serving the country's entire population of 45 million people; his request for votes "was predicated on a developmental peace model that was not condescending to any tribe."[16] Kenyatta ultimately won the August 2017 election with 54 percent of the popular vote, and a political scientist from the University of Nairobi specifically attributed the win to Kenyatta's "scores in infrastructure development, citing the 480-km standard gauge railway (SGR) put into operation."[17]

However, Kenyatta did not emerge from the contest entirely unscathed. In 2013, his rival, Raila Odinga, had succeeded in focusing public attention on Kenyatta's failure to stamp out corruption. In his second term, Kenyatta corrected course, appointing a zealous anti-corruption crusader to lead the Department of Public Prosecutions (DPP).[18] To the surprise of the Chinese government, the SGR – Beijing's largest infrastructure project in Kenya – became a target of the DPP's anti-corruption drive. According to *Reuters*,

Kenyan authorities . . . arrested the head of the agency that manages public land and the boss of the state railway on suspicion of corruption over land allocation for the new $3-billion flagship Nairobi-Mombasa railway. . . . Also arrested was Atanas Kariuki Maina, managing director of the Kenya Railways Corporation. . . . The investigation that led to the arrests centers on allegations that officials siphoned taxpayer money through [fraudulent] compensation claims for land used for the railway.[19]

---

[15] Wissenbach and Wang (2017: 24). According to BBC (2018), the "railway line was central to President Uhuru Kenyatta's reelection strategy, launched only months before the presidential poll last year."

[16] The New Times (2017). By contrast, the opposition candidate (Raila Odinga) adopted a slogan of "10-million-strong" – a reference to his party's goal of winning 10 million votes from the country's 19.6 million eligible voters (The New Times 2017).

[17] The New Times (2017).

[18] Indeed, in the run-up to the election (between December 2016 and June 2017), satisfaction with the country's direction on corruption declined sharply – from 49 percent to 34 percent – among likely Kenyatta voters (Arriola, Choi, and Rateng 2017).

[19] Malalo (2018). Three months later, SGR was embroiled in another scandal. Several CRBC employees were indicted on charges that they had bribed Kenyan government officials to facilitate a railway ticketing scam. John Githongo, the country's former permanent secretary for governance and ethics, told the *Financial Times* that we "knew from the very beginning that this was a lemon of a project and it is simply becoming more and more apparent every day" (Pilling and Feng 2018).

As the circuitous journey of the SGR project illustrates, Chinese development projects can generate complex externalities. While the project itself had a bounded set of economic objectives, it appears to have had spillover effects – on the natural environment, on electoral politics, and even on anti-corruption efforts.

The tale of the SGR project also underscores a key point from the previous chapter: China's transition from benefactor to banker has dramatically increased the stakes for host countries. At the turn of the century, Beijing was still primarily funding relatively small projects via grants and highly concessional loans. However, over the past twenty years, we have witnessed an unprecedented expansion in the country's overseas development program – and the size of the individual projects supported by the program – as China's policy banks and state-owned commercial banks have doubled down on the provision of non-concessional and semi-concessional loans to low- and middle-income countries. Kenya is a case in point. During the first ten years of our study period (2000–2009), China Eximbank provided US$61.6 million a year (on average) for road, rail, and bridge projects in Kenya. However, in the last five years of our study period (2010–2014), it provided US$700 million a year (on average) for such projects. Chapter 7 demonstrated that large, debt-financed Chinese development projects have benefits: they substantially improve socioeconomic outcomes in the near term, especially in Africa. But the scale and commercial orientation of China's overseas lending activities also present risks, which some host countries manage effectively. Others do not. As this chapter demonstrates, Chinese debt-financed development projects tend to increase corruption and conflict. However, we also provide evidence that some of the risks posed by these projects (like environmental degradation) can be mitigated. The choices made by host countries matter; they can influence the scope and the severity of the negative, unintended consequences of Chinese development projects. The lesson for those who primarily bank with Beijing is clear: Chinese debt-financed development projects affect the polities, societies, and ecosystems of borrower countries in complex ways, and the risks that these projects pose need to be proactively addressed.

Chapter 7 tested whether Chinese development finance is *effective*. In this chapter, we seek to determine whether Chinese development finance is *safe*. In modern medical research involving human subjects, clinical trials are undertaken to evaluate the efficacy and safety of new treatments. In principle, rigorous and responsible evaluations of international development projects should be no different, since the "treatments" in question can have many side effects.[20]

One risk is that foreign development projects might undercut or overtax domestic capacity in recipient countries. As we discussed in Chapter 7, aid agencies and development banks can weaken the capacity and performance of host government institutions by poaching top talent from the public sector or by providing distortionary wage top-ups to bureaucrats and politicians.[21] International development finance, which is highly fragmented and complex, can also place a heavy administrative burden on recipient country bureaucracies, which may not have the capacity to deal with dozens of donors and creditors and govern effectively at the same time.[22]

Another risk is that foreign aid and credit will undermine the accountability of government institutions. When domestic public expenditures are out of step with the public's needs, taxpayers can register their dissatisfaction in various ways: by protesting, voting, or leaving the locality or country where they reside. But projects financed by international development organizations are not paid for by taxes, and people living in developing countries do not have many ways of holding international development organizations accountable for the quality and quantity of goods and services they provide. Consequently, large windfalls of external aid and credit may sever the accountability relationship between governors and governed, making it easier for public officials to use their positions for private gain.[23] A separate but related concern is that international development organizations spend billions of dollars each year to increase the capacities of state institutions in host countries – for example, by training and equipping judges, legislators, police officers, and tax officials – but agents of the state can use these expanded

---

[20] One of these potential side effects is "Dutch Disease": the possibility that international development finance increases demand for imports of domestically scarce goods, thereby resulting in an appreciation of the nominal exchange rate and an overvaluation of the real exchange rate, which can make a country's exports less competitive in international markets. However, since Chapter 7 has already explored in some detail the economic impacts of Chinese development finance, we focus here on political, social, and environmental side effects.

[21] Knack and Rahman (2007) show that donor fragmentation reduces bureaucratic quality and argue that this problem increases in magnitude with the number of donors a recipient government faces. See Gehring, Michaelowa, Dreher, and Spörri (2017) for a more recent and nuanced view.

[22] The time and energy that politicians and bureaucrats in recipient countries use to obtain and distribute "cheap money" from external sources could instead be used to invest in economically productive activities.

[23] Moore (1998); Moss and Subramanian (2005).

capacities for good (enforcing the rule of law and delivering public services) or ill (enriching themselves via predation).

Another risk is that some governments may use international development finance to insulate themselves from the consequences of bad policies; without looming consequences, governments might delay or avoid policy reforms.[24] Consider a situation in which a government with low baseline levels of institutional quality, an underdeveloped tax base, and limited access to private capital is hit by crisis. In the absence of foreign aid or debt, it will almost certainly need to implement policy reforms. But if foreign sponsors and creditors are willing to support the government during its crisis, the country's politicians and bureaucrats can avoid difficult policy adjustments. While some foreign donors and lenders have tried to mitigate this risk by linking financial disbursements to specific policy reform commitments, this strategy has produced disappointing results:[25] when countries do not "own" reforms, they often renege or backtrack soon after funding is disbursed.[26]

Yet another risk is that foreign funding can intensify conflicts over assets and public goods. Foreign funding introduces more resources (such as cash and commodities) that warring factions can misappropriate to feed, pay, or equip soldiers. Even promises of outside funding could strengthen the incentive for rebels and would-be rebels to engage in conflict (since they increase the expected spoils of military victory). According to Harvard University's Nathan Nunn and Northwestern University's Nancy Qian, US food aid has increased the incidence and duration of civil conflict.[27] Richard Bluhm and colleagues, who focus on bilateral aid from a larger set of Western donors, arrive at a relatively similar set of results.[28]

One final risk is that development projects will negatively impact the natural environment. Conservationists and environmental advocacy groups warn that large-scale development projects often deplete and degrade water, air, soil, and forest resources, although foreign funders and recipient governments maintain that development projects are increasingly designed and implemented in environmentally sensitive ways.[29]

---

[24] Dreher and Gehring (2012) summarize the literature on aid and reforms. They conclude that the evidence across a large number of studies is mixed, at best.

[25] See, for example, Dollar and Svensson (2000); Dreher (2009).

[26] See, for example, Vreeland (2003, 2006).

[27] Nunn and Qian (2014). However, see also Christian and Barrett's (2017) methodological note of caution.

[28] They find that aid increases the chance that preexisting conflicts will escalate, but it has no effect on conflict in truly peaceful societies (Bluhm, Gassebner, Langlotz, and Schaudt 2021).

[29] Laurance, Peletier-Jellema, Geenen et al. (2015); Buchanan, Donald, Parks et al. (2018).

As we noted in previous chapters, China's critics and rivals claim that its development projects are especially likely to produce these kinds of negative side effects. They have flagged a wide array of concerns; in this chapter, we will focus on four specific concerns that have dominated debate among policymakers, journalists, and scholars. The first is that Chinese aid and debt undermine democratic governance, weaken public sector institutions, and fuel corruption.[30] The second is that funding from the Chinese government could trigger or intensify violent conflict. The third is that Chinese development projects accelerate environmental degradation.[31] The fourth is that Chinese development finance undermines Western development finance by creating an alternative source of funding, which gives developing countries the option of avoiding policies and project safeguards that are politically costly but ultimately beneficial in terms of long-term development.

In the remainder of this chapter, we expose these claims to empirical scrutiny. Leveraging some of the data and methods we introduced in earlier chapters, we measure the effects of Chinese development projects on corruption and other aspects of institutional quality in host countries (at national and subnational scales). Further, we assess whether and to what extent Chinese development projects affect violent conflict in recipient societies. We again test this question at the national level and in subnational localities that receive financial support from China. Additionally, with country-level indicators of environmental quality, we test whether Chinese development projects degrade the natural environment. We introduce our findings alongside the results of a new study that evaluates the forest cover impacts of Chinese development finance at subnational scales in two ecological hotspots: the Mekong Delta and the Great Lakes region of Africa.[32]

Finally, we bring new evidence to bear on the popular claim that Chinese development finance undermines the effectiveness of traditional sources of development finance. We do so by building upon earlier work in which we sought to understand how Chinese development projects may impinge upon the effectiveness of World Bank funding at the country level;[33] we perform several statistical tests that examine whether development finance from the World Bank registers different levels of economic growth in countries that are Chinese "darlings" (major recipients of development finance from Beijing) and Chinese "orphans" (countries

[30] Our finding from Chapter 5 suggests that this concern may have merit since Beijing's debt-financed projects do indeed favor more corrupt and authoritarian governments.
[31] Kurlantzick (2006); Bosshard (2007); Taylor (2007); Kynge (2016).
[32] BenYishay, Parks, Runfola, and Trichler (2016).
[33] Dreher, Fuchs, Parks et al. (2021).

that have not received large amounts of funding from Beijing). We present similar results at the subnational level, using one of the core outcome variables (per capita nighttime light output) from Chapter 7. Finally, we test whether the receipt of Chinese development finance has any bearing on the negative side effects that World Bank projects can produce, such as corruption, conflict, authoritarian rule, and environmental degradation.

## Governance

The Chinese government pursues a policy of non-interference in the domestic affairs of sovereign governments, which implies that it allocates aid and credit without considering the quality of governance in other countries. Our results in Chapter 5 confirm that Chinese aid neither favors nor disfavors countries based on their regime types, their track records of fighting corruption, or their levels of political stability. However, Chinese debt is an entirely different story: it actually *favors* more corrupt countries, less democratic countries, and countries with fewer constraints on executive power. Beijing's policy of non-interference raises a number of concerns.

One concern is that credit from Chinese state-owned banks could help the political leaders of borrower countries dilute, delay, or dismantle governance reforms. There is some evidence that aid has this effect. As Sarah Bermeo, a political scientist at Duke University, shows, aid from democratic donors is associated with a higher probability of democratic transition, while aid from six authoritarian donors is negatively correlated with the probability of democratization.[34] Similarly, Erasmus Kersting and Christopher Kilby – development economists at Villanova University – find that bilateral aid from Western sources improves democratic governance, while aid from authoritarian donors has the opposite effect.[35] However, the existing literature is primarily focused on aid rather than debt.

Because Chinese funding is so readily available now, there are fewer incentives for developing countries to implement the policy and institutional reforms that Western donors often require – reforms intended to promote long-term economic growth and effective public service

---

[34] Bermeo (2011).

[35] Kersting and Kilby (2014). Likewise, Li (2017), who uses a synthetic control group approach, finds that major recipients of Chinese development finance are less likely than other countries to make democratic governance gains. Ping, Wang, and Chang (2021) show that China's resource-related development projects diminish the capacity of recipient countries' horizontal (legislative and judicial) institutions but have little effect on electoral restraints on the executive (vertical accountability).

delivery.[36] According to one study, the receipt of Chinese development finance actually reduces the number of policy conditions that developing countries must accept when they borrow from the World Bank; however, development finance from the OECD-DAC has no such effect.[37] Kurt Annen and Steven Knack, two development economists, have published another study that may help explain this relationship.[38] They find that in recent years, OECD-DAC development finance has become more sensitive to the quality of policies and institutions in recipient countries, but this relationship is compromised when a country received large-scale funding from the Chinese government (in excess of US$2 billion).

Another key concern is that Chinese government funding fosters corruption in recipient countries. Ann-Sofie Isaksson of the University of Gothenburg and Andreas Kotsadam of the University of Oslo recently investigated whether development projects from different sources might fuel local corruption in the areas where they are implemented.[39] They merge a subnationally geo-referenced version of our dataset with geocoded Afrobarometer survey data on experiences with corruption; the survey includes data from nearly 100,000 respondents in thirty African countries. The authors find that local corruption is more prevalent around Chinese development project sites; they found no additional corruption around World Bank development project sites.[40] These findings do not explain *why* development finance from different sources seems to produce different local corruption outcomes. One reason might be that not all funders have equally robust institutional safeguards – for example, competitive bidding, citizen feedback mechanisms, and blacklisting of corrupt firms – in place. The World Bank has a whole host of provisions in its loan documentation and procurement guidelines that are designed to deter bribery and fraudulent

---

[36] Policy and institutional quality are important determinants of public investment efficiency (Denizer, Kaufmann, and Kraay 2013; Presbitero 2016) and economic growth (Humphreys and Bates 2005; Jones and Olken 2005).

[37] Hernandez (2017) estimates 15 percent fewer World Bank conditions for every 1 percent increase in Chinese aid. This finding comports with more direct evidence provided in other recent work (Brazys and Vadlamannati 2021); Watkins (2021) reports that compliance with World Bank project conditions decreases when countries receive larger funding from China. On the question of whether, when, and why the World Bank encourages de jure or de facto institutional reforms, see Andrews (2013); Smets and Knack (2016); Buntaine, Parks, and Buch (2017).

[38] Annen and Knack (2020).    [39] Isaksson and Kotsadam (2018a).

[40] Isaksson and Kotsadam (2018a). Findley, Milner, and Nielson (2017) provide experimental evidence that Ugandan citizens prefer development projects financed by USAID over those financed by China due to concerns about transparency and corruption.

behavior among contractors.[41] China, by contrast, has a relatively weak and underdeveloped set of anti-corruption safeguards for its overseas development projects.

China's existing system for designing and implementing projects has two key weaknesses that create a permissive environment for corruption. The first is a domestic vulnerability: informal ties between the Chinese government officials who review project proposals and the Chinese contractors who bid to implement projects that are approved. This vulnerability in the system was recently exposed when five high-ranking Chinese foreign aid officials from MOFCOM – the director general of the Department of Foreign Aid, three deputy directors of divisions within the Department of Foreign Aid, and the director general of the Department of International Trade and Economic Affairs – were charged with corruption and relieved of their duties.[42] One of the officials who had direct oversight of the project bidding process was caught accepting lavish gifts from Chinese contracting companies.

The second vulnerability in the system is the way in which project proposals are sourced from recipient countries. As we explained in Chapter 6, China's largest overseas financing institutions typically ask political leaders rather than technocrats from borrower countries to formulate project proposals and submit them for appraisal. Chinese contractors with a significant in-country presence know that this is how projects get approved, so they have an incentive to "game the system" by colluding with the political leaders responsible for submitting project proposals. A growing body of anecdotal evidence suggests that these contractors first identify a project that they are uniquely well positioned to implement and that will benefit the leader with whom they are colluding; then, they inflate the cost of the project to increase their profit and cover the expense of any potential side payment(s) to the leader and/or the leader's relatives and allies; finally, they ask the leader to present the candidate project to Beijing

---

[41] World Bank (2014). It also has a blacklisting policy whereby firms that are caught engaging in fraudulent, corrupt, or collusive practices can be debarred permanently or temporarily from bidding on World Bank contracts. A growing number of World Bank projects also include mechanisms (e.g., anonymous hotlines, citizen charters and report cards, crowdsourcing, and SMS feedback platforms) for citizens to sound the alarm if they witness or suspect corruption.

[42] Zhang and Smith (2017). The authorities in Beijing are clearly aware of the problem. In 2014, as part of President Xi Jinping's broader anti-corruption campaign, the Chinese Communist Party's Central Disciplinary Committee reviewed existing practices at MOFCOM and quickly zeroed in on the corruption risks that plague its overseas project portfolio (MOFCOM 2014b). Several years later, President Xi gave a speech in which he announced that "[w]e will ... strengthen international cooperation on anticorruption in order to build the Belt and Road Initiative with integrity" (Abi-Habib 2018).

as an official priority of the recipient government without leaving any "contractor fingerprints" on the proposal submission.[43]

Yet another possibility is that donors and lenders from different countries transmit different values and norms to the politicians, firms, and citizens in areas near their development projects. Isaksson marshals evidence in support of this argument.[44] She finds that individuals who live near World Bank project sites are more likely to report having attended a community meeting in the past year, but individuals who live near Chinese project sites are not.[45] Isaksson, working jointly with Kotsadam, has also demonstrated that Chinese projects do not increase local corruption by expanding economic activity around project sites, which increases the plausibility of their argument that local corruption increases due to norm transmission from the donor country.[46]

In summary, the existing body of evidence suggests that critics of Chinese development finance may be right: it seems to discourage policy reform, weaken public sector institutions, and fuel corruption.[47] However, given that these empirical conclusions are based on very different causal inference strategies and relatively small samples (that are sometimes specific to a single region), we decided to reevaluate them with our dataset of Chinese development projects, a battery of different governance outcome measures, and a consistent causal inference strategy (the one that we introduced in Chapter 7). Figure 8.1 summarizes our statistical findings with partial leverage plots.[48] The lines of best fit represent the average estimated effects of Chinese development projects on various governance outcomes. Panels A and B show how the number of Chinese development projects affects levels of corruption and democratic accountability at the country level, using data for the entire world over the 2000–2014 period.[49] We employ the same statistical approach as in the previous chapter, using predicted development finance rather than actual development finance, which allows us to interpret the slopes of the best-fit lines as causal effects rather than mere correlations (under the

---

[43] Dornan and Brant (2014); Zhang and Smith (2017); Parks (2019).

[44] Isaksson (2017).

[45] Isaksson and Kotsadam (2018b) also provide evidence that the implementation of Chinese development projects reduces public participation in trade unions in nearby areas.

[46] Isaakson and Kotsadam (2018a).

[47] In addition to the papers discussed earlier, Bader (2015a, 2015b) investigates whether Chinese development finance extends the tenure of authoritarian regimes, with mixed results. There is no significant effect on average; Chinese projects increase the longevity of party-based regimes but lead to the collapse of non-party-based regimes.

[48] Table A8.1 provides more detailed results.

[49] Details on data sources and model specifications can be found in the notes of our appendix tables.

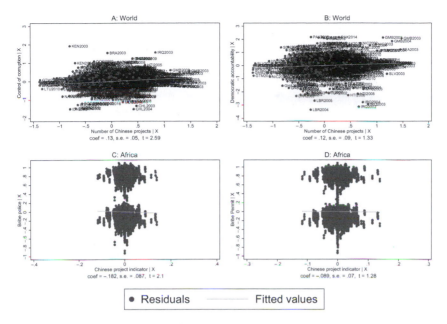

Figure 8.1 Chinese development projects, corruption, and democratic accountability

*Notes:* The figure shows partial leverage plots corresponding to columns 1–4 in Table A8.1. See the notes for this table for details on data and methods.

assumptions outlined in Appendix 7B). Our results show some evidence that the quality of governance improves with the number of Chinese development projects. More specifically, our statistical models suggest that exposure to an additional Chinese development project improves the absence-of-corruption indicator by 0.13 points. However, there is no significant effect on democratic accountability.[50]

In Panels C and D, we revisit the subnational findings of Isaksson and Kotsadam (using their original sample). They used a causal inference strategy that compares differences in experienced corruption between "posttreatment" individuals (i.e., those with active Chinese projects near their place of residence) and "control" individuals (i.e., those with planned

---

[50] We take both indices from the PRS Group's International Country Risk Guide (ICRG). The effect on democratic accountability is less precisely estimated but similar in magnitude to the absence-of-corruption effect. The absence-of-corruption indicator ranges between 0 and 6, with a mean of 2. The democratic accountability indicator ranges between 0 and 6, with a mean of 3.6. See Table A8.3 for descriptive statistics.

but not-yet-active Chinese projects near their place of residence). This is arguably more of an apples-to-apples comparison than simply comparing people who live in places with active Chinese projects with people who live in places that never receive Chinese projects. However, localities that receive Chinese projects today could still be systematically different from localities that receive Chinese projects tomorrow; if such site selection biases exist, it becomes more difficult to disentangle cause and effect.[51] We address this endogeneity issue by using the same causal inference strategy that we used in Chapter 7; we rely on the predicted number of Chinese projects to explain outcomes rather than the actual number of Chinese projects. We first construct a binary indicator that takes a value of one if a Chinese government-funded project was undertaken within 50 kilometers of the household being interviewed two years before the interview date.[52] We use the same outcome measures as Isaksson and Kotsadam: measures of whether survey respondents, during the past year, "had to pay a bribe, give a gift, or do a favor to government officials in order to" (a) "avoid a problem with the police (like passing a checkpoint or avoiding a fine or arrest)" or (b) "get a document or a permit."[53]

Our findings (in panels C and D) are consistent with those reported in panels A and B; however, at first glance, they appear to be inconsistent with those reported by Isaksson and Kotsadam: we find that local exposure to a Chinese development project reduces the probability that survey respondents will report paying bribes to the police in the past year by 18.2 percentage points and reduces the probability that survey respondents will report paying bribes to obtain permits by 8.9 percentage points.[54]

However, an interesting pattern emerges when we separate out Chinese aid and Chinese debt.[55] While both types of financial flows seem to reduce corruption at the country level, we find evidence of heterogeneous effects at the local level: Chinese debt-financed development projects fuel

---

[51] For example, police and the judiciary might fight corruption in a region less vigorously when it is the birth region of the leader who is currently in power if elite corruption benefits that leader. The increased development finance the region receives because of its status as a birth region would then be attributed to increased corruption, when in fact there is no causal effect of development projects on corruption; instead, birth region may have a causal effect on both corruption and development projects.

[52] Following our empirical strategy in Chapter 7, we build our instrumental variables as the interactions of two variables: our reserve- and input-based indicators for the availability of Chinese funding and the probability that the ADM1 region the household is located in receives such funding. We hold everything constant that does not vary within regions or years.

[53] Isaksson and Kotsadam (2018a: 149).     [54] The latter effect is imprecisely estimated.

[55] We do not report these results in tables, but they are available upon request.

corruption in nearby geographic areas, while Chinese aid-financed development projects have the opposite effect.[56]

These impacts should be interpreted in light of several other findings that we uncovered in previous chapters. First, recall from Chapters 4 and 5 that Chinese debt-financed development projects favor more corrupt countries and involve much larger sums of money than Chinese aid-financed projects. Second, recall from Chapter 2 that Beijing expects its debt-financed projects, but not its aid-financed projects, to support revenue-generating assets. Third, recall from Chapter 7 that Chinese debt-financed projects generate particularly high levels of economic activity – and they do so within only a few years' time. These facts help put our findings on the corruption impacts of Chinese aid- and debt-financed development projects into context. Chinese aid projects probably pose fewer corruption risks because they involve relatively small sums of money, generate little revenue, and are not implemented in settings that are particularly conducive to corruption. In contrast, Chinese debt-financed projects present higher risks of corruption because they involve big-ticket, revenue-generating projects that result in a large number of commercial transactions in a relatively short period of time and are often located in areas especially conducive to corruption.

What, then, should we conclude? Certainly that Chinese development projects do not increase corruption across the board. But we should also note that Beijing's borrowers face a trade-off between *efficacy* and *safety*. Chinese debt-financed development projects are attractive because they improve socioeconomic outcomes in the near term, but these rewards need to be weighed against the risks. Corruption is one of the risks of banking with Beijing, but as we explain next, it is not the only one.

### Violent Conflict

As we noted earlier in this chapter, some scholars have argued that Chinese development finance fuels conflict – especially in fragile states – by creating stronger incentives for rebels and would-be rebels to seek military victory (and the spoils that come with it).[57] Yet there are also ways in which Chinese development finance might reduce conflict. Beijing provides aid without regard for the quality of governance in recipient countries (as we saw in Chapter 5), and previous research demonstrates that abrupt withdrawals of Western aid make civil conflict

---

[56] The power of our instruments is substantially larger compared with the regressions that focus on all development finance, with a first-stage F-statistic above 8.3 in the ODA regressions and above 44 in the OOF regressions.
[57] Campbell, Wheeler, Attree et al. (2012); Kishi and Raleigh (2016).

more likely. Therefore, if China is willing and able to fill the void created by a large-scale Western aid withdrawal (as we saw in the case of Sri Lanka in Chapter 1), its funding might serve as a "shock absorber."[58] Yet another possibility is that the positive effect of Chinese development finance on income (documented in Chapter 7) increases the opportunity costs of fighting and thereby reduces violent conflict.

In this section, we build on the work of Richard Bluhm and colleagues, who have analyzed bilateral aid from OECD-DAC sources on various types of conflict.[59] They show that Western aid increases the risk that existing small conflicts will escalate to armed conflict, but that it does not ignite conflict in peaceful societies. By adding our measure of the number of Chinese development projects and the variables required for our identification strategy (from Chapter 7) to their replication dataset, we estimate the causal effects of Chinese development projects on various types of conflict (small, armed, and civil war around the globe during the 2002–2010 period.[60]

In Table 8.1, we use a "transition matrix" to summarize these effects at the country level and at the various stages of conflict, following the approach taken by Bluhm and his colleagues.[61] The entries in the table report the probabilities of moving from the state that is indicated in the corresponding row (e.g., "peace") to the state that is indicated in the corresponding column (e.g., "armed conflict") as a consequence of one additional Chinese development project. The estimated effects that we report in Table 8.1 show that no matter the level of conflict in the previous year, Chinese development projects reduce the probability of peace and increase the risk of armed conflict and civil war. For example, the "Peace-Peace" entry (the figure −3.623 in the upper-left cell) suggests that the receipt of one additional Chinese development project reduces the probability of a peaceful country remaining peaceful by about 3.6 percentage points. However, all of these effects are estimated imprecisely, so we cannot confidently conclude that there are effects of Chinese development projects on peace and conflict at the country level.

---

[58] Strange, Dreher, Fuchs et al. (2017).

[59] Bluhm, Gassebner, Langlotz, and Schaudt (2021) use a dynamic ordered probit estimator that controls for unobserved heterogeneity and corrects for the endogeneity of aid using a control function approach.

[60] We thank Richard Bluhm, Martin Gassebner, Sarah Langlotz, and Paul Schaudt for sharing their complete dataset and code with us.

[61] Column 5 of Appendix Table A8.1 shows the detailed regression results. The effect of development projects on conflict is lower if the recipient country experienced a small conflict in the year before, and the effect of aid on development projects does not differ depending on whether the country was at peace the year before (the omitted category) or experienced armed conflicts or civil war.

Table 8.1  *Transition matrix: Partial effect of Chinese development projects*

|  | To State | | | |
| --- | --- | --- | --- | --- |
| *From State* | Peace | Small Conflict | Armed Conflict | Civil War |
| Peace | −3.623 | 2.206 | 1.360 | 0.057 |
|  | (2.791) | (1.739) | (1.081) | (0.076) |
| Small Conflict | −2.212 | 1.036 | 1.088 | 0.087 |
|  | (3.813) | (1.808) | (1.900) | (0.186) |
| Armed Conflict | −3.501 | 0.312 | 2.598 | 0.591 |
|  | (4.415) | (1.119) | (3.340) | (0.824) |
| Civil War | −2.034 | −1.349 | 1.600 | 1.782 |
|  | (4.113) | (2.287) | (3.059) | (3.866) |

*Notes:* The table shows average partial effects corresponding to column 5 in Table A8.1. Panel bootstrap standard errors in parentheses, computed with 500 replications. See the notes of Table A8.1 for details on data and methods.

In an additional set of statistical models, we estimate the effects of aid- and debt-financed Chinese development projects separately.[62] Our results for Chinese aid mirror those that we just summarized, but our results for Chinese debt are quite different, providing stronger grounds for concern. We find that the receipt of an additional Chinese debt-financed development project substantially increases the probability of moving from a state of peace to a state of civil war. This statistical result reinforces our earlier point that Chinese debt-financed development projects present a trade-off between efficacy and safety. That is, while our previous results show significant positive economic growth effects from loans, these same flows increase the risk of negative externalities (like corruption and conflict).

These results beg the question: why would Chinese debt, but not aid, fuel violent conflict? Chinese debt is generally used to finance big-ticket linear infrastructure projects like roads and railways. These connective infrastructure projects expand the territorial reach of the host government, making it easier for agents of the state to access rural and remote areas. This higher level of access could, in turn, facilitate violent conflict by making it easier for state agents to confront rebel groups, tribal leaders, gangs, or foreign-backed militias who govern territorial enclaves. It could also indirectly promote violence if agents of the state use their expanded capacity to engage in rent-seeking and predation, thereby fueling local

[62] We do not show these tables here, to reduce clutter. They are available on request.

grievances and increasing the willingness of local residents to take up arms.

Another recent study investigates how Chinese aid, in particular, might influence conflict in Africa. Using the data on Chinese aid that we introduce in this book, Kai Gehring at the University of Bern, Lennart Kaplan at the University of Göttingen, and Melvin Wong at Leibniz

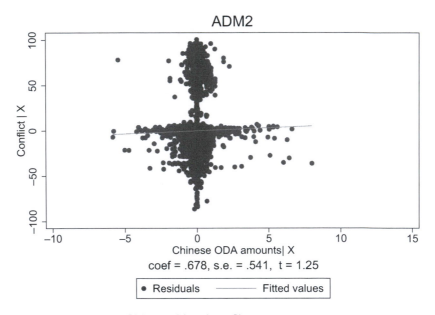

Figure 8.2  Chinese aid and conflict
*Notes:* The figure shows a partial leverage plot corresponding to column 6 in Table A8.1. See the notes of this table for details on data and methods.

University Hannover show that, on average, Chinese aid has no significant effect on lethal conflict at subnational scales in Africa.[63] We replicate their results at the district level, focusing on the effect of Chinese aid in monetary terms (as Gehring and colleagues do).[64] The results shown in Figure 8.2 and column 6 of Table A8.1 are in line with theirs and with our

[63] Gehring, Kaplan, and Wong (2019). We thank Kai Gehring, Lennart Kaplan, and Melvin Wong for sharing their data with us.

[64] We do so because Gehring, Kaplan, and Wong (2019) evaluate the effects of Chinese aid in monetary terms rather than in project count terms. Also, data on Chinese debt and total Chinese development finance are not included in the replication materials.

country-level results. We find that, on average, there is no effect of Chinese aid on conflict.[65]

## Natural Environment

We now turn to whether, when, and how development projects – financed by China or by traditional donors and lenders – affect the natural environment. There are relatively few studies that rigorously confront this question with empirical data. However, the growing availability of subnationally geo-referenced data on aid and outcomes has opened up new opportunities: social scientists can now estimate the environmental impacts of aid at local rather than national scales. These data are attractive from a causal inference standpoint because locations within countries face a common set of conditions; this makes it easier to identify "treated" and "comparison" cases that are sufficiently similar to estimate a credible counterfactual. In addition, panel studies can address long-standing concerns about confounding and omitted variables in a more convincing way using these data: they can exploit variation in the precise timing of development project exposure across subnational locations and net out the effects of other variables that would otherwise make it difficult to identify a cause-and-effect relationship.[66]

In a recent collaboration with Ariel BenYishay and colleagues at William & Mary, we used these geospatial impact evaluation methods to examine how Chinese development finance affects environmental outcomes.[67] We first merged geo-referenced data on Chinese infrastructure projects in two countries – Cambodia and Tanzania – with annual satellite observations on forest cover change. We then used a quasi-experimental panel framework – covering 26,716 initially forested areas observed annually from 1982 to 2014 – to identify changes in forest cover caused by exposure to Chinese infrastructure projects. We estimated the impact of Chinese infrastructure projects by comparing the pre- and post-intervention

---

[65] Gehring, Kaplan, and Wong (2019) include a number of control variables that we omit from the regressions here. They also find no effects of Chinese aid on the likelihood of demonstrations, strikes, and riots, but some evidence that Chinese aid increases government repression. Also focusing on Africa, Iacoella, Martorano, Metzger, and Sanfilippo (2021) find that protests, but not other forms of political participation, are more likely in the vicinity of Chinese projects.

[66] Panel studies like BenYishay, Parks, Runfola et al. (2016) that include time-fixed effects and fixed effects at fine geographic scales (e.g., 5 kilometers x 5 kilometers grid cells) account for the year-specific impacts on outcomes that affect all geographic units at the same time and the time-invariant characteristics of every small geographic unit in the analysis. Controlling for the time-invariant features of each small geographic area, in effect, allows each of those areas to serve as its own counterfactual.

[67] BenYishay, Parks, Runfola et al. (2016).

change in forest cover for the treated group (exposure to Chinese infrastructure projects) relative to a comparison group (no exposure to Chinese infrastructure projects).[68] We also explored whether the impacts of these projects varied across different types of forest governance regimes. Contrary to conventional wisdom, we do not find strong evidence that Chinese infrastructure projects consistently damage nearby forests. In areas where large tracts of forested land have been granted to natural resource sector investors and the enforcement of environmental laws and regulations is exceptionally weak, we find that Chinese infrastructure projects damaged nearby forests. But areas under formal forest protection experienced little or no deforestation from nearby Chinese infrastructure projects. These findings suggest that Chinese infrastructure projects need not lead to widespread environmental damage when nearby ecosystems are appropriately protected, and that domestic environmental governance plays a crucial role in moderating the effects of Chinese infrastructure projects on conservation outcomes.[69]

To estimate the potential environmental impacts of Chinese development projects at a global scale, we merge our country-level dataset with (a) the World Bank's measure of the quality of host country environmental policies and institutions (a 1–6 scale, where higher values indicate stronger policies and institutions) and (b) three environmental quality outcomes – net forest depletion, particulate emission damage, and carbon dioxide damage (all measured as a percentage of host country GNI).[70] We again use the predicted (rather than the actual) number

---

[68] We do this by using an annual treatment status variable and netting out two factors: the effect of variables that do not vary within districts over time or affect all districts equally in a year, and pre-trends at the individual 5 kilometers x 5 kilometers area level.

[69] In a set of companion studies, Runfola, BenYishay, Tanner et al. (2017), Zhao, Kemper, and Runfola (2017), and Buchanan, Donald, Parks et al. (2018) merge geo-referenced World Bank project data with remotely sensed forest cover change data and use matching methods to evaluate the forest cover and conservation impacts of World Bank projects. Three key findings emerge from these studies. First, there is a great deal of geographic variation in environmental impacts of World Bank projects; they can have positive, negative, and neutral impacts on nearby forests and biodiversity. Second, World Bank projects that are subjected to the organization's most stringent environmental safeguards – the vast majority of which are infrastructure projects – do not damage local ecosystems. Third, when environmental risks that can be readily mitigated are identified at the project preparation stage, World Bank projects tend to actually *improve* conservation outcomes (or reduce deforestation) in nearby areas.

[70] The measure of the quality of host country environmental policies and institutions (with a 1–6 scale, where higher values indicate stronger policies and institutions) comes from the World Bank's Country Policy and Institutional Assessment (CPIA). It aims to "assess the extent to which environmental policies foster the protection and sustainable use of natural resources and the management of pollution." See https://datacatalog .worldbank.org/cpia-policy-and-institutions-environmental-sustainability-rating-1low-6high-0, last accessed November 17, 2020. The construction of the three environmental

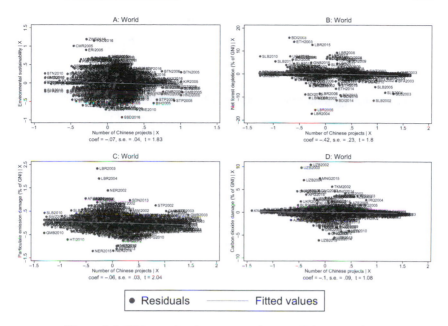

Figure 8.3 Chinese development projects and the natural environment
*Notes:* The figure shows partial leverage plots corresponding to columns 7–10 in Table A8.1. See the notes of this table for details on data and methods.

of Chinese development projects to estimate causal effects. We find mixed results. Figure 8.3 and Table A8.1 (columns 7–10) suggest that Chinese development projects reduce the quality of environmental policies and institutions in host countries but improve two of the three environmental quality outcomes – namely, net forest depletion and

quality variables – all of which are measured as a percentage of host country GNI – is described in Lange, Wodon, and Carey (2018). Net forest depletion is "calculated as the product of unit resource rents and the excess of roundwood harvest over natural growth"; "if growth exceeds harvest, this figure is zero." Carbon dioxide ($CO_2$) damage is measured as the "cost of damage as a result of carbon dioxide emissions from fossil fuel use and the manufacture of cement, estimated to be US\$30 per ton of $CO_2$ (the unit damage in 2014 U.S. dollars for $CO_2$ emitted in 2015) times the number of tons of $CO_2$ emitted." Air pollution damage is measured as the "cost of damage as a result of exposure of a country's population to air pollution, including ambient concentrations of particulate matter measuring less than 2.5 microns in diameter (PM2.5), indoor concentrations of air pollution in households cooking with solid fuels, and ambient ozone pollution"; "damage costs are calculated as forgone labor output caused by premature death from pollution exposure."

particulate emission damage. In quantitative terms, our statistical models indicate that an additional Chinese development project reduces the measure of host country environmental policies and institutions by 0.07 points, while reducing damage from forest depletion by 0.42 and from particulate emission by 0.06 percentage points of GNI. The results are weaker when we focus exclusively on Chinese aid projects: the effect on particulate emission damage remains, but the other effects become statistically insignificant. While our overall results for forest depletion are broadly consistent with those that BenYishay and his colleagues report at subnational scales, the negative effect on host country policies and institutions suggests that Chinese development projects might degrade environmental quality in more indirect ways and over longer time horizons. However, our results rely on a substantially smaller sample than the other regressions related to environmental outcomes, so they should be interpreted as suggestive rather than definitive.

### A Threat to Western Development Finance?

Finally, we assess the popular claim that development finance from China is undoing the gains achieved by Western donors and lenders. This is a relatively new line of empirical inquiry, and the findings from some recent contributions to the literature are seemingly contradictory. For example, one study finds that Chinese development finance has blunted the democratizing effects of Western aid to sub-Saharan Africa, which suggests that Western aid conditionality might work only when recipient countries have no alternative financing options (like Chinese aid or debt).[71] However, another recent study finds no evidence that Chinese development finance weakens the ability of the United States to use its leverage over weaker countries to encourage participation in the US-led anti-human trafficking regime.[72]

New research also tests the extent to which Chinese development finance competes with traditional sources. Some studies have concluded that China "has not had [a] 'game changing' impact on traditional development finance."[73] However, as we previously noted, there is evidence that recipients of Chinese aid receive World Bank loans with fewer conditions.[74] Another study by Chris Humphrey and Katharina Michaelowa from the University of Zurich finds that the level and sector allocation of World Bank and African

---

[71] Li (2017).    [72] Kavakli (2019).
[73] Humphrey and Michaelowa (2019: 15). Also see Arcand and Chauvet (2001).
[74] Hernandez (2017).

Development Bank (AfDB) lending changes in countries that receive non-concessional development finance (debt) from China, but not in countries that receive concessional development finance (aid) from China.[75] Similarly, Alexandra Zeitz of Concordia University investigates how Chinese development finance affects the type of development finance provided by the World Bank.[76] She finds that the World Bank reacts to Chinese competition by emulating how Beijing allocates its funds – specifically, by redirecting a larger proportion of its lending to infrastructure-intensive sectors.[77]

Building upon our previous work,[78] we first test whether the effects of World Bank projects vary across countries or subnational jurisdictions that receive high and low levels of financial support from China. We then test whether the presence of Chinese development projects in a country or subnational locality makes development finance from the World Bank less effective at promoting our main outcomes of interest: economic growth, sound policies and institutions, environmental quality, and political stability. We use the same statistical approach as in Chapter 7 to investigate the popular claim that access to Chinese development finance reduces the effectiveness of World Bank development finance: we examine the effects of World Bank development finance on various outcomes and compare countries that have received a major influx of Chinese development finance to countries that have not. To do so, we replicate the analyses introduced in this chapter and the previous chapter for the World Bank across three samples: the full sample, the subsample of Chinese "darlings," and the subsample of Chinese "orphans." One concern is that whether a country becomes a Chinese orphan or darling is likely not exogenous, as China's resource allocation decisions are made according to commercial, geopolitical, and need-based criteria, as we demonstrated in Chapter 5. To address this concern, we rely on an approach we have introduced in previous work: we use the number of Chinese development projects that we predict a country or district will receive – based on the exogenous variables discussed in Chapter 7 – rather than the actual number of projects. This allows us to define the sample of countries that China neglects.[79]

---

[75] Humphrey and Michaelowa (2019).    [76] Zeitz (2021).

[77] Zeitz (2021) does not find that the United States reacts to Chinese competition in a similar way. Vadlamannati, Li, Brazys and Dukalskis (2019) show that US executive directors at a wide variety of multilateral development banks are more likely to support loan packages to countries that receive little Chinese development finance but have joined the BRI; they see this as evidence that the United States will compete with Chinese funding in countries it might still be able to "win over."

[78] Dreher, Fuchs, Parks et al. (2021).

[79] Dreher, Fuchs, Parks et al. (2021). Specifically, we use the first-stage regression results from our analyses for China to split the sample.

We define "orphans" as countries that our statistical models predict would receive an average annual number of projects that falls below the median of the distribution over the sample period. This cutoff level corresponds to four projects. Analogously, we define "darlings" as those that the models predict to receive more than four projects at the country-year level. We then test whether the results differ between these samples.[80]

We present our results in Table A8.2, with panel A reporting results for the full sample, panel B reporting results only for Chinese darlings, and panel C reporting results only for Chinese orphans. With the exception of one statistical model (the model that focuses on corruption at subnational scales), we measure World Bank development finance in monetary terms rather than numbers of projects (since the monetary data are readily available).[81] Columns 1–6 of panel A reproduce results from Chapter 7 for growth, luminosity, mortality, and spatial inequality for the sake of comparison. The additional columns in Table A8.2 provide the results for institutional quality, conflict, and the natural environment.

Recall from Chapter 7 that World Bank funding has no effect on economic growth at the country level. It increases nightlight per capita at the district level but also increases infant mortality at national and subnational scales. Our new results show that World Bank funding has no significant effect on institutional quality or conflict at either national or subnational scales. We also find no effect of World Bank funding on the quality of environmental policies and institutions, forest depletion, or $CO_2$ emissions.[82]

Our results provide only weak evidence that Chinese development projects dampen the positive effects of financial support from traditional sources. For the World Bank, when we compare the results between the groups of Chinese darlings and orphans, we find that most coefficients are not statistically different across the samples.[83] This result is consistent

[80] Running seemingly unrelated estimations, we compute Wald tests to identify statistically significant differences in the effect sizes of the coefficients across the two samples.

[81] We also follow the original studies in using either commitments or disbursements. We report detailed definitions in the notes to the table.

[82] We do find that World Bank projects increase particulate air pollution, as measured by the forgone labor output caused by premature deaths due to fine particulate matter (PM2.5) exposure. A 10 percent increase in financial support from the World Bank leads to a 6 percent increase in the cost of PM2.5 damage as a percentage of recipient country GNI.

[83] Four exceptions stand out. First, we find that the effect of World Bank funding on infant mortality at the country level is driven by the sample of countries that do not receive substantial amounts of financial support from China. Second, the reverse holds true at subnational scales. Third, the receipt of World Bank funding increases local corruption in countries that receive substantial inflows of Chinese development finance more than in countries that do not. Fourth, the effect of World Bank funding on particulate emission damage seems to be driven by the Chinese orphans sample. Taken together, these results

with our earlier results on economic growth effects of World Bank development finance at the country level.[84] Nor do we find that development finance from the OECD-DAC (as a whole), the IBRD, or the IDA has a differential effect on economic growth in countries that do and do not receive substantial funds from China. When we focus on aid from the United States, the results are mixed.[85] However, on balance, the claim that Chinese development finance systematically impairs the effectiveness of development finance from traditional sources is not supported by our findings.

## Conclusion: Beware of Banking on Beijing

We began this chapter by telling the story of the China Eximbank-financed standard gauge railway project in Kenya. But that story is not yet finished. After the completion of the 475-kilometer railway in June 2017, the Kenyan authorities turned their attention to another potential phase of the project that would extend the railway by an additional 262 kilometers – from Naivasha in Central Rift Valley to the port city of Kisumu. President Kenyatta traveled to Beijing in April 2019 to request another China Eximbank loan worth approximately US$3.7 billion, but his request was rejected.[86] Several factors seem to have been at play. First, Kenya's debt-to-GDP ratio had risen to dangerous levels. When the Chinese government began ramping up its lending to Kenya in 2009, the ratio stood at approximately 45 percent. However, by 2018, it had crept up to 60 percent. Countries with rising debt-to-GDP ratios in excess of 50–60 percent tend to experience economic growth slowdowns, and Kenya's status placed it among the dozen or so BRI participants at risk of debt distress.[87]

---

indicate that World Bank development finance outcomes are worse in the presence of Chinese finance in two of the four exceptions.

[84] Dreher, Fuchs, Parks et al. (2021).

[85] The growth effect of US aid is positive whether or not we exclude Chinese darlings, but its effect on growth is larger in the sample focusing on China's orphans.

[86] Olingo (2019). After Kenyatta came home empty-handed, the Chinese ambassador to Kenya was asked about the Kenyan president's expectation that he would secure a new loan commitment from China Eximbank for the SGR; the ambassador reportedly said, "I really don't know where those expectations came from" (Herbling and Li 2019).

[87] Chudik, Mohaddes, Pesaran, and Raissi (2017); Hurley, Morris, and Portelance (2019). Not all debt is created equal: if a government carries a debt-to-GDP ratio of 60 percent but most of the loans that it has contracted are on concessional (below market rate) terms, it is less vulnerable than a government with a debt-to-GDP ratio of 60 percent that has primarily contracted loans on commercial (market rate) terms. Here again, Kenya is in a perilous position; an increasing proportion of its public debt will need to be paid back on commercial or semi-concessional terms. Indeed, one of the two China Eximbank loans

Second, China's policy banks were facing pressure from Chinese authorities to better manage their own balance sheets and apply more stringent economic viability (or "bankability") standards to incoming project proposals. These changes in the authorizing environment affected the funding prospects for a second phase of the SGR project.[88] The first phase of the project was premised on the assumption that railway revenue (and revenue from a new levy on imports) would be used to repay the two China Eximbank loans contracted by the Kenyan government. However, the railway did not turn a profit, and Beijing took note.[89] An unnamed source with knowledge of ongoing negotiations between China Eximbank and the Kenyan authorities recently told *Bloomberg News* that "China now requires high-quality projects and a more thorough feasibility study, [and] the process of approving loans has slowed in general, but it doesn't mean the [second phase of the SGR] project is terminated."[90]

Third, the SGR may be evolving from a political asset to a political liability from Beijing's perspective. After the implementation of the first phase of the project, Kenyan officials lavished praise on the Chinese government. Public sentiment toward China also improved considerably: whereas 61 percent of Kenyans approved of China in 2014 according to the Gallup World Poll (2017), 71 percent approved of China in 2016. However, after the SGR became embroiled in a corruption scandal in 2017, public support for China declined sharply.[91] A letter from Kenya's auditor general to the Kenya Ports Authority was leaked in December 2018 to a local media outlet and made matters worse;[92] it suggested that the Port of Mombasa's assets were collateral that could be seized if the Kenyan government could not repay its loans to China Eximbank. It also suggested that the Kenyatta administration had waived its sovereign immunity rights to make this pledge of collateral. The possibility that Beijing could seize a strategic asset like the Port of

---

secured by the Kenyan government to finance the first phase of SGR construction was provided at commercial borrowing rates: LIBOR plus a 3.6 percent margin and a 15-year maturity.

[88] At the Second Belt and Road Forum for International Cooperation in April 2019, Xi Jinping announced that China would "adopt widely accepted rules and standards and encourage participating companies to follow general international rules and standards in project development, operation, procurement and tendering and bidding." See www.fmprc.gov.cn/mfa_eng/zxxx_662805/t1658424.shtml, last accessed November 17, 2020.

[89] Herbling and Li (2019).    [90] Ibid.

[91] China's public approval rating in the Gallup World Poll (2017) declined from 71 percent in 2016 to 62 percent in 2017.

[92] Mwere (2018).

Mombasa provoked a public outcry in Kenya, forcing the Kenyatta administration to defend the project and its relationship with China. President Kenyatta dismissed the criticism that he had mortgaged the Port of Mombasa to Beijing as "pure propaganda" and said the following:

I will continue to borrow to develop the country.... If you want a copy of the [SGR loan] contract we have with China I can get it to you tomorrow.... We are opening up roads across the country and a railway line that never existed 50 years ago. The debt we are incurring is for development projects that will not only benefit this generation but future ones as well.[93]

All of these factors likely contributed to China's denial of President Kenyatta's request in 2019. They also underscore a key development that we have not yet discussed: while we have demonstrated in this chapter that Chinese development projects – particularly those financed by debt – can create governance externalities for recipient countries, they can also create unintended consequences for the Chinese government. As Beijing contemplates the future direction of the BRI and its overseas development program more generally, the story of the first phase of the SGR project, with its intended and unintended effects, may provide a glimpse of the rewards and risks that lie ahead. In the next chapter, we turn our attention to the question of how China's new position as a global lender of first resort has created a tension between its political and economic ambitions.

---

[93] CGTN Africa (2018).

## Appendix 8.A
## Tables

Table A8.1 *Chinese development finance and various outcomes*

| | (1) | (2) | (3) | (4) | (5) | (6) | (7) | (8) | (9) | (10) |
|---|---|---|---|---|---|---|---|---|---|---|
| | Control Corruption | Democratic Accountability | Bribe Police | Bribe Permit | Conflict | Conflict | Env., Pol., & Inst. | Forest Depl. | PM 2.5 Emissions | $CO_2$ Emissions |
| | World | World | Africa/ 55km$^2$ | Africa/ 55km$^2$ | World | Africa/ ADM2 | World | World | World | World |
| Panel A: 2SLS estimates – Dependent variable indicated in column header | | | | | | | | | | |
| Chinese OF (t–2) | 0.130** | 0.120 | −0.182** | −0.089 | 0.178 | 0.678 | −0.069* | −0.420* | −0.060** | −0.095 |
| | (0.050) | (0.090) | (0.087) | (0.070) | (0.145) | (0.541) | (0.038) | (0.233) | (0.029) | (0.088) |
| (log) Population (t–1) | −1.105* | −1.089 | | | −1.793 | 0.000 | 1.673*** | 2.651 | −2.414*** | 2.435** |
| | (0.574) | (0.944) | | | (2.677) | (0.000) | (0.617) | (2.851) | (0.452) | (1.020) |
| Small conflict*lagged state | | | | | −0.0958* | | | | | |
| | | | | | (0.0540) | | | | | |

|  | Chinese financing (t-2) |
| --- | --- |
| Armed conflict*lagged state | -0.0520 |
|  | (0.0832) |
| Civil conflict*lagged state | -0.0577 |
|  | (0.246) |
| Small conflict, lagged state | 0.783*** |
|  | (0.150) |
| Armed conflict, lagged state | 1.627*** |
|  | (0.323) |
| Civil conflict, lagged state | 2.683*** |
|  | (0.604) |

**Panel B: First-stage estimates – Dependent variable: Chinese financing (t-2)**

| | | | | | | | | | | |
| --- | --- | --- | --- | --- | --- | --- | --- | --- | --- | --- |
| Reserves*probability (t-3) | 2.276 | 2.276 | 2.420*** | 2.406*** | -0.0.18 | -24.140** | -0.073 | 1.459 | 0.733 | 0.789 |
|  | (2.595) | (2.595) | (0.780) | (0.779) | (4.175) | (9.934) | (2.630) | (2.449) | (2.505) | (2.367) |
| Input*probability (t-3) | 1.194** | 1.194** | -0.337*** | -0.335*** | 1.227 | -2.510* | 1.078** | 1.205*** | 1.344*** | 1.298*** |
|  | (0.463) | (0.463) | (0.111) | (0.111) | (0.576) | (1.358) | (0.447) | (0.396) | (0.413) | (0.389) |
| (log) Population (t-1) | 2.663 | 2.663 |  |  | 7.323 | 4.762 |  | 2.523 | 2.547 | 2.496 |
|  | (1.715) | (1.715) |  |  | (1.484) | (3.221) |  | (1.568) | (1.603) | (1.540) |

Table A8.1  (cont.)

| | | | | | | | | | | |
|---|---|---|---|---|---|---|---|---|---|---|
| Number of countries | 102 | 102 | 30 | 30 | 112 | 45 | 85 | 144 | 135 | 149 |
| Number of regions | | | 438 | 438 | | 5,853 | | | | |
| Number of observations | 1,399 | 1,399 | 89,968 | 90,049 | 1,008 | 70,148 | 918 | 1,814 | 1,740 | 1,879 |
| Kleibergen-Paap F | 34.00 | 34.00 | 4.92 | 4.86 | 27.58 | 31.15 | 10.48 | 40.94 | 38.72 | 41.77 |

*Notes:* The dependent variables, their range, and sources are (1) control of corruption (0–6, ICRG), (2) democratic accountability (0–6, ICRG), (3) bribe payments to police in the past year (0/1, Isaksson and Kotsadam 2018a), (4) bribe payments to obtain permits in the last year (0/1, Isaksson and Kotsadam 2018a), (5) ordinal measure of conflict (0–3, with "no conflict" being the omitted category and measuring a truly peaceful society, "small conflict," with at least one purge, assassination, riot, or guerrilla warfare but less than 25 battle-related deaths (BRD) in a year, "armed conflict," between 25 and 1,000 BRD, "civil war," more than 1,000 BRD, Bluhm, Gassebner, Langlotz, and Schaudt 2021), (6) conflict incidence (0/1, with at least five BRD in a region and year, Gehring, Kaplan, and Wong 2019), (7) CPIA policy and institutions for environmental sustainability rating (1–6, World Bank WDI), with higher values indicating more sustainable policies and institutions, (8) net forest depletion in percentage of GNI (World Bank WDI), (9) particulate emission damage in percentage of GNI (World Bank WDI), and (10) carbon dioxide damage in percentage of GNI (World Bank WDI). "Chinese OF" denotes the number of Chinese government–financed projects in columns 1–2, 5, and 7–10, a binary indicator for at least one OF project in columns 3–4, and (log) p.c. ODA in column 6. The instrumental variables are interactions of the de-trended first factor of China's production of aluminum, cement, glass, iron, steel, and timber, and its net change in international reserves with a recipient's probability to receive official finance. The probability to receive official finance is defined as the share of years in the sample period a country has received at least one OF project in columns 1–2, 5, and 7–10, per ADM1 region in columns 3 and 4; column 6 uses a cumulative probability at the ADM2 level. Columns 1–2 and 7–10 include fixed effects for countries and years, columns 3–4 for ADM1 regions and years, and column 6 for country-years and ADM2 regions. Column 5 applies Bluhm, Gassebner, Langlotz, and Schaudt's (2021) dynamic ordered probit estimator, removing unobserved heterogeneity with quasi fixed effects. The control function approach includes the residual from the first stage. Sample periods are (1)–(2) 2002–2016, (3)–(4) 2002–2013, (5) 2002–2010, (6) 2003–2014, (7) 2005–2016, (8)–(10) 2002–2015. Standard errors are reported in parentheses and are clustered at the level of (1)–(2), (6)–(10) country, and (3)–(4) enumeration areas. Column 5 bootstraps standard errors using 500 repetitions. *, **, ***: significant at the 10, 5, 1 percent levels, respectively.

Table A8.2 *World Bank development finance and various outcomes*

| | (1) | (2) | (3) | (4) | (5) | (6) | (7) | (8) |
|---|---|---|---|---|---|---|---|---|
| | Growth p.c. World | Light p.c. World, ADM2 | Mortality World | Mortality World, 55km$^2$ | Gini World | Gini World, ADM2 | Corruption World | Democracy World |
| **Panel A: 2SLS estimates – Full sample** | | | | | | | | |
| World Bank OF (t−2) | −0.125 | 0.020* | 1.150** | 5.799*** | 0.003 | 0.004** | 0.057 | 0.004 |
| | (0.189) | (0.011) | (0.449) | (2.005) | (0.003) | (0.002) | (0.043) | (0.053) |
| (log) Population (t−1) | 5.593** | −0.519*** | −47.335*** | | −0.063 | −0.006 | −0.228 | −0.083 |
| | (2.707) | (0.066) | (8.930) | | (0.059) | (0.004) | (0.517) | (0.928) |
| **Panel B: 2SLS estimates – "Aid darlings"** | | | | | | | | |
| World Bank OF (t−2) | −0.209 | 0.003 | −1.018 | 12.502** | −0.000 | 0.004 | 0.081 | 0.006 |
| | (0.213) | (0.014) | (0.613) | (6.290) | (0.003) | (0.002) | (0.055) | (0.077) |
| (log) Population (t−1) | 8.175** | −0.485*** | −64.998*** | | −0.109** | −0.002 | −0.283 | −0.769 |
| | (4.094) | (0.066) | (9.154) | | (0.043) | (0.006) | (0.725) | (1.112) |
| **Panel C: 2SLS estimates – "Aid orphans"** | | | | | | | | |
| World Bank OF (t−2) | 0.029 | 0.020* | 1.109** | −0.177 | 0.001 | 0.003 | 0.075 | −0.075 |
| | (0.197) | (0.011) | (0.503) | (1.831) | (0.003) | (0.002) | (0.056) | (0.100) |
| (log) Population (t−1) | 4.543 | −0.535** | −33.091** | | −0.062 | −0.011 | −0.154 | 1.351 |
| | (3.583) | (0.089) | (15.284) | | (0.091) | (0.008) | (0.928) | (2.158) |
| First year | 2000 | 2002 | 2000 | 1998 | 2000 | 2002 | 2000 | 2000 |
| Last year | 2016 | 2013 | 2015 | 2016 | 2013 | 2013 | 2016 | 2016 |
| Number of countries | 152 | 130 | 153 | 54 | 148 | 130 | 103 | 103 |

Table A8.2 (*cont.*)

| | | | | | | | | |
|---|---|---|---|---|---|---|---|---|
| Number of regions | | 35,764 | | 6,407 | | 32,895 | | |
| Number of obs. (full) | 2,370 | 413,635 | 2,303 | 624,738 | 1,970 | 359,637 | 1,618 | 1,618 |
| Number of obs. (darling) | 1,195 | 224,406 | 1,184 | 309,775 | 1,046 | 181,739 | 1,098 | 1,098 |
| Number of obs. (orphan) | 1,141 | 185,324 | 1,087 | 309,085 | 896 | 174,375 | 503 | 503 |
| Kleibergen–Paap F (f/d/o) | 9.3/6.4/6.4 | 14.0/9.7/8.7 | 8.3/4.3/6.5 | 8.1/2.5/4.3 | 13.2/ 5.7/15.0 | 13.2/8.1/9.7 | 5.6/4.6/3.0 | 5.6/4.6/3.0 |
| Prob > chi2 | 0.42 | 0.37 | 0.00 | 0.00 | 0.68 | 0.94 | 0.93 | 0.46 |

Table A8.2 (continued)

| | (9) Bribe Police Africa | (10) Bribe Permit Africa, ADM2 | (11) Conflict Africa | (12) Conflict Africa, ADM2 | (13) Env. Pol & Inst World | (14) Forest Depl. World | (15) PM 2.5 Emiss. World | (16) CO2 Emiss. World |
|---|---|---|---|---|---|---|---|---|
| **Panel A: 2SLS estimates – Full sample** | | | | | | | | |
| World Bank OF (t−2) | 0.115 | 0.137 | 0.0150 | −0.067 | −0.004 | −0.126 | 0.062*** | −0.145 |
| | (0.099) | (0.094) | (0.025) | (0.131) | (0.020) | (0.101) | (0.022) | (0.115) |
| (log) Population (t−1) | | | 0.819 | 0.000 | 1.289** | 2.081 | −2.433*** | 2.401* |
| | | | (1.205) | (0.000) | (0.589) | (2.273) | (0.520) | (1.240) |
| **Panel B: 2SLS estimates – "Aid darlings"** | | | | | | | | |
| World Bank OF (t−2) | 0.201 | 0.309 | 0.0124 | −0.190* | −0.061 | −0.025 | 0.015 | −0.222 |
| | (0.272) | (0.251) | (0.030) | (0.108) | (0.072) | (0.029) | (0.022) | (0.165) |
| (log) Population (t−1) | | | 1.567 | 0.000 | −1.047 | −0.662 | −3.486*** | 6.081*** |
| | | | (1.878) | (0.000) | (2.445) | (2.047) | (0.740) | (2.222) |
| **Panel C: 2SLS estimates – "Aid orphans"** | | | | | | | | |
| World Bank OF (t−2) | −0.137** | −0.091 | 0.036 | −0.039 | 0.010 | −0.222 | 0.085** | −0.037 |
| | (0.062) | (0.063) | (0.046) | (0.140) | (0.010) | (0.164) | (0.036) | (0.043) |

Table A8.2  (cont.)

| (log) Population (t−1) | | | | | | | |
|---|---|---|---|---|---|---|---|
| | | −0.0458 | −0.000 | 2.012** | 6.381 | −1.619* | 0.466 |
| | | (1.772) | (0.000) | (0.868) | (5.288) | (0.865) | (0.715) |
| First year | 2002 | 2002 | 1997 | 1998 | 2005 | 2000 | 2000 | 2000 |
| Last year | 2013 | 2013 | 2010 | 2014 | 2016 | 2015 | 2015 | 2015 |
| Number of countries | 30 | 30 | 112 | 45 | 85 | 145 | 136 | 151 |
| Number of regions | 458 | 458 | | 5,853 | | | | |
| Number of obs. (full) | 90,021 | 90,098 | 1,568 | 99,413 | 918 | 2,098 | 2,018 | 2,175 |
| Number of obs. (darling) | 45,813 | 45,798 | 854 | 49,676 | 463 | 1,115 | 1,077 | 1,125 |
| Number of obs. (orphan) | 43,219 | 43,311 | 714 | 48,621 | 443 | 955 | 909 | 1,018 |
| Kleibergen–Paap F (f/ d/o) | 7.6/3.0/15.1 | 7.6/3.0/15.3 | 144/76/71 | 57.4/75.94/23.98 | 8.4/1.2/8.4 | 11.7/11.5/12 | 12.0/10.8/10.7 | 12.4/11.8/13 |
| Prob > chi2 | 0.19 | 0.09 | n.a. | 0.90 | 0.18 | 0.17 | 0.01 | 0.24 |

*Notes:* See Table A8.1. World Bank Official Finance (OF) is measured as (log) commitments from the IDA and IBRD (constant 2010 US$, and a value of one added before taking logs) in columns 1, 3, 5, 7, 8, 11, and 13–16. We use logged disbursements in constant US$ in columns 2, 4, 6, and (from IDA only) 12; columns 9 and 10 use a binary indicator for projects starting. Aid orphans are defined as countries that are predicted to receive an average number of projects per year below the median of the distribution over the sample period according to the corresponding regression including Chinese development finance, and aid darlings as those that are predicted to receive more (at the country-year level, the relevant cutoff is four projects). The instrumental variables are the IBRD's equity-to-loans ratio and the IDA's "funding position," both interacted with the share of years in the 2000–2014 period a country or district received funding from these institutions. *, **, ***: significant at the 10, 5, 1 percent levels, respectively.

Table A8.3  *Descriptive statistics*

| | count | mean | sd | min | max |
|---|---|---|---|---|---|
| **Sample of Table A8.1, column 1** | | | | | |
| Chinese OF projects | 1,399 | 2.10 | 3.13 | 0.00 | 35.00 |
| Number of OOF/vague projects | 1,399 | 0.61 | 1.53 | 0.00 | 31.00 |
| Chinese ODA projects | 1,399 | 1.50 | 2.33 | 0.00 | 24.00 |
| Population | 1,399 | 44,492,138 | 130,000,000 | 483,044 | 1,320,000,000 |
| **Sample of Table A8.1** | | | | | |
| Control corruption World | 1,399 | 2.01 | 0.66 | 0.00 | 4.5 |
| Democratic accountability World | 1,399 | 3.60 | 1.52 | 0.00 | 6.00 |
| Bribe Police | 89,968 | 0.13 | 0.33 | 0.00 | 1.00 |
| Bribe Permit | 90,049 | 0.14 | 0.35 | 0.00 | 1.00 |
| Chinese project started | 89,968 | 0.10 | 0.30 | 0.00 | 1.00 |
| Conflict World | 1,008 | 0.47 | 0.81 | 0.00 | 3.00 |
| Conflict Africa ADM2 | 70,148 | 2.08 | 14.28 | 0 | 100 |
| (log) Chinese p.c. ODA | 70,148 | −4.29 | 2.32 | −4.61 | 20.37 |
| Env., Pol., & Inst. World | 918 | 3.12 | 0.55 | 1 | 4.50 |
| Forest Depl. World | 1,814 | 1.73 | 4.38 | 0 | 40.82 |
| PM 2.5 Emissions World | 1,740 | 1.09 | 1.07 | 0.10 | 6.95 |
| $CO_2$ Emissions World | 1,879 | 1.62 | 1.77 | 0.12 | 21.42 |
| **Sample of Table A8.2** | | | | | |
| World Bank OF | 2,370 | 10.06 | 9.31 | 0.00 | 22.66 |
| (log) World Bank p.c. ODA | 70,148 | 3.18 | 8.41 | −4.61 | 19.14 |
| Growth p.c. World | 2,370 | 2.85 | 5.22 | −62.23 | 56.88 |
| Light p.c. World, ADM2 | 413,635 | −3.06 | 1.09 | −4.61 | 8.11 |
| Mortality World | 2,234 | 38.91 | 27.70 | 3.40 | 143.30 |
| Mortality World, 55km$^2$ | 624,738 | 49.83 | 142.16 | 0.00 | 1000 |
| Gini World | 1,920 | 0.54 | 0.21 | 0.02 | 0.95 |
| Gini World, ADM2 | 360,173 | 0.36 | 0.20 | 0.00 | 0.91 |

# 9    Banking on the Belt and Road
## The Future of Global Development Finance

### The BRI at Twenty Years: A Thought Experiment

The year is 2033. The BRI was launched two decades ago, but China is no longer the lender of first resort for most developing countries. Enthusiasm for the initiative – among BRI member countries and key stakeholders in China – has vanished. Many governments that initially joined have publicly withdrawn or quietly curtailed their participation. China's staunchest clients remain engaged, but even they have reservations about the wisdom of the BRI. Many are saddled with unproductive public investment projects and struggling to service their debts. Public sentiment toward China has soured, and many governments now view their participation in BRI as a political liability rather than an asset. But they worry about the consequences of alienating an important patron and creditor. China has also assumed a defensive posture. Lacking the goodwill that it possessed at the beginning of BRI, it must now use carrots and sticks to prevent states from abandoning the initiative. Western donors and lenders watch from the sidelines with a sense of bemusement. They encouraged China to "multilateralize" the BRI by establishing a common set of project appraisal standards, procurement guidelines, fiduciary controls, transparency policies, and social/environmental safeguards that other aid agencies and development banks could support. But Beijing chose to go it alone. It rejected these "Western" approaches to development finance and ignored calls to publish detailed information about BRI projects. China bet on its fast and flexible approach to infrastructure finance, hoping that it would prove so compelling that traditional donors and lenders would jump on the bandwagon and co-finance BRI projects. But it miscalculated. Its model was insufficiently attractive to enlist the participation of the other major players in the bilateral and multilateral development finance market. Nor was it

This chapter draws selectively upon prose and argumentation from Parks (2019).

sufficiently appealing to sustain elite and public support in partner countries.

Following two decades of declining growth rates, China's economy is now substantially weaker than it was during the early days of BRI. Its policy banks and state-owned commercial banks faced top-down pressure from party leaders and bottom-up pressure from cash-poor BRI participant countries to fast-track big-ticket infrastructure projects with minimal red tape. But many of these projects were poorly designed; as a result, the banks are now dealing with an unsustainable stock of nonperforming loans, leaving them with two equally unattractive choices: restructure the debts of the least creditworthy countries or throw good money after bad by offering new loans to help borrowers repay old loans. With lower-than-expected reflows entering the coffers of China Development Bank, China Eximbank, and the "big 4" state-owned commercial banks, the People's Bank of China sees the writing on the wall and decides to intervene. It recapitalizes the banks once, and then again and again. As the country's foreign exchange reserves dwindle, fiscally conservative voices within China grow louder. They call upon the banks to rein in their overseas lending activities and find common cause with the Chinese public, which sees ample evidence of waste and corruption in BRI projects and has a declining appetite for overseas entanglements. As populist and isolationist pressures mount, China's political leadership concludes that it no longer has domestic support for its international ambitions.

Now consider an alternative scenario. It's 2033, and there is no longer much talk in Western capitals about China being a rogue donor or lender that threatens the coherence and stability of the global development finance regime. Instead, policy discussions in Washington, London, and Brussels focus on how to collaborate with Beijing in mutually beneficial ways. The BRI has become a shared project involving a broad coalition of bilateral aid and export credit agencies, multilateral development banks, and commercial banks around the globe. Beijing and its peers have agreed to use a common set of standards and safeguards. Consequently, few development finance institutions outside of China think of BRI co-financing as a high-risk, low-return proposition. Instead, they view it as an opportunity to support bankable, high-impact projects that they would not be able to finance on their own.

Chinese and non-Chinese development finance institutions have developed strong working relationships characterized by trust and mutual understanding, and it has become obvious that they have a shared interest in solving a wide array of problems that affect all parties to these transactions. All lenders want to be adequately protected from repayment risk and ensure that their borrowers are engaging in responsible debt management practices. They all want to avoid corruption and cost over-run problems as well as the reputational risk associated with projects that cause social and environmental harm. They all want contractors to be selected based on merit. Robust monitoring and evaluation systems are a "no-brainer," since each co-financier has an interest in being able to respond to concerns raised by shareholders, legislative overseers, and third-party monitors.

Getting to this point was not easy. After several frustrating years of courting potential co-financiers of BRI projects without success, Beijing realized that its ambition to become a leader of the global development finance regime would require that governments and intergovernmental organizations actually follow its lead. But neither multilateral develop-ment banks nor bilateral aid agencies were initially eager to do so. They needed to be convinced that projects they co-financed with China would be well designed and well supervised. So, during the early years of BRI implementation, Beijing began to work with the other big lenders and donors to establish common rules and standards for project design and implementation, monitoring and evaluation, and transparency. Now, after many years of voluntary compliance with these rules and standards, China is reaping the benefits: fewer nonperforming loans, higher-impact projects, and lower levels of reputational risk in host countries. At this point, no one really thinks of China as a rule breaker. If anything, most of its peers and partners around the globe believe that China is either a rule maker or rule taker, and these perceptions have a knock-on effect: they make it significantly easier and cheaper for China to exercise leadership in the global development finance regime. Rather than having to use carrots and sticks to induce cooperation, China is reaping the benefits of attrac-tional influence: countries are working with China because they respect and admire it, not because they want to secure concessions from it or avoid the consequences of antagonizing an important creditor.[1]

These two scenarios sit at opposite ends of the spectrum of possible outcomes. However, it is possible that in 2033, China will find itself in an intermediate scenario. Perhaps Beijing will decide to selectively multilateralize the BRI – for example, by strengthening some of its social and environmental safeguards to address a key concern of potential co-financiers while continuing to position the BRI as a signature Chinese foreign policy initiative that creates commercial advantages for the country's state-owned enterprises. In a scenario like this one, Beijing

---

[1] On the issue of why global leadership via hard power is more expensive than global leadership via soft power, see Nye (2004) and Lake (2009).

might be able to sustain the BRI without achieving widespread buy-in from multilateral institutions or the OECD-DAC countries.

It is also important to remember that Beijing cannot fully control the destiny of BRI. Its ultimate success will depend on elite and popular support in BRI member states and the actions of China's allies and rivals. As we write this book several years into the BRI experiment, it is clear that Beijing has important choices to make in the coming years. These choices will shape the future of the BRI and the extent to which China can establish itself as a leader of the global development finance regime.

In the remainder of this chapter, we pick up where our empirical chapters left off – around 2014 – and review the first six years of implementation under the BRI. We briefly explain how China's evolution from benefactor to banker, in conjunction with its push for expanded influence on the global stage, led to the adoption of the BRI. We then consider some strategic choices that Beijing will need to confront, which will in turn determine whether the ultimate outcomes of the BRI more closely resemble the first or the second scenario that we just described. We also consider whether and why China might choose to comply with – or help redesign – international development finance rules and standards.

## Banking on the Belt and Road

When China introduced the BRI in 2013, we knew it was signaling an ambitious shift in its foreign policy. This became increasingly clear in subsequent years, such as in 2017, when the BRI was enshrined in the constitution of the Chinese Communist Party during the 19th Party Congress, and in 2021, when the BRI featured prominently in China's long-awaited third white paper on development assistance (State Council 2021). However, we also felt a sense of déjà vu. China's transformation into a global development banker occurred because of the implementation of the Going Out strategy. That strategy was expressly designed to support China's own economic development, and the BRI looked like another forceful response to economic challenges that China faced at home.

Around 2010 – a decade after Going Out was launched – China's leadership anticipated several threats to the country's future economic growth.[2] China was initially buoyed by a relatively strong response in the aftermath of the 2008 global financial crisis, but optimism eventually gave way to concerns about economic and political stability.[3] Chinese

---

[2] The Chinese government's political legitimacy rests upon its ability to sustain economic growth (e.g., Zhao 2009).

[3] In her recent book, Min Ye of Boston University characterizes the BRI as a crisis response and places it in a comparative framework alongside the Going Out policy as well as China's

companies borrowed heavily in the aftermath of the crisis and corporate debt levels were steadily rising. Also, due to increasing labor costs, China understood that it would eventually lose its comparative advantage in labor-intensive manufacturing; global investors were increasingly turning to Southeast Asia and other parts of the developing world as alternative manufacturing bases.[4] Party leadership was apparently divided on macro-economic policy, but there was a consensus that industrial overproduction remained a serious problem that could hobble China's future economic growth.[5] The authorities were also keen to avoid the "middle income trap," a well-known phenomenon in which a middle-income economy gets stuck at a certain level of development, and determined to see the country move up the global value chain and transition onto a more sustainable economic growth path. They later coalesced around a "Made in China 2025" initiative, which sought to establish China as a global leader in high-tech manufacturing – competitive in both domestic and international markets.[6]

Enter the BRI. Initially termed the "One Belt, One Road" (OBOR) in English, the authorities launched the initiative in part to help Chinese companies reduce their costs by moving low-end manufacturing processes to poorer countries with cheaper labor. This strategy supports "Made in China 2025" by allowing Chinese firms to focus on selling high-end products to domestic and foreign customers.[7] The BRI also builds upon the Going Out strategy by helping Chinese state-owned enterprises offshore industrial production facilities and stimulate demand for domestically oversupplied industrial inputs in markets outside of China.[8] Creating additional demand for the implementation of overseas projects

"Western Development" strategy (Ye 2020). China's leaders also felt a strong sense of encirclement by the United States, which at the time was pursuing a "Pivot to Asia" and negotiating the Trans-Pacific Partnership (TPP). The United States later withdrew its support for the TPP, which is now known as the Comprehensive and Progressive Agreement for Trans-Pacific Partnership.

[4] Overholt (2010).    [5] E.g., Naughton (2016).

[6] Wubbeke, Meissner, Zenglein et al. (2016).

[7] It also supports the development of the "Digital Silk Road," which was first introduced in 2015. See OECD (2018); Greene and Triolo (2020).

[8] Yafei (2014); Stanway (2015); Cai (2017). This offshoring strategy began with the adoption of the Going Out strategy, but it has become more explicit and sophisticated over time. The Chinese authorities eventually developed a special term that they use to describe it (国际产能合作), which roughly translates as "International Capacity Cooperation." The central government pairs individual Chinese provinces that suffer from specific types of industrial overproduction problems with countries that they believe can help address these problems by hosting relocated production facilities. Hebei province, which produces more steel than any other Chinese province, is a case in point. The central government directed it to shutter 240 of its 400 steel mills by 2020. It also put in place a set of targets for reductions in cement, aluminum, and glass production (Xinhua 2014; Lian and Burton 2017). Then, the central government paired Hebei province with

also helps Chinese companies secure new contracts and pay down domestic debts that began mounting after the 2008 global financial crisis.[9] Another source of continuity between the Going Out strategy and the BRI is the emphasis on foreign currency-denominated lending. Even after fifteen years of using excess foreign currency reserves to support overseas development projects, China still holds nearly US$3 trillion in foreign currency reserves. The BRI seeks to provide bankable projects where surplus dollars and euros can be invested.[10] Finally, China's historically underdeveloped western provinces such as Xinjiang, Tibet, Qinghai, and Gansu have been repositioned as important stops along the overland belt portion of the BRI, creating an opportunity to integrate these provinces into regional economic networks and address long-standing regional inequalities.[11] The Going Out strategy tethered China's domestic economic future to developing country markets, and the BRI follows a similar economic logic.

## BRI as a Soft Power Initiative

However, when the BRI was unveiled, we also sensed that major change was afoot. The decision to launch the BRI in late 2013 was an important milestone signaling China's ambition to position itself as a major world power and project influence around the globe. Western politicians and pundits speculated that President Xi Jinping was abandoning the "hide your capabilities and bide your time" strategy and seeking to reestablish China as a great power. At the time, Beijing's actions and rhetoric reinforced the perception that BRI was a *bilateral* initiative designed to advance China's own interests. Xi Jinping argued that "[w]e should increase China's soft power, give a good Chinese narrative, and better communicate China's message to the world."[12] Echoing this point, a senior MOFCOM official announced that "the work of foreign aid relates to China's image. We cannot tolerate any negligence or projects of poor quality."[13] During the early years of the BRI, the Chinese government also became more intentional about cultivating its brand – from the prominent placement of "China Aid" placards at project sites to the participation of global leaders at summits in Beijing – and broadcasting positive messages

a specific set of countries (Kazakhstan, Serbia, and Nigeria) that it envisioned as potential destinations for relocated production facilities, and it enlisted the support of the China Development Bank and China Eximbank to support joint industrial production ventures between Chinese state-owned enterprises and firms in these countries (Kenderdine and Ling 2018).

[9] Jiang (2020).    [10] He (2018).    [11] Cai (2017).    [12] People's Daily (2014).
[13] MOFCOM (2014a).

about its overseas activities.[14] Finally, unlike the Going Out policy, the BRI was personal. Many analysts consider the BRI as the signature policy initiative of Xi Jinping. The link between China's paramount leader and the BRI makes it difficult for Chinese firms and government agencies to identify and openly criticize problematic elements of the initiative that could undermine its ultimate success.[15]

Indeed, during the BRI era, the Chinese government made a series of unforced errors, which tarnished its international reputation and forced it to assume a defensive posture. Sri Lanka was the canary in the coal mine. As we described in Chapter 1, Beijing overplayed its hand in Sri Lanka and inadvertently provoked a public backlash. Then, in the face of swirling questions about "white elephants" and rampant corruption in the Sri Lankan president's home district, China made a bad situation worse by purchasing a distressed asset: the seaport in Hambantota. This move was widely characterized by international media outlets as an example of Chinese "debt trap diplomacy" – plying a foreign government with easy credit for a big-ticket project and then offering to forgive its debts in exchange for ownership of a strategic asset.[16]

Beijing's public diplomacy debacle in Sri Lanka foreshadowed a problem that would soon plague its broader BRI portfolio: its vulnerability to miscalculation in countries with strong institutions of democratic oversight. In at least a dozen countries where BRI projects faced high levels of media and parliamentary scrutiny, China encountered

---

[14] It did so by leveraging social media channels and cultivating journalists to encourage positive media coverage of their accomplishments. It also forged content-sharing partnerships with radio stations, television channels, and newspapers and invested in telecommunication systems in host countries to facilitate the transmission of information to its target audiences (Custer, Russell, DiLorenzo et al. 2018; Custer, Sethi, Solis et al. 2019).

[15] Swaine (2015); He (2018).

[16] In 2017, Brahma Chellaney, a professor of strategic studies at the New Delhi-based Center for Policy Research, coined the phrase "debt trap diplomacy" and used the Hambantota "debt-for-equity" deal to popularize the notion that China engages in predatory lending (Chellaney 2017). However, China's actions vis-à-vis the Hambantota port do not constitute clear-cut evidence of predation or entrapment (Bräutigam 2019). China Eximbank initially offered the Sri Lankan government several loans for the development of the Hambantota port (worth more than US$1 billion); when the port proved to be commercially nonviable under host-country ownership, the Sri Lankan government could not service its loans to China Eximbank. Then, a Chinese state-owned enterprise called China Merchant Port Holdings (CMPH) offered to effectively convert the debt into equity by providing a cash payment of US$1.1 billion to Sri Lanka's government in exchange for an 85 percent ownership stake in the port and the right to operate and develop it for 99 years (IMF 2018). CMPH therefore absorbed the risk of managing a stranded asset that would have otherwise been borne by the Sri Lankan government. The final 99-year concession agreement also expressly forbids Chinese military activity at the port without the host government's invitation.

difficult questions about opaque loan agreements, collusion and illicit payments between host country politicians and Chinese contractors, and artificially inflated project costs.[17] However, rather than openly addressing these concerns in responsive ways, Beijing turned to a strategy that it has used for decades: catering to the interests of political leaders in these countries. Its strategy backfired. Democratically elected politicians in Africa, Asia, Latin America, and Europe increasingly felt compelled to cancel or mothball high-profile BRI projects because major changes in public sentiment made it difficult to maintain close relations with China.[18]

During this period, Chinese state-owned banks and insurance providers also saw growing signs of asset distress and default risk in the BRI project portfolio, which threatened to undermine the government's financial yield maximization strategy (described in Chapters 2 and 7).[19] Several big-ticket infrastructure projects – such as a China Eximbank-financed railway from Addis Ababa to the Port of Djibouti – failed to generate sufficient revenue to service the loans that financed their construction, which in turn forced Chinese state-owned banks to restructure loans to allow borrowers to make their payments. It also forced the China Export and Credit Insurance Corporation (Sinosure) to write off major losses.[20] These loan restructurings and losses had a chastening effect. In 2016, an official with China's National Development and Reform Commission (NDRC) told the *Financial Times* that "these days we need viable projects and a good return. We don't want to back losers." Then, in September 2018, Xi Jinping gave a speech in which he issued a clear warning to would-be borrowers: financing from China is "not to be spent

---

[17] Concerns about the opaque nature of Chinese debt imposed particularly heavy reputational costs on China (Aamir 2018; Custer, Russell, DiLorenzo et al. 2018; Bloomberg News 2019; Hausmann 2019; Osaki 2019).

[18] These countries include, but are not limited to, Brazil, Ecuador, Kazakhstan, Kenya, the Kyrgyz Republic, Malaysia, the Maldives, Montenegro, Pakistan, Uganda, and Zambia (Abi-Habib 2018; Balding 2018; Mambetova and Kilner 2018; Montenegro 2018; Bisenov 2019; Custer and Tierney 2019; Mundy and Hille 2019; Ofstad and Tjønneland 2019; Wright and Hope 2019).

[19] During this period, Beijing acknowledged that its project appraisal standards were in need of revision. It expressed particular interest in the use of ex ante cost-benefit analysis to vet incoming project proposals (e.g., IMF 2014: 4, 2015: 53; Gabuev 2017; Jiang 2018) – a standard practice among many bilateral and multilateral development finance institutions but not among Chinese donors and lenders. As we mentioned in Chapter 6, the World Bank, the Asian Development Bank, the Inter-American Development Bank, the European Union, and the US government's Millennium Challenge Corporation (MCC) all use some form of cost-benefit analysis to vet candidate projects (Warner 2010: 57).

[20] For example, in the case of the China Eximbank-financed Djibouti-Addis Ababa Railway Project, Sinosure wrote off approximately US$1 billion in losses (Pilling and Feng 2018). See also Kynge (2016).

on any vanity projects but in places where they count the most."[21] The chief economist of Sinosure went even further, characterizing the due diligence procedures that China's policy banks use to assess the economic viability of projects as "downright inadequate."[22]

## Can Beijing Multilateralize the BRI?

After sailing into strong headwinds for several years, Beijing altered its course. One of the first signs of change came when President Xi announced in 2017 that "[w]e will . . . strengthen international cooperation on anticorruption in order to build the Belt and Road Initiative with integrity."[23] Then, in 2018, Beijing financed the creation of a China-IMF Capacity Development Center to train Chinese government officials on debt sustainability frameworks (DSFs) in low-income countries and other BRI-related policy issues.[24] A year later, the government announced that it would team up with eight multilateral institutions – the World Bank, the Inter-American Development Bank, the Asian Development Bank, the European Bank for Reconstruction and Development, the European Investment Bank, the International Fund for Agricultural Development, Corporación Andina de Fomento, and the Asian Infrastructure Investment Bank – to establish a Multilateral Cooperation Center for Development Finance. The center's mandate would be to (a) invest in more upstream project preparation work; (b) build the capacity of lenders and borrowers to more effectively manage and mitigate risks related to debt sustainability, procurement, corruption, and environmental and social issues; and (c) facilitate greater information sharing and coordination between Chinese and non-Chinese development finance institutions.[25] A month later, in

[21] Financial Times (2016) and Shepherd and Blanchard (2018).
[22] Pilling and Feng (2018).
[23] Abi-Habib (2018). The authorities in Beijing were certainly aware of the problem well before Xi Jinping's speech. In 2014, as part of the government's broader anti-corruption campaign, the CCP Central Disciplinary Committee reviewed existing practices at MOFCOM and quickly zeroed in on the corruption risks that plague its overseas project portfolio (MOFCOM 2014b). The Chinese government is currently seeking to address these risks through top-down audits (Belt & Road News 2019).
[24] In 2019, China also announced the adoption of a DSF for all projects implemented under the BRI (Morris, Parks, and Gardner 2020; Zettelmeyer 2020). This announcement followed a flurry of reports about possible debt distress in BRI borrower countries. A 2018 study found that roughly fifteen BRI member countries had crossed – or were in danger of crossing – critical debt sustainability thresholds (Hurley, Morris, and Portelance 2019). Shortly thereafter, another study concluded that "more than two dozen countries now owe more than 10 percent of their GDP to the Chinese government" (Horn, Reinhart, and Trebesch 2019: 13).
[25] See www.aiib.org/en/about-aiib/who-we-are/partnership/_download/collaboration-on-matters.pdf, last accessed November 17, 2020.

April 2019, President Xi gave a speech at the Second Belt and Road Forum for International Cooperation where he announced that China would "adopt widely accepted rules and standards and encourage participating companies to follow general international rules and standards in project development, operation, procurement and tendering and bidding."[26] Taken together, these actions and rhetorical commitments signaled that Beijing was preparing to pivot away from its traditional role of status quo challenger and move toward a new and far less familiar role: champion of international rules and standards. Beijing's bid to make the BRI a *multilateral* initiative also signaled that the Chinese government had ambitions to play a leadership role in the global development finance market.[27]

## A Leader without Followers Is Not a Leader

But herein lies a fundamental challenge: leadership requires followership and there are few indications that OECD-DAC donors or multilateral development banks are ready to jump on the BRI bandwagon. If anything, we have witnessed a role reversal in the relationship between China and the traditional players in the international development finance market: Beijing now finds itself in the position of courting the same multilateral institutions and Western powers that courted it during the pre-BRI period. China is not only seeking co-financiers and collaborators but also a seat at the table in shaping the rules and norms of a new development finance regime.

For the better part of the past twenty years, Beijing has positioned itself as an alternative source of financing for governments that would prefer not to deal with OECD-DAC donors or multilateral development banks. It has tacitly encouraged low-income and middle-income countries to bypass the prevailing rules and norms of the global development finance regime by bankrolling large-scale infrastructure projects with less "hassle," offering relatively fast and flexible project preparation procedures, less stringent environmental and social safeguards, and no competitive bidding requirements. It has openly criticized Western donors and multilateral creditors for conditioning financial disbursements on the adoption of specific reforms – like the passage of road maintenance legislation to ensure that there are adequate funds earmarked for the long-run upkeep of capital infrastructure projects – and positioned itself as a more flexible and

[26] See www.fmprc.gov.cn/mfa_eng/zxxx_662805/t1658424.shtml, last accessed November 17, 2020.
[27] The Economist (2017c); Igoe (2018b); Russel and Berger (2019).

responsive financier that treats the policy autonomy of host countries as sacrosanct.

It has also spurned nearly all invitations to negotiate a set of stable, transparent, and mutually acceptable international development finance rules and norms. In 2006, China was invited to join the Paris Club as a full-fledged member because of its status as an increasingly important sovereign lender. It rejected this offer and chose instead to be an "ad hoc participant," placing it "under no obligation to act in solidarity with Paris Club members or even to inform the Paris Club about the management of its credit activities."[28] Then, in 2011, the donor community encouraged China to comply with a common set of aid transparency standards. China's negotiators rejected this proposal, stating that the "principle of transparency should apply to north-south cooperation, but . . . it should not be seen as a standard for south-south cooperation."[29] Nor have efforts to negotiate a mutually acceptable set of export financing rules – which would supplement or supersede the OECD's "Gentleman's Agreement" on Officially Supported Export Credits – borne much fruit.[30] Since the turn of the century, Western powers and multilateral institutions have courted China, and China has coyly rejected their advances.

In the absence of any meaningful cooperation with China, the "incumbents" of the international development finance regime have chosen to act as though Beijing is not a major player. They have pursued debt-restructuring deals without knowing whether or when China would offer new loans to the same borrowers or how existing loans might be restructured. They have insisted that all infrastructure projects have strong environmental and social safeguards without knowing whether China was offering to finance the same projects without such safeguards. They have demanded policy concessions in exchange for budget support without knowing whether recipient governments were considering alternative offers from China with no such concessions. And they have offered export credits on terms that were consistent with their own Gentlemen's Agreement without knowing if China was undercutting such initiatives by blending export finance with development finance (e.g., grants and concessional loans).

China, for its part, seems perfectly content to pursue a "go-it-alone" strategy. For the past two decades, it has financed major infrastructure projects shortly after Western donors and lenders passed on the very same projects because of inadequate environmental risk mitigation measures.[31]

[28] Hurley, Morris, and Portelance (2019).    [29] Tran (2011a).
[30] Xu and Carey (2014).
[31] Gray and Kutenbach (2012); Laurance, Peletier-Jellema, Geenen et al. (2015).

It has pushed for commodity-backed loan arrangements with "sovereign guarantee" provisions that reduce the likelihood that borrower country debts to other bilateral and multilateral creditors will be repaid.[32] It has even sweetened the terms of its export financing deals by linking them to the provision of grants and concessional loans, thereby undermining Western governments that voluntarily comply with the Gentlemen's Agreement.

Thus, from the perspective of would-be BRI collaborators, China's past actions betray its present rhetoric. Beijing may be interested in multilateralizing the BRI, but its bid to assume a leadership position in the global development finance regime is difficult to reconcile with its apparent disinterest in negotiating and abiding by a set of shared rules and standards over the past twenty years. The key obstacle to collaboration, then, is the absence of trust.

Trust promotes cooperation by increasing communication and information sharing, reducing uncertainty and transaction costs, fostering norms of reciprocity, and generating stable expectations about future behavior.[33] However, in international relations, trust is in short supply because neither governments nor multilateral institutions have access to third-party contract enforcement mechanisms.[34] Consequently, governments and multilateral institutions that contemplate the possibility of collaboration must convince each other that they will honor commitments, and they must forge "self-enforcing" agreements. They must "decide whom to make agreements with, and on what terms, largely on

---

[32] In 2007, a consortium of Chinese companies entered into a joint venture with two state-owned Congolese mining companies. Under the terms of the original US$9.2 billion "Sicomines" deal, a US$3.2 billion mining investment was approved, with future profits from the investment earmarked to underwrite the reimbursement of a credit line for US$6 billion worth of infrastructure projects (Bräutigam 2010b; Jansson 2011, 2013; Mthembu-Salter 2012). China Eximbank agreed to help finance the deal, and two Chinese state-owned enterprises (CREC and Sinoyhdro) agreed to implement the infrastructure projects. The International Monetary Fund (IMF) and other creditors sounded the debt sustainability alarm, questioning China's request for a sovereign guarantee, whereby the Congolese government would be obligated to repay its Chinese loans even if the net operating profits from the mining investment were insufficient for repayment (Manson 2010; Mthembu-Salter 2012). According to Jansson (2013: 155), "[i]t was this sovereign guarantee that provoked particular concern with the IMF and the Paris Club donors, who feared that China [would] burden the Congolese state with [US] $9 billion of new debt." However, they also took issue with the fact that China's request for a sovereign guarantee was effectively a request for "preferred creditor" status, wherein its debts would be repaid before other bilateral and multilateral debts.

[33] Keohane (1984); Putnam (1993); Kydd (2000).

[34] Kydd (2007: 3) defines trust as "a belief that the other side is trustworthy, that is, willing to reciprocate cooperation, and mistrust as a belief that the other side is untrustworthy, or prefers to exploit one's cooperation." For the seminal discussion of this point, see Keohane (1984) and Oye (1986).

the basis of their expectations about their partners' willingness and ability to keep their commitments."[35] One way to do this is by sending each other "costly signals" of reassurance. These signals are particularly effective at building trust when they are observable, irreversible, noncontingent, and costly to the sender.[36] Such signals "serve to separate the trustworthy types from the untrustworthy types; trustworthy types will send them, [and] untrustworthy types will find them too risky to send."[37] Therefore, China may need to identify signals that would be sufficiently credible – and costly to its own interests – to induce a collaborative response from traditional donors and creditors.

### What Can China Do to Overcome Its Trust Deficit with Traditional Donors and Creditors?

The Chinese government has not had much success in finding traditional donors and lenders who are willing to join forces and support the BRI for at least three reasons: (a) its reluctance to share detailed information about its financial and implementation arrangements with host governments; (b) its track record of independently financing, designing, and implementing projects rather than adhering to common standards and disciplines; and (c) its go-it-alone approach to solving sovereign debt management problems. During the next phase of BRI implementation, the authorities in Beijing will confront a set of decisions related to these three issues, and the decisions that they take will send important signals to traditional donors and creditors. Whether the incumbents that maintain the existing international development finance regime will interpret those signals as sufficiently costly and credible to justify collaboration is an open question.

#### *Revisit the Costs and Benefits of Transparency*

China's secrecy places it at a reputational disadvantage with its peers in the development finance market. Michael Findley, a professor of government at the University of Texas, and his coauthors completed a field experiment in Uganda in which they randomly assigned descriptions of development projects financed by different donors, including China, the United States, the World Bank, and the African Development Bank. They asked approximately 3,000 members of the public a battery of attitudinal questions about whether they would support or oppose aid

---

[35] Keohane (1984: 105).    [36] Spence (1973); Rose and Spiegel (2011).
[37] Kydd (2000: 326).

from the donor in question.[38] The experiment also measured a set of behavioral outcomes to determine whether study participants would take costly actions that were consistent with their stated preferences. These outcomes included participants signing a paper copy of a petition (or not) and using their own money to send a text message (or not) to convey their project preferences. The results of the experiment indicate that host country citizens prefer development projects financed by USAID, the World Bank, and the African Development Bank to those financed by China. An investigation of the underlying reasons that account for this difference in attitudes suggests that the public trusts and favors donors and lenders who make it easy to monitor their projects, and that the opposite is true of nontransparent suppliers of development finance.[39]

These findings should give the Chinese authorities pause. Under the auspices of the BRI, they are conducting a costly international campaign to "win hearts and minds" in the hopes that more favorable public perceptions of China will "filter up and influence elite policy to be more amenable to [Chinese] interests."[40] However, Beijing may be spending its way to international disrepute by shielding its projects from public scrutiny.[41]

Beijing's transparency allergy is likely also undermining the performance of its development projects. Dan Honig, a professor at the Johns Hopkins SAIS, and his colleagues have analyzed 23,000 development projects financed by 12 bilateral and multilateral institutions in 148 countries between 1980 and 2016. They find that strong "access to information" (ATI) policies and institutions within aid agencies and development banks produce substantially better-performing projects.[42] Other studies have shown that more easily monitored development projects are less vulnerable to capture and corruption.[43] Transparency generally leads to better project outcomes because staff within development

---

[38] As they explain in their study, "[t]he projects were co-financed by multiple countries and agencies, which allowed us to manipulate the donor presented – naming possible contributors one at a time in separate conditions – to the subjects as well as the type of project without using active deception" (Findley, Milner, and Nielson 2017b: 318–319).

[39] Findley, Milner, and Nielson (2017).    [40] Brazys and Dukalskis (2019: 567).

[41] One of Beijing's stated reasons for having a foreign assistance program is to project a positive public image abroad (Chen 2010; Custer, Russell, DiLorenzo et al. 2018; Zhang 2018; Custer, Sethi, Solis et al. 2019). On the question of whether Chinese aid is a cost-effective way to win hearts and minds or an expensive irony, see Wellner, Dreher, Fuchs et al. (2020), Blair, Marty, and Roessler (2021), and Eichenauer, Fuchs, and Brückner (2021).

[42] ATI policies and institutions are particularly effective in conjunction with bottom-up methods of project oversight, such as civic monitoring and independent media scrutiny (Honig, Lall, and Parks 2020).

[43] Winters (2014); Carlson and Seim (2020).

finance institutions and their local counterparts in developing countries design and supervise projects more carefully when they anticipate public scrutiny.

For China, the consequences of its opacity are far-reaching because it creates risk aversion among potential collaborators in the international development finance market. Beijing's would-be collaborators do not need evidence from a randomized controlled trial in Uganda or a multiyear 148-country study to know that shrouding one's activities in secrecy is a reputational liability.[44] The pages of major international newspapers are filled with examples of the price that China pays for its secrecy. For instance, in 2018, the *Financial Times* reported that "Pakistan's government has not made public the details of project agreements with China, which contain information about the financing models … [and the] result has been mounting public discontent and intense criticism in Pakistan."[45]

Before agreeing to co-finance BRI projects with China, OECD-DAC and multilateral suppliers of development finance will almost certainly weigh the potential consequences of joining forces with the world's least transparent (and most controversial) donor and creditor.[46] It is possible that China's reputational toxicity will spill over onto traditional donors and lenders; it is also possible that China will more successfully safeguard its own brand by spreading reputational risk across a larger group of donors and lenders. Neither of these outcomes is particularly attractive to would-be collaborators, and Beijing's aversion to transparency may thus make collaboration with traditional donors and creditors less likely.[47] On the flip side, if China were to reverse course and embrace aid and debt transparency, it would send a costly signal to would-be collaborators.

### Reconsider the Value of Adhering to Common Standards and Disciplines

The Chinese authorities are increasingly aware of the benefits of international coordination and harmonization,[48] and they have signaled preliminary interest in modernizing their monitoring and evaluation systems

---

[44] Honig and Weaver (2019) demonstrate that donors are sensitive to these types of reputational pressures and adopt transparency measures to improve their performance in this annual benchmarking exercise.

[45] Aamir (2018).    [46] Publish What You Fund (2020).

[47] In other words, Beijing's aversion to transparency may increase the "risk premium" that traditional donors and creditors use when they weigh the benefits and the costs of working with China.

[48] Varrall (2016); Zhang (2018).

and strengthening their procurement guidelines, fiduciary controls, and social and environmental safeguards.[49] But if Beijing wants to convince traditional donors and lenders to participate in BRI, its grant-giving and lending institutions will most likely need to adhere to standards and safeguards that are acceptable to donors and lenders outside of China.

This does not necessarily mean that China must blindly accept all of the "gold-plated" standards and safeguards of OECD-DAC aid agencies and multilateral development banks. However, it does imply that China will need to work with its OECD-DAC and multilateral counterparts to (a) harmonize their standards and safeguards and (b) demonstrate its commitment to enforcing these standards and safeguards. Credible enforcement will be especially crucial, because this is where the biggest gap exists between Chinese practices and the practices of would-be BRI collaborators.

By way of illustration, consider environmental safeguards. China Development Bank and China Eximbank – the two largest sources of Chinese development finance for overseas infrastructure projects – have already adopted many of the same de jure environmental safeguards that are used by the major multilateral development banks. These include ex ante environmental impact assessments (EIA), project reviews, compliance with host country environmental laws and regulations, and ex post EIAs.[50] However, Chinese state-owned banks and their multilateral and OECD-DAC peers diverge in their de facto application of these safeguards.[51] In a comparative case study of a World Bank-financed hydroelectric dam project and a China Eximbank-financed hydroelectric dam project in Cameroon, Yunnan Chen and David Landry of the Johns Hopkins School for Advanced International Studies found the following:

Both China Eximbank and the World Bank have upped their game in prioritizing environmental norms and standards. However ... the strictness with which they are applied differ. The World Bank ... has prioritized its safeguard policies and

---

[49] Abi-Habib (2018); Igoe (2018b); Carey and Ladislaw (2019). A case in point was the admission in 2014 by the deputy director-general of MOFCOM's Department of Foreign Aid that "[w]e have long emphasized project implementation but neglected evaluation" and "Western aid practice is a very important reference point for us" (MOFCOM 2014a).

[50] BenYishay, Parks, Runfola et al. (2016). Gallagher (2013: 9) points to the following rationale for the adoption of these environmental safeguards: "[t]o the extent that local skepticism and protests result in delays or even loss of projects, environment-related political risk can severely affect the bottom line of the major Chinese policy banks." As Compagnon and Alejandro (2013) also note, these policy banks understand that the success of China's Going Out strategy increasingly depends on their ability to show critics and important market actors that they (and their contractors) are interested in protecting the natural environment.

[51] Dollar (2018).

demonstrated the political will to enforce them.... While [environmental] impact assessments and mitigation plans were a condition for loan disbursement [from China Eximbank], their monitoring and enforcement were largely the responsibility of the [Cameroonian government], for better or worse, thereby exposing a gap between theory and practice.

The authors conclude that "[t]here is a trade-off ... between Chinese and Western financing: while financing from China is disbursed faster, it poses a higher risk of issues arising during the implementation stage. Conversely, [World Bank development] finance featured a tougher approval process, but the construction process was a smoother one."[52]

Given these large baseline differences, a likely concern among China's would-be collaborators is that Beijing will pay lip service to international standards and safeguards but not strictly enforce them in its own projects. Beijing could preempt such concerns by choosing to "show rather than tell." That is, if Chinese donors and lenders co-finance, co-design, and co-implement projects with OECD-DAC and multilateral institutions, they would enable their collaborators to assess the credibility of Beijing's commitments to following a common set of standards and safeguards. Let's say, for instance, that China Eximbank approaches the United Kingdom's FCDO about jointly undertaking a large-scale BRI project that is fraught with social, environmental, and fiduciary risk but could deliver major socioeconomic dividends.[53] FCDO would insist upon a rigorous cost-benefit analysis and an environmental and social impact assessment, and its parliamentary oversight body would require that FCDO adapt the design of the project based on the results and recommendations of those studies – changes that would likely delay project implementation and conflict with the political interests of host government officials.[54] Then, FCDO would probably want to subject the project to international competitive bidding, which might result in the selection of a non-Chinese contractor. During implementation, FCDO would probably also want to ensure that a robust monitoring and evaluation system was in place so that it could track the intended and unintended

---

[52] Chen and Landry (2018: 569).

[53] The Chinese and British governments are potential BRI collaborators. In 2013, DFID and MOFCOM created the China International Development Research Network (CIDRN) to promote greater awareness and understanding of China's overseas development practices and impacts (Stallings and Kim 2017: 156). China Development Bank has also courted the United Kingdom's Commonwealth Development Corporation (CDC) to participate in BRI projects. (Author interview with a senior CDC official on March 23, 2019.)

[54] FCDO, for example, "requires[s] a statement of evidence from rigorous studies to support new proposals, and ... how the proposed [project] will collect the needed evidence if it doesn't exist" (White 2019).

effects of the project. FCDO's principals in the UK Parliament would require that all of these monitoring and evaluation data be made public, whether or not they painted FCDO and its co-financiers in a favorable light. One can think of multiple reasons why China Eximbank might get cold feet at any one of these stages in the project cycle. However, forging a deep and enduring collaboration would ultimately require that China Eximbank and FCDO coalesce around a mutually acceptable set of behavioral rules and norms.

In summary, efforts to co-finance, co-design, and co-implement projects would be costly signals from the Chinese government financing institutions to aid agencies and development banks outside of China, showing that Beijing is strongly committed to following a common set of project appraisal standards, procurement guidelines, fiduciary controls, and social and environmental safeguards.[55] Making these kinds of concessions would also begin to shift the prevailing assumptions of China's would-be collaborators, evidencing Beijing's broader commitment to compliance with international rules and norms.

### Revisit the Wisdom of a Go-It-Alone Approach to Solving Sovereign Debt Management Problems

Sovereign debt management is another area ripe for trust-building efforts.[56] Beijing is now the world's largest official creditor; as such, it has a special interest in making sure that borrowers repay their loans. Debt-distressed borrowers who owe large sums of money to Chinese and non-Chinese creditors pose an acute threat to Beijing. Those who can no longer service their loans typically engage with their largest creditors to seek an orderly debt restructuring that is acceptable to all relevant parties.[57] For the past sixty-five years, the Paris Club has served as the main negotiating venue for these kinds of settlements. However, as we previously noted, China has rejected multiple invitations to join the Paris Club.

When a sovereign debt resolution is not undertaken in a coordinated manner, a host of problems can arise: creditors may be tempted to engage in bad faith behavior, such as buying distressed sovereign debt for pennies

---

[55] Previous studies demonstrate that the quality of project preparation is an important determinant of final project outcomes (Denizer, Kaufmann, and Kraay 2013; Kilby 2015). Therefore, China's unwillingness to share information arguably limits the quality of the projects that can enter its pipeline in the first place.

[56] Group of Seven (2006); Lagarde (2018); Strauss (2018); Kawanami (2019).

[57] The risk of "disorderly" sovereign debt resolution includes discontinuation of debt service payments to some creditors but not others, and the pursuit of litigation by individual creditors to free-ride on already completed restructurings.

on the dollar to gain greater leverage in negotiations, and borrowers may be tempted to impose capital controls and suspend the convertibility of bank deposits. Lack of coordination may stoke fears about the stability of the banking sector. These conditions could produce a full-blown sovereign debt crisis that would leave all or most creditors worse off. Therefore, as sovereign debt sustainability problems in the developing world become more acute, China will have a growing incentive to share information and coordinate with other creditors – at least in principle.

A recent policy report from the Center for Global Development explains why information sharing and coordination between Chinese and non-Chinese lenders have become increasingly important: "[t]here is no aggregate reporting on the Chinese government's credit exposure to other sovereigns" and "[i]t is unambiguously the case that China is the largest sovereign-to-sovereign creditor in the world," so "[f]or the existing Paris Club members, there needs to be clear recognition that the list of the world's largest sovereign creditors looks different today than it did in 1956 when the club formed." The authors of the report argue that "[i]f the club is to continue to be effective in providing a public good to developed and developing countries alike, then China, along with a prospective class of emerging sovereign creditors, cannot continue to be outside the fold."[58]

However, to date, China has shown little interest in restructuring debt in a coordinated way, either through the Paris Club or any other multilateral mechanism. Its state-owned banks have sought to mitigate the risk of disorderly sovereign debt resolution with defensive, go-it-alone measures. It has contractually prohibited borrowers from rescheduling their outstanding Chinese debts through the Paris Club.[59] It has also used collateralization to effectively make its debts more "senior" than debts contracted with other creditors.[60]

[58] Hurley, Morris, and Portelance (2019: 158).
[59] Gelpern, Horn, Morris et al. (2021) undertake a detailed review of the terms and conditions in 100 Chinese loan contracts and find that approximately 80 percent of these contracts include explicit "No Paris Club" clauses, which guarantee that a borrower's outstanding obligations will not be subject to Paris Club debt rescheduling agreements (or the debt rescheduling agreements of any other creditor or group of creditors). Many Chinese loan contracts use some derivation of the following language: "the Borrower hereby represents, warrants and undertakes that its obligations and liabilities under this Agreement are independent and separate from those stated in agreements with other creditors (official creditors, Paris Club creditors, or other creditors), and the Borrower shall not seek from the Lender any kind of comparable terms and conditions which are stated or might be stated in agreements with other creditors."
[60] Gelpern, Horn, Morris et al. (2021) provide evidence that Chinese state-owned banks are significantly more likely than all other types of official creditors to collateralize the loans that they issue. They also demonstrate that Chinese state-owned banks have a strong preference for collateralizing on fully liquid ("grab and go") assets rather than

Not surprisingly, these practices have driven a wedge between China and traditional creditors. In January 2020, Jeromin Zettelmeyer, the deputy director of the IMF's Strategy and Policy Review Department, announced that his organization's "number one message" to the Chinese authorities is as follows:

If you are a big lender, there is no free-riding.... If you fail to be transparent, you make it more difficult for everyone else – borrowers and lenders – to take the right decisions, which makes it more likely that there will be a big blow up, which makes it more likely that you as the big lender will get hurt. So, your transparency decisions can actually influence outcomes.[61]

He also reported that the IMF has told Chinese authorities to "go easy on collateral" and "get ready for ... restructurings."[62]

Therefore, Beijing has an opportunity to signal its trustworthiness to other participants in the global development finance regime by revising its approach to sovereign debt management and crisis resolution. Whether the signals that it sends are perceived to be costly or cheap will likely determine the willingness of its would-be collaborators to participate in a multilateralized version of the BRI.

## Final Reflections

If China wants to persuade its peers that it is ready to make a strategic pivot and multilateralize the BRI, it must negotiate a mutually agreeable set of international rules and standards and demonstrate its commitment to compliance with them. Doing so would allow would-be collaborators to judge China's credibility as a leader of the global development finance regime. Therefore, the success of Beijing's trust-building efforts will have a significant influence on the outcomes that are ultimately achieved via

physical (illiquid) assets that can only be recovered through a judicial process. As a result, Beijing has more leverage than other lenders, and it is more likely to be repaid on a priority basis if its borrowers experience a liquidity or solvency crisis.

[61] Zettelmeyer (2020).

[62] Elaborating on this point, he noted that "what we are seeing since roughly the late 2000s is the third boom-bust cycle in international finance since the Second World War. The first was the first big boom-bust cycle of the 1980s driven ... mostly by bank lending to Latin America. Then we had one mostly to emerging markets and based on bond financing ... that went bust around 2000.... This is number three. This time we have this very interesting mix of non-Paris club, semi-concessional official borrowing, commercial borrowing, and with one very large lender playing a role. So, unless history has changed completely, this cycle is going to come to end, and when it does, there will be a wave of defaults, and we are seeing the beginning of that wave." He also warned that "if a lot of debt is collateralized, that really impedes access to unsecured [debt] financing in a crisis. That could go as far as complicating crisis resolution with the help of official financing, such as the IMF and the World Bank" (Zettelmeyer 2020).

BRI – and whether China finds itself in a situation that is more like the first or second scenario that we described at the beginning of this chapter.

But the success of a more inclusive and revitalized development finance regime does not rest solely on the shoulders of Beijing. OECD-DAC aid agencies and multilateral development finance institutions cannot afford to rest on their laurels or assume that current international rules and standards are the only basis for collaboration with Beijing. After World War II, these donors and lenders functioned like a cartel. They created a set of international rules and norms to promote their shared aims in the developing world; through the OECD-DAC, the Paris Club, and other organizations, they granted and denied membership to "new" donors and lenders based on whether they could credibly commit to the prevailing rules and norms of the international development finance regime. However, China never sought membership in this cartel. It chose instead to create and follow a different set of behavioral rules and norms, which gave developing countries a greater ability to "shop around" for alternative sources of funding. The cartel has not fared well in this competition, especially since the turn of the century. Large swathes of the developing world are now banking on Beijing – not Washington, Brussels, or London – for their highest-priority development projects. Therefore, if "traditional" donors and creditors wish to avert a crisis of confidence and relevance, they will need to rewrite international development finance rules and norms in ways that accommodate Beijing's interests and more effectively account for the preferences of low-income and middle-income countries.

# Postscript: Analysis of China's Overseas Development Program During the BRI Era With an Updated Dataset

In this book, we introduced and analyzed the 1.0 version of AidData's global dataset of Chinese ODA- and OOF-financed projects. Shortly after we completed our manuscript (Chapters 1–9), we collaborated with AidData to publish a new (2.0) version of the dataset based upon an improved version of the TUFF methodology (Custer et al. 2021).[1] The 2.0 dataset, which was published in September 2021, captures 13,427 Chinese ODA- and OOF-financed projects worth US$843.1 billion across 165 countries.[2] These projects were financed by more than 330 Chinese government institutions and state-owned entities. The dataset covers projects approved (i.e., officially committed) between 2000 and 2017—and implemented between 2000 and 2021—in every low-income, lower-middle income, and upper-middle income country and territory across Africa, Asia, Oceania, the Middle East, Latin America and the Caribbean, and Central and Eastern Europe.[3]

Just as the 1.0 dataset was built on the foundations of earlier versions of the TUFF methodology, the construction of the 2.0 dataset targeted several areas for improvement. Expanding the volume and diversity of official sources was a major point of emphasis. To facilitate the construction of the 2.0 dataset, we worked with a team of more than 130 faculty, staff, and students at AidData over a five-year period (2017–2021) to

---

[1] Recall from Chapter 4 that the 1.0 version of the dataset catalogued 5,466 projects in 138 countries, of which our analyses include 4,327 projects worth US$351.7 billion. The 2.0 version of the TUFF methodology can be accessed via https://www.aiddata.org/publications/aiddata-tuff-methodology-version-2-0; the 2.0 dataset is accessible via https://www.aiddata.org/data/aiddatas-global-chinese-development-finance-dataset-version-2-0.

[2] In total, the 2.0 dataset identifies Chinese government-financed projects in 145 countries. It also identifies 20 additional countries where systematic searches were undertaken but no evidence of Chinese government-financed projects was found.

[3] 10,849 of the 13,427 records in the dataset are formally approved, active, and completed projects. These projects are collectively worth US$843.1 billion. The remaining 2,577 projects in the 2.0 dataset are (i) projects that secured official financial or in-kind commitments from China but were subsequently suspended or cancelled; (ii) projects that secured pledges of financial or in-kind support from official sector institutions in China but never reached the formal approval (official commitment) stage; and (iii) so-called "umbrella" projects that are designed to support multiple, subsidiary projects.

increase the TUFF methodology's use of unredacted grant, loan, export credit, debt cancellation, and debt rescheduling agreements published in government registers and gazettes; official records extracted from the information management systems of host countries; annual reports published by Chinese state-owned banks and enterprises; Chinese Embassy and Ministry of Commerce websites; and reports published by parliamentary oversight institutions in host countries.

This enhanced focus on official sources resulted in a more comprehensive and detailed dataset that draws upon an expanded and more diverse set of sources. Whereas the 1.0 dataset drew upon approximately 15,000 unique sources, the 2.0 dataset draws upon more than 63,000 unique sources.[4] In the 1.0 dataset, the average project record was based upon 3.6 sources. By comparison, the average project record in the 2.0 dataset is based upon 6.8 sources. The 2.0 dataset also makes more extensive use of official sources from China and recipient countries: 62 percent of the project records in the 1.0 dataset are underpinned by at least 1 official source; however, in the 2.0 dataset, this figure has increased to 89 percent.[5]

A key feature of the 2.0 dataset is its comprehensive scope. It not only covers all regions and sectors, but also all sources and types of financial and in-kind transfers from government and state-owned institutions in China.[6] The projects in the 2.0 dataset are supported by 334 unique official sector institutions in China, including central government agencies (like the Ministry of Commerce, the Ministry of Foreign Affairs, and the Ministry of Agriculture), regional and local government agencies (like

[4] In total, the dataset was assembled with 91,356 sources (including 63,464 unique sources in more than a dozen languages, of which 34,075 are official sources). To expose our coding and categorization choices to public scrutiny and enable replicable research findings, we disclose all the sources that were used to construct the dataset at the project level.

[5] The 2.0 dataset was assembled primarily with open-source materials in seven languages: Chinese, English, Spanish, French, Portuguese, Russian, and Arabic. However, in countries where the official "language of government" is not one of these seven languages, we used local language sources—for example, Farsi sources in Iran, Vietnamese sources in Vietnam, and Dutch sources in Suriname.

[6] There are other datasets that capture official financial transfers from China to a single sector (e.g., energy) or region (e.g., Latin America), or that only track certain types of financial flows (e.g., loans) and funding sources (e.g., China's policy banks). See, for example, the Chinese Loans to Africa Database maintained by Boston University and the China Africa Research Initiative at the Johns Hopkins University School of Advanced International Studies (SAIS-CARI), the China's Global Energy Finance Database and China's Overseas Development Finance Database maintained by Boston University, the China-Latin America Finance Database maintained by Boston University and Inter-American Dialogue, the China-Latin America Commercial Loans Tracker maintained by Inter-American Dialogue, and the Pacific Aid Map maintained by the Lowy Institute. For a comparison of AidData's 2.0 dataset to other Chinese development finance datasets, see Table A-1 in Malik et al. (2021).

Chongqing Municipal Health Commission and Tianjin Municipal Government), state-owned enterprises (like China National Petroleum Corporation, China National Aero-Technology Import & Export Corporation, and China Machinery Engineering Corporation), state-owned policy banks (like China Development Bank and China Eximbank), state-owned commercial banks (like Bank of China, China Construction Bank, and the Industrial and Commercial Bank of China), state-owned funds (like the Silk Road Fund), and non-profit government organizations (like Hanban and the China Foundation for Poverty Alleviation).

Several additional improvements were made possible by the scale, diversity, and quality of the sourcing that underpins the 2.0 dataset: (1) more detailed information about the terms and conditions that govern financial agreements between official sector institutions in China and recipient institutions in developing countries, (2) more precise measurement of the implementation of projects over time and geographic space, (3) identification of the agencies responsible for project implementation and measurement of their characteristics, and (4) the inclusion of more detailed narrative descriptions that detail how Chinese development projects are being designed, implemented, monitored, and evaluated.

The 2.0 dataset provides more detailed information on the terms and conditions that govern the financing agreements issued by Chinese state-owned entities. Of the 3,103 loans, buyer's credits, or seller's credits that are captured in the dataset, 2,757 identify a transaction amount, 1,659 have a known interest rate, 1,940 have a known maturity length, and 1,285 have a known grace period. These details ensure accurate measurements of financial concessionality levels according to the OECD–DAC guidelines for ODA and OOF. For 50 percent of the loans, buyer's credits, and seller's credits (and 56 percent of the debt in monetary terms) in the 2.0 dataset, we obtained the three key pricing details that are needed to measure financial concessionality levels with the OECD–DAC grant element calculator. By way of comparison, only 29 percent of the loans and export credits in the 1.0 dataset included all three of these pricing details.[7] Another important feature of the 2.0 dataset is the inclusion of five new variables that measure commitment fees, management fees, and the use of three types of repayment safeguards (collateral, credit

---

[7] Whereas 35 percent of the loans and export credits in the 1.0 dataset identified an interest rate, this figure has increased to 53 percent in the 2.0 dataset. Similarly, 37 percent of the loans and export credits in the 1.0 dataset identified a maturity length and 28 percent identified a grace period, but these coverage rates have increased to 63 percent and 41 percent, respectively, in the 2.0 dataset.

insurance, and third-party repayment guarantees).[8] The 2.0 dataset also documents the monetary value and timing of disbursements and repayments; the establishment of special purpose vehicles (SPVs) and subsidiary on-lending arrangements; and the monetary value and timing of underlying commercial contracts.[9] Additionally, the 2.0 dataset provides stable URLs to a large number of unredacted grant, loan, buyer's credit, seller's credit, debt forgiveness, and debt rescheduling agreements whenever they were successfully retrieved. AidData previously published a subset of these financing agreements at the time of the publication of the "How China Lends" study in April 2021 (Gelpern et al. 2021).[10] However, the 2.0 dataset provides the full set of unredacted financing agreements.

Another key area of improvement is the precise measurement of project implementation over time and geographic space. The 2.0 dataset identifies the calendar days when implementation commenced for 5,539 projects and the calendar days when implementation concluded for 6,061 projects. By comparison, the 1.0 dataset only identifies implementation start dates for 745 projects and project completion dates for 906 projects.[11] The 2.0 dataset also provides substantially more precise location information about Chinese development projects. Whereas the 1.0 dataset used a point-based geocoding methodology to identify the physical locations of Chinese development projects, the 2.0 dataset provides these data with a higher level of spatial measurement precision. The physical boundaries and exact locations of schools, hospitals, stadiums, government buildings, power plants, and factories are represented with polygons. Similarly, polygons are used to represent the geographical scope of special economic zones, industrial

---

[8] More specifically, the 2.0 dataset catalogues three different types of "credit enhancements" used by Chinese state-owned lenders to increase their repayment prospects: (i) formal and informal pledges of collateral that can be seized in the event the borrower defaults on its repayment obligations, (ii) the issuance of any repayment guarantees by parties other than the borrower, and (iii) the acquisition of credit insurance (typically but not exclusively from Sinosure).

[9] We also made special efforts to document the debt cancellation and rescheduling actions of Chinese state-owned lenders. With the 1.0 version of our dataset, Horn et al. (2019: 32) identify 140 Chinese debt cancellation and rescheduling actions between 2000 and 2017. They find that these types of actions are far more common among official Chinese creditors than private external creditors (banks and bondholders). However, the 2.0 version of our dataset identifies an even larger number (212) of debt cancellation and rescheduling actions by Chinese state-owned lenders during the same 18-year period: 134 debt cancellation actions in 64 countries and 78 debt rescheduling actions in 36 countries.

[10] In total, Gelpern et al. (2021) analyzed 100 loan contracts issued by Chinese state-owned lenders. See https://www.aiddata.org/how-china-lends for more details.

[11] The 2.0 dataset also provides information on the originally scheduled project implementation start dates and completion dates, so that users can determine whether projects have been implemented on schedule, behind schedule, or ahead of schedule.

parks, mining concessions, protected areas, and plots of land under culti-vation. Line vectors (i.e., "squiggly" lines) are provided to capture the exact routes of roads, bridges, tunnels, railways, power lines, canals, and pipe-lines. Technically-savvy users can now access these data via GeoJSON files, which can be easily merged with georeferenced outcome and covari-ate data to undertake various types of analysis at subnational scales.[12] With calendar day-level information on the timing of project implementation and exact location details, users of the 2.0 dataset can now measure the spatio-temporal rollout of project implementation with a high level of precision.

The 2.0 dataset also provides more information about the organ-izations responsible for implementing Chinese government-financed projects.[13] In the 1.0 version of the dataset, we were able to identify implementing agencies for 29 percent of projects (1,272 out of 4,373 projects) worth US$223 billion. However, in the 2.0 dataset, we have managed to identify implementing agencies for 63 percent of the projects (6,886 out of 10,849 projects) worth US$682 billion. In total, we identify 3,523 implementing agencies. The 2.0 dataset also includes two new variables related to the characteristics of the agencies responsible for project implementation: "Implementing Agencies Type" and "Implementing Agencies Origin."[14] Across

---

[12] In total, for 3,285 projects that have physical footprints or involve specific locations, the 2.0 dataset extracts point, polygon, and line vector data via OpenStreetMap URLs and provides a corresponding set of GeoJSON files. An important caveat is that we are only able to provide these geospatial details for the subset of projects in the 2.0 dataset that have physical footprints (e.g., roads, railways, transmission lines) or involve activities at specific locations (e.g., medical teams stationed at a given hospital, equipment given to park rangers to patrol a well-demarcated protected area). Out of the 13,427 projects in the 2.0 dataset, 3,285 projects (worth US$410 billion) have corresponding GeoJSON files and OpenStreetMap URLs. AidData has made the complete set of GeoJSON files along with usage tips, and related documentation accessible via https://github.com/aid data/china-osm-geodata.

[13] This is particularly true for large, "implementation-intensive" projects. Many different types of transactions in the 2.0 dataset that are not "implementation-intensive," such as cash grants, commodity (e.g., oil, coal, rice, corn, wheat) donations, equipment dona-tions, balance of payments support, pre-export finance facilities, debt forgiveness, schol-arships, and trainings.

[14] The "Implementing Agencies Type" variable captures the type of agency responsible for implementing the project activities. Each implementing agency is assigned to one of ten categories: Government Agency, State-Owned Bank, State-Owned Company, State-Owned Fund, Intergovernmental Organization, Special Purpose Vehicle/Joint Venture, Private Sector, NGO/CSO/Foundation, Other, or No Organization Type Specified. The "Implementing Agencies Origin" variable indicates the origin of the implementing agency with respect to whether it is from the financier country, the recipient country, or another country. Each receiving agency is assigned to one of the following categories: China, Recipient Country, or Other.

the 3,523 implementing agencies in the 2.0 dataset, we identify 1,045 government agencies (30 percent), 958 state-owned companies (27 percent), 554 private sector organizations (16 percent), and 189 special purpose vehicles/joint ventures (5 percent). The remaining 770 implementing agencies (22 percent) consist of non-governmental organizations (NGOs), inter-governmental organizations (IGOs), and organizations that we could not reliably assign to a category ("unspecified"). 35 percent of these implementing agencies are from China, while 58 percent are from host countries. 7 percent are neither from China nor the host country where the project is based (e.g., IGOs).[15]

Another unique feature of the 2.0 dataset is the large amount of qualitative information (in the "description" field) that it provides about the various risks and challenges that arose during project design and implementation (e.g., protests, scandals, and public health restrictions); how funding, receiving, implementing, and accountable institutions responded to these risks and challenges; project achievements and failures; contractor performance vis-à-vis deadlines and deliverables; and findings from project audits and evaluations. The average length of each project narrative in the 2.0 dataset is 144 words. When all of the narratives are stitched together, they are as long as 19 full-length books (1.93 million words).[16]

An AidData policy report, entitled *Banking on the Belt and Road*, provides an extensive, 166-page analysis of the 2.0 dataset and we encourage readers to consult this publication (Malik et al. 2021). However, by way of introduction, we will highlight five key patterns and trends from the 2.0 dataset that directly relate to the findings of this book.[17]

---

[15] The 2.0 dataset also provides more detailed information about the broader set of organizations that are involved in Chinese ODA- and OOF-financed projects, including 334 official sector institutions in China that provide funding and/or in-kind support, 460 co-financing institutions (some of which are traditional bilateral and multilateral agencies that have chosen to participate in syndicated loans or other types of consortia with Chinese counterparts), 2,450 recipient institutions, and 227 "accountable agencies" that provide repayment guarantees, credit insurance policies, and collateral which can be seized in the event of default.

[16] AidData has created individual webpages (with stable URLs) for each project—and project narrative—on the china.aiddata.org website.

[17] The 2.0 dataset includes significant historical revisions based upon new sources of information. Therefore, the summary statistics from the 1.0 dataset (used in Chapters 1–9) cannot be directly compared to the summary statistics from the 2.0 dataset (referenced in this postscript).

First, China's overseas development finance program dramatically expanded after the BRI was introduced in 2013. During the pre-BRI era (2000–2012), China and the U.S. were overseas spending rivals: average annual development finance commitments from China amounted to US$32 billion and average annual development finance commitments from the U.S. were roughly on par (nearly US$34 billion). We documented the same basic pattern in Chapter 4 (using the 1.0 dataset). However, the 2.0 dataset calls attention to a trend that was not yet apparent when we first wrote this book: During the first five years of BRI implementation, China outspent the U.S. on a more than 2-to-1 basis. More specifically, between 2013 and 2017, average annual development finance commitments from China amounted to US$85.4 billion and average annual development finance commitments from the U.S. amounted to US$37 billion.[18]

Second, Beijing's 21st century transition from benefactor to banker rapidly accelerated during the BRI era. We documented the beginning of this trend in Chapter 4. However, once the BRI was introduced, China doubled down on its effort to become the global lender of first resort for low-income and middle-income countries: whereas China issued 5.3 dollars of debt for every dollar of aid during the thirteen-year period preceding the BRI (2000–2012), it issued more than 9 dollars of debt for every dollar of aid during five years of BRI implementation (2013–2017).[19]

Third, Beijing's "policy banks"—China Eximbank and China Development Bank—led a major expansion in overseas lending in the run-up to the BRI. However, since 2013, state-owned commercial banks—including Bank of China, the Industrial and Commercial Bank of China, and China Construction Bank—have played an increasingly important role, with their overseas lending activities increasing 5-fold during the first five years of BRI implementation. The number of "mega-projects"—financed with loans worth US$500 million or more—being approved each year also tripled between 2013 and 2017.[20] In an average year during the 13-year

---

[18] With AidData's 1.0 dataset and several other sources, Horn et al. (2019: 14) demonstrate that China became the world's largest official creditor to the developing world, surpassing both the World Bank and the IMF, in 2011 (Horn et al. 2019: 14). However, analysis of AidData's 2.0 dataset demonstrates that, even after establishing itself as the world's largest official creditor, China continued to dramatically increase the size of its overseas lending program during the first five years of the BRI.

[19] In 2000 (the first full year following the adoption of the "Going Out" strategy), the 2.0 dataset indicates that China issued 1.7 dollars of debt for every dollar of aid in 2000.

[20] The 2.0 dataset demonstrates that the average monetary value of a loan from an official sector institution in China increased by 27 percent during the first five years of the BRI. Whereas the average monetary value of a loan during the pre-BRI era (2000–2012) was

period preceding the BRI (2000–2012), Beijing approved 11 loans worth more than US$500 million. By contrast, in an average year during the first five years of BRI implementation (2013–2017), Beijing approved 36 loans worth more than US$500 million.

Fourth, to pool credit risk and support projects that they would not otherwise finance on their own, China's state-owned policy banks and commercial banks have increasingly collaborated via lending syndicates and other co-financing arrangements during the BRI era. At the turn of the century (2000), the 2.0 dataset indicates that virtually no official sector lending from China was co-financed. However, by 2017, 32 percent of Beijing's overseas lending portfolio was co-financed.[21] The 2.0 dataset also reveals that, as China has financed bigger projects and taken on higher levels of credit risk, it has put in place stronger repayment safeguards: only 31% of the country's overseas lending portfolio benefited from credit insurance, a pledge of collateral, or a third-party repayment guarantee during the early 2000s (2000–2003), but this figure increased to 58 percent during the first five years of BRI implementation (2013–2017). Among these so-called "credit enhancements," collateralization is the most popular tool among Chinese state-owned lenders: at least 44 percent of official sector lending from China is collateralized, while at least 17 percent is backed by a repayment guarantee and at least 13 percent is insured.[22] When the stakes are especially high, collateralization is Beijing's "go-to" risk mitigation tool: 40 of the 50 largest loans in the 2.0 dataset are collateralized.[23]

Fifth, an important but poorly understood feature of China's overseas development finance program during the BRI era is the rise of "hidden" debt and the fall of sovereign debt. We alluded to this trend in Chapter 2 during our discussion of Chinese lending to SPVs in Pakistan. However, given that the recipient agency variable

---

US$258 million, it was US$328 million during the first five years of the BRI (2013–2017).

[21] This trend was not discoverable in the 1.0 dataset due to insufficiently complete data on co-financing with Chinese and non-Chinese institutions.

[22] We use the "at least" qualifier because AidData only codes loans and export credits as being collateralized, guaranteed, or insured when it has evidence that one of these credit enhancements was issued. However, there are almost certainly collateralized, guaranteed, or insured transactions in the 2.0 dataset that are not identified as such because no such evidence was identifiable.

[23] We also find evidence that Chinese state-owned lenders favor collateralization when they lend to countries that pose especially high levels of fiduciary risk: 83 percent of China's collateralized lending between 2000 and 2017 supported countries within the bottom quartile of the WGI Control of Corruption Index.

in the 1.0 dataset suffered from high levels of missingness, we were not able to systematically measure the changing composition of recipient (borrowing) institutions in China's overseas lending portfolio when we first wrote this book. The 2.0 dataset addresses this shortcoming. It documents a sharp decline in China's official sector lending to government agencies (from 55 percent in 2000 to 30 percent in 2017), which coincided with a sharp increase in China's official sector lending to SPVs, state-owned companies, state-owned banks, and private sector institutions (from 31 percent in 2000 to 68 percent in 2017). These debts incurred by SPVs, state-owned companies, state-owned banks, and private sector institutions, for the most part, do not appear on government balance sheets. However, most of them benefit from explicit or implicit forms of host government liability protection, which has blurred the distinction between private and public debt and created major public financial management challenges for low-income and middle-income countries.[24]

Finally, after writing this book, several research institutions—including but not limited to the China Africa Research Initiative at the Johns Hopkins University School of Advanced International Studies and the Boston University Global Development Policy Center—published new Chinese development finance datasets. These datasets are more limited in scope, focusing on a particular region, sector, or set of funding sources. For a comparison of AidData's 2.0 dataset of Chinese ODA- and OOF-financed projects

---

[24] In some cases, Chinese state-owned creditors have lent to a private company or SPV but demanded that the host government issue a sovereign guarantee in support of the loan, which means that the loan issued could become a public debt that host country taxpayers are responsible for repaying (if the borrower goes bankrupt or the project in question does not generate sufficient revenue). In other cases, they have lent to a state-owned enterprise in the host country (or an SPV that is wholly or partially-owned by a state-owned enterprise in the host country) without demanding a sovereign guarantee, thereby creating uncertainty about who will assume responsibility for repayment in the event that the borrower goes bankrupt or defaults on its obligations. Another practice that has become increasingly popular is issuing a loan to an SPV or private sector institution without requiring a formal repayment guarantee from the host government but demanding a guaranteed return on equity from the host government. In principle, this type of loan is not a public sector liability since the borrower is an independent legal entity and the host government has no repayment obligation in the event of default. However, in practice, a host government-guaranteed return on equity implies that the borrower will be able to consistently service its Chinese debts, which is tantamount to an explicit loan repayment guarantee that that host government does not need to disclose.

to other Chinese development finance datasets, see Table A-1 in Malik et al. (2021). AidData plans to extend, expand, and improve this dataset in the future. Therefore, interested readers should monitor the aiddata.org website for future iterations of the dataset and the TUFF methodology.

# References

Aamir, Adnan. 2018. China's Belt and Road Plans Dismay Pakistan's Poorest Province. *Financial Times*. June 14. Accessed at www.ft.com/content/c4b78fe0-5399-11e8-84f4-43d65af59d43.

Abbas, Ali S., Nazim Belhocine, Asmaa A. Elganainy, and Mark Horton. 2010. A Historical Public Debt Database. IMF Working Paper 10/245. Washington, DC: International Monetary Fund. Accessed at www.imf.org/en/Publications/WP/Issues/2016/12/31/A-Historical-Public-Debt-Database-24332.

Abi-Habib, Maria. 2018. How China Got Sri Lanka to Cough Up a Port. *New York Times*. June 25. Accessed at www.nytimes.com/2018/06/25/world/asia/china-sri-lanka-port.html.

Acemoglu, Daron, and James Robinson. 2012. Fancy Schools. Why Nations Fail Blog. February 27. Accessed at http://whynationsfail.com/blog/2012/2/27/fancy-schools.html.

Acharya, Amitav. 2014. Who Are the Norm Makers? The Asian-African Conference in Bandung and the Evolution of Norms. *Global Governance* 20 (3): 405–417.

Acker, Kevin, Deborah Bräutigam, and Yufan Huang. 2020. Debt Relief with Chinese Characteristics. SAIS-CARI Policy Brief 46. Washington, DC: Johns Hopkins SAIS. Accessed at www.sais-cari.org/publications-policy-briefs.

African Development Bank (AfDB), Organisation for Economic Co-operation and Development (OECD), United Nations Development Program (UNDP), and United Nations Economic Commission for Africa (UNECA). 2011. *African Economic Outlook 2011*. Tunis, Tunisia: AfDB. Accessed at www.afdb.org/fileadmin/uploads/afdb/Documents/Generic-Documents/Media_Embargoed_Content/ENAEO_2011_embargo%206%20Juin.pdf.

African Development Bank (AfDB). 2014a. Study on Quality of Bank Financed Road Projects. Abidjan, Côte d'Ivoire: AfDB. Accessed at www.afdb.org/fileadmin/uploads/afdb/Documents/Events/ATFforum/Study_on_the_quality_of_Bank_Financed_Road_Projects_-_AfDB.pdf.

African Development Bank (AfDB). 2014b. Kenya: Nairobi-Thika Highway Improvement Project. Abidjan, Côte d'Ivoire: AfDB. Accessed at www.afdb.org/fileadmin/uploads/afdb/Documents/Project-and-Operations/Presidential_awards_2014_-_Kenya_-_Nairobi_-_Thika_Highway_Improvement_Project.pdf.

African Development Bank (AfDB). 2016. PCR Evaluation Note for Public Sector Operations: Nairobi-Thika Highway Improvement Project. Abidjan,

Côte d'Ivoire: AfDB. Accessed at https://evrd.afdb.org/documents/docs/EN_PN10706.pdf.

African Development Fund (ADF). 2007. Appraisal Report: Nairobi-Thika Highway Improvement Project. Tunis, Tunisia: AfDB. Accessed at www.afdb.org/fileadmin/uploads/afdb/Documents/Project-and-Operations/Kenya_-_Nairobi-Thika_Highway_Improvement_Project_-_Appraisal_Report.PDF.

Afrobarometer. 2015. Chinese Engagement in Tanzania: Is It Considered Positive or Negative by Tanzanians? Findings from the Afrobarometer Round 6 Survey in Tanzania. Presentation delivered in Dar es Salaam on February 25. Accessed at http://afrobarometer.org/sites/default/files/media-briefing/tanzania/tan_r6_presentation2_china.pdf.

Ahmed, Faisal Z. 2012. The Perils of Unearned Foreign Income: Aid, Remittances, and Government Survival. *American Political Science Review* 106 (1): 146–165.

AidData. 2013. A Rejoinder to Rubbery Numbers on Chinese Aid. The First Tranche: AidData's Blog. May 1. Accessed at www.aiddata.org/blog/a-rejoinder-to-rubbery-numbers-on-chinese-aid.

AidData. 2017. *World Bank Geocoded Research Release Level 1 v1.4.2.* Williamsburg, VA: AidData at William & Mary. Accessed at http://aiddata.org/research-datasets.

Alden, Chris, and Cristina Alves. 2008. History & Identity in the Construction of China's Africa Policy. *Review of African Political Economy* 35(115): 43–58.

Alesina, Alberto, and David Dollar. 2000. Who Gives Foreign Aid to Whom and Why? *Journal of Economic Growth* 5(1): 33–63.

Allen-Ebrahimian, Bethany. 2017. Russia Is the Biggest Recipient of Chinese Foreign Aid. *Foreign Policy*. October 11. Accessed at http://foreignpolicy.com/2017/10/11/russia-is-the-biggest-recipient-of-chinese-foreign-aid-north-korea.

Anaxagorou, Christiana, Georgios Efthyvoulou, and Vassilis Sarantides. 2020. Electoral Motives and the Subnational Allocation of Foreign Aid in Sub-Saharan Africa. *European Economic Review* 127: 103430.

Anderlini, Jamil. 2009. China to Deploy Foreign Reserves. *Financial Times.* July 21. Accessed at www.ft.com/content/b576ec86-761e-11de-9e59-00144feabdc0.

Anderlini, Jamil, and Justine Lau. 2009. China's Stimulus Is Working but Social Unrest Fears Persist. *Financial Times.* June 13.

Andreoni, Antonio. 2017. Anti-Corruption in Tanzania: A Political Settlements Analysis. ACE Working Paper 1. London: University of London. Accessed at https://eprints.soas.ac.uk/24853/1/ACE-WorkingPaper001-TZ-AntiCorruption-171102_final%20revised.pdf.

Andreula, Nicolo, Alberto Chong, and Jorge B. Guillen. 2009. Institutional Quality and Fiscal Transparency. IDB Working Paper 36. Washington, DC: Inter-American Development Bank. Accessed at www.econstor.eu/bitstream/10419/89153/1/IDB-WP-125.pdf.

Andrews, Matt. 2013. *The Limits of Institutional Reform in Development.* Cambridge: Cambridge University Press.

Aneez, Shihar. 2016. Chinese Query Sri Lanka Allegations of Corruption in Contracts. Reuters, November 2. Accessed at www.reuters.com/article/sri-lan

ka-china/chinese-query-sri-lanka-allegations-of-corruption-in-contracts-idUSL4N1D256S.

Annen, Kurt, and Stephen Knack. 2020. Better Policies from Policy-Selective Aid? *World Bank Economic Review*. Forthcoming. Accessed at https://doi .org/10.1093/wber/lhaa017.

Ansar, Atif, Bent Flyvbjerg, Alexander Budzier, and Daniel Lunn. 2016. Does Infrastructure Investment Lead to Economic Growth or Economic Fragility? Evidence from China. *Oxford Review of Economic Policy* 32(3): 360–390.

Arcand, Jean-Louis, and Lisa Chauvet. 2001. Foreign Aid, Rent-Seeking Behavior, and Civil War. Working Paper. Clermont-Ferrand, France: Université d'Auvergne (CERDI CNRS). Accessed at www.researchgate.net/p rofile/Jean-Louis-Arcand/publication/228696996_Foreign_Aid_Rent-Seekin g_Behavior_and_Civil_War/links/0deec522f2ed3e9954000000/Foreign-Aid-Rent-Seeking-Behavior-and-Civil-War.pdf.

Argaw, Bethlehem A. 2017. Regional Inequality of Economic Outcomes and Opportunities in Ethiopia: A Tale of Two Periods. UNU-WIDER Working Paper 118. Helsinki, Finland: World Institute for Development Economic Research (UNU-WIDER). Accessed at www.wider.unu.edu/publication/regi onal-inequality-economic-outcomes-and-opportunities-ethiopia.

Arriola, Leonardo R., Donghyun Danny Choi, and Victor Rateng. 2017. The Key to Kenya's Close Election: The Power of Partisanship. *Washington Post*. August 7. Accessed at www.washingtonpost.com/news/monkey-cage/wp/2017/08/07/heres-how-partisanship-not-the-economy-is-shaping-kenyas-close-election.

Asian Development Bank. 2013. Myanmar Agriculture, Natural Resources, and Environment Initial Sector Assessment, Strategy, and Road Map. Mandaluyong City, Philippines: Asian Development Bank. Accessed at http://themimu .info/sites/themimu.info/files/documents/Report_Myanmar_Agriculture_Enviro nment_Assement_and_Road_Map_Apr2013.pdf.

Asian Development Bank. 2017. Meeting Asia's Infrastructure Needs. Mandaluyong City, Philippines: Asian Development Bank. Accessed at www .adb.org/sites/default/files/publication/227496/special-report-infrastruc ture.pdf.

Asmus, Gerda, Andreas Fuchs, and Angelika Müller. 2018. Russia's Foreign Aid Re-Emerges. The First Tranche: AidData's Blog. Accessed at http://aiddata .org/blog/russias-foreign-aid-re-emerges.

Asmus, Gerda, Andreas Fuchs, and Angelika Müller. 2020. BRICS and Foreign Aid. In Soo Yeon Kim (ed.), *The Political Economy of the BRICS Countries*, Volume 3: *BRICS and the Global Economy*. Singapore: World Scientific: 139–177.

Asmus, Gerda, Vera Z. Eichenauer, Andreas Fuchs, and Bradley Parks. 2021. Does India Use Development Finance to Compete with China? A Subnational Analysis. AidData Working Paper 110. Williamsburg, VA: AidData at William & Mary.

Athukorala, Prema-chandra, and Sisira Jayasuriya. 2013. Economic Policy Shifts in Sri Lanka: The Post-Conflict Development Challenge. *Asian Economic Papers* 12(2): 1–28.

Bader, Julia. 2015a. China, Autocratic Patron? An Empirical Investigation of China as a Factor in Autocratic Survival. *International Studies Quarterly* 59: 23–33.

Bader, Julia. 2015b. Propping up Dictators? Economic Cooperation from China and Its Impact on Authoritarian Persistence in Party and Non-Party Regimes. *European Journal of Political Research* 54(4): 655–672.

Baker, Peter. 2015. Obama, on China's Turf, Presents U.S. as a Better Partner for Africa. *New York Times*. July 29. Accessed at www.nytimes.com/2015/07/30/world/africa/obama-on-chinas-turf-presents-us-as-a-better-partner-for-africa.html.

Balding, Christopher. 2018. Why Democracies Are Turning against Belt and Road: Corruption, Debt, and Backlash. *Foreign Affairs*. October 24. Accessed at www.foreignaffairs.com/articles/china/2018-10-24/why-democracies-are-turning-against-belt-and-road.

Balestri, Sara, and Mario A. Maggioni. 2014. Blood Diamonds, Dirty Gold and Spatial Spill-Overs: Measuring Conflict Dynamics in Western Africa. *Peace Economics, Peace Science and Public Policy* 20(4): 551–564.

Banik, Dan. 2019. Coordinating Chinese Aid in a Globalized World. Policy Brief. Carnegie-Tsinghua Center for Global Policy. Accessed at https://carnegietsinghua.org/2019/01/06/coordinating-chinese-aid-in-a-globalized-world-pub-78058.

Banuri, Sheheryar, Stefan Dercon, and Varun Gauri. 2017. Biased Policy Professionals. World Bank Policy Research Working Paper 8113. Washington, DC: World Bank. Accessed at https://openknowledge.worldbank.org/handle/10986/27611.

Barkan, Joel D., and Michael Chege. 1989. Decentralising the State: District Focus and the Politics of Reallocation in Kenya. *Modern African Studies* 27(3): 431–453.

Barron, Manuel, and Maximo Torero. 2014. Household Electrification: Short-Term Effects with Long-Term Implications. Working Paper. University of California Berkeley: Department of Agricultural and Resource Economics.

Barta, Patrick. 2012. Cambodia Says No Strings Attached in Recent Chinese Aid. *Wall Street Journal*. September 6. Accessed at www.wsj.com/articles/BL-SEAB–1127.

Bartke, Wolfgang. 1989. *The Economic Aid of the PR China to Developing and Socialist Countries*. Munich, Germany: K.G. Saur.

BBC. 2009. China's Global Reach: Lending More Than the World Bank. BBC News. December 11. Accessed at www.bbc.co.uk/news/mobile/business–16092634.

BBC. 2015a. Full Transcript of BBC Interview with President Barack Obama. BBC News. July 24. Accessed at www.bbc.com/news/world-us-canada–33646542.

BBC. 2015b. Nepal Earthquake: India and China Pledge Millions in Aid. BBC News. June 25. Accessed at www.bbc.com/news/world-asia–33266422.

BBC. 2017. Kenya Opens Nairobi-Mombasa Madaraka Express Railway. BBC News. May 31. Accessed at www.bbc.com/news/world-africa–40092600.

BBC. 2018. Africa Live: Barbecues "Fuel Nigeria Deforestation." BBC News. July 16. Accessed at www.bbc.com/news/live/world-africa-44844937/page/3.

Bearak, Max. 2015. Sri Lankan Ex-President's Vanity Airport Project Grounded by Cash Crunch. *Al-Jazeera America*. March 31. Accessed at http://america.al

jazeera.com/articles/2015/3/31/Sri-Lankan-ex-presidents-vanity-airport-pro
ject-grounded-by-cash-crunch.html.

Bearce, David H., and Daniel C. Tirone. 2010. Foreign Aid Effectiveness and the Strategic Goals of Donor Governments. *Journal of Politics* 72(3): 837–851.

Beattie, Alan, and Eoin Callan. 2006. China Lends Where the World Bank Fears to Tread. *Financial Times*. December 8. Accessed at https://m.ftchinese.com/s tory/001008349/en?archive.

Beck, Thorsten, George Clarke, Alberto Groff, Philip Keefer, and Patrick Walsh. 2001. New Tools in Comparative Political Economy: The Database of Political Institutions. *World Bank Economic Review* 15(1): 165–176.

Belt & Road News. 2019. Despite US Rejection & Indian Objection, BRI Projects Set to Become "Project of the Millennium." May 5. Accessed at www .beltandroad.news/2019/05/05/despite-us-rejection-indian-objection.

Ben-Artzi, Ruth. 2017. IOs and Peer Pressure: An Examination of the Development Assistance Committee (DAC). Paper presented at the 10th Annual Conference on the Political Economy of International Organizations, Bern, January 12–14. Accessed at www.peio.me/wp-content/uploads/2016/12/ PEIO10_paper_111.pdf.

BenYishay, Ariel, Matthew DiLorenzo, and Carrie Dolan. 2019. The Economic Efficiency of Aid Targeting. Mimeo.

BenYishay, Ariel, Bradley Parks, Daniel Runfola, and Rachel Trichler. 2016. Forest Cover Impacts of Chinese Development Projects in Ecologically Sensitive Areas. AidData Working Paper 32. Williamsburg, VA: AidData at William & Mary.

BenYishay, Ariel, Bradley Parks, Rachel Trichler, Christian Baehr, Daniel Aboagye, and Punwath Prum. 2019. Building on a Foundation Stone: The Long-Term Impacts of a Local Infrastructure and Governance Program in Cambodia. Stockholm, Sweden: Sweden's Expert Group for Aid Studies (EBA).

BenYishay, Ariel, Daniel Runfola, Rachel Trichler, Carrie Dolan, Seth Goodman, Bradley Parks, Jeffery Tanner, Silke Heuser, Geeta Batra, and Anupam Anand. 2017. A Primer on Geospatial Impact Evaluation Methods, Tools, and Applications. AidData Working Paper 44. Williamsburg, VA: AidData at William & Mary.

Berman, Eli, Jacob Shapiro, and Joseph Felter. 2011. Can Hearts and Minds Be Bought? The Economics of Counterinsurgency in Iraq. *Journal of Political Economy* 119(4): 766–819.

Bermeo, Sarah Blodgett. 2011. Foreign Aid and Regime Change: A Role for Donor Intent. *World Development* 39(11): 2021–2031.

Bermeo, Sarah Blodgett. 2016. Aid Is Not Oil: Donor Preferences, Heterogeneous Aid, and the Aid-Democratization Relationship. *International Organization* 70(1): 1–32.

Berthélemy, Jean-Claude, and Ariane Tichit. 2004. Bilateral Donors' Allocation Decisions: A Three Dimensional Panel Analysis. *International Review of Economics and Finance* 13(3): 253–274.

Bigsten, Arne, and Sven Tengstam. 2015. International Coordination and the Effectiveness of Aid. *World Development* 69: 75–85.

Bisenov, Naubet. 2019. Kazakh President's Upcoming Beijing Trip Stokes Sino-Phobia. *Nikkei Asian Review*. September 10. Accessed at https://asia.nikkei.co m/Politics/International-relations/Kazakh-president-s-upcoming-Beijing-trip-stokes-Sino-phobia.

Biswas, Rajiv. 2015. Reshaping the Financial Architecture for Development Finance: The New Development Banks. LSE Global South Unit Working Paper 2/2015. London: London School of Economics and Political Science.

Bitzer, Jürgen, and Erkan Gören. 2018. Foreign Aid and Subnational Development: A Grid Cell Analysis. AidData Working Paper 55. Williamsburg, VA: AidData at William & Mary.

Bjørnskov, Christian, and Martin Rode. 2020. Regime Types and Regime Changes: A New Dataset. *Review of International Organizations* 15: 531–551.

Blair, Robert A., Robert Marty, and Philip Roessler. 2021. Foreign Aid and Soft Power: Great Power Competition in Africa in the Early Twenty-first Century. *British Journal of Political Science*. Forthcoming. Accessed at https://doi.org/10.1017/S0007123421000193.

Blake, Robert. 2006. Sri Lanka: Huge Push to Develop the President's Home District. Wikileaks. December 18. Accessed at https://wikileaks.org/plusd/cabl es/06COLOMBO2086_a.html.

Blake, Robert. 2007. MCC in Sri Lanka: Majority of Indicators Probably Now Below International Standards. Wikileaks. January 4. Accessed at http://wiki leaks.wikimee.net/cable/2007/01/07COLOMBO147.html.

Bloomberg News. 2019. China's Belt and Road Gets a Reboot to Boost Its Image. October 30. Accessed at www.bloomberg.com/news/articles/2019-08-14/chin a-s-belt-and-road-is-getting-a-reboot-here-s-why-quicktake.

Bluhm, Richard, Axel Dreher, Andreas Fuchs, Bradley Parks, Austin Strange, and Michael J. Tierney. 2020. Connective Financing: Chinese Infrastructure Projects and the Diffusion of Economic Activity in Developing Countries. AidData Working Paper 103. Williamsburg, VA: AidData at William & Mary.

Bluhm, Richard, Martin Gassebner, Sarah Langlotz, and Paul Schaudt. 2021. Fueling Conflict? (De)escalation and Bilateral Aid. *Journal of Applied Econometrics* 36(2): 244–261.

Bluhm, Richard, and Melanie Krause. 2018. Top Lights: Bright Cities and Their Contribution to Economic Development. AidData Working Paper 67. Williamsburg, VA: AidData at William & Mary.

Bohara, Alok K., Neil J. Mitchell, and Mani Nepal. 2006. Opportunity, Democracy, and the Exchange of Political Violence: A Subnational Analysis of Conflict in Nepal. *Journal of Conflict Resolution* 50(1): 108–128.

Bolton, John. 2019. China, Africa and Washington's Weird Worry. *Guardian*. January 31. Accessed at https://guardian.ng/opinion/china-africa-and-washingtons-weird-worry.

Bommer, Christian, Axel Dreher, and Marcello Perez-Alvarez. 2019. Home Bias in Humanitarian Aid. CEPR Discussion Paper DP13957. London: Centre for Economic Policy Research.

Bonfatti, Roberto, and Steven Poelhekke. 2017. From Mine to Coast: Transport Infrastructure and the Direction of Trade in Developing Countries. *Journal of Development Economics* 127: 91–108.

Bosshard, Peter. 2007. China's Role in Financing African Infrastructure. Berkeley, CA: International Rivers Network. Accessed at www.irn.org/files/p df/china/ChinaEximBankAfrica.pdf.

Boyce, Tucker. 2017. *The China-Pakistan Economic Corridor: Trade Security and Regional Implications.* SANDIA Report SAND2017-0207. Albuquerque, NM, and Livermore, CA: Sandia.

Bräutigam, Deborah. 2009. *The Dragon's Gift: The Real Story of China in Africa.* New York: Oxford University Press.

Bräutigam, Deborah. 2010a. China, Africa and the International Aid Architecture. African Development Bank Group Working Paper 107. Tunis, Tunisia: African Development Bank.

Bräutigam, Deborah. 2010b. Chinese Refineries in Nigeria, Chad, Niger & Ghana: The Sudan Model? The China-Africa Research Initiative Blog. December 11. Accessed at www.chinaafricarealstory.com/2010/12/chinese-refineries-in-nigeria-chad.html.

Bräutigam, Deborah. 2011. Aid "with Chinese Characteristics": Chinese Foreign Aid and Development Finance Meet the OECD-DAC Regime. *Journal of International Development* 23(5): 752–764.

Bräutigam, Deborah. 2012. China in Africa: Investors, Not Infesters. *China Economic Quarterly* 16(3): 22–27.

Bräutigam, Deborah. 2013. Rubbery Numbers for Chinese Aid to Africa. China in Africa Blog. April 30. Accessed at www.chinaafricarealstory.com/2013/04/rubbery-numbers-on-chinese-aid.html.

Bräutigam, Deborah. 2019. Misdiagnosing the Chinese Infrastructure Push. *The American Interest.* April 4. Accessed at www.the-american-interest.com/2019/04/04/misdiagnosing-the-chinese-infrastructure-push.

Bräutigam, Deborah, and Kevin Gallagher. 2014. Bartering Globalization: China's Commodity-Backed Finance in Africa and Latin America. *Global Policy* 5(3): 346–352.

Bräutigam, Deborah, and Jyhjong Hwang. 2016. Eastern Promises: New Data on Chinese Loans in Africa, 2000 to 2014. SAIS-CARI Working Paper 4. Washington, DC: Johns Hopkins SAIS.

Bräutigam, Deborah, and Jyhjong Hwang. 2019. Great Walls over African Rivers: Chinese Engagement in African Hydropower Projects. *Development Policy Review* 37(3): 313–330.

Brazys, Samuel, and Alexander Dukalskis. 2019. Rising Powers and Grassroots Image Management: Confucius Institutes and China in the Media. *Chinese Journal of International Politics* 12(4): 557–584.

Brazys, Samuel, and Krishna Chaitanya Vadlamannati. 2021. Aid Curse with Chinese Characteristics? Chinese Development Flows and Economic Reforms. *Public Choice* 188: 407–430.

Brazys, Samuel, Johan A. Elkink, and Gina Kelly. 2017. Bad Neighbors? How Co-located Chinese and World Bank Development Projects Impact Local Corruption in Tanzania. *Review of International Organizations* 12: 227–253.

Brewster, David. 2014. Beyond the "String of Pearls": Is There Really a Sino-Indian Security Dilemma in the Indian Ocean? *Journal of the Indian Ocean Region* 10(2): 133–149.

Briggs, Ryan C. 2012. Electrifying the Base? Aid and Incumbent Advantage in Ghana. *Journal of Modern African Studies* 50(4): 603–624.

Briggs, Ryan C. 2014. Aiding and Abetting: Project Aid and Ethnic Politics in Kenya. *World Development* 64: 194–205.

Briggs, Ryan C. 2016. Does Chinese Aid Target the Poorest? Working paper.

Briggs, Ryan C. 2017. Does Foreign Aid Target the Poorest? *International Organization* 71(1): 187–206.

Briggs, Ryan C. 2018a. Poor Targeting: A Gridded Spatial Analysis of the Degree to Which Aid Reaches the Poor in Africa. *World Development* 103: 133–148.

Briggs, Ryan C. 2018b. Leaving No One Behind? A New Test of Subnational Aid Targeting. *Journal of International Development* 30(5): 904–910.

Briggs, Ryan C. 2021. Why Does Aid Not Target the Poorest? *International Studies Quarterly* 65(3): 739–752.

British Geological Survey. 2016. *World Mineral Statistics Data*. Keyworth, Nottingham: British Geological Survey. Accessed at www.bgs.ac.uk/mineral suk/statistics.

Broich, Tobias. 2017. Do Authoritarian Regimes Receive More Chinese Development Finance Than Democratic Ones? Empirical Evidence for Africa. *China Economic Review* 46: 180–207.

Bruederle, Anna, and Roland Hodler. 2018. Nighttime Lights as a Proxy for Human Development at the Local Level. *PLoS ONE* 13(9): e0202231.

Buchanan, Graeme M., Paul F. Donald, Bradley Parks, Brian O'Donnell, John Swaddle, Lukasz Tracewski, Daniel Runfola, and Stuart H. M. Butchart. 2018. The Local Impacts of World Bank Development Projects Near Sites of Conservation Significance. *Journal of Environment and Development* 27(3): 299–322.

Budjan, Angelika, and Andreas Fuchs. Forthcoming. Democracy and Aid Donorship. *American Economic Journal: Economic Policy*. Accessed at www .aeaweb.org/articles?id=10.1257/pol.20180582&&from=f.

Bueno de Mesquita, Bruce, and Alastair Smith. 2007. Foreign Aid and Policy Concessions. *Journal of Conflict Resolution* 51(2): 251–284.

Bueno de Mesquita, Bruce, and Alastair Smith. 2009a. A Political Economy of Aid. *International Organization* 63(2): 309–340.

Bueno de Mesquita, Bruce, and Alastair Smith. 2009b. Political Survival and Endogenous Institutional Change. *Comparative Political Studies* 42(2): 167–197.

Bueno de Mesquita, Bruce, and Alastair Smith. 2010. Leader Survival, Revolutions and the Nature of Government Finance. *American Journal of Political Science* 54(4): 936–950.

Bulow, Jeremy. 2002. First World Governments and Third World Debt. *Brookings Papers on Economic Activity* 1: 229–255.

Bun, Maurice, and Teresa D. Harrison. 2019. OLS and IV Estimation of Regression Models Including Endogenous Interaction Terms. *Econometric Reviews* 38(7): 814–827.

Buntaine, Mark. 2016. *Giving Aid Effectively: The Politics of Environmental Performance and Selectivity at Multilateral Development Banks*. Oxford: Oxford University Press.

Buntaine, Mark T., Bradley Parks, and Benjamin P. Buch. 2017. Aiming at the Wrong Targets: The Difficulty of Improving Domestic Institutions with International Aid. *International Studies Quarterly* 61(2): 471–488.

Bunte, Jonas B., Harsh Desai, Kanio Gbala, Bradley Parks, and Daniel Runfola. 2018. Natural Resource Sector FDI, Government Policy, and Economic Growth: Quasi-Experimental Evidence from Liberia. *World Development* 107: 151–162.

Burgess, G. Thomas, and Christopher Lee. 2010. Mao in Zanzibar: Nationalism, Discipline, and the (De) Construction of Afro-Asian Solidarities. In Christopher Lee (ed.), *Making a World after Empire: The Bandung Moment and Its Political Afterlives*. Athens: Ohio University Press: 196–234.

Burgess, Robin, Remi Jedwab, Edward Miguel, Ameet Morjaria, and Gerard Padró i Miquel. 2015. The Value of Democracy: Evidence from Road Building in Kenya. *American Economic Review* 105(6): 1817–1851.

Burnside, Craig, and David Dollar. 2000. Aid, Policies, and Growth. *American Economic Review* 90(4): 847–868.

Business Daily Africa. 2018. Big Projects Drive China Steel Demand. March 27. Accessed at www.businessdailyafrica.com/corporate/shipping/Big-projects-drive-China-steel-demand/4003122-4360614-wq9hdcz/index.html.

Busse, Matthias, Ceren Erdogan, and Henning Mühlen. 2016. China's Impact on Africa – The Role of Trade, FDI and Aid. *Kyklos* 69(2): 228–262.

Cai, Peter. 2017. Understanding China's Belt and Road Initiative. Analyses. Sydney: The Lowy Institute for International Policy.

Campbell, Ivan, Thomas Wheeler, Larry Attree, Dell M. Butler, and Bernardo Mariani. 2012. China and Conflict-Affected States: Between Principle and Pragmatism. London: Saferworld.

Carey, Lachlan, and Sarah Ladislaw. 2019. Chinese Multilateralism and the Promise of a Green Belt and Road. CSIS Brief. Washington, DC: Center for Strategic and International Studies.

Carlson, Elizabeth, and Brigitte Seim. 2020. Honor Among Chiefs: An Experiment on Monitoring and Diversion Among Traditional Leaders in Malawi. *Journal of Development Studies* 56(8): 1541–1557.

Carnegie, Allison, and Nikolay Marinov. 2017. Foreign Aid, Human Rights, and Democracy Promotion: Evidence from a Natural Experiment. *American Journal of Political Science* 61(3): 671–684.

Carnegie, Allison, and Cyrus Samii. 2019. International Institutions and Political Liberalization: Evidence from the World Bank Loans Program. *British Journal of Political Science* 49(4): 1357–1379.

Carter, Becky. 2017. A Literature Review on China's Aid. K4D Helpdesk Report. Brighton, UK: Institute of Development Studies.

Carter, Brett L. 2016. Repression and Foreign Aid in Autocracies: Exploiting Debt Relief Negotiations in Post-Cold War Africa. AidData Working Paper #29. Williamsburg, VA: AidData at William & Mary.

Casey, Katherine. 2015. Crossing Party Lines: The Effects of Information on Redistributive Politics. *American Economic Review* 105(8): 2410–2448.

Cervellati, Matteo, Elena Esposito, Uwe Sunde, and Song Yuan. 2020. Malaria and Chinese Economic Activities in Africa. *Journal of Development Economics*. Forthcoming. Accessed at https://doi.org/10.1016/j.jdeveco.2021.102739.

CGTN Africa. 2018. Kenyan Major Port Not Mortgaged to China, Uhuru Says. December 29. Accessed at https://africa.cgtn.com/2018/12/29/104322.

Chan, Ho Fai, Bruno S. Frey, Ahmed Skali, and Benno Torgler. 2019. Political Entrenchment and GDP Misreporting. CESifo Working Paper 7653. Munich, Germany: CESifo.

Chaturvedi, Sachin. 2008. Emerging Patterns in Architecture for Management of Economic Assistance and Development Cooperation: Implications and Challenges for India. RIS Discussion Paper 139. New Delhi, India: Research and Information System for Developing Countries.

Chaudhuri, Rudra. 2018. The Making of an "All Weather Friendship": Pakistan, China and the History of a Border Agreement: 1949–1963. *International History Review* 40(1): 41–64.

Chauvet, Lisa, Flore Gubert, and Sandrine Mesplé-Somps. 2013. Aid, Remittances, Medical Brain Drain and Child Mortality: Evidence Using Inter and Intra-Country Data. *Journal of Development Studies* 48(12): 801–818.

Cheibub, José Antonio, Jennifer Gandhi, and James Raymond Vreeland. 2010. Democracy and Dictatorship Revisited. *Public Choice* 143: 67–101.

Chellaney, Brahma. 2017. China's Debt Trap Diplomacy. *Project Syndicate*. January 23. Accessed at www.project-syndicate.org/commentary/china-one-belt-one-road-loans-debt-by-brahma-chellaney-2017-01?barrier=accesspaylog.

Chen, Chuan, and Ryan J. Orr. 2009. Chinese Contractors in Africa: Home Government Support, Coordination Mechanisms, and Market Entry Strategies. *Journal of Construction Engineering and Management* 135(11): 1201–1210.

Chen, Deming. 2010. Nuli kaichuang yuanwai gongzuo xin jumian [Working Hard to Promote Chinese Foreign Aid]. *Qiu Shi* 19: 42–44.

陈其林 [Chen, Qilin]. 2016. 耿飚将军与中巴友谊 [General Geng Biao and Sino-Pakistani Friendship]. 炎黄春秋杂志 [*Yanhuang Chunqiu Magazine*] 9.

Chen, Shaohua, Ren Mu, and Martin Ravallion. 2009. Are There Lasting Impacts of Aid to Poor Areas? *Journal of Public Economics* 93(3–4): 512–528.

Chen, Yunnan, and David Landry. 2018. Capturing the Rains: Comparing Chinese and World Bank Hydropower Projects in Cameroon and Pathways for South-South and North-South Technology Transfer. *Energy Policy* 115: 556–571.

Cheng, Zhangxi, and Ian Taylor. 2017. *China's Aid to Africa: Does Friendship Really Matter?* London: Routledge.

Cheng, Zhiming, and Russell Smyth. 2016. Why Give It Away When You Need It Yourself? Understanding Public Support for Foreign Aid in China. *Journal of Development Studies* 52(1): 53–71.

Cheung, Yin-Wong, Jakob de Haan, Xing Wang Qian, and Shu Yu. 2014. The Missing Link: China's Contracted Engineering Projects in Africa. *Review of Development Economics* 18(3): 564–580.

Chin, Gregory T. 2012. China as a "Net Donor": Tracking Dollars and Sense. *Cambridge Review of International Affairs* 25(4): 579–603.

Chin, Gregory T., and Kevin P. Gallagher. 2019. Coordinated Credit Spaces: The Globalization of Chinese Development Finance. *Development and Change* 50(1): 245–274.

China Daily. 2010. Zhou Enlai Announces Eight Principles of Foreign Aid. August 13. Accessed at www.chinadaily.com.cn/china/2010-08/13/con tent_11149131.htm.

China Daily. 2017. Diplomatic Skills Boost China's Global Role. October 23. Accessed at http://english.chinamil.com.cn/19thCNC/2017-10/23/con tent_7796135.htm.

Chowdhury, Debasish Roy. 2015. Passive Investor to Partner in Crime: How China Lost the Plot in Sri Lanka. *South China Morning Post.* March 29. Accessed at www.scmp.com/business/china-business/article/1750377/passive-investor-partner-crime-how-china-lost-plot-sri-lanka.

Chowdhury, Debasish Roy. 2018. Driven by India into China's New Arms, Is Nepal the New Sri Lanka? *South China Morning Post.* February 25. Accessed at www.scmp.com/week-asia/geopolitics/article/2134532/driven-india-chinas-ar ms-nepal-new-sri-lanka.

Christian, Paul, and Christopher Barrett. 2017. Revisiting the Effect of Food Aid on Conflict: A Methodological Caution. Policy Research Working Paper 8171. Washington, DC: World Bank.

Chudik, Alexander, Kamiar Mohaddes, M. Hashem Pesaran, and Mehdi Raissi. 2017. Is There a Debt-Threshold Effect on Output Growth? *Review of Economics and Statistics* 99(1): 135–150.

CIA. 1975–1976, 1981–1984. *Communist Aid to Less Developed Countries of the Free World.* CIA Intelligence Handbook. Washington, DC: Central Intelligence Agency.

CIA. 1980. *Communist Aid to Non-Communist Less Developed Countries.* CIA Intelligence Handbook. Washington, DC: Central Intelligence Agency.

Civelli, Andrea, Andrew Horowitz, and Arilton Teixeira. 2018. Foreign Aid and Growth: A Sp P-VAR Analysis Using Satellite Sub-National Data for Uganda. *Journal of Development Economics* 134: 50–67.

Clemens, Michael, and Michael Kremer. 2016. The New Role for the World Bank. *Journal of Economic Perspectives* 30(1): 53–76.

Clemens, Michael A., Steven Radelet, Rikhil R. Bhavnani, and Samuel Bazzi. 2012. Counting Chickens When They Hatch: Timing and the Effects of Aid on Growth. *Economic Journal* 122(561): 590–617.

Clinton, Hillary Rodham. 2014. *Hard Choices.* New York: Simon & Schuster.

Cohen, John M. 1995. *Ethnicity, Foreign Aid, and Economic Growth in Sub-Saharan Africa: The Case of Kenya.* HIID Development Paper 520. Cambridge, MA: Harvard Institute for International Development.

Collier, Paul. 2007. *The Bottom Billion: Why the Poorest Countries Are Failing and What Can Be Done about It.* Oxford: Oxford University Press.

Compagnon, Daniel, and Audrey Alejandro. 2013. China's External Environmental Policy: Understanding China's Environmental Impact in Africa and How It Is Addressed. *Environmental Practice* 15(3): 220–227.

Coppedge, Michael, John Gerring, Staffan I. Lindberg, Svend-Erik Skaaning, and Jan Teorell. 2015. *V-Dem Comparisons and Contrasts with Other Measurement Projects.* Varieties of Democracy (VDem) Project. Gothenburg, Sweden: V-Dem Institute.

Copper, John F. 1979. China's Foreign Aid in 1978. *Occasional Paper/Reprints Series in Contemporary Asian Studies 8.* Baltimore: University of Maryland School of Law.

Copper, John F. 1981. China's Foreign Aid in 1979–80. *Occasional Paper/Reprints Series in Contemporary Asian Studies 5.* Baltimore: University of Maryland School of Law.

Copper, John F. 2016. *China's Foreign Aid and Investment Diplomacy,* Volume II: *History and Practice in Asia, 1950–Present.* Basingstoke, UK: Palgrave Macmillan.

Corkin, Lucy. 2011. Redefining Foreign Policy Impulses Toward Africa: The Roles of the MFA, the MOFCOM and China Exim Bank. *Journal of Current Chinese Affairs* 40(4): 61–90.

Corkin, Lucy. 2013. *Uncovering African Agency: Angola's Management of China's Credit Lines.* Surrey, UK: Ashgate.

Crabtree, James. 2012. Sri Lanka: A Tight Grip on the Controls. *Financial Times.* October 31. Accessed at www.ft.com/content/ab3d4758-229e-11e2-b606-00144feabdc0.

Craig, Tim, and Simon Denyer. 2015. From the Mountains to the Sea: A Chinese Vision, a Pakistani Corridor. *Washington Post.* October 23. Accessed at www.washingtonpost.com/world/asia_pacific/from-the-mountains-to-the-sea-a-chinese-vision-a-pakistani-corridor/2015/10/23/4e1b6d30-2a42-11e5-a5ea-cf74396e59ec_story.html?utm_term=.b87eeb8394fc

Crouigneau, Françoise, and Richard Hiault. 2006. World Bank Hits at China Over Lending. *Financial Times.* October 23. Accessed at www.ft.com/content/ea6cd650-62d8-11db-8faa-0000779e2340.

Cruz, Cesi, Philip Keefer, and Julien Labonne. 2018. Buying Informed Voters: New Effects of Information on Voters and Candidates. Working Paper. Accessed at https://julienlabonne.files.wordpress.com/2018/05/ppcrv_052018_web.pdf.

Cruz, Cesi, Philip Keefer, Julien Labonne, and Francesco Trebbi. 2018. Making Policies Matter: Voter Responses to Campaign Promises. Working Paper. Accessed at https://julienlabonne.files.wordpress.com/2018/08/making_promises_matter_08222018_web.pdf.

Cruz, Cesi, and Christina J. Schneider. 2017. Foreign Aid and Undeserved Credit Claiming. *American Journal of Political Science* 61(2): 396–408.

Cruzatti, John, Axel Dreher, and Johannes Matzat. 2020. Chinese Aid and Health at the Country and Local Level. AidData Working Paper 97. Williamsburg, VA: AidData at William & Mary.

Cummings, Clare, and Beatrice Obwocha. 2018. At the Crossroads: The Politics of Road Safety in Nairobi. London and Washington, DC: Overseas Development Institute and the World Resources Institute.

Custer, Samantha, Axel Dreher, Thai-Binh Elston, Andreas Fuchs, Siddharta Ghose, Joyce Jiahui Lin, Ammar A. Malik, Bradley C. Parks, Brooke Russell, Kyra Solomon, Austin Strange, Michael J. Tierney, Katherine Walsh, Lincoln Zaleski, and Sheng Zhang. 2021. Tracking Chinese Development Finance: An Application of AidData's TUFF 2.0 Methodology. Williamsburg, VA: AidData at William & Mary.

Custer, Samantha, Matthew DiLorenzo, Takaaki Masaki, Tanya Sethi, and Ani Harutyunyan. 2018. *Listening to Leaders: Is Development Cooperation Tuned-in or Tone-Deaf?* Williamsburg, VA: AidData at William & Mary.

Custer, Samantha, Brooke Russell, Matthew DiLorenzo, Mengfan Cheng, Sid Ghose, Jake Sims, Jennifer Turner, and Harsh Desai. 2018. *Ties that Bind: Quantifying China's Public Diplomacy and Its "Good Neighbor" Effect.* Williamsburg, VA: AidData at William & Mary.

Custer, Samantha, Tanya Sethi, Jonathan A. Solis, Joyce Jiahui Lin, Siddhartha Ghose, Anubhav Gupta, Rodney Knight, and Austin Baehr. 2019. *Silk Road Diplomacy: Deconstructing Beijing's Toolkit to Influence South and Central Asia.* Williamsburg, VA: AidData at William & Mary.

Custer, Samantha, and Michael J. Tierney. 2019. China's Global Development Spending Spree: Winning the World One Yuan at a Time? In Ashley Tellis (ed.), *Strategic Asia 2019: China's Expanding Strategic Ambitions.* Washington, DC: The National Bureau of Asian Research: 311–341.

Daily News Sri Lanka. 2014. China's Contribution to Sri Lanka's Economic Growth Is Unprecedented. September 17. Accessed at https://mfa.gov.lk/chinas-contribution-to-srlankas-economic-growth-is-unprecedented-president.

Davies, Martyn, Hannah Edinger, Nastasya Tay, and Sanusha Naidu. 2008. How China Delivers Development Assistance to Africa. Stellenbosch, South Africa: Centre for Chinese Studies, University of Stellenbosch.

Davies, Penelope. 2007. *China and the End of Poverty in Africa – Towards Mutual Benefit?* Sundyberg, Sweden: Diakonia, Alfaprint.

Davison, William. 2012. As Ethiopia Looks beyond Strongman Meles, Fears of Instability. *The Christian Science Monitor.* August 22. Accessed at www.csmonitor.com/World/Africa/2012/0822/As-Ethiopia-looks-beyond-strongman-Meles-fears-of-instability.

de Freytas-Tamura, Kimiko. 2017. Kenyans Fear Chinese-Backed Railway Is Another "Lunatic Express." *New York Times.* June 8. Accessed at www.nytimes.com/2017/06/08/world/africa/kenyans-fear-chinese-backed-railway-is-another-lunatic-express.html.

De Luca, Giacomo, Roland Hodler, Paul A. Raschky, and Michele Valsecchi. 2018. Ethnic Favoritism: An Axiom of Politics? *Journal of Development Economics* 132: 115–129.

De, Rajlakshmi, and Charles Becker. 2015. The Foreign Aid Effectiveness Debate: Evidence from Malawi. AidData Working Paper 6. Williamsburg, VA: AidData at William & Mary.

Deininger, Klaus, Lyn Squire, and Swati Basu. 1998. Does Economic Analysis Improve the Quality of Foreign Assistance? *World Bank Economic Review* 12(3): 385–418.

Deng, Shulian, Jun Peng, and Cong Wang. 2013. Fiscal Transparency at the Chinese Provincial Level. *Public Administration* 91(4): 947–963.

Denizer, Cevdet, Daniel Kaufmann, and Aart Kraay. 2013. Good Countries or Good Projects? Macro and Micro Correlates of World Bank Project Performance. *Journal of Development Economics* 105: 288–302.

Deutsche Welle. 2006. German Development Minister Criticizes China's Africa Policy. October 23. Accessed at http://dw.com/p/9HKg.

Devarajan, Shantayanan, Andrew Sunil Rajkumar, and Vinaya Swaroop. 1999. What Does Aid to Africa Finance? Policy Research Working Paper 2092. Washington, DC: World Bank.

Dietrich, Simone, Minhaj Mahmud, and Matthew S. Winters. 2018. Foreign Aid, Foreign Policy, and Domestic Government Legitimacy: Experimental Evidence from Bangladesh. *Journal of Politics* 80(1): 133–148.

DiLorenzo, Matthew, and Mengfan Cheng. 2019. Political Turnover and Chinese Development Cooperation. *Chinese Journal of International Politics* 12 (1): 123–151.

Dimitriou, Harry T., Nicholas Low, Sophie Sturup, Genevieve Zembri, Elisabeth Campagnac, George Kaparos, Pantoleon Skayannis, Yasunori Muromachi, Seiji Iwakura, Kazuya Itaya, and Mendel Giezen. 2014. What Constitutes a "Successful" Mega Transport Project? *Planning Theory & Practice* 15(3): 389–430.

Dinkelman, Taryn. 2011. The Effects of Rural Electrification on Employment: New Evidence from South Africa. *American Economic Review* 101(7): 3078–3108.

Djankov, Simeon. 2016. The Rationale Behind China's Belt and Road Initiative. In Simeon Djankov, and Sean Miner (eds.), *China's Belt and Road Initiative: Motives, Scope, and Challenges*. PIIE Briefing 16-2. Washington, DC: Peterson Institute for International Economics: 6–10.

Do, Quoc-Anh, Trang Nguyen, and Anh N. Tran. 2017. One Mandarin Benefits the Whole Clan: Hometown Favoritism in an Authoritarian Regime. *American Economic Journal: Applied Economics* 9(4): 1–29.

Doig, Will. 2019. The Belt and Road Initiative Is a Corruption Bonanza. *Foreign Policy*. January 15. Accessed at https://foreignpolicy.com/2019/01/15/the-belt-and-road-initiative-is-a-corruption-bonanza.

Dolan, Carry B., Ariel BenYishay, Karen Grépin, Jeffery Tanner, April Kimmel, David Wheeler, and Gordon McCord. 2019. The Impact of an Insecticide Treated Bednet Campaign on All-Cause Child Mortality: A Geospatial Impact Evaluation from the Democratic Republic of Congo. *PLoS ONE* 14(2): e0212890.

Dolan, Carry B., and Kaci Kennedy McDade. 2020. Pulling the Purse Strings: Are there Sectoral Differences in Political Preferencing of Chinese Aid to Africa? *PLoS ONE* 15(4): e0232126.

Dollar, David. 2008. Supply Meets Demand: Chinese Infrastructure Financing in Africa. World Bank Blog. Accessed at http://blogs.worldbank.org/eastasiapacific/supply-meets-demand-chinese-infrastructure-financing-in-africa.

Dollar, David. 2018. Is China's Development Finance a Challenge to the International Order? *Asian Economic Policy Review* 13(2): 283–298.

Dollar, David, and Victoria Levin. 2006. The Increasing Selectivity of Foreign Aid, 1984–2003. *World Development* 34(12): 2034–2046.

Dollar, David, and Lant Pritchett. 1998. *Assessing Aid: What Works, What Doesn't and Why*. Oxford: Oxford University Press.

Dollar, David, and Jakob Svensson. 2000. What Explains the Success or Failure of Structural Adjustment Programmes? *Economic Journal* 110(466): 894–917.

Dornan, Matthew, and Philippa Brant. 2014. Chinese Assistance in the Pacific: Agency, Effectiveness and the Role of Pacific Island Governments. *Asia and the Pacific Policy Studies* 1(2): 349–363.

Dou, Eva. 2017. The Big Winner From China's Foreign-Aid Frenzy: China. *Wall Street Journal*. October 11. Accessed at www.wsj.com/articles/when-it-comes-to-foreign-aid-chinas-taking-care-of-business–1507694463.

Doucouliagos, Hristos. 2019. The Politics of International Aid. In Roger Congleton, Bernard Grofman, and Stefan Voigt (eds.), *Oxford Handbook of Public Choice*, Volume 2. Oxford: Oxford University Press: 697–724.

Doucouliagos, Hristos, and Martin Paldam. 2009. The Aid Effectiveness Literature: The Sad Results of 40 Years of Research. *Journal of Economic Surveys* 23(3): 433–461.

Downs, Erica. 2011. Testimony before the U.S.-China Economic & Security Review Commission. April 13. Accessed at www.uscc.gov/hearings/2011hearings/written_testimonies/11_04_13_wrt/11_04_13_downs_testimony.pdf.

Dreher, Axel. 2009. IMF Conditionality: Theory and Evidence. *Public Choice* 141 (1–2): 233–267.

Dreher, Axel, Vera Eichenauer, and Kai Gehring. 2018. Geopolitics, Aid, and Growth: The Impact of UN Security Council Membership on the Effectiveness of Aid. *World Bank Economic Review* 32(2): 268–286.

Dreher, Axel, and Andreas Fuchs. 2015. Rogue Aid? An Empirical Analysis of China's Aid Allocation. *Canadian Journal of Economics* 48(3): 988–1023.

Dreher, Axel, Andreas Fuchs, Roland Hodler, Bradley Parks, Paul A. Raschky, and Michael J. Tierney. 2019. African Leaders and the Geography of China's Foreign Assistance. *Journal of Development Economics* 140: 44–71.

Dreher, Axel, Andreas Fuchs, Roland Hodler, Bradley Parks, Paul Raschky, and Michael J. Tierney. 2021. Is Favoritism a Threat to Chinese Aid Effectiveness? A Subnational Analysis of Chinese Development Projects. *World Development* 139: 105291.

Dreher, Axel, Andreas Fuchs, Andreas Kammerlander, Lennart Kaplan, Charlotte Robert, and Kerstin Unfried. 2021. Light of Their Lives: Country Leaders' Spouses and Regional Favoritism. Mimeo.

Dreher, Axel, Andreas Fuchs, and Peter Nunnenkamp. 2013. New Donors. *International Interactions* 39(3): 402–415.

Dreher, Axel, Andreas Fuchs, Bradley Parks, Austin M. Strange, and Michael J. Tierney. 2018. Apples and Dragon Fruits: The Determinants of Aid and Other Forms of State Financing from China to Africa. *International Studies Quarterly* 62(1): 182–194.

Dreher, Axel, Andreas Fuchs, Bradley Parks, Austin Strange, and Michael J. Tierney. 2021. Aid, China, and Growth: Evidence from a New Global

Development Finance Dataset. *American Economic Journal: Economic Policy*, 13(2): 135–174.

Dreher, Axel, and Martin Gassebner. 2013. Greasing the Wheels of Entrepreneurship? The Impact of Regulations and Corruption on Firm Entry. *Public Choice* 155: 413–432.

Dreher, Axel, and Kai Gehring. 2012. Does Aid Buy (Economic) Freedom? In James Gwartney, Robert Lawson, and Joshua Hall (eds.), *Economic Freedom of the World: 2012 Annual Report*. Vancouver, Canada: Fraser Institute: 219–246.

Dreher, Axel, Stephan Klasen, James Raymond Vreeland, and Eric Werker. 2013. The Costs of Favoritism: Is Politically Driven Aid Less Effective? *Economic Development and Cultural Change* 62(1): 157–191.

Dreher, Axel, Valentin Lang, and Katharina Richert. 2019. The Political Economy of International Finance Corporation Lending. *Journal of Development Economics* 140: 242–254.

Dreher, Axel, Valentin Lang, and Sebastian Ziaja. 2018. Foreign Aid. In Thomas Risse, Tanja Börzel, and Anke Draude (eds.) *The Oxford Handbook of Governance and Limited Statehood*. Oxford: Oxford University Press: 394–415.

Dreher, Axel, and Sarah Langlotz. 2020. Aid and Growth: New Evidence Using an Excludable Instrument. *Canadian Journal of Economics* 53(3): 1162–1198.

Dreher, Axel, and Steffen Lohmann. 2015. Aid and Growth at the Regional Level. *Oxford Review of Economic Policy* 31(3–4): 420–446.

Dreher, Axel, Anna Minasyan, and Peter Nunnenkamp. 2015. Government Ideology in Donor and Recipient Countries: Does Political Proximity Matter for the Effectiveness of Aid? *European Economic Review* 79: 80–92.

Dreher, Axel, Peter Nunnenkamp, and Rainer Thiele. 2008. Does US Aid Buy UN General Assembly Votes? A Disaggregated Analysis. *Public Choice* 136(1–2): 139–164.

Dreher, Axel, Peter Nunnenkamp, and Rainer Thiele. 2011. Are "New" Donors Different? Comparing the Allocation of Bilateral Aid Between NonDAC and DAC Donor Countries. *World Development* 39(11): 1950–1968.

Dunning, Thad. 2004. Conditioning the Effects of Aid: Cold War Politics, Donor Credibility, and Democracy in Africa. *International Organization* 58(2): 409–423.

Duo, Yu. n.d. Export-Import Bank of China Introduction to "Two Concessional" Loan Export-Import Bank of China. Beijing, China: Export-Import Bank of China. Accessed at www.dropbox.com/s/i5nau9n07ohkizt/39 2125610-Export-Import-Bank-of-China-pptx.pdf?dl=0.

Dutt, Pushan, and Daniel Traca. 2010. Corruption and Bilateral Trade Flows: Extortion or Evasion? *Review of Economics and Statistics* 92(4): 843–860.

Easterly, William, and Ross Levine. 2003. Tropics, Germs, and Crops: The Role of Endowments in Economic Development. *Journal of Monetary Economics* 50 (1): 3–39.

Easterly, William, and Tobias Pfutze. 2008. Where Does the Money Go? Best and Worst Practices in Foreign Aid. *Journal of Economic Perspectives* 22(2): 29–52.

Egreteau, Renaud. 2008. India and China Vying for Influence in Burma – A New Assessment. *India Review* 7(1): 38–72.

Eichenauer, Vera Z., Andreas Fuchs, and Lutz Brückner. 2021. The Effects of Trade, Aid and Investment on China's Image in Latin America. *Journal of Comparative Economics* 49(2): 483–498.

Eichenauer, Vera Z., Andreas Fuchs, Sven Kunze, and Eric Strobl. 2020. Distortions in Aid Allocation of United Nations Flash Appeals: Evidence from the 2015 Nepal Earthquake. *World Development* 136: 105023.

Eisenman, Joshua. 2018. Comrades-in-Arms: The Chinese Communist Party's Relations with African Political Organisations in the Mao Era, 1949–76. *Cold War History* 18(4): 429–445.

Ejdemyr, Simon, Eric Kramon, and Amanda Lea Robinson. 2018. Segregation, Ethnic Favoritism, and the Strategic Targeting of Local Public Goods. *Comparative Political Studies* 51(9): 1111–1143.

Ellis, Robert Evan. 2019. Latin America and China: Choosing Self-interest. December 23. Accessed at https://theglobalamericans.org/2019/12/latin-america-and-china-choosing-self-interest.

Elvidge, Christopher D., Kimberly E. Baugh, Eric A. Kihn, Herbert W. Kroehl, Ethan R. Davis, and Chris W. Davis. 1997. Relation Between Satellite Observed Visible-Near Infrared Emissions, Population, Economic Activity and Electric Power Consumption. *International Journal of Remote Sensing* 18 (6): 1373–1379.

Engelsma, Brian, Helen V. Milner, and Weiyi Shi. 2017. Political Competition in Recipient Countries and the Allocation of Chinese Aid: Evidence from Kenya and Zambia. Paper prepared for the Tracking International Aid and Investment from Developing and Emerging Economies Workshop, Heidelberg University, Germany.

Evrensel, Ayse Y. 2004. Lending to Developing Countries Revisited: Changing Nature of Lenders and Payment Problems. *Economic Systems* 28: 235–256.

Export-Import Bank of China [China Eximbank]. 2002. 中国进出口银行统计年鉴 [*Annual Statistical Yearbook of Export-Import Bank of China*]. Beijing, China: China Eximbank.

Export-Import Bank of China. [China Eximbank] n.d. Government Concessional Loan & Preferential Buyer's Credit Brochure. Beijing, China: China Eximbank. Accessed at www.dropbox.com/s/sptor0fju165k3j/3921256 21-GovernmentConcessional-Loan-PreferentialBuyer-sCredit-Brochure-pdf.pdf?dl=0.

Export-Import Bank of the United States. 2017. Report to the U.S. Congress on Global Credit Competition for the Period January 1, 2016 through December 31, 2016. Washington, DC: Export-Import Bank of the United States. Accessed at www.exim.gov/sites/default/files/reports/EXIM-Competitiveness-Report_June2017.pdf.

Faria, Andre, and Paolo Mauro. 2009. Institutions and the External Capital Structure of Countries. *Journal of International Money and Finance* 28(3): 367–391.

Fay, Marianne, Michael Toman, Daniel Benitez, and Stefan Csordas. 2011. Infrastructure and Sustainable Development. In Shahrokh Fardoust, Yongbeom Kim, and Claudia Sepúlveda (eds.), *Post-Crisis Growth and Development*. Washington, DC: World Bank.

Faye, Michael, and Paul Niehaus. 2012. Political Aid Cycles. *American Economic Review* 102(7): 3516–3530.

Fernholz, Tim. 2013. Revealed: $75 Billion in Previously Secret Chinese Aid to Africa. *Quartz*. April 29. Accessed at https://qz.com/79355/revealed-75-billion-in-previously-secret-chinese-aid-to-africa.

Ferree, Karen E., Clark C. Gibson, and James D. Long. 2014. Voting Behavior and Electoral Irregularities in Kenya's 2013 Election. *Journal of Eastern African Studies* 8(1): 153–172.

Financial Times. 2016. China Rethinks Developing World Largesse as Deals Sour. October 13. Accessed at www.ft.com/content/5bf4d6d8-9073-11e6-a72e-b428cb934b78.

Findley, Michael G., Adam S. Harris, Helen V. Milner, and Daniel L. Nielson. 2017. Who Controls Foreign Aid? Elite versus Public Perceptions of Donor Influence in Aid-Dependent Uganda. *International Organization* 71(4): 633–663.

Findley, Michael G., Helen V. Milner, and Daniel L. Nielson. 2017. The Choice among Aid Donors: The Effects of Multilateral versus Bilateral Aid on Recipient Behavioral Support. *Review of International Organizations* 12(2): 307–334.

Findley, Michael G., Josh Powell, Daniel Strandow, and Jeff Tanner. 2011. The Localized Geography of Foreign Aid: A New Dataset and Application to Violent Armed Conflict. *World Development* 39(11): 1995–2009.

Finkel, Steven E., Aníbal Pérez-Liñán, and Mitchell A. Seligson. 2007. The Effects of US Foreign Assistance on Democracy Building, 1990–2003. *World Politics* 59(3): 404–439.

Fisher, Max. 2017. Myanmar, Once a Hope for Democracy, Is Now a Study in How It Fails. *New York Times*. October 19. Accessed at www.nytimes.com/20 17/10/19/world/asia/myanmar-democracy-rohingya.html.

Fleisher, Belton, Haizheng Li, and Min Qiang Zhao. 2010. Human Capital, Economic Growth, and Regional Inequality in China. *Journal of Development Economics* 92(2): 215–231.

Flyvbjerg, Bent, Mette Skamris Holm, and Søren Buhl. 2002. Underestimating Costs in Public Works Projects: Error or Lie? *Journal of the American Planning Association* 68(3): 279–295.

Foster, Vivien, William Butterfield, Chuan Chen, and Nataliya Pushak. 2008. *Building Bridges: China's Growing Role as Infrastructure Financier for sub-Saharan Africa*. Washington, DC: World Bank.

Fowler, Valerie. 2009. Sri Lanka's Economic Policy Focuses on Government Led Development; Sees Future in Asia. Wikileaks. November 25. Accessed at https://wikileaks.org/plusd/cables/09COLOMBO1067_a.html.

Fowler, Valerie. 2010. Hambantota Port Complex: Will Sri Lanka Realize the Dream? Wikileaks. February 9. Accessed at https://wikileaks.org/plusd/cables/10COLOMBO103_a.html.

Francken, Nathalie, Bart Minten, and Johan F. M. Swinnen. 2012. The Political Economy of Relief Aid Allocation: Evidence from Madagascar. *World Development* 40(3): 486–500.

French, Howard W. 2014. Into Africa: China's Wild Rush. *New York Times*. May 16. Accessed at www.nytimes.com/2014/05/17/opinion/into-africa-chinas-wild-rush.html.

Freund, Caroline, and Michael Ruta. 2018. *Brief: Belt and Road Initiative*. March 29. Washington, DC: World Bank. Accessed at hwww.worldbank.org/en/topic/regional-integration/brief/belt-and-road-initiative.

傅道鹏 [Fu, Daopeng]. 2003. 官方发展援助研究 [Research on Official Development Assistance]. Doctoral Research, Ministry of Finance and Science Research Institute.

Fuchs, Andreas, and Marina Rudyak. 2019. The Motives of China's Foreign Aid. In Ka Zeng (ed.), *Handbook of the International Political Economy of China*. Cheltenham, UK: Edward Elgar: 391–410.

Fuchs, Andreas, and Krishna Chaitanya Vadlamannati. 2013. The Needy Donor: An Empirical Analysis of India's Aid Motives. *World Development* 44: 110–128.

Furukawa, Mitsuaki. 2018. Management of the International Development Aid System: The Case of Tanzania. *Development Policy Review* 36(1): 270–284.

Gabuev, Alexander. 2017. Belt and Road to Where? Moscow, Russia: Carnegie Moscow Center. December 8. Accessed at https://carnegie.ru/2017/12/08/belt-and-road-to-where-pub–74957.

Galiani, Sebastian, Stephen Knack, Lixin C. Xu, and Ben Zou. 2017. The Effect of Aid on Growth: Evidence from a Quasi-Experiment. *Journal of Economic Growth* 22(1): 1–33.

Gallagher, Kevin P. 2013. *Profiting from Precaution: How China's Policy Banks Can Enhance Social and Environmental Standards*. Paulson Policy Memorandum. Chicago: Paulson Institute at the University of Chicago.

Gallagher, Kevin P., and Amos Irwin. 2014. Exporting National Champions: China's Outward Foreign Direct Investment Finance in Comparative Perspective. *China & World Economy* 22(6): 1–21.

Gallup. 2017. Gallup World Poll. Available at www.gallup.com/analytics/232838/world-poll.aspx.

Gardner, Alysha, Joyce Lin, Scott Morris, and Brad Parks. 2020. Bargaining with Beijing: A Tale of Two Borrowers. Washington, DC: AidData and the Center for Global Development.

Ge, Yang. 2018. "Belt and Road" Projects Require Right Mix of Stakeholder Participation: Experts. *Caixin*. January 24. Accessed at www.caixinglobal.com/2018-01-24/belt-and-road-projects-require-right-mix-of-stakeholder-participation-experts-101202470.html.

Gehring, Kai, Lennart Kaplan, and Melvin H. L. Wong. 2019. China and the World Bank: How Contrasting Development Approaches Affect the Stability of African States. AidData Working Paper 70. Williamsburg, VA: AidData at William & Mary.

Gehring, Kai, Katharina Michaelowa, Axel Dreher, and Franziska Spörri. 2017. Do We Know What We Think We Know? Aid Fragmentation and Effectiveness Revisited. *World Development* 99: 320–334.

Gelpern, Anna, Sebastian Horn, Scott Morris, Bradley C. Parks, and Christoph Trebesch. 2021. How China Lends: A Rare Look into 100 Debt Contracts with Foreign Governments. Peterson Institute for International Economics, Kiel Institute for the World Economy, Center for Global Development, and AidData at William & Mary.

Ghossein, Tania, Bernard Hoekman, and Anirudh Shingal. 2018. Public Procurement in the Belt and Road Initiative. MTI Discussion Paper 10. Washington, DC: World Bank.

Gilmore, Elisabeth, Nils Petter Gleditsch, Päivi Lujala, and Jan Ketil Rød. 2005. Conflict Diamonds: A New Dataset. *Conflict Management and Peace Science* 22 (3): 257–292.

Goodman, Seth, Ariel BenYishay, Zhonghui Lv, and Daniel Runfola. 2019. GeoQuery: Integrating HPC Systems and Public Web-based Geospatial Data Tools. *Computers & Geosciences* 122: 103–112.

Government of Sri Lanka, 2012. *Global Partnership Towards Development 2012.* Colombo, Sri Lanka: External Resources Department, Ministry of Finance and Planning. Accessed at https://web.archive.org/web/20170329053452/http://www.erd.gov.lk/files/ERDBudget_English2012.pdf.

Government of Tanzania, 1969. *Second Five-Year Plan for Economic and Social Development, 1969–1974.* Volumes 1–4. Dar Es Salaam, Tanzania: Government of Tanzania.

Gray, Denis D., and Elaine Kutenbach. 2012. China Is Top Dam Builder, Going Where Others Won't. *Washington Examiner.* December 19. Accessed at www.washingtonexaminer.com/china-is-top-dam-builder-going-where-others-wont.

Green, Mark. 2019. Testimony by USAID Administrator on the FY 2020 Foreign Assistance Budget and Policy Priorities. April 9. Committee on Foreign Affairs, U.S. House of Representatives. Accessed at https://docs.house.gov/meetings/FA/FA00/20190409/109304/HHRG-116-FA00-Transcript-20190409.pdf.

Greene, Robert, and Paul Triolo. 2020. Will China Control the Global Internet via Its Digital Silk Road? *SupChina*, May 8.

Greßer, Christina, and David Stadelmann. 2021. Evaluating Water- and Health-Related Development Projects: A New Cross-Project and Micro-Based Approach. *Journal of Development Studies* 57(7): 1221–1239.

Grimm, Michael, Robert Sparrow, and Luca Tasciotti. 2015. Does Electrification Spur the Fertility Transition? Evidence from Indonesia. *Demography* 52(5): 1773–1796.

Grimm, Sven. 2013. Aid Dependency as a Limitation to National Development Policy? The Case of Rwanda. In William Brown and Sophie Harman (eds.), *African Agency in International Politics.* New York: Routledge: 81–96.

Group of Seven (G-7). 2006. Statement by G7 Finance Ministers and Central Bank Governors. September 16. Accessed at www.g7.utoronto.ca/finance/fm060916.htm.

Guerrero, Dorothy. 2017. Chinese Investment in Europe in the Age of Brexit and Trump. Working Paper. Amsterdam, Netherlands: Transnational Institute. Accessed at www.tni.org/en/publication/chinese-investment-in-europe-in-the-age-of-brexit-and-trump.

Halper, Stefan, 2010. *The Beijing Consensus: How China's Authoritarian Model Will Dominate the Twenty-First Century*. New York: Basic Books.

Hamdi, Abdelrahim. 2005. Al-waraqa Al-Iqtisadiyya Li'l-Mu'tamar Alwatani Al-HʾakimʾBi'l-Sudan [The Economic Paper for the Ruling National Congress: Future of Foreign Investment in Sudan]. Unpublished Manuscript. Khartoum, Sudan.

Harrison, Graham, and Sarah Mulley with Duncan Holtom. 2009. Tanzania: A Genuine Case of Recipient Leadership in the Aid System? In Lindsay Whitfield (ed.), *The Politics of Aid: African Strategies for Dealing with Donors*. Oxford: Oxford University Press: 271–298.

Hausmann, Ricardo. 2019. China's Malign Secrecy. *Project Syndicate*. January 2. Accessed at www.project-syndicate.org/commentary/china-development-finance-secrecy-by-ricardo-hausmann-2019-01?barrier=accesspaylog.

Hawkins, Darren, Dan Nielson, Anna Bergevin, Ashley Hearn, and Becky Perry. 2010. *Codebook for Assembling Data on China's Development Finance, Version 1.0*. Provo, UT and Williamsburg, VA: Brigham Young University and College of William and Mary. Accessed at www.aiddata.org/research/china.

He, Baogang. 2018. The Domestic Politics of the Belt and Road Initiative and Its Implications. *Journal of Contemporary China* 28(116): 180–195.

He, Yafei. 2014. China's Overcapacity Crisis Can Spur Growth through Overseas Expansion. *South China Morning Post*. January 8. Accessed at www.scmp.com/comment/insight-opinion/article/1399681/chinas-overcapacity-crisis-can-spur-growth-through-overseas.

Headey, Derek. 2008. Geopolitics and the Effect of Foreign Aid on Economic Growth: 1970–2001. *Journal of International Development* 20(2): 161–180.

Helleiner, Gerry. 2002. Emerging Relationships between Poor Countries and External Sources of Finance: The Case of Tanzania. *International Journal* 57 (2): 227–232.

Henderson, J. Vernon, Adam Storeygard, and David Weil. 2012. Measuring Economic Growth from Outer Space. *American Economic Review* 102(2): 994–1028.

Herbling, David, and Dandan Li. 2019. China's Built a Railroad to Nowhere in Kenya. *Bloomberg News*. July 18. Accessed at www.bloomberg.com/news/features/2019-07-19/china-s-belt-and-road-leaves-kenya-with-a-railroad-to-nowhere.

Hernandez, Diego. 2017. Are "New" Donors Challenging World Bank Conditionality? *World Development* 96: 529–549.

Hicks, Robert, Bradley Parks, Timmons Roberts, and Michael J. Tierney. 2008. *Greening Aid? Understanding the Environmental Impact of Development Assistance*. Oxford: Oxford University Press.

Hirono, Miwa, and Shogo Suzuki. 2014. Why Do We Need "Myth-Busting" in the Study of Sino-African Relations? *Journal of Contemporary China* 23(87): 443–461.

Hirschman, Albert O. 1958. *The Strategy of Economic Development*. New Haven, CT: Yale University Press.

Hodler, Roland, and Paul A. Raschky. 2014. Regional Favoritism. *Quarterly Journal of Economics* 129(2): 995–1033.

Hollyer, James R., B. Peter Rosendorff, and James Raymond Vreeland. 2011. Democracy and Transparency. *Journal of Politics* 73(4): 1191–1205.

Holslag, Jonathan. 2011. China and the Coups: Coping with Political Instability in Africa. *African Affairs* 110(440): 367–386.

Hong, Eunsuk, and Laixiang Sun. 2006. Dynamics of Internationalization and Outward Investment: Chinese Corporations' Strategies. *China Quarterly* 187: 610–634.

Honig, Daniel, Ranjit Lall, and Bradley Parks. 2020. When Does Transparency Improve Performance? Evidence from 20,000 Public Projects in 183 Countries. AidData Working Paper 100. Williamsburg, VA: AidData at William & Mary.

Honig, Daniel, and Catherine Weaver. 2019. A Race to the Top? The Aid Transparency Index and the Social Power of Global Performance Indicators. *International Organization* 73(3): 579–610.

Hook, Steven, and Jessie G. Rumsey. 2016. The Development Aid Regime at Fifty: Policy Challenges Inside and Out. *International Studies Perspectives* 17(1): 55–74.

Horn, Sebastian, Carmen M. Reinhart, and Christoph Trebesch. 2019. China's Overseas Lending. NBER Working Paper No. 26050. Cambridge, MA: National Bureau of Economic Research.

Hornby, Lucy, and Tom Hancock. 2018. China Pledge of $60bn Loans to Africa Sparks Anger at Home. *Financial Times*. September 4. Accessed at www.ft.com /content/fb7436d6-b006-11e8-8d14-6f049d06439c.

Horvath, Janos, 1976. *Chinese Technology Transfer to the Third World*. New York: Praeger.

Huang, Hao, and Yehua Dennis Wei. 2016. Spatial Inequality of Foreign Direct Investment in China: Institutional Change, Agglomeration Economies, and Market Access. *Applied Geography* 69: 99–111.

Huang, Meibo. 2015. How Government Loans Promote FDI: Japanese Yen Loans and Chinese Government Preferential Loans. Presentation at the Chinese Overseas Finance Conference, Johns Hopkins University, Washington, DC. Accessed at www.sais-cari.org/event-details/2015/4/10/chin ese-overseas-finance-conference-2015.

Hühne, Philipp, Birgit Meyer, and Peter Nunnenkamp. 2014. Who Benefits from Aid for Trade? Comparing the Effects on Recipient versus Donor Exports. *Journal of Development Studies* 50(9): 1275–1288.

Humphrey, Chris, and Katharina Michaelowa. 2019. China in Africa: Competition for Traditional Development Finance Institutions? *World Development* 120: 15–28.

Humphreys, Macartan, and Robert Bates. 2005. Political Institutions and Economic Policies: Lessons from Africa. *British Journal of Political Science* 35 (3): 403–428.

Hurley, John, Scott Morris, and Gailyn Portelance. 2019. Examining the Debt Implications of the Belt and Road Initiative from a Policy Perspective. *Journal of Infrastructure Policy and Development* 3(1): 139–175.

Iacoella, Francesco, Bruno Martorano, Laura Metzger, and Marco Sanfilippo. 2021. Chinese Official Finance and Political Participation in Africa. *European Economic Review* 136: 103741.

Igoe, Michael. 2018a. USAID Adopts a Hard Line on China's Development Approach. *Devex*. September 18. Accessed at www.devex.com/news/usaid-adopts-a-hard-line-on-china-s-development-approach–93453.

Igoe, Michael. 2018b. Will the World Bank Push China's Belt and Road Initiative in the Right Direction? *Devex*. November 2. Accessed at www.devex.com/news/will-the-world-bank-push-china-s-belt-and-road-initiative-in-the-right-direction–93657.

International Development Association (IDA). 2015. Management's Discussion & Analysis and Financial Statements. June 30. Washington, DC: World Bank. Accessed at https://ida.worldbank.org/sites/default/files/images/ida_financial_statements_jun_15.pdf.

International Monetary Fund (IMF). 2014. Niger Staff Report for the 2014 Article IV Consultation and Fourth and Fifth Reviews Under the Extended Credit Facility Arrangement and Request for Waiver of Nonobservance of Performance Criteria and Modification of Performance Criteria. Washington, DC: IMF. Accessed at www.imf.org/external/pubs/ft/dsa/pdf/2015/dsacr1563.pdf.

International Monetary Fund (IMF). 2015. First Review Under the Policy Support Instrument – Staff Report; Press Release; and Statement by the Executive Director for the United Republic of Tanzania. IMF Country Report 15/14. Washington, DC: IMF. Accessed at www.imf.org/external/pubs/ft/scr/2015/cr1514.pdf.

International Monetary Fund (IMF). 2017. Nepal Staff Report for the 2017 Article IV Consultation – Debt Sustainability Analysis. Washington, DC: IMF. Accessed at www.imf.org/external/pubs/ft/dsa/pdf/2017/dsacr1774.pdf.

International Monetary Fund (IMF). 2018. Sri Lanka 2018 Article IV Consultation and Fourth Review Under the Extended Arrangement Under the Extended Arrangement, IMF Country Report 18/175. Washington, DC: IMF. Accessed at www.imf.org/~/media/Files/Publications/CR/2018/cr18175.ashx.

Inveen, Cooper. 2017. President's Iron-Fist Methods Raise Fears for Future of Democracy in Sierra Leone. *Guardian*. October 20. Accessed at www.theguardian.com/global-development/2017/oct/20/president-ernest-bai-koroma-iron-fist-methods-raise-fears-for-future-of-democracy-in-sierra-leone-march-election.

Ioannidis, John P. A., Tom D. Stanley, and Hristos Doucouliagos. 2017. The Power of Bias in Economics Research. *Economic Journal* 127: F236–F265.

Isaksson, Ann-Sofie. 2017. Geospatial Analysis of Aid: A New Approach to Aid Evaluation. Stockholm, Sweden: Expert Group on Aid Studies.

Isaksson, Ann-Sofie, and Andreas Kotsadam. 2018a. Chinese Aid and Local Corruption. *Journal of Public Economics* 159: 146–159.

Isaksson, Ann-Sofie, and Andreas Kotsadam. 2018b. Racing to the Bottom? Chinese Development Projects and Trade Union Involvement in Africa. *World Development* 106(C): 284–298.

Isham, Jonathan, and Daniel Kaufmann. 1999. The Forgotten Rationale for Policy Reform: The Productivity of Investment Projects. *Quarterly Journal of Economics* 114(1): 149–184.

Isham, Jonathan, Daniel Kaufmann, and Lant Pritchett. 1997. Civil Liberties, Democracy, and the Performance of Government Projects. *World Bank Economic Review* 11(2): 219–242.

Ispahani, Mahnaz. (1989). *Roads and Rivals: The Political Uses of Access in the Borderlands of Asia.* Ithaca, NY: Cornell University Press.

Jablonski, Ryan. 2014. How Aid Targets Votes: The Effect of Electoral Strategies on the Distribution of Foreign Aid. *World Politics* 66(2): 293–330.

Jackson, Steven F. 1995. China's Third World Foreign Policy: The Case of Angola and Mozambique, 1961–93. *China Quarterly* 142: 388–422.

Jacobson, Harold K., and Michel Oksenberg. 1990. *China's Participation in the IMF, the World Bank, and GATT: Toward a Global Economic Order.* Ann Arbor: University of Michigan Press.

Jansson, Johanna. 2011. *The Sicomines Agreement: Change and Continuity in the Democratic Republic of Congo's International Relations.* SAIIA Occasional Paper 97. Johannesburg, South Africa: South African Institute of International Affairs. Accessed at https://media.africaportal.org/documents/saiia_OP_97.pdf.

Jansson, Johanna. 2013. The Sicomines Agreement Revisited: Prudent Chinese Banks and Risk-Taking Chinese Companies. *Review of African Political Economy* 40(135): 152–162.

Jean, Neal, Marshall Burke, Sang Michael Xie, W. Matthew Davis, David B. Lobell, and Stefano Ermon. 2016. Combining Satellite Imagery and Machine Learning to Predict Poverty. *Science* 353(6301): 790–794.

Jedwab, Remi, and Alexander Moradi. 2016. The Permanent Effects of Transportation Revolutions in Poor Countries: Evidence from Africa. *Review of Economics and Statistics* 98(2): 268–284.

Jenke, Libby, and Christopher Gelpi. 2017. Theme and Variations: Historical Contingencies in the Causal Model of Interstate Conflict. *Journal of Conflict Resolution* 61(1): 2262–2284.

Jenkins, Glenn. 1997. Project Analysis and the World Bank. *American Economic Review* 87(2): 38–42.

Jensen, Nathan M. 2003. Democratic Governance and Multinational Corporations: Political Regimes and Inflows of Foreign Direct Investment. *International Organization* 57(3): 587–616.

季崇威 [Ji, Chongwei]. 1992. 关于成立进出口银行问题——在`中国外贸发展与改革'研讨会上的发言 [On Establishing the Export-Import Bank of China: A Speech at the Workshop "Reform and Development of China's Foreign Trade"].国际贸易 *[International Trade]* 8.

Jiang, Xueqing. 2018. Nonpublic Sector at the Forefront of BRI Efforts. *China Daily.* November 17. Accessed at www.chinadaily.com.cn/a/201811/17/WS5 bef7d58a310eff30328944d.html.

Jiang, Yuan. 2020. Understanding the Intersection of the Belt and Road Initiative and China's Supply-Side Structural Reform. *Jamestown Foundation China Brief* 20(17).

金言文 [Jin, Yanwen]. 1988. 对我国对外经济技术合作发展战略问题的探讨 [An Exploration of Strategic Issues Regarding the Development of China's Foreign Economic and Technical Cooperation].国际经济合作 *[International Economic Cooperation]* 9: 3–9.

Johnston, Lauren, and Marina Rudyak. 2013. China's "Innovative and Pragmatic" Foreign Aid: Shaped by and now Shaping Globalisation. In Ligang Song, Ross Garnaut, Cai Fang, and Lauren Johnston (eds.), *China's New Sources of Economic Growth* (Vol. 2). Acton: Australian National University Press: 431–451.

Jones, Benjamin F., and Benjamin A. Olken. 2005. Do Leaders Matter? National Leadership and Growth since World War II. *Quarterly Journal of Economics* 120 (3): 835–864.

Jones, Lee. 2014. The Political Economy of Myanmar's Transition. *Journal of Contemporary Asia* 44(1): 144–170.

Kao, Michael Y. M. 1988. Taiwan's and Beijing's Campaigns for Unification. In Harvey Feldman, Michael Y. M. Kao, and Ilpyong J. Kim (eds.), *Taiwan in a Time of Transition*. New York: Paragon House: 175–200.

Kaplan, Stephen B. 2016. Banking Unconditionally: The Political Economy of Chinese Finance in Latin America. *Review of International Political Economy* 23 (4): 643–676.

Kapstein, Ethan, and Jacob N. Shapiro. 2019. Catching China by the Belt (and Road). *Foreign Policy*. April 20. Accessed at https://foreignpolicy.com/2019/04/20/catching-china-by-the-belt-and-road-international-development-finance-corp-beijing-united-states.

Kaufmann, Daniel, Aart Kraay, and Massimo Mastruzzi. 2004. Governance Matters III: Governance Indicators for 1996, 1998, 2000, and 2002. *World Bank Economic Review* 18(2): 253–287.

Kavakli, Kerim Can. 2019. Does the Rise of China Weaken Global Governance? Evidence from the Anti-Trafficking Regime. Mimeo. Milan, Italy: Bocconi University.

Kawanami, Takeshi. 2019. World Bank Chief Calls for Transparency in China's Foreign Lending. *Nikkei Asian Review*. June 11. Accessed at https://asia.nikkei.com/Editor-s-Picks/Interview/World-Bank-chief-calls-for-transparency-in-China-s-foreign-lending.

Kenderdine, Tristan, and Han Ling. 2018. International Capacity Cooperation – Financing China's Export of Industrial Overcapacity. *Global Policy* 9(1): 41–52.

KARA and CSUD. 2012. The Social/Community Component of the Analysis of the Thika Highway Improvement Project. Kenya Alliance of Resident Associations and Center for Sustainable Urban Development. Accessed at http://csud.ei.columbia.edu/files/2012/11/KARA-report_FINAL.pdf.

Kenya National Assembly. 2014. Report of the Departmental Committee on Transport, Public Works, and Housing on the Statement Sought by Hon. Hezron Awiti, MP, on the Tendering and Construction of the Standard Gauge Railway from Mombasa to Malaba. Nairobi, Kenya: Kenya National Assembly. Accessed at www.dropbox.com/s/sk2aubk0btyumso/Transport-Committee-FINAL-REPORT-ON-Standard-Gauge-Railway.pdf?dl=0.

Kenya National Bureau of Statistics (KNBS). 2015. *Economic Survey 2015*. Nairobi, Kenya: KNBS.

Kenya National Bureau of Statistics (KNBS). 2017. *Economic Survey 2017*. Nairobi, Kenya: KNBS.

Keohane, Robert, 1984. *After Hegemony: Cooperation and Discord in the World Political Economy*. Princeton, NJ: Princeton University Press.

Kersting, Erasmus, and Christopher Kilby. 2014. Aid and Democracy Redux. *European Economic Review* 67: 125–143.

Khadka, Narayan. 1997. Foreign Aid to Nepal: Donor Motivations in the Post–Cold War Period. *Asian Survey* 37(11): 1044–1061.

Khomba, Daniel Chris, and Alex Trew. 2017. Aid and Growth in Malawi. AidData Working Paper 42. Williamsburg, VA: AidData at William & Mary.

Kilby, Christopher. 2009. The Political Economy of Conditionality: An Empirical Analysis of World Bank Loan Disbursements. *Journal of Development Economics* 89(1): 51–61.

Kilby, Christopher. 2011. Informal Influence in the Asian Development Bank. *Review of International Organizations* 6(3–4): 223–257.

Kilby, Christopher. 2013. The Political Economy of Project Preparation: An Empirical Analysis of World Bank Projects. *Journal of Development Economics* 105: 211–225.

Kilby, Christopher. 2015. Assessing the Impact of World Bank Preparation on Project Outcomes. *Journal of Development Economics* 115(C): 111–123.

Kilby, Christopher, and Axel Dreher. 2010. The Impact of Aid on Growth Revisited: Do Donor and Recipient Characteristics Make a Difference? *Economics Letters* 107(3): 338–340.

Kim, Samuel S. 1979. *China, the United Nations and World Order*. Princeton, NJ: Princeton University Press.

Kim, Samuel S. 1981. Whither Post-Mao Chinese Global Policy? *International Organization* 35(3): 433–465.

King, Gary. 1995. Replication, Replication. *PS: Political Science and Politics* 28(3): 444–452.

Kishi, Roudabeh, and Clionadh Raleigh. 2016. Chinese Official Finance and State Repression in Africa. ACLED Working Paper. Accessed at www.acleddata.com/wp-content/uploads/2017/04/Chinese-Aid-Repression.pdf.

Kitano, Naohiro. 2016. Estimating China's Foreign Aid II: 2014 Update. JICA-RI Working Paper 131. Tokyo, Japan: Japan International Cooperation Agency. Accessed at www.jica.go.jp/jica-ri/publication/workingpaper/wp_131.html.

Klitgaard, Robert. 1990. *Tropical Gangsters: One Man's Experience with Development and Decadence in Deepest Africa*. New York: Basic Books.

Knack, Stephen, and Aminur Rahman. 2007. Donor Fragmentation and Bureaucratic Quality in Aid Recipients. *Journal of Development Economics* 83 (1): 176–197.

Knack, Stephen, F. Halsey Rogers, and Nicholas Eubank. 2011. Aid Quality and Donor Rankings. *World Development* 39(11): 1907–1917.

Knutsen, Tora, and Andreas Kotsadam. 2020. The Political Economy of Aid Allocation: Aid and Incumbency at the Local Level in Sub Saharan Africa. *World Development* 127: 104729.

Kobayashi, Takaaki. 2008. Evolution of China's Aid Policy. JBICI Working Paper 27. Tokyo, Japan: Japan Bank for International Cooperation. Accessed at www.jica.go.jp/jica-ri/IFIC_and_JBICI-Studies/jica-ri/english/publication/archives/jbic/report/working/pdf/wp27_e.pdf.

Kong, Bo, and Kevin P. Gallagher. 2017. Globalizing Chinese Energy Finance: The Role of Policy Banks. *Journal of Contemporary China* 26(108): 834–851.

Kosack, Stephen. 2003. Effective Aid: How Democracy Allows Development Aid to Improve the Quality of Life. *World Development* 31(1): 1–22.

Kotsadam, Andreas, Gudrun Østby, Siri A. Rustad, Andreas F. Tollefsen, and Henrik Urdal. 2018. Development Aid and Infant Mortality: Micro-level Evidence from Nigeria. *World Development* 105: 59–69.

Kragelund, Peter. 2011. Back to BASICs? The Rejuvenation of Non-traditional Donors' Development Cooperation with Africa. *Development and Change* 42 (2): 585–607.

Kumarage, Amal. 2014. The Real Cost of Highway Development: Who Has Got the Numbers Right? *Sunday Times*. December 21. Accessed at www.sundaytimes.lk/141221/Cost%20of%20Expressways.pdf.

Kurlantzick, Joshua. 2006. Beijing's Safari: China's Move into Africa and Its Implications for Aid, Development, and Governance. Carnegie Endowment Policy Outlook 29. Washington, DC: Carnegie Endowment for International Peace.

Kurlantzick, Joshua. 2007. *Charm Offensive: How China's Soft Power Is Transforming the World*. New Haven, CT: Yale University Press.

Kuziemko, Ilyana, and Eric Werker. 2006. How Much Is a Seat on the Security Council Worth? Foreign Aid and Bribery at the United Nations. *Journal of Political Economy* 114(5): 905–930.

Kydd, Andrew. 2000. Trust, Reassurance, and Cooperation. *International Organization* 54(2): 325–357.

Kydd, Andrew. 2007. *Trust and Mistrust in International Relations*. Princeton, NJ: Princeton University Press.

Kynge, James. 2016. China Becomes Global Leader in Development Finance. *Financial Times*. May 17. Accessed at www.ft.com/content/b995cc7a-1c33-11e6-a7bc-ee846770ec15#axzz490q596xJ.

Labonne, Julien. 2016. Local Political Business Cycles: Evidence from Philippine Municipalities. *Journal of Development Economics* 121: 56–62.

Lagarde, Christine. 2018. Belt and Road Initiative: Strategies to Deliver in the Next Phase. Speech by the IMF Managing Director at the 2018 IMF-PBC Conference in Beijing, China. Accessed at www.imf.org/en/News/Articles/2018/04/11/sp041218-belt-and-road-initiativestrategies-to-deliver-in-the-next-phase.

Lake, David. 2009. *Hierarchy in International Relations*. Ithaca, NY: Cornell University Press.

Lammers, Ellen. 2007. How Will the Beijing Consensus Benefit Africa? *The Broker*. Accessed at www.thebrokeronline.eu/how-will-the-beijing-consensus-benefit-africa.

Lancaster, Carol. 2007. The Chinese Aid System. CGD Essay. June. Washington, DC: Center for Global Development, Accessed at www.cgdev.org/publication/chinese-aid-system.

Lang, Valentin. 2021. The Economics of the Democratic Deficit: The Effect of IMF Programs on Inequality. *Review of International Organizations* 16: 599–623.

Lange, Glenn-Marie, Quentin Wodon, and Kevin Carey (eds.). 2018. *The Changing Wealth of Nations 2018: Building a Sustainable Future.* Washington, DC: World Bank.

Large, Daniel. 2008. Beyond "Dragon in the Bush": The Study of China-Africa Relations. *African Affairs* 107(426): 45–61.

Larmer, Brook. 2017. What the World's Emptiest International Airport Says About China's Influence. *New York Times Magazine.* September 13. Accessed at www.nytimes.com/2017/09/13/magazine/what-the-worlds-emptiest-international-airport-says-about-chinas-influence.html.

Laurance, William F., Anna Peletier-Jellema, Bart Geenen, Harko Koster, Pita Verweij, Pitou Van Dijck, Thomas E. Lovejoy, Judith Schleicher, and Marijke Van Kuijk. 2015. Reducing the Global Environmental Impacts of Rapid Infrastructure Expansion. *Current Biology* 25(7): R259–R262.

Lee, Ching Kwan. 2017. *The Specter of Global China Politics, Labor, and Foreign Investment in Africa.* Chicago: University of Chicago Press.

Lee, Christopher J. (ed.). 2010. *Making a World after Empire: The Bandung Moment and Its Political Afterlives.* Athens: Ohio University Press.

Lekorwe, Mogopodi, Anyway Chingwete, Mina Okuru, and Romaric Samson. 2016. China's Growing Presence in Africa Wins Largely Positive Popular Reviews. Afrobarometer Dispatch No. 122. October 24. Accessed at http://afrobarometer.org/publications/ad122-chinas-growingpresence-africa-wins-largely-positive-popular-reviews.

Lengauer, Sara. 2011. China's Foreign Aid Policy: Motive and Method. *Culture Mandala: Bulletin of the Centre for East-West Cultural & Economic Studies* 9(2): 35–81.

Lessmann, Christian. 2013. Foreign Direct Investment and Regional Inequality: A Panel Data Analysis. *China Economic Review* 43: 129–149.

李凤亭 [Li, Fengting]. 1992. 创建国家进出口银行为改革开放服务 [Creating a National Export-Import Bank to Serve Reform and Opening].国际贸易 *[International Trade]* 8: 6–8.

Li, Jing, Aloysius Newenham-Kahindi, Daniel M. Shapiro, and Victor Z. Chen. 2013. The Two-Tier Bargaining Model Revisited: Theory and Evidence from China's Natural Resource Investments in Africa. *Global Strategy Journal* 3(4): 300–321.

Li, Xiaojun. 2017. Does Conditionality Still Work? China's Development Assistance and Democracy in Africa. *Chinese Political Science Review* 2(2): 201–220.

Li, Yuanxin. 2019. The Growth Effects of Chinese Development Assistance in Sub-Saharan Africa: An Empirical Analysis. Mimeo. Accessed at https://ssrn.com/abstract=3370159.

Lian, Ruby and Melanie Burton. 2017. China Orders Aluminum, Steel Cuts in War on Smog. *Reuters.* March 1. Accessed at www.reuters.com/article/us-china-pollution/china-orders-aluminum-steel-cuts-in-war-on-smog-idUSKBN1683G6.

Licht, Amanda A. 2010. Coming into Money: The Impact of Foreign Aid on Leader Survival. *Journal of Conflict Resolution* 54(1): 58–87.

Lim, Darren J., and Rohan Mukherjee. 2017. What Money Can't Buy: The Security Externalities of Chinese Economic Statecraft in Post-War Sri Lanka. *Asian Security* 15(2): 73–92.

Lin, Teh-Chang. 1993. The Foreign Aid Policy of the People's Republic of China: A Theoretical Analysis. Doctoral Dissertation. DeKalb: Northern Illinois University.

Lipin, Michael. 2016. Who Has an Edge in the South China Sea: China or US? *Voice of America News*. June 7. Accessed at www.voanews.com/a/who-has-an-edge-in-south-china-sea-china-or-us/3364876.html.

Liu, Bingyu. 2017. Regulation of Chinese Infrastructure Companies' Environmental and Social Impacts in Host Countries Overseas: A Study of the Chinese-Built Standard Gauge Railway Project in Kenya. *South African Journal of Environmental Law and Policy* 23(1): 101–141.

Lujala, Päivi. 2009. Deadly Combat over Natural Resources: Gems, Petroleum, Drugs, and the Severity of Armed Civil Conflict. *Journal of Conflict Resolution* 53(1): 50–71.

Lujala, Päivi, Jan Ketil Rød, and Nadia Thieme. 2007. Fighting over Oil: Introducing a New Dataset. *Conflict Management and Peace Science* 24(3): 239–256.

Lum, Thomas, Hannah Fischer, Julissa Gomez-Granger, and Anne Leland. 2009. China's Foreign Aid Activities in Africa, Latin America, and Southeast Asia. Congressional Research Service Report for Congress. February 25. Washington, DC: Congressional Research Service. Accessed at https://sgp.fas.org/crs/row/R40361.pdf.

Lusaka Times. 2018. Zambia Risks Asset Seizure by Chinese, Says Global Ratings Firm Moody's. November 28. Accessed at www.lusakatimes.com/2018/11/28/zambia-risks-asset-seizure-by-chinese-says-global-ratings-firm-moodys.

Magee, Christopher S. P., and John A. Doces. 2015. Reconsidering Regime Type and Growth: Lies, Dictatorships, and Statistics. *International Studies Quarterly* 59(2): 223–237.

Makoye, Kizito. 2014. Ex-CEO of Tanzania Ports Faces Fraud Charges over Bloated Chinese Contract. *Thomson Reuters Foundation News*. July 15. Accessed at https://news.trust.org/item/20140715205110-works/?source=fiOtherNews2.

Makundi, Hezron, Huib Huyse, and Patrick Develtere. 2017. Negotiating the Technological Capacity in Chinese Engagements: Is the Tanzanian Government in the Driving Seat? *South African Journal of International Affairs* 24(3): 331–353.

Malalo, Humphrey. 2018. Kenya Arrests Two Top Officials for Suspected Corruption over New $3 Billion Railway. *Reuters*. August 11. Accessed at www.reuters.com/article/us-kenya-corruption-railway/kenya-arrests-two-top-officials-for-suspected-corruption-over-new-3-billion-railway-idUSKBN1KW07L.

Malik, Ammar A., Bradley Parks, Brooke Russell, Joyce Lin, Katherine Walsh, Kyra Solomon, Sheng Zhang, Thai-Binh Elston, and Seth Goodman. 2021. Banking on the Belt and Road: Insights from a New Global Dataset of 13,427 Chinese Development Projects. Williamsburg, VA: AidData at William & Mary.

Malik, J. Mohan. 1994. Sino-Indian Rivalry in Myanmar: Implications for Regional Security. *Contemporary Southeast Asia* 16(2): 137–156.

Mambetova, Altynai, and James Kilner. 2018. Kyrgyzstan Grows Wary of China Amid Corruption Probe. July 4. *Nikkei Asian Review*. Accessed at https://asia.nikkei.com/Politics/International-relations/Kyrgyzstan-grows-wary-of-China-amid-corruption-probe.

Manova, Katrina. 2013. Credit Constraints, Heterogeneous Firms, and International Trade. *Review of Economic Studies* 80(2): 711–744.

Manson, Katrina. 2010. Interview – Congo Defends $6 Bln China Deal, Awaits Funds. *Reuters*. October 27. Accessed at https://de.reuters.com/article/congo-democratic-china-idAFLDE69Q10C20101027.

Markovits, Daniel, Austin Strange, and Dustin Tingley. 2019. Foreign Aid and the Status Quo: Evidence from Pre-Marshall Plan Aid. *Chinese Journal of International Politics* 12(4): 585–613.

Marshall, Monty G., Ted Gurr, and Keith Jaggers. 2013. *Polity IV Project: Political Regime Characteristics and Transitions, 1800–2012*. Vienna, VA: Center for Systemic Peace.

Martinez, Luis. 2021. How Much Should We Trust the Dictator's GDP Growth Estimates? BFI Working Paper 2021-78. Chicago: University of Chicago.

Martorano, Bruno, Laura Metzger, and Marco Sanfilippo. 2020. Chinese Development Assistance and Household Welfare in Sub-Saharan Africa. *World Development* 129: 104909.

Marty, Robert, Carrie B. Dolan, Matthias Leu, and Daniel Runfola. 2017. Taking the Health Aid Debate to the Subnational Level: The Impact and Allocation of Foreign Health Aid in Malawi. *BMJ Global Health* 2(1): e000129.

Marty, Robert, Seth Goodman, Michael Le Few, Carrie B. Dolan, Ariel BenYishay, and Dan Runfola. 2019. Assessing the Causal Impact of Chinese Aid on Vegetative Land Cover in Burundi and Rwanda Under Conditions of Spatial Imprecision. *Development Engineering* 4: 100038.

Marx, Benjamin. 2018. Elections as Incentives: Project Completion and Visibility in African Politics. Mimeo. Accessed at https://drive.google.com/file/d/1aSDEhq-ZGlUcX5QxWbb-0bAcAdSUXlKc/view.

Masaki, Takaaki. 2018. The Political Economy of Aid Allocation in Africa: Evidence from Zambia. *African Studies Review* 61(1): 55–82.

Masaki, Takaaki, Bradley Parks, Jörg Faust, Stefan Leiderer, Matthew D. DiLorenzo. 2021. Aid Management, Trust, and Development Policy Influence: New Evidence from a Survey of Public Sector Officials in Low-Income and Middle-Income Countries. *Studies in Comparative International Development* 56: 364–383.

Mattlin, Mikael, and Matti Nojonen. 2015. Conditionality and Path Dependence in Chinese Lending. *Journal of Contemporary China* 24(94): 701–720.

Mauk, Ben. 2019. Can China Turn the Middle of Nowhere into the Center of the World Economy? *New York Times*. January 29. Accessed at www.nytimes.com/interactive/2019/01/29/magazine/china-globalization-kazakhstan.html.

Mawdsley, Emma. 2013. *From Recipients to Donors: The Emerging Powers and the Changing Development Landscape*. London: Zed Books.

McCullough, Bruce, and Ross McKitrick. 2009. *Check the Numbers: The Case for Due Diligence in Policy Formation*. Studies in Risk & Regulation. February. Calgary, Alberta: Fraser Institute.

McDonald, Kristen, Peter Bosshard, and Nicole Brewer. 2009. Exporting Dams: China's Hydropower Industry Goes Global. *Journal of Environmental Management* 90: S294–S302.

McGreal, Chris. 2007. Chinese Aid to Africa May Do More Harm than Good, Warns Benn. *Guardian*. February 7. Accessed at www.theguardian.com/world/2007/feb/08/development.topstories3.

McGuirk, Rod. 2018. Australia Details Investment in Pacific as China Clout Grows. *AP News*. November 7. Accessed at https://apnews.com/article/cf3404ef6f4b404197e83066179aa4f4.

Mehmood, Sultan, and Avner Seror. 2019. The Political Economy of Foreign Aid and Growth: Theory and Evidence. ESI Working Paper 19–10. Orange, CA: Chapman University. Accessed at https://digitalcommons.chapman.edu/esi_working_papers/268.

Minasyan, Anna, Peter Nunnenkamp, and Katharina Richert. 2017. Does Aid Effectiveness Depend on the Quality of Donors? *World Development* 100: 16–30.

Ministry of Finance. 1994–2017. 中国财政年鉴 *[Finance Yearbook of China]*. Beijing, China: 中国财政杂志社 [China Finance Magazine].

Ministry of Finance and Planning. 2016. National Five Year Development Plan 2016/17–2020/21. Dar es Salaam, Tanzania: Ministry of Finance and Planning.

Ministry of Foreign Affairs. 1990. 周恩来外交文选 [Selected Diplomatic Memoirs of Zhou Enlai]. 中华人民共和国外交部 [Ministry of Foreign Affairs of the People's Republic of China]. 中央文献出版社 [Zhongyang wenxian chubanshe].

Ministry of Foreign Affairs. 2014a. *China's Initiation of the Five Principles of Peaceful Co-Existence*. Beijing, China: Ministry of Foreign Affairs of the People's Republic of China. Accessed at www.fmprc.gov.cn/mfa_eng/ziliao_665539/3602_665543/3604_665547/t18053.shtml.

Ministry of Foreign Affairs. 2014b. *Chairman Mao Zedong's Theory on the Division of the Three World and the Strategy of Forming an Alliance Against an Opponent*. Beijing, China: Ministry of Foreign Affairs of the People's Republic of China. Accessed at www.fmprc.gov.cn/mfa_eng/ziliao_665539/3602_665543/3604_665547/t18008.shtml.

Ministry of Foreign Affairs. 2020. Diplomatic Allies. Taipei, Taiwan: Ministry of Foreign Affairs of the Republic of China. Accessed at www.mofa.gov.tw/en/AlliesIndex.aspx?n=DF6F8F246049F8D6&sms=A76B7230ADF29736.

Minoiu, Camelia, and Sanjay G. Reddy. 2010. Development Aid and Economic Growth: A Positive Long-Run Relation. *Quarterly Review of Economics and Finance* 50(1): 27–39.

Mitchell, Ian, and Caitlin McKee. 2018. *How Do You Measure Aid Quality and Who Ranks Highest?* November 15. Washington, DC: Center for Global Development. Accessed at www.cgdev.org/blog/how-do-you-measure-aid-quality-and-who-ranks-highest.

MOFCOM. 1990, 1996, 1999. *Almanac of China's Foreign Economic Relations and Trade.* Hong Kong, China: China Foreign Economic Relations and Trade Publishing House.

MOFCOM. 2014a. MOFCOM Held a Media Debriefing on the Measures for the Administration of Foreign Aid. Beijing, China: Ministry of Commerce. Accessed at www.mofcom.gov.cn/article/fbhfn/fbh2014/201412/2014120082 4824.shtml.

MOFCOM. 2014b. Announcement from MOFCOM's Party Committee on Inspection and Improvement. Beijing, China: Ministry of Commerce. June 11. Accessed at www.mofcom.gov.cn/article/ae/ai/201406/20140600620 170.shtml.

Molenaers, Nadia, Anna Gagiano, and Lodewijk Smets. 2017. Introducing a New Data Set: Budget Support Suspensions as a Sanctioning Device: An Overview from 1999 to 2014. *Governance* 30(1): 143–152.

Monson, Jamie. 2006. Defending the People's Railway in the Era of Liberalization: Tazara in Southern Tanzania. *Africa: Journal of the International African Institute* 76(1): 113–130.

Monson, Jamie. 2009. *Africa's Freedom Railway: How a Chinese Development Project Changed Lives and Livelihoods in Tanzania.* Bloomington: Indiana University Press.

Monson, Jamie. 2010. Working Ahead of Time: Labor and Modernization During the Construction of the TAZARA Railway, 1968–1986. In Christopher Lee (ed.), *Making a World after Empire: The Bandung Moment and Its Political Afterlives.* Athens: Ohio University Press: 235–265.

Montenegro, Javier. 2018. El Gobierno de Correa Ocultó la Deuda en Petroecuador. *Diario Expreso.* January 3. Accessed at https://web.archive.org/web/20180731211027/http://www.expreso.ec/actualidad/el-gobierno-de-cor rea-oculto-la-deuda-en-petroecuador-CM1943501.

Montinola, Gabriela R. 2010. When Does Aid Conditionality Work? *Studies in Comparative International Development* 45(3): 358–382.

Moore, Mick. 1998. Death without Taxes: Democracy, State Capacity, and Aid Dependence in the Fourth World. In Mark Robinson, and Gordon White (eds.), *Towards a Democratic Developmental State.* Oxford: Oxford University Press: 84–125.

Moravcsik, Andrew M. 1989. Disciplining Trade Finance: The OECD Export Credit Arrangement. *International Organization* 43(1): 173–205.

Morgan, Pippa, and Yu Zheng. 2019. Tracing the Legacy: China's Historical Aid and Contemporary Investment in Africa. *International Studies Quarterly* 63(3): 558–573.

Morgenthau, Hans. 1962. A Political Theory of Foreign Aid. *American Political Science Review* 56(2): 301–309.

Morley, Joanna. 2017. " ... Beggars Sitting on a Sack of Gold": Oil Exploration in the Ecuadorian Amazon as Buen Vivir and Sustainable Development. *International Journal of Human Rights* 21(4): 405–441.

Morris, Scott, Brad Parks, and Alysha Gardner. 2020. Chinese and World Bank Lending Terms: A Systematic Comparison across 157 Countries and 15 Years. CGD Policy Paper 170. Washington, DC: Center for Global Development.

Accessed at www.cgdev.org/publication/chinese-and-world-bank-lending-terms-systematic-comparison.

Moser, Christine. 2008. Poverty Reduction, Patronage or Vote Buying? The Allocation of Public Goods and the 2001 Election in Madagascar. *Economic Development and Cultural Change* 57(1): 137–162.

Moss, Todd, Gunilla Pettersson, and Nicolas van de Walle. 2007. An Aid-Institutions Paradox? A Review Essay on Aid Dependency and State Building in Sub-Saharan Africa. In William Easterly (ed.), *Reinventing Foreign Aid.* Cambridge: Cambridge University Press: 255–281.

Moss, Todd J., and Arvind Subramanian. 2005. After the Big Push? Fiscal and Institutional Implications of Large Aid Increases. CGD Working Paper 71. Washington, DC: Center for Global Development. Accessed at www.cgdev.org/publication/after-big-push-fiscal-and-institutional-implications-large-aid-increases-working-paper.

Mthembu-Salter, Gregory. 2012. Goodwill and Hard Bargains: The DRC, China and India. SAIIA Occasional Paper 114. Johannesburg, South Africa: South African Institute of International Affairs. Accessed at https://saiia.org.za/research/goodwill-and-hard-bargains-the-drc-china-and-india/.

Mu, Ren, and Xiaobo Zhang 2014. Do Elected Leaders in a Limited Democracy Have Real Power? Evidence from Rural China. *Journal of Development Economics* 107(C): 17–27.

Muchapondwa, Edwin, Daniel Nielson, Bradley Parks, Austin M. Strange, and Michael J. Tierney. 2014. "Ground-Truthing" Chinese Development Finance in Africa: Field Evidence from South Africa and Uganda. UNU-WIDER Working Paper 2014/031. Helsinki, Finland: UNU-WIDER. Accessed at www.wider.unu.edu/sites/default/files/wp2014-031.pdf.

Muchapondwa, Edwin, Daniel Nielson, Bradley Parks, Austin M. Strange, and Michael J. Tierney. 2016. "Ground-Truthing" Chinese Development Finance in Africa: Field Evidence from South Africa and Uganda. *Journal of Development Studies* 52(6): 780–796.

Mundy, Simon, and Kathrin Hille. 2019. The Maldives Counts the Cost of Its Debts to China: The Government Joins a Backlash Against Beijing-Financed Infrastructure Projects. *Financial Times.* February 10. Accessed at www.ft.com/content/c8da1c8a-2a19-11e9-88a4-c32129756dd8.

Murshed, S. Mansoob, and Scott Gates. 2005. Spatial-horizontal Inequality and the Maoist Insurgency in Nepal. *Review of Development Economics* 9(1): 121–134.

Mwase, Ngila. 1983. The Tanzania-Zambia Railway: The Chinese Loan and the Pre-Investment Analysis Revisited. *Journal of Modern African Studies* 21(3): 535–543.

Mwase, Nkunde, and Yongzheng Yang. 2012. BRICs' Philosophies for Development Financing and Their Implications for LICs. IMF Working Paper 12/74. Washington, DC: International Monetary Fund. Accessed at www.imf.org/external/pubs/ft/wp/2012/wp1274.pdf.

Mwere, David. 2018. China May Take Mombasa Port over Sh227bn SGR Debt: Ouko. *Daily Nation.* December 20. Accessed at https://mobile.nation.co.ke/news/Chinese-may-take-Mombasa-Port–Ouko/1950946-4902162-item-1-cv5rc2z/index.html.

Naím, Moises. 2007. Rogue Aid. *Foreign Policy* 159 (March/April): 95–96.

国家统计局 [National Bureau of Statistics]. 1999. 新中国五十年统计资料汇编 [Comprehensive Statistical Data and Materials on Fifty Years of New China]. Beijing, China: 中国统计出版社 [China Statistics Press].

国家统计局 [National Bureau of Statistics]. 2017. 中国统计年鉴2017 [China Statistical Yearbook 2017]. Beijing, China: 中国统计出版社 [China Statistics Press].

Naughton, Barry. 2016. Supply-side Structural Reform: Policy-Makers Look for a Way Out. *China Leadership Monitor* 49: 1–13.

New Spotlight. 2018. China to Help Reopen Tatopani Border Point. March 16. Accessed at www.spotlightnepal.com/2018/03/16/china-help-reopen-tatopani-border-point.

New York Times. 2007. Patron of African Misgovernment. February 19. Accessed at www.nytimes.com/2007/02/19/opinion/19mon1.html.

Newhouse, David Locke, Pablo Suarez Becerra, and Dung Thi Thuy Doan. 2016. *Sri Lanka – Poverty and Welfare: Recent Progress and Remaining Challenges*. Washington, DC: World Bank.

Ng'wanakilala, Fumbuka. 2015. Tanzanian President Suspends Rail Chief Pending Probe into Tender. *Reuters*. December 22. Accessed at https://cn.reuters.com/article/tanzania-corruption-railway/tanzanian-president-suspends-rail-chief-pending-probe-into-tender-idUKL1N14B19W20151222.

Nielson, Daniel L., and Michael J. Tierney. 2003. Delegation to International Organizations: Agency Theory and World Bank Environmental Reform. *International Organization* 57(2): 241–276.

Nielson, Daniel L., Bradley Parks, and Michael J. Tierney. 2017. International Organizations and Development Finance: Introduction to the Special Issue. *Review of International Organizations* 12(2): 157–169.

Nizalova, Olena Y., and Irina Murtazashvili. 2016. Exogenous Treatment and Endogenous Factors: Vanishing of Omitted Variable Bias on the Interaction Term. *Journal of Econometric Methods* 5(1): 71–77.

Nowak-Lehmann D., Felicitas, Inmaculada Martínez-Zarzoso, Stephan Klasen, and Dierk Herzer. 2009. Aid and Trade – A Donor's Perspective. *Journal of Development Studies* 45(7): 1184–1202.

Nunn, Nathan, and Nancy Qian. 2014. U.S. Food Aid and Civil Conflict. *American Economic Review* 104(6): 1630–1666.

Nunnenkamp, Peter, and Hannes Öhler. 2011. Throwing Foreign Aid at HIV/AIDS in Developing Countries: Missing the Target? *World Development* 39 (10): 1704–1723.

Nunnenkamp, Peter, Hannes Öhler, and Andrés Maximiliano Sosa. 2017. Need, Merit and Politics in Multilateral Aid Allocation: A District-Level Analysis of World Bank Projects in India. *Review of Development Economics* 21(1): 126–156.

Nye, Joseph. 2004. *Soft Power: The Means to Success in World Politics*. New York: Public Affairs.

Odokonyero, Tonny, Robert Marty, Tony Muhumuza, Alex T. Ijjo, and Godfrey Owot Moses. 2018. The Impact of Aid on Health Outcomes in Uganda. *Health Economics* 27(4): 733–745.

OECD. 1987. *The Aid Programme of China*. Paris, France: Organisation for Economic Co-operation and Development.

OECD. 2015. Making Development Co-operation Fit for the Future: A Survey of Partner Countries. OECD Development Co-operation Working Paper 20. Paris, France: Organisation for Economic Co-operation and Development. Accessed at https://doi.org/10.1787/5js6b25hzv7h-en.

OECD. 2018. China's Belt and Road Initiative in the Global Trade, Investment and Finance Landscape. In *OECD Business and Finance Outlook 2018*. Paris, France: Organisation for Economic Co-operation and Development: 3–44.

Office of the President of the United States. 2017. National Security Strategy of the United States of America. Accessed at www.whitehouse.gov/wp-content/uploads/2017/12/NSS-Final-12-18-2017-0905.pdf.

Office of the White House. 2018. Remarks by Vice President Pence on the Administration's Policy Toward China at the Hudson Institute. October 4. Accessed at www.whitehouse.gov/briefings-statements/remarks-vice-president-pence-administrations-policy-toward-china.

Ofstad, Arve, and Elling Tjønneland. 2019. Zambia's Looming Debt Crisis – Is China to Blame? CMI Insight 2019/01. Bergen, Norway: Chr. Michelsen Institute.

Öhler, Hannes, Mario Negre, Lodewijk Smets, Renzo Massari, and Željko Bogetić. 2019. Putting Your Money Where Your Mouth Is: Geographic Targeting of World Bank Projects to the Bottom 40 Percent. *PLoS ONE* 14(6): e0218671.

Öhler, Hannes, and Peter Nunnenkamp. 2014. Needs-Based Targeting or Favoritism? The Regional Allocation of Multilateral Aid within Recipient Countries. *Kyklos* 67(3): 420–446.

Okoth, Edwin. 2019. SGR Pact with China a Risk to Kenyan Sovereignty, Assets. *Daily Nation*. January 13. Accessed at www.nation.co.ke/news/Hidden-traps-in-SGR-deal-with-China/1056-4932764-ebw46r/index.html.

Olingo, Allan. 2019. Kenya Fails to Secure $3.6b from China for Third Phase of SGR Line to Kisumu. *The East African*. April 27. Accessed at www.theeastafrican.co.ke/business/Kenya-fails-to-secure-loan-from-China-for-third-phase-of-SGR/2560-5090192-2o0y9j/index.html.

Osaki, Tomohiro. 2019. In Blow to China, Japan's "Quality Infrastructure" to Get Endorsement at Osaka G20. *The Japan Times*. June 25. Accessed at www.japantimes.co.jp/news/2019/06/25/business/economy-business/blow-china-japans-quality-infrastructure-get-endorsement-osaka-g20/#.Xg9ATRdKjyI.

Overholt, William H. 2010. China in the Global Financial Crisis: Rising Influence, Rising Challenges. *The Washington Quarterly* 33(1): 21–34.

Oye, Kenneth A. (ed.). 1986. *Cooperation Under Anarchy*. Princeton, NJ: Princeton University Press.

Page, Jeremy, and Saeed Shah. 2018. China's Global Building Spree Runs into Trouble in Pakistan. *Wall Street Journal*. July 22. Accessed at www.wsj.com/articles/chinas-global-building-spree-runs-into-trouble-in-pakistan-1532280460.

Pant, Harsh V. 2017. China's Moment in Nepal: Implications for India. *The Diplomat*. December 27. Accessed at https://thediplomat.com/2017/12/chinas-moment-in-nepal-implications-for-india.

Park, Hyo-Sung. 2016. China's RMB Internationalization Strategy: Its Rationales, State of Play, Prospects and Implications. Harvard Kennedy School M-RCBG Associate Working Paper 63. Accessed at www .hks.harvard.edu/centers/mrcbg/publications/awp/awp63.

Parker, George, and Alan Beattie. 2006. EIB Accuses China of Unscrupulous Loans. *Financial Times*. November 29. Accessed at www.ft.com/content/5894 73b6-7f14-11db-b193-0000779e2340.

Parks, Bradley. 2019. *Chinese Leadership and the Future of BRI: What Key Decisions Lie Ahead?* CGD Note. Washington, DC: Center for Global Development.

Parks, Bradley, and Caroline Davis. 2019. When Do Governments Trade Domestic Reforms for External Rewards? Explaining Policy Responses to the Millennium Challenge Corporation's Eligibility Standards. *Governance* 32(2): 349–367.

Parks, Bradley, Scott Morris, Joyce Lin, and Alysha Gardner. 2020. *Bargaining with Beijing: A Tale of Two Borrowers*. Washington, DC: Center for Global Development.

Parks, Bradley, and Austin M. Strange. 2019. Autocratic Aid and Governance: What We Know, Don't Know, and Need to Know. *Annals of Comparative Democratization* 17(2): 12–16.

Paxton, Pamela, and Stephen Knack. 2012. Individual and Country-Level Factors Affecting Support for Foreign Aid. *International Political Science Review* 33(2): 171–192.

Pedregosa, Fabian, Gaël Varoquaux, Alexandre Gramfort, Vincent Michel, Bertrand Thirion, Olivier Grisel et al. 2011. Scikit-learn: Machine Learning in Python. *Journal of Machine Learning Research* 12: 2825–2830.

Peebles, Patrick. 2015. *Historical Dictionary of Sri Lanka*. Lanham, MD: Rowman & Littlefield Publishers.

Pehnelt, Gernot. 2007. The Political Economy of China's Aid Policy in Africa. Jena Economic Research Paper 2007–51. Jena, Germany: University of Jena.

Pehrson, Christopher J. 2006. String of Pearls: Meeting the Challenge of China's Rising Power Across the Asian Littoral. Carlisle Papers in Security Strategy, July. Accessed at https://css.ethz.ch/en/services/digital-library/publications/pub lication.html/27007.

Pence, Michael. 2018. Notable & Quotable: No Belt, Just Open Road. *Wall Street Journal*. November 19. Accessed at www.wsj.com/articles/notable-quotable-no -belt-just-open-road–1542672745.

People's Daily. 2014. Xi Eyes More Enabling Intl' Environment for China's Peaceful Development (3). November 30. Accessed at http://en.people.cn/n/2 014/1130/c90883-8815967-3.html.

Perdue, David, Roy Blunt, John Cornyn, Tom Cotton, Ted Cruz, Steve Daines et al. 2018. Letter to Steven T. Mnuchin and Michael R. Pompeo. August 3. Washington, DC: United States Senate. Accessed at www.dropbox.com/s/zkob zyvctkh0825/IMF%20China%20Belt%20and%20Road%20Initiative%20Let ter.pdf?dl=0.

Perlez, Jane, and Yufan Huang. 2017. Behind China's $1 Trillion Plan to Shake Up the Economic Order. *New York Times*. May 13. Accessed at www .nytimes.com/2017/05/13/business/china-railway-one-belt-one-road-1-tril lion-plan.html.

Perroux, Francois. 1950. Economic Space: Theory and Applications. *Quarterly Journal of Economics* 64(1): 89–104.

Pew Research Center. 2013. As Sequester Deadline Looms, Little Support for Cutting Most Programs. February 22. Accessed at www.peoplepress.org/2013/02/22/as-sequester-deadline-looms-little-support-for-cutting-most-programs.

Pilling, David, and Emily Feng. 2018. Chinese Investments in Africa Go Off the Rails. *Financial Times*. December 5. Accessed at www.ft.com/content/82e77d8a-e716-11e8-8a85-04b8afea6ea3.

Ping, Szu-Ning, Yi-Ting Wang, and Wen-Yang Chang. 2021. The Effects of China's Development Projects on Political Accountability. *British Journal of Political Science*. Forthcoming. Accessed at https://doi.org/10.1017/S0007123420000381.

Pinkovskiy, Maxim, and Xavier Sala-i-Martin. 2016. Lights, Camera . . . Income! Illuminating the National Accounts-Household Surveys Debate. *Quarterly Journal of Economics* 131(2): 579–631.

Policy Forum. 2018. A Review of the Performance of Tanzania's Prevention and Combating of Corruption Bureau, 2007–16. Dar es Salaam, Tanzania: Policy Form. Accessed at www.policyforum-tz.org/sites/default/files/PCCB%20%20REPORT%20FINAL.pdf.

Poole, Peter Andrews. 1966. Communist China's Aid Diplomacy. *Asian Survey* 6 (11): 622–629.

Presbitero, Andrea F. 2016. Too Much and Too Fast? Public Investment Scaling-up and Absorptive Capacity. *Journal of Development Economics* 120: 17–31.

Publish What You Fund. 2020. *Aid Transparency Index 2020*. London: Publish What You Fund.

Putnam, Robert D. 1993. *Making Democracy Work*. Princeton, NJ: Princeton University Press.

Qiang, Zhai. 1992. China and the Geneva Conference of 1954. *The China Quarterly* 129: 103–122.

Rai, Kul B. 1980. Foreign Aid and Voting in the UN General Assembly, 1967–1976. *Journal of Peace Research* 17(3): 269–277.

Rajan, Raghuram G., and Arvind Subramanian. 2008. Aid and Growth: What Does the Cross-Country Evidence Really Show. *Review of Economics and Statistics* 90(4): 643–665.

Raleigh, Clionadh, Andrew Linke, Håvard Hegre, and Joakim Karlsen. 2010. Introducing ACLED-Armed Conflict Location and Event Data. *Journal of Peace Research* 47(5): 651–660.

Randt Jr., Clarke T. 2007. Subject: Fifth Generation Star Li Keqiang Discusses Domestic Challenges, Trade Relations with Ambassador. US Department of State Cable. March 15. Available at https://archive.org/details/07BEIJING1760.

Rauhala, Emily. 2015. China Rushes Aid to Nepal After Deadly Earthquake; Taiwan Is Turned Away. *Time*. April 27. Available at http://time.com/3836182/china-nepal-earthquake-taiwan-geopolitics.

Reilly, James. 2012. A Norm-Taker or a Norm-Maker? Chinese Aid in Southeast Asia. *Journal of Contemporary China* 21(73): 71–91.

Reilly, James. 2015. The Role of China as an Education Aid Donor. Background Paper Prepared for the Education for All Global Monitoring Report 2015.

Paris, France: UNESCO. Accessed at https://unesdoc.unesco.org/ark:/48223/pf0000232475.

Reinhart, Carmen, and Kenneth Rogoff. 2004. Serial Default and the "Paradox" of Rich to Poor Capital Flows. *American Economic Review* 94(2): 52–58.

Republic of Kenya. 2014a. Special Report on the Procurement and Financing of the Construction of Standard Gauge Railway from Mombasa to Nairobi (Phase I). Public Investments Committee of the National Assembly of the Republic of Kenya. Nairobi: National Assembly of the Republic of Kenya. Accessed at https://africog.org/wp-content/uploads/2017/06/PIC-REPORT.pdf.

Republic of Kenya. 2014b. Report of the Departmental Committee on Transport, Public Works and Housing on the Tendering and Construction of the Standard Gauge Railway from Mombasa to Malaba. Nairobi: National Assembly of the Republic of Kenya. Accessed at https://africog.org/wp-content/uploads/2017/06/Transport-Committee-FINAL-REPORT-ON-Standard-Gauge-Railway.pdf..

Reuters. 2017. China Hopes Sri Lanka Fosters Good Atmosphere for Projects. May 16. Accessed at https://af.reuters.com/article/worldNews/idAFKCN18D036.

Reuters. 2018. China's Xi Offers Fresh $295 Million Grant to Sri Lanka. July 22. Accessed at www.reuters.com/article/us-sri-lanka-china-grant/chinas-xi-offers-fresh-295-million-grant-to-sri-lanka-idUSKBN1KC0D8.

Rich, Timothy S. 2009. Status for Sale: Taiwan and the Competition for Diplomatic Recognition. *Issues & Studies* 45(4): 159–188.

Roessler, Phillip. 2013. Chinese Development Finance and Strategies of Political (and Territorial) Survival in Sudan. The First Tranche: AidData's Blog. Accessed at www.aiddata.org/blog/chinese-development-finance-and-strategies-of-political-and-territorial-survival-in-sudan.

Roessler, Phillip, Yannick Pengl, Rob Marty, Kyle Titlow, and Nicholas van de Walle. 2020. The Cash Crop Revolution, Colonialism and Legacies of Spatial Inequality: Evidence from Africa. CSAE Working Paper Series 2020–12. Oxford: University of Oxford. Accessed at https://ideas.repec.org/p/csa/wpaper/2020-12.html.

Rose, Andrew K., and Mark M. Spiegel. 2011. The Olympic Effect. *Economic Journal* 121(553): 652–677.

Rosenstein-Rodan, Paul N. 1943. Problems of Industrialization of Eastern and South-Eastern Europe. *Economic Journal* 53 (210/211): 202–211.

Ross, Dennis. 2018. Iranians Are Mad as Hell About Their Foreign Policy. January 2, 2018. *Foreign Policy*. Accessed at https://foreignpolicy.com/2018/01/02/iranians-are-mad-as-hell-about-their-foreign-policy.

Rudyak, Marina. 2019. *The Ins and Outs of China's International Development Agency*. September 2. Washington, DC: Carnegie Endowment for International Peace. Accessed at https://carnegieendowment.org/2019/09/02/ins-and-outs-of-china-s-international-development-agency-pub-79739.

Runfola, Daniel, Ariel BenYishay, Jeffery Tanner, Graeme Buchanan, Jyoteshwar Nagol, Matthias Leu et al. 2017. A Top-Down Approach to Estimating Spatially Heterogeneous Impacts of Development Aid on Vegetative Carbon Sequestration. *Sustainability* 9(3): 409.

Russel, Daniel R., and Blake Berger. 2019. *Navigating the Belt and Road Initiative*. Washington, DC: Asia Society Policy Institute.

Sanghi, Apurva, and Dylan Johnson. 2016. Deal or No Deal: Strictly Business for China in Kenya? World Bank Policy Research Working Paper #7614. Washington, D.C.: The World Bank. Accessed at https://openknowledge .worldbank.org/handle/10986/24159.

Sato, Jin, Hiroaki Shiga, Takaaki Kobayashi, and Hisahiro Kondoh. 2011. Emerging Donors from a Recipient Perspective: An Institutional Analysis of Foreign Aid in Cambodia. *World Development* 39(12): 2091–2104.

Schraeder, Peter J., Steven Hook, and Bruce Taylor. 1998. Clarifying the Foreign Aid Puzzle. *World Politics* 50(2): 294–323.

Schultz, Kai. 2017. Sri Lanka, Struggling With Debt, Hands a Major Port to China. *New York Times*. December 12. Accessed at www.nytimes.com/2017/ 12/12/world/asia/sri-lanka-china-port.html.

Schwemlein, James. 2018. Pakistan's Economic Turmoil Threatens China's Ambitions. August 16. *Foreign Policy*. Accessed at https://foreignpolicy.com /2018/08/16/pakistans-economic-turmoil-threatens-chinas-ambitions-cpec.

Shapiro, Isaac. 2000. Trends in US Development Aid and the Current Budget Debate. Center on Budget and Policy Priorities. Accessed at www.cbpp.org/a rchives/4-25-00bud.htm.

Shen, Gordon C., and Victoria Y. Fan. 2014. China's Provincial Diplomacy to Africa: Applications to Health Cooperation. *Contemporary Politics* 20(2): 182–208.

Shepard, Wade. 2016. The Story Behind the World's Emptiest International Airport. *Forbes*. May 18. Available at www.forbes.com/sites/wadeshepard/201 6/05/28/the-story-behind-the-worlds-emptiest-international-airport-sri-lankas -mattala-rajapaksa.

Shepherd, Christian, and Ben Blanchard. 2018. China's Xi Offers Another $60 Billion to Africa, but Says No to "Vanity" Projects. *Reuters*. September 3. Accessed at www.reuters.com/article/china-africa/chinas-xi-says-funds-for- africa-not-for-vanity-projects-idUSL3N1VO018.

石林 [Shi, Lin ]. 1989. 当代中国的对外经济合作 [*Contemporary China's Foreign Economic Cooperation*]. Beijing, China: 中国社会科学出版社 [China Social Sciences Press].

Shi, Yulong. 2018. BRI's Image Being Tarred by False Claims. *China Daily*. October 25. Accessed at http://global.chinadaily.com.cn/a/201810/25/WS5b d10250a310eff303284606.html.

Shinn, David H. 2006. Africa, China and Health Care. *Inside Asia* 3–4: 14–16.

Sirisena, Maithripala. 2014. Compassionate Government, Maithri: A Stable Country. Election Manifesto of Maithripala Sirisena, New Democratic Front. Accessed at https://web.archive.org/web/20181104214644/http://www .priu.gov.lk/presidential_manifestos/Manifesto-EN.pdf.

Small, Andrew. 2015. *The China Pakistan Axis: Asia's New Geopolitics*. New York: Oxford University Press.

Smets, Lodewijk, and Stephen Knack. 2016. World Bank Lending and the Quality of Economic Policy. *Journal of Development Studies* 52(1): 72–91.

Smith, Colby. 2018. Belt and Road, or Debt Trap? *Financial Times*. July 24. Accessed at https://ftalphaville.ft.com/2018/07/24/1532410200000/Belt-and-Road–or–debt-trap.

Song, Wei. 2015. Seeking New Allies in Africa: China's Policy Towards Africa During the Cold War as Reflected in the Construction of the Tanzania-Zambia Railway. *Journal of Modern Chinese History* 9(1): 46–65.

Sonntag, Diana. 2010. *AIDS and Aid: A Public Good Approach*. Berlin, Germany: Springer Physica.

Sovacool, Benjamin K., Saroj Dhakal, Olivia Gippner, and Malavika Jain Bambawale. 2011. Halting Hydro: A Review of the Socio-Technical Barriers to Hydroelectric Power Plants in Nepal. *Energy* 36(5): 3468–3476.

Spence, Michael. 1973. Job Market Signaling. *Quarterly Journal of Economics* 87 (3): 355–374.

*Sri Lanka Mirror*. 2017. Matara-Mattala Expressway: Corruption More than Before. March 25. Accessed at www.srilankamirror.com/news/2442-matara-mattala-expressway-corruption-more-than-before.

Srinivasan, Meera. 2017. India Keen to Run Sri Lanka Airport. *The Hindu*. August 11. Accessed at www.thehindu.com/news/international/india-keen-to-run-sri-lanka-airport/article19476394.ece.

Stallings, Barbara, and Eun Mee Kim. 2017. China as a Non-Traditional Asian Donor. In Barbara Stallings, and Eun Mee Kim (eds.), *Promoting Development: The Political Economy of East Asian Foreign Aid*. Singapore: Palgrave: 117–162.

Stanway, David. 2015. Update1 – Going Abroad the Solution to China's Overcapacity Woes – Ministry Official. *Reuters*. July 22. Accessed at www.reuters.com/article/china-industry-overcapacity-idUSL3N10230E20150722.

State Council. 2011. White Paper on China's Foreign Aid. Beijing, China: Information Office of the State Council. Accessed at http://gov.cn/english/offi cial/.2011-04/21/content1849913.htm.

State Council. 2013. Guidelines to Resolve Serious Overcapacity Problems. Overcapacity. State Decree No. 41. Beijing, China: Information Office of the State Council. Accessed at www.gov.cn/zwgk/2013-10/15/content_2507143.htm.

State Council. 2014. China's Foreign Aid. Beijing, China: Information Office of the State Council. Accessed at http://news.xinhuanet.com/english/china/2014-07/10/c_133474011.htm.

State Council. 2015a. Premier Pushes International Capacity Cooperation. August 12. Accessed at http://english.www.gov.cn/premier/news/2015/08/12/content_281475166618531.htm.

State Council. 2015b. Hebei Should Export Production Capacity, Premier Says. March 8. Accessed at http://english.www.gov.cn/premier/news/2015/03/08/content_281475067740335.htm.

State Council. 2015c. Guiding Opinions on Promoting International Capacity Cooperation and Equipment Manufacturing, State Decree No. 30. Accessed at www.gov.cn/zhengce/content/2015-05/16/content_9771.htm.

State Council. 2021. China's International Development Cooperation in the New Era. Beijing, China: Information Office of the State Council. Accessed at www.xinhuanet.com/english/2021-01/10/c_139655400.htm.

Straits Times of Singapore. 2018. Samoa Rejects China Pacific Debt Forgiveness Call. August 20. Accessed at www.straitstimes.com/asia/east-asia/samoa-rejects-china-pacific-debt-forgiveness-call.

Strange, Austin, Axel Dreher, Andreas Fuchs, Bradley Parks, and Michael J. Tierney. 2017. Tracking Underreported Financial Flows: China's Development Finance and the Aid-Conflict Nexus Revisited. *Journal of Conflict Resolution* 61(5): 935–963.

Strange, Austin, Siddhartha Ghose, Brooke Russell, Mengfan Cheng, and Bradley Parks. 2017. AidData's Methodology for Tracking Underreported Financial Flows. Version 1.3. Williamsburg, VA: AidData at William & Mary. Accessed at http://docs.aiddata.org/ad4/pdfs/AidDataTUFF_Methodo logy_1.3.pdf.

Strange, Austin, Bradley Parks, Michael J. Tierney, Andreas Fuchs, Axel Dreher, and Vijaya Ramachandran. 2013. China's Development Finance to Africa: A Media-Based Approach to Data Collection. CGD Working Paper 323. Washington, DC: Center for Global Development. Accessed at www.cgdev.o rg/publication/chinas-development-finance-africa-media-based-approach-dat a-collection.

Strangio, Sebastian. 2014. *Hun Sen's Cambodia*. New Haven, CT: Yale University Press.

Stratfor. 2018. Wary of China, India Shares Its Largesse with Neighbors. April 24. Austin, TX: Stratfor Enterprises. Accessed at https://worldview.strat for.com/article/india-china-aid-neighbors-nepal-bhutan-sri-lanka-maldives-ba ngladesh-seychelles.

Strauss, Delphine. 2018. IMF Faces China Debt Dilemma as Low Income Nations Seek Help. *Financial Times*. November 22. Accessed at www.ft.com/ content/6a0002ba-ecd9-11e8-89c8-d36339d835c0.

Sun, Yun. 2013. Chinese Investment in Myanmar: What Lies Ahead, Stimson Issue Brief No 1. Accessed at www.stimson.org/2013/chinese-investment-myanmar-what-lies-ahead/.

Sun, Yun. 2014. *Africa in China's Foreign Policy*. Washington, DC: Brookings Institution.

Suzuki, Susumu, Volker Krause, and J. David Singer. 2002. The Correlates of War Project: A Bibliographic History of the Scientific Study of War and Peace, 1964-2000. *Conflict Management and Peace Science* 19(2): 69–107.

Svensson, Jakob. 1999. Aid, Growth and Democracy. *Economics & Politics* 11(3): 275–297.

Swaine, Michael D. 2015. Chinese Views and Commentary on the "One Belt, One Road" Initiative. *China Leadership Monitor* 47(2): 31–24.

Swann, Christopher, and William McQuillen. 2006. China to Surpass World Bank as Top Lender to Africa. *Bloomberg News*. November 3.

Swedlund, Haley J. 2017a. *The Development Dance: How Donors and Recipients Negotiate the Delivery of Foreign Aid*. Ithaca, NY: Cornell University Press.

Swedlund, Haley J. 2017b. Is China Eroding the Bargaining Power of Traditional Donors in Africa? *International Affairs* 93(2): 389–408.

Tang, Keyi, and Yingjiao Shen. 2020. Do China-Financed Dams in Sub-Saharan Africa Improve the Region's Social Welfare? A Case Study of the Impacts of Ghana's Bui Dam. *Energy Policy* 136: 111062.

Tan-Mullins, May. 2016. Chinese Perception of Soft Power: The Role of Media in Shaping Chinese Views and Discourses on Foreign Aid to Africa. In Xiaoling Zhang, Herman Wasserman, and Winston Mano (eds.), *China's Media and Soft Power in Africa: Promotion and Perceptions*. New York: Palgrave Macmillan: 107–120.

Tarnoff, Curt, and Marian Lawson. 2011. Foreign Aid: An Introduction to U.S. Programs and Policy. CRS R40213. Washington, DC: Congressional Research Service. Accessed at www.everycrsreport.com/files/20110210_R40213_2705 77bfb8efb9044920eae5ec56d650fce6ca54.pdf.

Taylor, Ian. 1998. China's Foreign Policy Towards Africa in the 1990s. *Journal of Modern African Studies* 36(3): 443–460.

Taylor, Ian. 2007. China's Environmental Footprint in Africa. *China Dialogue*. February 2. Accessed at www.chinadialogue.net/article/show/single/en/741-China-s-environmentalfootprint-inAfrica.

Taylor, Jay. 1974. *China and Southeast Asia: Peking's Relations with Revolutionary Movements*. New York: Praeger Publishers.

Thacker, Strom C. 1999. The High Politics of IMF Lending. *World Politics* 52(1): 38–75.

The Citizen. 2017. JPM Confirms Turkey Role in Railway Project. January 24. Accessed at www.thecitizen.co.tz/news/JPM-confirms-Turkey-role-in-railway-project/1840340-3784882-t8jm50/index.html.

The Economic Times. 2019. China, Maldives Clash over Mounting Chinese Debt as India Warms Up to Male. July 8. Accessed at https://economictimes.india times.com/news/international/world-news/china-maldives-clash-over-mount ing-chinese-debt-as-india-warms-up-to-male/articleshow/70127479.cms? from=mdr.

The Economist. 2009. An (Iron) Fistful of Help: Development Aid from Authoritarian Regimes. June 6. Accessed at http://www.economist.com/node/ 13799239.

The Economist. 2010. The Colombo Consensus: Brotherly Love, Massive Aid and No Questions Asked. July 8. Accessed at www.economist.com/node/ 16542629.

The Economist. 2012. A Dangerous Year: Unrest in China. January 28. Accessed at www.economist.com/briefing/2012/01/28/a-dangerous-year.

The Economist. 2016. Misplaced Charity. June 11. Accessed at www.economist .com/news/international/21700323-development-aid-best-spent-poor-well-go verned-countries-isnt-where-it.

The Economist. 2017a. A Thousand Golden Stars: China Goes to Africa. July 20. Accessed at www.economist.com/middle-east-and-africa/2017/07/20/china-goes-to-africa.

The Economist. 2017b. Why Cambodia Has Cosied Up to China. January 21. Accessed at www.economist.com/news/asia/21715010-and-why-it-worries-cambodias-neighbours-why-cambodia-has-cosied-up-china.

The Economist. 2017c. What Is China's Belt and Road Initiative? May 15. Accessed at www.economist.com/the-economist-explains/2017/05/14/what-is-chinas-belt-and-road-initiative.

The Economist. 2018. Tanzania's Rogue President. March 15. Accessed at www.economist.com/middle-east-and-africa/2018/03/15/tanzanias-rogue-president.

The Nepalese Voice. 2017. Chinese Bank Renews Loan Grace Period for Upper Trishuli 3A Hydro. September 24. Accessed at http://nepalesevoice.com/bussiness/chinese-bank-renews-loan-grace-period-for-upper-trishuli-3a-hydro.

The New Times. 2017. How President Kenyatta's Scores in Development Helped in Re-Election. August 16. Accessed at www.newtimes.co.rw/section/read/218123.

Tierney, Michael J., Daniel L. Nielson, Darren G. Hawkins, J. Timmons Roberts, Michael G. Findley, Ryan M. Powers et al. 2011. More Dollars than Sense: Refining Our Knowledge of Development Finance Using AidData. *World Development* 39(11): 1891–1906.

Tran, Mark. 2011a. Transparency Could Be the Sticking Point for China at Busan. The Guardian's Poverty Matters Blog. *Guardian.* November 14. Accessed at www.theguardian.com/global-development/poverty-matters/2011/nov/14/busan-aid-china-rejects-transparency.

Tran, Mark. 2011b. China and India to Join Aid Partnership on New Terms. *Guardian.* November 11. Accessed at www.theguardian.com/global-development/2011/dec/01/china-india-aid-partnership.

Tull, Dennis M. 2006. China's Engagement in Africa: Scope, Significance and Consequences. *Journal of Modern African Studies* 44(3): 459–479.

US Department of Defense. 2018. US National Defense Strategy 2018: Sharpening the American Military's Competitive Edge. August 11. Washington, DC: US Department of Defense. Accessed at https://dod.defense.gov/Portals/1/Documents/pubs/2018-National-Defense-Strategy-Summary.pdf.

US International Development Finance Corporation. 2019. The Launch of Multi-Stakeholder Blue Dot Network. November 4. Accessed at www.dfc.gov/media/opic-press-releases/launch-multi-stakeholder-blue-dot-network.

UNDP. 2015. China's Humanitarian Aid. Issue Brief. Beijing, China: United Nations Development Programme China. Accessed at www.cn.undp.org/content/china/en/home/library/south-south-cooperation/issue-brief–china-s-humanitarian-aid.html.

United States Agency for International Development (USAID). 2018. Press Release: US Agency for International Development Administrator Mark Green's Interview with C-SPAN's "Newsmakers" Host Susan Swain and *Washington Post*'s Carol Morello and *Wall Street Journal*'s Ben Kesling. November 26. Washington, DC: USAID. Accessed at www.usaid.gov/news-information/press-releases/nov-26-2018-administrator-mark-green-interview-cspan-newsmakers.

Upreti, Bishnu Raj. 2004. *The Price of Neglect: From Resource Conflict to Maoist Insurgency in the Himalayan Kingdom.* Kathmandu, Nepal: Bhrikuti Academic Publications.

Vadlamannati, Krishna Chaitanya, Arusha Cooray, and Samuel Brazys. 2018. Nothing to Hide: Commitment to, Compliance with, and Impact of the Special Data Dissemination Standard. *Economics & Politics* 30(1): 55–77.

Vadlamannati, Krishna Chaitanya, and Indra de Soysa. 2016. Do Resource-Wealthy Rulers Adopt Transparency-Promoting Laws? *International Studies Quarterly* 60(3): 457–474.

Vadlamannati, Krishna Chaitanya, Yuanxin Li, Samuel Brazys, and Alexander Dukalskis. 2019. Building Bridges or Breaking Bonds? The Belt and Road Initiative and Foreign Aid Competition. UCD Geary Institute for Public Policy Discussion Paper 2019/06. Dublin, Ireland: Geary Institute, University College Dublin. Accessed at www.ucd.ie/geary/static/publications/workingpapers/gearywp201906.pdf.

van de Walle, Dominique, and Ren Mu. 2007. Fungibility and the Flypaper Effect of Project Aid: Micro Evidence for Vietnam. *Journal of Development Economics* 84(2): 667–684.

van de Walle, Nicolas. 2007. Meet the New Boss, Same as the Old Boss? The Evolution of Political Clientelism in Africa. In Herbert Kitschelt, and Steven I. Wilkinson (eds.), *Patrons, Clients, and Policies*. New York: Cambridge University Press: 60–67.

Van Holt, Tracy, Jeffery Johnson, Shiloh Moates, and Kathleen Carley. 2016. The Role of Datasets on Scientific Influence within Conflict Research. *PLoS ONE* 11(4): e0154148.

Varrall, Merriden. 2016. Domestic Actors and Agendas in Chinese Aid Policy. *Pacific Review* 29(1): 21–44.

Velloor, Ravi. 2010. A Man Who Loves His Country. *The Straits Times of Singapore*. March 19. Accessed at http://archive1.english.news.lk/category-table/14314-qa-man-who-loves-his-countryq.html.

Verhoeven, Harry. 2015. *Water, Civilisation and Power in Sudan*. New York: Cambridge University Press.

Voeten, Erik, Anton Strezhnev, and Michael Bailey. 2009. United Nations General Assembly Voting Data (version 18). Harvard Dataverse. Available at https://dataverse.harvard.edu/dataset.xhtml?persistentId=doi:10.7910/DVN/LEJUQZ.

Vreeland, James Raymond. 2003. *The IMF and Economic Development*. New York: Cambridge University Press.

Vreeland, James Raymond. 2006. IMF Program Compliance: Aggregate Index Versus Policy Specific Research Strategies. *Review of International Organizations* 1(4): 359–378.

Vreeland, James Raymond, and Axel Dreher. 2014. *The Political Economy of the United Nations Security Council. Money and Influence*. New York: Cambridge University Press.

Wade, Abdoulaye. 2008. Time for the West to Practice What It Preaches. *Financial Times*. January 23. Accessed at www.ft.com/content/5d347f88-c897-11dc-94a6-0000779fd2ac.

Wade, Geoff. 2005. The Zheng He Voyages: A Reassessment. *Journal of the Malaysian Branch of the Royal Asiatic Society* 71(8): 37–58.

Wagstaff, Adam. 2011. Fungibility and the Impact of Development Assistance: Evidence from Vietnam's Health Sector. *Journal of Development Economics* 94 (1): 62–73.

Wahman, Michael, and Catherine Boone. 2018. Captured Countryside? Stability and Change in Sub-national Support for African Incumbent Parties. *Comparative Politics* 50(2): 189–216.

Wallace, Jeremy. 2016. Juking the Stats? Authoritarian Information Problems in China. *British Journal of Political Science* 46(1): 11–29.

Wang, Jenny Qu, Minquan Liu, Aming Liu, Tao Wei, and Hang Li. 2013. Global Health Governance in China: The Case of China's Health Aid to Foreign Countries. In Kelley Lee, Tikki Pang, and Yeling Tan (eds.), *Asia's Role in Governing Global Health*. London: Routledge: 39–65.

Wang, Yuan, and Uwe Wissenbach. 2019. Clientelism at Work? A Case Study of Kenyan Standard Gauge Railway Project. *Economic History of Developing Regions* 34(3): 280–299.

Wantchekon, Leonard. 2003. Clientelism and Voting Behavior: Evidence from a Field Experiment in Benin. *World Politics* 55(3): 399–422.

Warner, Andrew. 2010. *Cost-Benefit Analysis in World Bank Projects*. Independent Evaluation Group of the World Bank. Washington, DC: World Bank.

Watanabe, Shino. 2013. How Have Major Donors Affected China's Economic Development and Foreign Aid Policy? In Jin Sato, and Yasutami Shimomura (eds.), *The Rise of Asian Donors: Japan's Impact on the Evolution of Emerging Donors*. Abingdon, UK: Routledge: 87–113.

Watkins, Mitchell. 2021. Undermining Conditionality? The Effect of Chinese Development Assistance on Compliance with World Bank Project Agreements. *Review of International Organizations*. Accessed at https://link.springer.com/article/10.1007/s11558-021-09443-z

Wayoro, Didier, and Léonce Ndikumana. 2019. Impact of Development Aid on Infant Mortality: Micro-Level Evidence from Côte d'Ivoire. UMass Amherst Economics Working Papers 2019–07. Amherst: University of Massachusetts Amherst. Accessed at https://scholarworks.umass.edu/econ_workingpaper/265/.

Wehner, Joachim, and Paolo de Renzio. 2013. Citizens, Legislators, and Executive Disclosure: The Political Determinants of Fiscal Transparency. *World Development* 41(C): 96–108.

Wei, Liang-Tsai. 1982. *Peking Versus Taipei in Africa: 1960–1978*. Taipei, Taiwan: The Asia and World Institute: 382–390.

Weidmann, Nils B., and Sebastian Schutte. 2017. Using Night Lights for the Prediction of Local Wealth. *Journal of Peace Research* 54(2): 125–140.

Wellner, Lukas, Axel Dreher, Andreas Fuchs, Bradley Parks, Austin M. Strange, and Michael J. Tierney. 2020. Do China's Overseas Development Projects Buy Public Support for the Chinese Government? Mimeo.

Weng, Lingfei, and Jeffrey Sayer. 2019. Trap (陷阱) or Treat (馅饼)? The Africa-China Relationship. Presentation delivered to the University of British Columbia's Department of Forest and Conservation Sciences on March 13, Vancouver, Canada.

Werker, Eric. 2012. The Political Economy of Bilateral Foreign Aid. In Gerard Caprio (ed.), *Handbook of Safeguarding Global Financial Stability: Political,*

*Social, Cultural, and Economic Theories and Models.* London: Academic Press: 47–58.

White, Howard. 2019. The Twenty-First Century Experimenting Society: The Four Waves of the Evidence Revolution. *Palgrave Communications* 5(1): 1–7.

Wijedasa, Namini. 2016. China Gets Huge Projects in Polonnaruwa District. *Sunday Times.* May 29. Accessed at www.sundaytimes.lk/160529/news/china-gets-huge-projects-in-polonnaruwa-district-195355.html.

Willard, Anna. 2007. Paris Club Prods Kuwait and Saudi over Iraqi Debt. *Reuters.* September 27. Accessed at https://fr.reuters.com/article/us-debt-iraq-interview-idUSL2548938920070927.

Williams, Martin. 2017. The Political Economy of Unfinished Development Projects: Corruption, Clientelism, or Collective Choice? *American Political Science Review* 111(4): 705–723.

Williamson, Claudia R. 2008. Foreign Aid and Human Development: The Impact of Foreign Aid to the Health Sector. *Southern Economic Journal* 75(1): 188–207.

Willmott, Cort J., and Kenji Matsuura. 2001. *Terrestrial Air Temperature and Precipitation: Monthly and Annual Time Series (1950–1999).* Newark, DE: Center for Climatic Research, University of Delaware. Accessed at http://climate.geog.udel.edu/~climate/html_pages/README.ghcn_ts2.html.

Winters, Matthew. 2014. Targeting, Accountability and Capture in Development Projects. *International Studies Quarterly* 58(2): 393–404.

Wissenbach, Uwe. 2019. Kenya's Madaraka Express: An Example of the Decisive Chinese Impulse for African Mega-Infrastructure Projects. In Nuno Gil, Anne Stafford, and Innocent Musonda (eds.), *Duality by Design: The Global Race to Build Africa's Infrastructure.* Cambridge: Cambridge University Press.

Wissenbach, Uwe, and Yuan Wang. 2017. African Politics Meets Chinese Engineers: The Chinese-Built Standard Gauge Railway Project in Kenya and East Africa. SAIS-CARI Working Paper 13. Washington, DC: Johns Hopkins SAIS.

Wolf Jr., Charles, Xiao Wang, and Eric Warner. 2013. *China's Foreign Aid and Government-Sponsored Investment Activities: Scale, Content, Destinations and Implications.* Santa Monica, CA: Rand Corporation.

Wong, Catherine. 2017. Nepal Torn Both Ways as Standoff between China and India Continues. *South China Morning Post.* August 9. Accessed at www.scmp.com/news/china/diplomacy-defence/article/2106120/nepal-torn-both-ways-st and-between-india-and-china.

Wong, John, and Sarah Chan. 2003. China's Outward Direct Investment: Expanding Worldwide. *China: An International Journal* 1(2): 273–301.

Woods, Kevin. 2011. Ceasefire Capitalism: Military-Private Partnerships, Resource Concessions and Military–State Building in the Burma-China Borderlands. *Journal of Peasant Studies* 38(4): 747–770.

Wooldridge, Jeffrey M. 2015. Control Function Methods in Applied Econometrics. *Journal of Human Resources* 50(2): 420–445.

World Bank. 1994. *Operational Policy (OP) 10.04: Economic Evaluation of Investment Operations. World Bank Operational Manual: Operational Policies.* Washington, DC: World Bank.

World Bank. 2013. *A Poverty Profile for Sierra Leone*. Washington, DC: World Bank.

World Bank. 2014. *Strategic Framework for Mainstreaming Citizen Engagement in World Bank Group Operations*. Washington DC: World Bank.

World Bank. 2016. *World Development Indicators*. Washington, DC: World Bank.

World Bank. 2019. *Estimating the Impact of the Mojo-Hawassa Expressway. Development Impact Evaluation (DIME) Brief*. Washington, DC: World Bank.

World Bank. 2020. *International Debt Statistics Database*. September 27. Washington, DC: World Bank. Accessed at https://data.worldbank.org/products/ids.

Wright, Joseph. 2010. Aid Effectiveness and the Politics of Personalism. *Comparative Political Studies* 43(6): 735–762.

Wright, Tom, and Bradley Hope. 2019. WSJ Investigation: China Offered to Bail Out Troubled Malaysian Fund in Return for Deals; The Secret Discussions Show How China Uses Its Political and Financial Clout to Bolster Its Position Overseas. *Wall Street Journal*. January 7. Accessed at www.wsj.com/articles/how-china-flexes-its-political-muscle-to-expand-power-overseas–11546890449.

Wu, Rongwei, Degang Yang, Jiefang Dong, Lu Zhang, and Fuqiang Xia. 2018. Regional Inequality in China Based on NPP-VIIRS Night-Time Light Imagery. *Remote Sensing* 10(2): 240.

Wu, Xinbo. 2001. Four Contradictions Constraining China's Foreign Policy Behavior. *Journal of Contemporary China* 10(27): 293–301.

Wubbeke, Jost, Mirjam Meissner, Max J. Zenglein, Jaqueline Ives, and Bjorn Conrad. 2016. Made in China 2025: The Making of a High-Tech Superpower and Consequences for Industrial Countries. Mercator Institute for China Studies (MERICS) Papers on China No. 2. Accessed at https://merics.org/en/report/made-china-2025.

Xinhua News Agency. 2014. Chronology of Asian Infrastructure Investment Bank. April 1. Accessed at www.chinadaily.com.cn/business/2015-04/01/content_19966945.htm.

Xinhua News Agency. 2015. 习近平在巴基斯坦议会的演讲(全文) [Full text of Xi Jinping's Speech at Pakistan Meeting]. April 21. Accessed at www.mod.gov.cn/affair/2015-04/21/content_4585889_2.htm.

Xinhua News Agency. 2017. Socialism with Chinese Characteristics Enters New Era: Xi. October 18. Accessed at www.xinhuanet.com/english/2017-10/18/c_136688475.htm.

Xinhua News Agency. 2020. Rasuwagadhi-Kerung Border Crossing between Nepal, China to Reopen. July 5. Accessed at www.xinhuanet.com/english/2020-07/05/c_139190373.htm.

Xiong, Hou. 2017. China's Foreign Aid and Multilateral Development Organizations. In Hong Zhou and Hou Xiong (eds.), *China's Foreign Aid: 60 Years in Retrospect*. Singapore: Springer Nature: 49–95.

Xu, Jiajun, and Richard Carey. 2014. China's Development Finance: What Issues for Reporting and Monitoring Systems? *IDS Bulletin* 45(4): 102–113.

Xue, Lan. 2014. China's Foreign Aid Policy and Architecture. *IDS Bulletin* 45(4): 36–45.

Yao, Jing. 2019. Ambassador Yao Jing's Speech at the 5th CPEC Media Forum. Embassy of the People's Republic of China in the Islamic Republic of Pakistan. November 22. Accessed at http://pk.chineseembassy.org/eng/zbgx/t1718338 .htm.

Yarbrough, Beth, and Robert Yarbrough. 2014. *Cooperation and Governance in International Trade*. Princeton, NJ: Princeton University Press.

Ye, Min. 2020. *The Belt Road and Beyond: State-Mobilized Globalization in China: 1998–2018*. Cambridge: Cambridge University Press.

Yu, George T. 1977. China and the Third World. *Asian Survey* 17(11): 1036–1048.

Yu, Qiao. 2013. *Relocating China's Foreign Reserves*. Washington, DC: Brookings Institution.

Yung, Christopher D., Ross Rustici, Scott Devary, and Jenny Lin. 2014. *"Not an Idea We Have to Shun": Chinese Overseas Basing Requirements in the 21st Century*. Washington, DC: National Defense University Press.

Zeitz, Alexandra. 2021. Emulate or Differentiate? Chinese Development Finance, Competition, and World Bank Infrastructure Funding. *Review of International Organizations* 16: 265–292.

曾建业 [Zeng, Jianye]. 1996. 援外优惠贷款: 我国企业跨国经营融资新方式 [Government Concessional Loans: A New Method for Chinese Firms to Manage Transnational Finance]. 中国工业经济 *[China Industrial Economy]* 10.

Zettelmeyer, Jeromin. 2020. Public Remarks at the "The Economics of Belt and Road: Policy Implications of New and Emerging Research" Conference at the Center for Global Development. January 24. Accessed at www.cgdev.org/eve nt/economics-beltand-road-policy-implications-new-and-emerging-research.

Zhang, Chenying. 2011a. Sterilization in China: Effectiveness and Cost. The Wharton School, Finance Department, University of Pennsylvania. Accessed at https://faculty.wharton.upenn.edu/wp-content/uploads/2012/04/Sterilizatio nJun1.pdf.

張郁慧 [Zhang, Yuhui]. 2011b. 中国对外援助 *1950–2010 [Chinese Foreign Aid, 1950-2010]*. Beijing, China: 九州出版社 [Jiuzhou Pess].

Zhang, Denghua. 2018. A Tango by Two Superpowers: China-US Cooperation in Trilateral Aid and Implications for Their Bilateral Relations. *Asian Journal of Political Science* 26(2): 181–200.

Zhang, Denghua, and Graeme Smith. 2017. Foreign Aid System: Structure, Agencies, and Identities. *Third World Quarterly* 38(10): 2330–2346.

Zhang, Guang. 2004. The Determinants of Foreign Aid Allocation across China: The Case of World Bank Loans. *Asian Survey* 44(5): 691–710.

Zhao, Dingxin. 2009. The Mandate of Heaven and Performance Legitimation in Historical and Contemporary China. *American Behavioral Scientist* 53(3): 416–433.

Zhao, Hong. 2008. China and India: Competing for Good Relations with Myanmar. *Journal of East Asian Affairs* 22(1): 175–194.

Zhao, Jianin, Peter Kemper, and Daniel Runfola. 2017. Quantifying Heterogeneous Causal Treatment Effects in World Bank Development

Finance Projects. *Data Mining and Knowledge Discovery (ECML PKDD)*: 204–215. Accessed at www.aiddata.org/publications/quantifying-heterogeneous-causal-treatment-effects-in-world-bank-development-finance-projects.

Zhao, Jianzhi, and Yijia Jing. 2019. The Governance of China's Foreign Aid System: Evolution and Path Dependence. *Public Administration and Development* 39(4/5): 182–192.

Zhao, Suisheng, ed. 2004. *Chinese Foreign Policy: Pragmatism and Strategic Behavior*. New York: Routledge.

郑掷 [Zheng, Zhi]. 2009. 新疆生产建设兵团出国修筑中巴友谊公路纪实 [A Record of Xinjiang Production and Construction Corps' Trip Abroad to Construct the China-Pakistan Friendship Highway]. 中国新闻网[Chinanews.com]. Accessed at http://news.ifeng.com/mil/history/200907/0713_1567_124 6729_1.shtml.

Zhou, Hang. 2018. China-Britain-Uganda: Trilateral Development Cooperation in Agriculture. SAIS-CARI Working Paper 2018/20. Washington, DC: Johns Hopkins SAIS. Accessed at www.sais-cari.org/publications-working-papers.

周弘 [Zhou, Hong]. 2010. 中国援外六十年的回顾与展望 [60 Years of Chinese Aid: Reflections and Projections]. 外交评论: 外交学院学报 *[Foreign Affairs Review]* 27(5): 3–11.

Zhou, Hong, and Hou Xiong (eds.). 2013. *Chinese Foreign Aid: 60 Years in Retrospect*. Beijing, China: Social Sciences Academic Press.

朱稳根 [Zhu, Wengen]. 1997. 援外优惠贷款的现状, 问题及思考 [Government Concessional Loans: Current Status, Issues, and Thoughts]. 国际经济合作 *[Journal of International Economic Cooperation]* 3: 4–8.

# Index

Made in the USA
Monee, IL
19 May 2022

96698436R00219